D0079171

ORGANIZED MIRACLES

ORGANIZED MIRACLES

A Study of a Contemporary, Youth,
Communal, Fundamentalist
Organization

James T. Richardson
Mary White Stewart
Robert B. Simmonds

Transaction Books
New Brunswick, New Jersey

Copyright © 1979 by Transaction, Inc.
New Brunswick, New Jersey 08903

All rights reserved under International and Pan-American Copyright
Conventions. No part of this book may be reproduced or transmitted
in any form or by any means, electronic or mechanical, including
photocopy, recording, or any information storage and retrieval system,
without prior permission in writing from the publisher. All inquiries
should be addressed to Transaction Books, Rutgers—The State University, New Brunswick, New Jersey 08903.

Library of Congress Catalog Number: 78-55937
ISBN: 0-87855-284-7 (cloth)
Printed in the United States of America

Library of Congress Cataloging in Publication Data
Richardson, James T   1941-
   Organized miracles.

   Bibliography: p. 347
   Includes index.
   1. Christ Communal Organization.   I. Stewart,
Mary White, 1945-   joint author.   II. Simmonds,
Robert B., 1945-   joint author.   III. Title.
BV4407.3.R52   301.5′8   78-55937
ISBN 0-87855-284-7

306.6
R523b

DEDICATION

We dedicate this effort to the CCO members, whose life and work has gained our respect, and whose fine treatment of us has forcefully reminded us of the difficulties, even perils, of "objective" research.

Contents

Illustrations		ix
Preface		xi
Acknowledgements		xiii
Introduction		xv
Part A: An Organizational Analysis		1
Chapter 1	History and Beliefs of the Organization	5
Chapter 2	Organizational Evolution	41
Chapter 3	Analysis as a "Social Movement Organization"	105
Part B: Group Life and Culture		123
Chapter 4	Daily Life in CCO	127
Chapter 5	Sex Roles, Courtship, Marriage, Family Life, and Children	137
Part C: Individual Characteristics		167
Chapter 6	The Sisters and Brothers: A Profile	171
Chapter 7	Personality Assessment	185
Chapter 8	Alienation and Political Orientation	201
Part D: Conversion and Affiliation		227
Chapter 9	Conversion Models: A Critique, Extension, and Partial Test	231
Part E: Future of the Organization		275
Chapter 10	An Application of Kanter's Model to CCO	279

Appendix A: The Research Project: Methods, History,
and Special Features   295
Appendix B: Testing Specific "Movement Organization"
Hypotheses   329
About the Authors   347
Bibliography   349
Index   363

Illustrations

TABLES

Table 3.1 Goals, Membership Requirements, and Related Structural Characteristics of Social Movement Organizations   109

Table 3.2 Relationship of Characterization of Membership to Conditions of Membership   111

Table 3.3 Relationship of "Expressive-Instrumental" Orientation to "Inward-Outward" Focus of Organization   112

Table 3.4 Relationship of "Focus" of Organization to Conditions of Membership   114

Table 6.1 Hardest Drugs Used by Drug Users of CCO   180

Table 6.2 Comparison of CCO Prior Religious Affiliation with Religious Composition of U.S.   182

Table 7.1 Mean Standard ACL Scores for CCO Males (n = 66), Females (n = 17), and for the Combined Sample (n = 83)   189

Table 8.1 Relationship of Amount of Exposure, Level of Commitment, and Type of Religion   209

Table 8.2 Responses to Alienation Questions   215

Table 8.3 Political Self-Characterization Before and After Affiliation   218

Table 9.1 Relationship of Groups to American Society and the General Type of Ideology Espoused by the Groups   242

ix

Table 9.2 Relationship of Affective Ties with Nongroup Significant Others and Affective Ties with Group Members   254
Table 9.3 Relationship of Affective Ties with Nongroup Members and Evaluation of the Group with Significant Nongroup Others   254
Table 9.4 Relationship of Affective Ties with Group Members and Congruence of Group with Predispositions of Potential Converts   255
Table 10.1: Basic Elements of Kanter's (1972) Model of Commitment: Types, Mechanisms, and Effects   280
Table B.1: Results of a Test of the Zald and Ash (1966) Propositions Concerning Social Movement Organizations, with Zurcher and Curtis (1973) Results Included   337

FIGURES

Figure 1: Evolution and Relationship of Organization Goals   46
Figure 2: Outline of Positions and Lines of Authority in Formal Authority Structure   49
Figure 3: Outline and Lines of Authority in Task-Oriented "Steward Structure," with Differentiation between Local and Organization-Wide Tasks   53
Figure 4: Evolution of Methods of Organizational and Member Support, and Levels of Such Support   63
Figure 5: Evolution and Differentiation of Living Arrangements   69
Figure 6: Flow of a New Member Through the "Schools" for Resocialization, with Approximate Time Spent in Each   77
Figure 7: Evolution and Differentiation of Evangelism and Resocialization Methods   89

Preface

This book has been difficult to bring to a close, simply because of the rapid changes being continually experienced by the organization that is the subject of the work. Our observations of the organization over the past seven or so years has made us very aware of the dangers of reifying a temporary stage of development in the life of the organization. We did not want to "freeze the moment" and imply a degree of permanence that does not exist. However, we have felt for some time that we were studying something of possible widespread interest, and that much valuable information could be made available about the alternative life-style developed by the group. So, we have proceeded to write, and we hope readers agree that there is much of value to know about this organization and its members. We urge all readers, however, to be constantly reminded of the amazing flexibility and creativity of the group being described, and of the fundamental truth that, from a sociological point of view, this very willingness to change has perhaps been the key to the overall strength and stability of the organization. The picture presented herein, no matter how accurate and detailed, may be but a brief moment in the long-term history of the organization, and this needs to be understood.

Even if the present structure of the organization turns out to be fairly temporary, we think this book will make several contributions.

Perhaps the most obvious is the considerable historical and descriptive material here available about the development of one of the major groups to come out of the much-heralded Jesus movement and the widely publicized "commune movement." There is a paucity of scholarly treatments of the movement and its specific groups, and on the newer communal religious groups, thus forcing lay persons and scholars alike to rely on more journalistic accounts. We hope our account will help rectify this dearth of solid information, although we would caution readers not to assume that all movement groups and religious communes are alike. Such is not the case, and we have attempted to make some comparisons with other groups where differences were obvious.

We also think that our work makes contributions to several areas of theoretical development in sociology, social psychology, and even psychology (personality assessment). Specifically, we have tested ideas from the "movement organization" literature of social movement research, along with applying many theoretical notions from the growing literature on communes. We have also examined questions about the types of people who join in such movements, and include a presentation of some of the only personality assessment available on members of such groups. We pay particular attention to the relationship of past drug usage and political involvement to the decision to affiliate with the group, since such questions have been prevalent in more popular discussions of such groups. We also expend considerable time discussing the concept of "alienation" and then applying it to participants in the group studied. A major focus of the work that is more social psychological is our examination of the conversion and resocialization processes used in the organization. This material should be of interest to many readers, given the recent controversy over alleged "brainwashing" by new religious groups and the just as controversial "deprogramming" that has developed in reaction to the new religions. The rather detailed appendix dealing with our experiences in doing this challenging and interesting research project will, we hope, also make some contribution to what may be the beginnings of a new specialized field of research—the interdisciplinary study of the many new religious groups that have developed in our society and other societies as well.

As is obvious from the last paragraph, we have attempted to do many things in this book, and to write simultaneously for several different audiences. Perhaps some will say that we attempted too much, but we hope that most who read our work will be pleased with our efforts.

Acknowledgements

By far, our largest debt is to the many members of CCO who allowed us to intrude into their lives, sometimes repeatedly. Without their willingness to cooperate with us, even when they thought us somewhat strange and misguided in our dedication to research, a study of this type would have been impossible. We are also appreciative of support, both direct and indirect, received from the University of Nevada, Reno. Direct support has been in the form of a Research Advisory Board grant of $2,300 used in the summer 1972, research, along with two small travel grants from the Social Psychology Doctoral Program Committee for other research trips. Indirect support from UNR has included secretarial help and some incidental help with duplicating and such. The first author is especially appreciative of a sabbatical spent at the London School of Economics, during which the major organization of this book was developed.

All the authors would like to acknowledge the support and help of their families, a few of whom had begun to think this book a never-ending siege. The patience and help of spouses, children, and parents is appreciated.

A number of people deserve thanks for directly helping in various way with this project, including interviewers Fred Kautz, Michael

Tissier, Bill May, Tom Perkins, Lori Backman and Maren Hungerford, the latter two of whom also aided in data analysis and coding. Rob Foss and Linda Globig helped with the data analysis; Doris Ginsberg made invaluable suggestions concerning questionnaire construction; and Caroline Simmonds aided with the indexing. Several colleagues at the University of Nevada, Reno, gave support of various kinds, including serving on graduate committees. These include Gerald Ginsburg, Carl Backman, Lyle Warner, Rebecca Stafford, John Marschall, Paul McReynolds, David Harvey, and Anne Howard. And we would like to express our appreciation to those of the secretarial staff who helped with typing and other such tasks. We are especially grateful to Sunny Minedew, who served as something of an administrative assistant-secretary for much of this project, and to Peggy Sagen, who did much of the final typing.

The research effort has been aided in many ways by the interest and suggestions of fellow researchers involved in studying religion. It would be impossible to name all who have helped in this manner, but we want especially to mention David Martin and Eileen Barker of the London School of Economics; Jim Beckford, University of Durham; Peter Jarvis, University of Surrey; Roy Wallis, Queens at Belfast; Rex Davis, formerly at the World Council of Churches in Geneva, now at Lincoln Cathedral, England; and Geoffrey Nelson, Birmingham Polytechnic. Within the United States, special thanks is due Meredith McGuire, Dick Anthony, Tom Robbins, Allan Eister, Pat McNamara, and Benton Johnson for their encouragement and assistance.

J.R.T.
M.W.S
R.B.S

Reno, Nevada
Fall 1977

Introduction

In the late 1960s, a nearly unbelievable event occurred on the West Coast of America. Thousands of young Americans became involved with one of the most unpredicted social movements in the history of this country—the so-called Jesus movement, accepting a brand of fundamentalist-oriented Christianity that many thought was dead. This movement was related in some important ways to other new religious movements of that time (see Needleman, 1970; Glock & Bellah, 1976) and also to the "commune movement" (see Rigby, 1974; Kanter, 1972b, among others), but it had some crucial differences which will be explicated. This Jesus movement started on the West Coast in places like San Francisco, the Los Angeles area, and Seattle, and quickly attracted much attention from commentators who had so recently been reporting a sharply contrasting phenomenon, the violent explosions of political sentiment on college campuses. This unique and puzzling Jesus movement rapidly gained prominence and large numbers of participants, and stayed "in the news" for several years, only gradually dropping from "sight." Sporadic attention has been given the movement since, over such issues as alleged "brainwashing" of young people who become members, and there have been several state and federal government investigations of various recruitment and financial practices of movement groups (see Charity Frauds Bureau,

1974; Californial Legislature Senate Select Committee on Children and Youth, 1974). Also, a rather well-publicized "countermovement" has developed under the name "deprogramming" (See Shupe, Spielman, & Stigall, 1977).

Aside from this negative and indirect kind of occasional publicity, there has been little attention given to the movement since the early years of its development, especially in the more scholarly publications. (All such writing known to the authors is listed in the bibliography.) Some early treatments of the beginnings of some segments of the movement were quite informative (especially Enroth, Ericson, & Peters, 1972), but little of lasting value has been produced since, except for a few journal articles which typically focused on specific groups in the movement. Thus the American public, both lay and scholarly, is rather uninformed about what has happened to the movement in the ten years of its existence. Few people realize that the movement is "alive and well." Several of its groups have achieved a remarkable degree of strength and stability and must now be considered more or less permanent fixtures on the religious scene in America, and even around the world. This book focuses on one major JM-derived organization that has received relatively little publicity, except for the "anonymous" attention focused on the group by our own publications.

Few people realize the extent to which the larger Jesus movement has penetrated other parts of the world, with groups in some 70 countries at present (see Richardson, 1975; Balswick, 1974; Davis & Richardson, 1976, for more details on the international scope of the movement). There seems to be little appreciation of the fact that several hundred thousand young people in America and around the world have had quite meaningful and sometimes life-changing experiences through the movement, and that thousands of these young people still remain in the Jesus movement groups that have managed to survive and even prosper.[1]

Just the *numbers* of participants alone would make continued study of this phenomenon worthwhile, but other considerations even add to the need for more attention to be focused on the movement and its groups and organizations. The *timing* of the movement is one such interesting aspect; it occurred at a time when many thought American society might well disintegrate, and it may well have made an important contribution to the "cooling off" that America experienced in the late 1960s and early 1970s. Also, the possible ties of the movement with *shifting attitudes* among younger members of modern societies warrant attention being paid to the movement in America and other countries around the world.

These broad questions aside, there are still many important reasons to study the Jesus movement groups. Much can be gained that is of interest to many areas of human endeavor. Religionists should be interested in the meaning of the movement from the point of view of changes in religious institutions, and in relating the movement to religious history. Theologians should find the beliefs shared by the movement to be of interest, especially since they *seem* "old-fashioned" but are viewed as "new and different" by most participants (see Balswick's 1974 discussion of this phenomenon). Psychologists might well be concerned about why people affiliated with movement groups, and about the "personality types" that would get involved with such strange happenings. Furthermore, they might desire to know what happens to the "personalities" of participants once they join. Do participants become more "self-actualized," more "dependent," or what? Are movement groups "therapeutic groups" or not? Social psychologists should be fascinated by the processes used by movement groups to "convert" and resocialize members, and to maintain certain "types" of members. They will also find the development of leadership structures in movement groups of interest. Sociologists should have a multitude of concerns with the movement. Family sociologists should appreciate that new family forms are being developed in the movement, and that everything from courtship patterns to child-rearing techniques to family financial support methods have been the subject of experimentation by some movement groups. Commune theorists can study the various ways that communes can be organized, and can learn much about utopian types of communal experiments that were so important to early American history, but which many thought had mostly "died out." Organization theorists should be intrigued by the development of new organizational forms, with fascinating changes taking place as the new organizations seek to survive. Social movement and collective behavior theorists obviously can find much of value in a study of this movement, as it offers an opportunity to test some crucial notions from such literature. Historical and sociological interest is heightened by the juxtaposition of the Jesus movement with other important movements. It followed closely on the heels of the massive antiwar and civil rights movements, and occurred at about the same time as some other important movements such as women's liberation. Social theorists can, in the movement, find a fertile field for testing ideas related to such important concepts as alienation and anomy. We will not even try to list prominent concerns of sociologists of religion that might well be better understood by close examination of this and related movements.

THE PURPOSE AND ORGANIZATION
OF THIS BOOK

This book is an attempt to answer several of the important questions mentioned and to furnish material related to other areas of study. The book is the result of more than six years of study which focused on one major movement organization—herein called Christ Communal Organization (CCO)—that has been little-chronicled in the popular media. Our writing also has been informed of other solid research on the movement. Hundreds of "person-hours" have been spent by the three of us—all sociologists and social psychologists—in this research project, details of which are presented in Appendix A. Two dissertations have come from the study (Harder, 1973; Simmonds, 1977), along with several publications and professional papers (see Bibliography for full listing), and we have accumulated what is probably the largest and most thorough set of data available on any movement group. Most of this data is as yet unpublished, and this book is an attempt to organize much of this material in a coherent form, so that scholars from the several disciplines referred to earlier can have a relatively definitive account of at least one large movement group. Also, we think the work presented herein makes contributions to some of the specific areas discussed. Particularly we would mention the areas of "movement organization" theory, general organization theory, conversion processes, personality assessment, "alienation" theory, commune theory, sociology of religion, and even research methods.

The book has six parts, each with a somewhat different focus. Part A gives the history and ideology of the organization studied, and also presents the elaborate differentiation that has taken place in the few years of CCO's existence. Chapter 2 is a detailed analysis of changes that have occurred in CCO, with some theoretical comments, and Chapter 3 is a critique and application of "movement organization" theorizing built on the seminal paper of Zald and Ash (1966), and later work by Curtis and Zurcher (1974) and Zurcher and Curtis (1973).

Part B focuses more on CCO "culture" and tries to give readers a glimpse of what life in CCO has been like over the ten years of its short history. Chapter 4 discusses the daily typical life experiences of most members, while Chapter 5 discusses the crucial configuration of the beliefs and behaviors that make up the CCO approach to sex roles, courtship, marriage, family life, and child rearing. In this chapter, we use the familism-collectivism conceptualization from the commune literature (see Kanter, 1973; and Talmon, 1973, especially) in an attempt to communicate the import of recent changes in this area of CCO life.

Part C focuses on the individual level of analysis. Chapter 6 presents a great deal of descriptive material on participants—their social backgrounds their experiences prior to affiliation, their attitudes about a number of things, and their drug usage histories. Chapter 7 presents some of our personality assessment data gained from an administration of the Adjective Check List (Gough & Heilbrun, 1965) to CCO members, and Chapter 8 discusses the important area of changes in political beliefs and values. This chapter also contains data gained from a preliminary attempt to apply Berger's (1967) concept of alienation in empirical research, an attempt which yielded some provocative findings.

Part D contains a major theoretical effort of our research. Chapter 9 contains a critique of the "conversion literature" of sociology of religion and social psychology, especially that of Lofland and Stark (1965) and Gerlach and Hine (1970), and presents an extension of such work that seems to fit better such phenomena as the Jesus movement.

We close the book with Part E, which returns to an organizational level of analysis with a detailed examination, from the perspective of "commune theory," of future prospects for the organization we studied. Kanter's (1972) work on commitment mechanisms is applied in this chapter, and we arrive at a very defensible prediction that CCO will indeed last for the foreseeable future.

Appendix A gives a history of the research project, which has continued for several years and has involved a number of people in several major data-gathering trips and visits to CCO communes and operations. In Appendix A, we address the question of why our research experience has been successful, especially in light of the problems discussed in the Robbins, Anthony, & Curtis (1973) paper analyzing the problematic situation they encountered in trying to study another movement group. Appendix B is a more detailed analysis of the "movement organization" hypotheses from the work discussed in Chapter 3.

ORIGINS OF THE JESUS MOVEMENT

Before moving into the material specifically related to CCO, it may be useful to discuss briefly the origins of the greater Jesus movement in America.[2] We use the Jesus movement as a general vehicle of

xx   Organized Miracles

analysis, even though we certainly consider CCO to be part of other movements as well (such as the "commune movement"). The general search for alternative life styles and values and the move away from some core values of modern industrial American society are amply illustrated by CCO. However, since group members readily identify with the Jesus movement, we will in this section accept their self-designation and focus on that movement. We think, however, that the brief analysis offered will also apply in part to an explanation of some of the broader concerns mentioned.

Some will not be so interested in this analysis, which has been presented in more detail before (Richardson, 1974) and may want to skip to Part A. Others less familiar with the movement may find such a discussion useful. This section makes use of Smelser's (1963) model of the development of social movements, and is thus to be viewed as a deliberately sociological analysis of the Jesus movement (and related phenomena). The brevity of this section necessitates taking some liberties in the direction of simplifying Smelser's theorizing on collective behavior. It is to be noted that he uses a "value-added" perspective which means, in short, that his analytical model is *not* to be interpreted chronologically, but instead that instances of collective behavior occur only because of certain configurations of his six major determinants.

Structural Conduciveness

Smelser's first determinant, *structural conduciveness,* can be used as both a "positive" and a "negative" factor to explain the Jesus movement. First, it should be noted that other types of movements, particularly political movements, were viewed by many in the late 1960s as *not* being acceptable to most segments of the society. Many university administrations and ther leaders and politicians attempted to stifle the many demonstrations that were occurring, and the inevitable result of confrontation politics was violence such as that at Kent State. In the minds of many, this violence indicated that in the late 1960s the structure of American society was no longer conducive to such political action on the part of the young people in that society, however well-educated, well-intentioned, or closely related they were to those in positions of power in the society. Traditional political channels had already been dismissed by most young people, since such channels had had little effect on stopping the war or on gaining civil rights for the disadvantaged.

Another major event was the expulsion of whites from the civil rights movement. Thus in the late 1960s, all major ongoing movements (civil rights, student protest, antiwar) were no longer perceived as very accessible to the unprecedented large groups of the "structurally unin-hibited" middle and upper class, college-age, white young people who demographers have noted were present in society. The unwillingness of most segments of society to condone the values and behaviors of the drug culture is yet another indication of the lack of structural conduciveness in American society for alternative forms of activity.

On the other hand, in American society, religion, particularly tradi-tional kinds of religion, nearly always has been positively sanctioned, allowed, and even encouraged. It is worth noting that the most rapidly growing churches in recent times have been fundamentalist-oriented (Kelley, 1972). This tradition has spawned a number of campus-re-lated groups such as Campus Crusade for Christ, Inter-Varsity Fellow-ship, Fellowship of Christian Athletes, and well-developed campus ministry programs whereby fundamentalism has had major contacts on university campuses and among youth groups. In short, traditional conservative religion has been encouraged and presented forcefully by many different groups to American youth.

Another factor is that many young people had experienced substan-tial religious socialization during their youth. (Many Jesus movement participants were part of the "children's revival" of the 1950s in Amer-ica; see Nash & Berger, 1962.) Further, the use of drugs had contrib-uted to an interest in things spiritual for many youths (see Clark, 1969), a factor that several observers have considered to be crucial not just to the Jesus movement, but also to other religious movements, such as those emphasizing the occult or eastern religions. The effect of this combination of positive and negative factors related to "con-duciveness" is that in the late 1960s, American society was structurally conducive to the onset of the Jesus movement (as well as certain other movements).

Structural Strain

We have seen in the last two decades many examples of *structural strain*, Smelser's second element, occurring in American society. The 1954 Supreme Court decision to desegregate public schools marked the beginning of an age of protest. In the late 1950s many college-age students involved themselves in activities that were supposed to do away with the racism that had been made a public issue by the Su-preme Court decision. Some young people went into the South to help desegregate schools and to confront racism in other institutional structures. They soon found out that Southern institutional structures were not so easily changed, and that they could literally "die trying." Many young whites became radicalized and upon their return to campus contributed to an ever-growing group of radicalized students ready to take issue with other felt problems confronting them.

These young people, part of a unique and large cadre of comparatively well-educated students, were further galvanized by the continued prosecution of the war in Vietnam. Few government leaders fully appreciated the explosive potential of a relatively well-informed generation of young men being forced by conscription to fight in a war that many of them believed was legally and morally wrong (not to mention stupid). Other issues, such as *in loco parentis* policies of universities and colleges also became involved in the protests.

The explosion of the student-protest/antiwar movement surprised many people, but in retrospect it seems so easily explicable that social scientists should be astonished at their naiveté in not having expected what took place. The protest movement grew to a very large size, involving literally hundreds of thousands of students at various times during the middle and late 1960s. The time of the Cambodian invasion saw nearly 500 colleges and universities shut down in the largest such action in American history.

However, structural strain continued because it became evident to many that the efforts of students and those who sympathized with them were relatively ineffectual.[3] The war, racism, and other problems continued. The ineffectiveness of the student protest movement in meaningfully modifying university structures or in stopping the war was dramatically demonstrated with the killings at Kent State and Jackson State, which let all the world—including participants in the student protest movement—know that "the State will kill its children." Another important segment of political action was completely closed to whites when Blacks excluded them from much of the civil rights movement, which was also viewed as relatively ineffectual. Thus political action undertaken by many to alleviate strains in the structure of American society actually contributed more strain to an already stressed society.

Many young people were already involved in experimentation with drugs, an involvement that often led to more personal "strains" (acquisition of drugs, addiction, etc.). Around 1967–68 and even before, a large number of young people began to "drop out" and "turn on." The "flower children" subculture presented a sharp contrast to the politically-oriented activist youth although the two groups overlapped considerably, but both evidenced strain in American society.

Patterns of Belief

The third element of Smelser's model is the *growth and spread of a generalized belief.* In the 1960s, a number of social problems demanded solution, but no pertinent solutions were immediately at hand. One general alternative was for concerned youths to refocus on other problems. Many did, in sociologically understandable ways, just this, moving into the more acceptable ecology movement or, for more militant females, the women's liberation movement. Others, particularly those with much previous religious socialization (and perhaps some who had exhausted other alternatives) moved to the Jesus movement. Those adopting the ideology of the Jesus movement reinterpreted the "strains" so that they were no longer problems, or at least problems over which the individual should exercise control in terms of changing society. Thus we saw an old message being presented to a new group, especially in California where the student protest movement had begun. Balswick (1974) has insightfully referred to this phenomena, using Mannheim's term, as a "fresh contact."

The message was that the problems of society were caused primarily not by structural misalignments, but by the sinfulness of man. This, of course, is the message of fundamentalism, a message made famous by a number of preachers in American history, most recently by Billy Graham. He and other spokesmen of fundamentalism indicate that such things as racism, Vietnam, and all other major problems derive directly from the fact that individuals are sinful. Fundamentalism, as an ideology, focuses on the individual instead of the structure, and this change of focus was just what many of the young people in our society were ready to accept. The other focus (structural) had not led to many easily discernible positive results. The fundamentalist perspective promised two ways of erasing the strains that were felt. One way, of course, was for everyone "to accept Jesus Christ as personal savior." Another part of the ideology, however, indicated that the world would end soon, making attempts to do anything but evangelize wasteful. Thus the "new" beliefs furnished an interpretation of the situation that was more personally "functional" for many, especially if they were predisposed toward such views or had had alternative views discounted.

The typical beliefs of Jesus movement groups (which will be discussed in more detail in Chapter 1) were usually similar in emphasis to the focus on the individual found in encounter and other "folk psychology" movements, the well-publicized movement to eastern religions by some previous campus radicals, the movement to drugs, and also the movement back into mainstream American society, with its still-current Horatio Alger myths of individual success. This "new" generalized belief seems to be a return to a general ideological motif that has long pervaded American history.

Precipitating Factors

We have already mentioned several things that could be classified as *precipitating factors,* the fourth determinant in Smelser's model, for the inception of the Jesus Movement. First, the very dramatic demonstrations—such as Kent State and Jackson State—of the extent to which some individuals and agencies of government were willing to go for the sake of order contributed to a dramatic increase of interest among a number of young people in other alternative forms of belief and behavior, such as that of the Jesus movement. Second the continual apparent failures of political action constituted a series of "small" precipitating events that may have been important cumulatively in the development of such interest. Every additional failure led to disillusionment by more and more people. Third, several groups (such as the Christian World Liberation Front, in Berkeley) and individual Jesus movement leaders (such as Blessit and Pederson) were independently and dramatically calling attention to their "new" perspective. Mass baptisms in the Pacific, carrying a cross across the country, and forceful witnessing by several such groups are examples of such "media-prone" events of the late 1960s. Some commentators would even suggest that the concentration of the media on a few unusual happenings by some fundamentalist self-appointed youth leaders sparked the Jesus movement We would disagree, but only in terms of the emphasis; obviously the media played a large role in publicizing and spreading the "new" generalized belief, with its attendant behavior. Related to this, several leaders of organizations such as Campus Crusade dropped out of their organizations and started ministering to the street people in more "hip" ways (Berkeley's Christian World Liberation Front started this way). Some major churches on the West Coast started programs (coffee houses, religious folk music groups, etc.) designed to reach the "drop out" youth. Fourth, one must also consider the more personal crises of members as individual precipitating events. Most Jesus movement researchers have found many participants who had bad experiences with drugs, some who were having sexual identity problems, others who had unwanted pregnancies or children, or who **had** contracted venereal disease, or who had been brought to grief in some other way by sexual activity and/or drug usage (see Harder, Richardson, & Simmonds, 1972; Adams & Fox, 1972; Gordon, 1974). Some had experienced considerable difficulties with their families or some sort of psychic difficulty in terms of defining a "meaning of life" for themselves. The confluence of all these "negative" and "positive" precipitating factors contributed greatly to the rise of the Jesus movement.

Leadership and Activity

The next element in the Smelser model is the element of *mobilization of participants for action*. How did the Jesus movement organize itself for self-maintenance in order to become a movement of import in American history? One key consideration was the type of leadership that developed, which was in most instances what would be called charismatic. That is to say, seldom did people in authority in the institutional church pick out individuals who then led parts of the movement. The leaders were usually self-appointed people such as Blessit, Sparks, and Pederson, the ex-Campus Crusade people, and many, many others across the United States who felt that they had something to offer and could convince enough people to develop at least a temporary following. This type of leadership is quite flexible and is situationally-oriented, and was of great importance in starting and maintaining groups within the movement.

Another important "mobilization" consideration is the communal life-style adopted by most branches of the Jesus movement, which quite often was dealing with persons who, for various reasons, were not able to stay at home with their families. They were people on the road—people who had "burned their bridges" because of involvements in political movements, drugs and sex, and because of a rejection of parental values. An obvious solution to the problem of a lack of community among these young people was a communally-oriented movement. The past decade has seen hundreds, even thousands of communes spring up across the face of America and many have a religious focus (see Zablocki, 1972). This natural growth of communal living for people who would otherwise be homeless furnished a surrogate family for many of the participants and a loving, caring atmosphere in which to live. The importance of the communal motif in changing people's views and behavior and in maintaining the new perspective should be obvious.

The media must also be mentioned again in conjunction with mobilization. Participants in some Jesus movement groups sometimes stage their own "media events" for publicity purposes. Others have developed widely read newspapers, some of which have been published by the hundreds of thousands. Still others, such as CCO, shun most publicity, but nonetheless gain members as a result of the attention of the media.

One last "organizational" point is that, even thought most leaders of the movement openly criticize the institutional church and society in general, alignments with both are not rare. Such ties have contributed much to the development and maintenance of the movement, even though its jargon is often anti-institutional (and especially anti-institutional church) in nature. Such ties between the movement groups and the institutional structure of society which are important in terms of "mobilization" also illustrate the last of Smelser's six elements—*social control*.

Social Control and the Jesus Movement

A society can respond to a social movement in many ways. It can repress and destroy it, radicalizing remnants of the movement and forcing them underground (i.e., the Weathermen). It can ignore the movement, allowing it to grow (or perhaps even die) from a lack of attention. However, a society can also welcome and even encourage a movement either directly or indirectly. In the main American society has seemed pleased with the advent of the Jesus movement. We have already mentioned the structural conduciveness of American society with reference to religious solutions to problems. A number of occurrences in America indicate that our society reacted positively to the movement itself, once it did begain. This is not withstanding the notoriety gained by some segments of the Jesus movement (especially the Alamo's Christian Foundation and the Children of God), which have been accused of kidnapping and brainwashing young people, and the publicity given to the "deprogrammers" involved in kidnapping and reconverting several hundred members of Jesus movement groups and other new religious groups as well. (CCO has had little problem with deprogramming so far.)

The institutional church has paid close attention to the Jesus movement, and mainly welcomed and even mimicked it. The news media in American society, which generally paid a great deal of attention to the Jesus movement at first, has usually responded favorably as well. There have been a number of dramatic encouragements both by lay leaders in society and by institutional church leaders, some of which will be described in Chapter 1.

At the same time that American society generally welcomed the

Jesus movement, it continued to discourage many other alternatives. Punitive drug laws, reactions to student political action, the growing disenchantment among whites concerning the civil rights movement, the generally bad economic situation in the United States, and similar factors worked together to discourage alternative types of action to both the Jesus movement and to other "harmless" movements such as ecology or eastern religion.

In sum it is quite easy to say that, in the main, American society has responded favorably to the Jesus movement. Apparently, most parents would prefer to see their sons and daughters involved in a fundamentalist religious commune than to see them involved in a political demonstration or with drugs (the deprogramming furor notwithstanding). Local, state, and even the federal agencies are apparently also willing to encourage in various ways the growth of the Jesus movement.

It is perhaps too cynical to suggest that the "power structure" realizes that those involved in the Jesus movement are no longer acting to change the structure of society, and that this is the reason for this indirect and direct encouragement. A more defensible explanation for the general support of the social structure for the movement probably involves a recognition by those in positions of authority that a similarity of values and goals is shared by the greater society and the movement. Whatever the explanation, available information indicates that this positiveness exists, and it is obviously very important to the movement.

NOTES

1. The size of the movement has been a point of debate. Hollenweger (1974) gives a summary of estimates of participants—estimates which vary from 300,000 to 3 million. What is meant by "participant" is also important, however, as some are full-time and fully-committed members, others are more like "hangers-on," and some move in and out of movement groups. Note, however, that a number of movement groups have continued to exist, which means they have a cadre of committed members and are continuing to attract new converts. The two largest and strongest JM groups are the Children of God (see David & Richardson, 1976) and the group studied in the research reported here, referred to with the pseudonym "Christ Communal Organization." However, a number of smaller "independent" groups also continue to exist, both in the United States and abroad.
2. This analysis will focus on the American scene. Those interested in the situation vis-à-vis the movement outside America are referred to a paper, "The Jesus Movement Outside America" (Richardson, 1975), which was based on a year's sabbatical research in the Western European area, to Balswick (1974), and to Corry (1973).

3. Only the passage of time can reveal what effects the student protest movement had on American society. We are only trying here to indicate that most participants seemed to accept a view that little if any meaningful change was occurring as a result of the massive actions associated with the protests.

PART A

AN ORGANIZATIONAL ANALYSIS

In this part we will deal with Christ Communal Organization (CCO) at an organizational level, leaving information on more individual and social psychological levels of analysis for later sections of the book. A first requirement for an analysis of CCO as an organization is a recounting of its history. The history is presented in enough detail to make clear what kind of organization CCO is and how it developed. Another essential feature of an organizational analysis is a discussion of group beliefs or ideology, and chapter 1 also contains an attempt to explain the modified form of fundamentalism that has been adopted and implemented by CCO. Chapter 1 closes with a descriptive delineation of major organizational differentiation that has occurred during the short history of CCO.

In chapter 2, we focus on changes in some major features of CCO as an organization. This chapter, which contains a number of diagrams that we think will be helpful to readers, focuses on changes in five major facets of CCO. These include (1) group aims and goals; (2) the leadership and authority structure of CCO; (3) CCO group and individual methods of financial support; (4) living arrangements; and (5) methods of member training and resocialization. While other areas of CCO organizational life might have been chosen for our analysis, these were felt by us to be major elements that should be examined,

3

and we think such a focus allows readers to gain an understanding of the type of organization that CCO was and has become in just a few short years. Also in this chapter are brief discussions of the CCO organization from the point of view of "church-sect" theory, commune typology theory, along with an analysis of the so-called "integrative hypothesis" vis-à-vis CCO.

In chapter 3 we examine, based particularly on the material from chapter 2, the CCO organizational changes in the light of the "movement organization" literature, which was given impetus by the widely-reprinted Zald and Ash (1966) paper. This chapter represents the first direct contribution of this book to sociological theory, for we think that our "test" of the ideas of Zald and Ash and others (Zurcher & Curtis, 1973; Curtis & Zurcher, 1974) in this tradition furnishes considerable useful information on which to build theory in the area of movement organizations. The material of chapter 3 is dealt with in more detail in Appendix B, which is a specific testing of the many hypotheses from the three major "movement organization" papers examined in chapter 3.

1

History and Beliefs of the Organization

GROUP HISTORY

The early history of this organization, herein called Christ Communal Organization (CCO), began in that cauldron of new social movements, Southern California in the late 1960s. It developed at about the time that several other prominent groups within the so-called Jesus movement were starting in the Southern California area. Among these are the Children of God (COG) led by Moses David Berg and fostered for a time by a television evangelist, the Alamo's Christian Foundation, and several others. The early history of the movement on the West Coast is best chronicled in Enroth, Ericson, and Peters (1972), and we will not attempt another detailed explanation of the exact relationship of the various groups, as our intent in this chapter is to focus on one as yet unchronicled organization's early history. It is worth noting, however, that there was some contact among these groups in the late 1960s, and that they were involved in doctrinal disputes and competition for members early in the movement's history. An understanding of this contributes to an understanding of the amazing differentiation within the movement during its early days—a little-understood heterogeneity that continues to this day. A history of CCO written especially for the organization's journal by the initial leader of the group (who still is the leader) documented some of these disputes. Two especially important disagreements were with the local Teen Challenge group (one of the offshoots of Wilkerson's *The Cross and the Switch-Blade*, 1968, approach), and with the Children of God, back before they were even called the COG.[1] Many other disagreements and leadership battles were also discussed in this history—battles that took place as CCO was attempting to define itself and establish boundaries of accepted beliefs and behaviors. That these battles were successful in the sense that a strong, well-defined organization resulted is evidenced by the size and strength of the organization, which now has over one thousand full-time members, established groups in about twenty-five states, and capital assets of nearly $2 million. How such a large and strong organization developed will be the focus of this first part of chapter 1 (along with a discussion of the theology or ideology of the group), with the latter part of the chapter being a somewhat more detailed description of the major financial and material holdings and operations of the organization as it exists today.

Early History [2]

The young man who still serves CCO as president of their nonprofit corporation and head of their "spiritual body" was converted in 1966 while living in Southern California.[3] For the first eighteen months of his new Christian existence (he was previously Catholic), he claims to have had no contact with other Christians who believed as he did. Subsequently, a person with similar beliefs started to work with the same firm, and a friendship built on the similarity of beliefs developed. This other person, still a CCO member in a leadership capacity, invited the leader-to-be to meet some other friends who agreed with them on doctrine, thus establishing contact with a now well-known person, Charles (Chuck) Smith, pastor of the famous Calvary Chapel Church in Costa Mesa, California. The CCO leader-to-be went along to a Bible study and was delighted to hear a group of people and a pastor who shared his beliefs. An immediate rapport was established between Pastor Smith and the leader-to-be. This bond continues to the present, with Pastor Smith being referred to by the leader as a "personal Elder," who serves as an advisor in times of "trials" and tough decisions.[4] This leader became involved with the developing ministry of Smith at his church, which was still quite small at the time of the initial encounter, and it was here that the leader received his training in a particular interpretation of Scripture. The experience of the leader of "baptism of the Holy Spirit" or "speaking in tongues" (glossolalia) also took place under Smith's tutelage, and it was Smith who later encouraged the leader to serve as elder in the first Christian commune opened and supported in part by Calvary Chapel. Smith encouraged the leader to minister to the hippie types in the area, a ministry that was already a "burden" of the leader. This first Christian house was called the House of Miracles, and it was opened on May 17, 1968, with Calvary Chapel furnishing the first $50 of the $90 monthly rent payments. Living expenses were also furnished by the church and friends of the church, as the leader was not working. The leader explained that he had felt led to grow a beard, which was a great "tool for witnessing" to the street people, but which effectively kept him from getting any kind of work in the area.

This house was an immediate success, and droves of youth began coming to get a meal, find a place to sleep, and to hear the "gospel message." Contact was established with another Christian house—the House of Acts in San Francisco, and one of the leaders in that group came for a while to aid in the new house ministry in Costa Mesa. During the first week, twenty-one people were converted, and by the end of the second week some fifty people were living in the house. The decision to establish a Christian house had obviously "struck a nerve," and converts continued to pour out of the drug subculture of the area and into this and other "Christian houses." One piece of dramatic evidence of the rapid growth and type of response involved one runaway young woman who was converted and then brought over fifty people to the house during the next three weeks! An early decision by the new elder to have all new converts begin to witness and evangelize immediately further increased the pressure on the meager facilities, a pressure aggravated by complaining neighbors who objected to "hippies" living in the area and sleeping "wall-to-wall" and in the backyard of the house.

During these early months of frequent conversion, overcrowding, and feverish activity, the basic structure and life-style of the organization began to emerge. Every day involved street witnessing by nearly all occupants, except those who were ill, working, or who were preparing food, and so on. Some new members quickly found jobs which would help support the group. The emphasis on work, which sharply distinguishes this group from some organizations that are a part of the Jesus movement, grew out of a Bible study on commitment. The group had been led earlier to accept the view that they should sell all their goods and depend on God for support. After they did this and were destitute, to quote the elder, "God ministered to us that we should go to work." And go to work they did, accepting any kind of work that required little skill, for few of the converts had any useful skills at all. This aspect of group life will be more fully discussed later, as it has greatly contributed to the continuance and success of the organization. Nightly Bible studies, usually led by the elder, also developed, during which those who were gathered in as a result of beach and street witnessing during the day were challenged to "accept Christ." These studies continue to this day throughout CCO, with all of its communes and families participating in a unified plan of nightly Bible study, supplemented now with some technical media aids, and led by many different "house pastors" who have been "raised up" within the group.

The success of the first House of Miracles led to the desire to establish others, and one was opened in Riverside when a derelict motel owned by a sympathetic businessman was rented and refurbished by members. This commune had four "elders," two of whom were youths of nineteen and seventeen years of age. The inexperience of its leadership notwithstanding, the house was made liveable quickly, with friends furnishing materials and the youthful members doing the work. During the first week of operation, some sixty-five youths were converted and baptized in the fish pond of the motel. By the end of summer 1968, over five hundred young people had been converted through this ministry, and the commune had outgrown its quarters.

New communal "Christian houses" were opened in several places soon thereafter. (Calvary Chapel is credited with helping to establish and support dozens of such Christian houses in the years that followed the first House of Miracles, but we will not attempt to describe all of these, as our interest is mainly on those that eventually formed the beginnings of CCO, on which we started research in late 1970). The next one of these "Christian houses" which was under the at first informal control (or at least influence) of the leader opened in Santa Ana in September of 1968. This facility actually replaced the first house in Costa Mesa since some neighbors there were complaining so strongly about the commune. Again the "brothers" and "sisters" had to repair the place and make it liveable, but by now they were getting used to this technique of obtaining housing. They were quite happy with this new house, as it "had a nice freeway not too far away . . . on a hitchhiking route," furnishing them with ready access to the itinerant youth population moving about the area. The house at Santa Ana also had a small garden plot, and it was here that the group got its first taste of such work.

At the end of the summer of 1968, the Riverside motel "house" was closed down due to disputes within the group. Such disputes were commonplace in the early history of the group (as with other such groups), and we have read and been told of arguments over such occurrences as new converts continuing to use and sell drugs while living in a house; members trying to gain control of part of the "body" (group) through "false doctrines" and direct challenges to the authority of the original leader; the use of alcohol; and an ambitious member trying to usurp authority over work teams and thereby control the money earned. Other difficulties arose because of critical neighbors, and at least once, members living at the house were attacked by a motorcycle gang trying to "sell protection." But in the face of all these problems, CCO persisted and began to establish boundaries of behavior and belief—boundaries that are now quite well-defined.

We will discuss in greater depth the authority structure that eventually developed and how it functions, but it should be noted here that many, if not most, of the present leaders of CCO (and their wives) came into the group by being converted in one of these early houses in 1968 and 1969. Some extremely energetic and talented young men and women were attracted to the group, and some have remained in the group, maintaining positions of top leadership ever since. We have met most of this cadre of leaders and can state unequivocally that they could be successes at about any endeavor they chose. Instead of becoming "secular" businessmen, teachers, or accountants, they committed themselves to the beliefs and goals of the original leader and became a strong and dependable team of workers ready to "try anything." This is not to say that *only* these young men could have accomplished what they have, or that *only* the "failures" and "weaklings" dropped out of the group. We are simply claiming that a dozen or so very capable people came together in the late 1960s and committed themselves to each other and to a way of life that has worked remarkably well for them since.[5]

Also in the fall of 1968, a new house was opened in Fontana, California, an important step for the new organization because of a two-acre garden plot, which caused some more CCO members to gain more experience in agriculture, an experience that was to prove invaluable later. Some married couples in Santa Ana also opened their homes to new converts. This first house outside California was established in November 1968, in Phoenix, Arizona. Both the Fontana and Phoenix houses were successful in attracting many converts. At one point, a person who was an elder in the Fontana house tried to take control of it and the Phoenix house, separating them from the other houses, but this plan was thwarted by energetic intervention of the original leader and other members.

Other new houses included one in Corona which was established in

January 1969 and lasted six months, and another in Riverside. Bible study groups which were noncommunal were also developed in some homes in the area. The new house in Riverside, which operated until September 1969, is especially interesting because it was opened in a unique way that has been used since a time or two in the expansion of the organization.[6] Some Christians who were part of the "body" of the House of Miracles houses made a deliberate decision to move into a commune full of "dopers." They immediately began witnessing to people and leading Bible studies, and soon converted a few residents. The other "unbelievers" decided to move, leaving the Christians with the facility. Meanwhile the Phoenix house had "backslid" and ceased to be a part of the informal group of communes being guided by the original leader (with the counsel of Reverend Smith).

Getting Organized

At this time the original leader asked for a more formal commitment from the four communal Christian houses that were involved so closely with each other—Fontana, Riverside, Corona, and Santa Ana. The pastors of all the houses gave a commitment, including even the Fontana house, which was still coheaded by a person with his own designs on leadership of the confederation of the four communes. Armed with these commitments, the leader solicited Reverend Smith to endorse his leadership and "to take oversight of us as a bishop and give us counsel; and he agreed." In a crucial meeting that followed, however, a great argument broke out as the Fontana leader tried to fight the attempt to organize four houses under the original leader. The Fontana leader used a strong attack accusing the leader of being too liberal about cigarette smoking (his wife, a new convert, still smoked, and also the leader allowed smoking areas for new members in the communes). Smith stopped this attack by simply disallowing it and led a Bible study instead. This instance of the exercise of authority by a member of the so-called institutional church was quite important to the establishment of this organization, a fact that should not be ignored. This kind of key involvement of "the institution" with such groups seems much more typical than some care to admit, but such ties exist nonetheless. In the case of Calvary Chapel's pastor, we accept that he is somewhat "on the fringe" of the traditional institutional church, but still would point out that his authority, which was at least partially derived from and legitimated by his position as pastor of the church, was very valuable in settling the internal dispute over control of the several houses. Only when such differences were settled and the leader was implicitly but effectively "anointed" by Smith could the organization begin to act more independently and take the actions that have led it to its present strong and solid position. As we have said, this tie with Calvary Chapel has loosened considerably since then, but the relationship was of great importance in the early history of the group.

The Big Move

Houses were still being opened in Southern California, an outreach which continues to this day, with houses presently in San Diego, Sacramento, and San Francisco (which has two houses—one for a "crash pad" and the other for quarters for new members). However, shortly after the leader was anointed he began to investigate a move to another Western state. In April 1969, the leader and several members moved from California, leaving some of the "stronger brothers" as pastors in the several California houses and Bible study fellowships that had been established there.

The move to the new state was made "under the guidance and protection of the Holy Spirit," according to the leader, who felt directed to go, accompanied by the person who had originally introduced him to Reverend Smith, to visit another area. They "put out the fleece," and were answered by a visiting man from that area who wanted them to move their ministry to his area. This person drove them several hundred miles and introduced them to a group of pastors of churches in his conservative denomination. At a meeting arranged for the leader to "tell his story," this group of pastors voted to give several hundred dollars to the group if they would come to the area and establish a house there. The person then loaned the two men a large van in which they returned to Southern California for those people "that the Lord had picked," to bring them to the new area.

That first contingent of people numbered about fifteen, including three married couples each with a small child, and several single "brothers." The group moved into a large house owned by the person who had arranged their earlier visit, a house outside a rather large city in the new state. Bad feelings immediately developed between the man and group members. Apparently this benefactor had plans to be in full control of the group, and he required (they claim) that all money received from churches to establish a house be given to him. This situation caused great distress among the group, and they began working to extract themselves from their dependency on the person. Some of the men started working and earned $200 for painting a house—

money that was used to rent a large vacant house that the leader had located in the nearby city by searching and reading legal documents in the city's house of records. First the three young families moved in, even though the house had no dishes, no silverware, no pots or pans, and no furniture except a few mattresses on the floor and cribs (brought from California) for the babies. There was not even enough money to buy food for the babies, and the first breakfast was bought for the group by an unexpected early morning visitor to the house.

The leader, because of the problematic situation of the group, "felt led" to go to a Salvation Army administrative office in the neighborhood to volunteer the group's services in ministering to itinerant youth. The Salvation Army administrator accepted the offer and in return offered baby food (someone had just donated a month's supply) and other needed items. The group immediately received a month's supply of food of all kinds, including berries, meat, sugar, spices, baby food, and other things. From a local Goodwill store they obtained free furniture for the entire house, along with dishes, silverware, and cooking utensils. In these two instances, we again see evidence of important ties between the Jesus movement and parts of the institutional structure of society—an institutional structure that was, it seems, usually willing to help a group of young people who accepted and practiced certain basic Christian tenets.

Soon after getting the first house in the new area established, the leader felt led to attempt to begin a new house, and a two man team, with only 65¢ between them, was sent to another urban area in the state. They first lived a few days with a sympathetic family, but soon again tried the tactic of moving into a "dopers" commune and converting them. Again the tactic was successful—the social order of that commune was destroyed and a new "Christian" one substituted with most of the members becoming "believers." Soon an opportunity developed to rent a house in this new town, and thus a new ministry was established quickly. At the time of the move to the new state, the name of the organization was changed, with House of Miracles not being used anymore or since. The new name (which we are pledged not to reveal, see note 3) has been used with all houses since, including the ones operating in California. This name change was an obvious expression of independence from Calvary Chapel influence.

Financial support for the two houses located in the new area was obtained by hiring out all able-bodied members as bean pickers at the impressive rate of 2½¢ a pound (about $5 a day for a good picker). This was the first large-scale hiring out of teams of workers by CCO to agricultural-related industries, a practice that has continued, greatly contributing to the financial strength of the organization. It should be noted that the area to which the organization moved had a rich agri-culture-based economy, with many operations making heavy use of itinerant laborers during harvest and planting seasons. CCO took full advantage of this situation, and its members easily supplanted the usual type of itinerant laborers in several types of agricultural enter-prises in the area. Some farmers and businessmen were anxious to hire them because they worked hard and were dependable, and a few particularly liked the Christian emphasis of the group as well.

The Start of a New Way of Life

At the end of the summer of 1969, CCO's members also got in-volved in fruit picking, with a great deal of energy being expended in apple picking particularly. One of the leaders had the idea that a large project such as apple picking should be sought to help pay the debts of members in all of the five or six CCO houses in the two states. Apparently these debts were considerable, and also troublesome, as the group's ideology included honesty as a basic tenet (which is an-other reason businessmen and potential employers like the group). Thus, nearly forty members loaded on a bus furnished by an apple company in an adjoining state and traveled to pick apples in order to earn enough money to clear the debts and allow the organization to establish a firmer economical base. This trip accomplished its purpose, even though some hostility was expressed toward the group by other workers. A building housing some of the workers was firebombed by an unknown party. Blame was placed on some of the other pickers in what may be an instance of possible friction between the group and the labor population that they were partially replacing. We are un-aware of other such difficulties, however, and the group's definition of what happened was that the other pickers were simply angered at the Christian witness of the group, which insisted on evangelizing every-one in sight, including the itinerant pickers frequenting the area.

At about this time, the leader had a vision which was destined to have a great impact on the future of the group. He was at the large house in the new area, sitting on a glass-enclosed porch, relaxing in the sun, and "seeking the Lord in prayer" when:

> The Spirit of the Lord descended on me and I received a vision, one of the few I have had in my Christian work. It was a strange one. It was like watching television, but without the tube. It was a whole picture, yet the surroundings of the room remained in-

tact. I beheld a big man with grey hair coming down from Northern ——— out of a large city; I presume ———. He proceeded from a white building, presumably a church, but it didn't seem like the churches I knew. He came to the house at ——— and said the Lord had sent him to ordain me. He also said that he had a fellowship in ———, and that the Lord had ministered to him to turn the legal papers of the fellowship over to me. The ——— ministry was then to use this nonprofit structure for the glory of God. At the end of the vision, I heard a voice saying, "I have opened an effectual door to you."

A month later, a person fitting the description visited the house with his son, a Bible college student, and then returned the next day claiming that he had been "sent by the Lord" to ordain the leader, and that legally he could do this, as he was an ordained minister himself. The organization journal recounts a frantic discussion that followed this announcement, with the leader and other members trying to find out what color the building he had was painted! They were using this test as a "sign," and when it turned out that the storefront building the man hailed from had indeed been painted white just two weeks before, there was great excitement in the group. Thus the leader was ordained as a legally recognized minister, with "the right to marry and bury." A short time later the same man, who himself affiliated with CCO (as perhaps its oldest member) and served as head of their cannery for a time, stated that he also felt led to turn over to the leader the articles of incorporation of a small nonprofit youth evangelism corporation that he headed and operated out of the aforementioned white building. After some consideration, the corporation was accepted, and the leader became president of the corporation, a post he holds to this day. The corporation has been an extremely useful legal vehicle in the development of the organization. The first payoff of nonprofit status was to save much of the apple-picking money, which came in just a few days after the transfer of the corporation was made, thus avoiding some taxes that would otherwise have been required. The nonprofit status has many other advantages, of course, including access to some federal food programs, the ability to purchase some goods below regular cost, and the general avoidance of many different kinds of taxes. This latter point was (and is) extremely important, as it allows the organization to operate with financial success some activities that would otherwise be only marginal or even failures. The value of this one type of support by society to the group is considerable, and is another key to their overall success. CCO continually strives to maintain its tax-exempt status.

Two other key people became secretary and treasurer (referred to in the group as Vice-President of Financial Affairs) of the corporation, and they too still serve in these capacities, along with being part of the board (called Pastors' Council) that now governs CCO's nationwide organization (more on this in chapter 2). From our observations, it seems that the young man brought from a California house to become head of financial operations for CCO has been of great value to the group. He organized the complicated business end of the organization, helped get the agricultural part of the group life functioning, and knows a great deal about the far-flung operations of the organization.[7]

The Move to "The Land"

One last item of CCO history that will be recounted here involves the purchase of the first real property by the group, which had heretofore been living only in rented or free quarters. The leader admits to having given serious consideration to moving the group to the eastern part of America where he was raised, as he felt few strong ties with either California or the new home state. He and his family were "allowed" to visit the East because of a small inheritance received by his wife (a use of the money sanctioned by Reverend Smith, who was still, in late 1969, personal counselor to the leader). Just prior to this visit, an opportunity to purchase some property in the new area developed. The person who had first brought them to the new state (and with whom they had had some initial difficulties) had been using some other converts from Calvary Chapel (converts not affiliated with CCO) in an attempt to develop a communal ministry under his control on some property that he owned. The effort had failed (we were told) because of arguments over doctrine between the young converts and the self-appointed leader, even though the CCO leader was at one point called in to mediate.

This man then offered the property to the CCO, saying that if they did not want it, he would develop it for housing. His price was $55,000 for the ninety-acre plot of "raw land" which was about twenty miles form the city where CCO was headquartered. The leader thought this opportunity was "of God" (even though such a sum of money was not readily available), and gained the support of his deacons and other members in making a commitment to purchase the property. The land sales contract stated that if the full price was paid off in a year's time, then no interest would be charged. This was accomplished several months early on May 5, 1970, somewhat to the apparent surprise of the seller. The group claims to have followed the example of George Mueller, a nineteenth-century Christian who founded several orphanages in England. They "told no one of our need," but prayed daily from December 1969 to May 1970 that the needed money would be forthcoming. During this time, well over $100,000 was raised, mostly from group members in the two houses in the new state of residence.

Getting the property was a utopian dream to which everyone was committed. Some of the members began to work on the property immediately after the initial commitment to purchase was made, preparing it for occupancy by clearing some of it and starting buildings. At the same time, pressure from city officials forced a move from the first house established in the new state (the house was in a residential, single-family zone, and some neighbors were bothered by the presence of the commune). An agreement was secured from the city to allow the house to operate until May 1, 1970, at which time the commune moved on to the new property, some six months after making the original agreement to purchase it. This piece of property, which is referred to within the group and in this book as "The Land," has been the center of organization life since that time and will be discussed in greater detail later in the book.

With the episode, we terminate this brief history section. We leave the recounting of the group's history at what might be called its "take-off point." What was just a handful of newly converted itinerant young people living a hand-to-mouth existence in a few crowded and ill-equipped communes in Southern California had, in just two years, become an organization with six growing communes in two states, one hundred or so full-time committed members developing into disciplined work teams, and a valuable piece of property on which to begin their new life. Using their willingness to work and their first property to best advantage, CCO leaders began an active program of property acquisition, as is illustrated by the many different facilities described in the last section of this chapter. But before describing CCO holdings in greater detail, we want to discuss briefly the beliefs shared by CCO members—beliefs held with enough dedication to help the group withstand many adversities.

GROUP BELIEFS[8]

The term beliefs used in this context refers to the cognitive aspects of the culture of the group. Thus we mean more than just theology as that term is usually construed. We want to discuss at a general level the belief system propounded by CCO, and also focus on some important specific elements of that belief system and attendant behaviors. In understanding the elements of the belief system, care should be taken not to assume that the system is totally logical, or that the system is internally consistent, especially as it is accepted by individual believers. The system itself, as propounded and continually embellished by the group "theologians" (leaders), is developing into a coherent system of thought, but such was not the case at first, such is still not totally the situation, and certainly individual members know and accept only parts of the system of thought. Most members do accept a common core of beliefs, and it is these shared beliefs that we will delineate most carefully.

Group Beliefs

In terms of theology, the group can with some effort be classified as fundamentalist, which means that they accept the virgin birth of Christ, his death on the cross for sinners, his resurrection, his eventual return (which is thought to be imminent), along with the notion that the Bible is the inspired word of God, able to be directly applied to all contemporary situations for direction and answers to specific problems and questions. But to say the group is fundamentalist is misleading, for some of these beliefs are held much more fervently than others, and in fact, such a listing of beliefs would probably not be completely accepted by many members as an accurate statement of their beliefs.[9] A better way to describe their beliefs would be to say that they are Jesus-centered and Bible-centered. The person of Jesus is emphasized, even though other elements of the Trinity, especially the Holy Spirit (defined as the active agent in glossolalia), are also accepted. The Bible is viewed as inerrant and is applied literally to all concrete situations facing them, using the "proof-texting" motif popular with conservative and fundamentalist groups.

This dual focus on Jesus and the Bible is strong in CCO. Jesus is defined as the person who can save anyone from anything, and great emphasis is put on experiencing and maintaining a personal relationship with Jesus. Prayers are constantly directed to him, and all potential converts are "pointed in his direction." Jesus is given credit for the rapid drug addiction cures of many in the group. The Bible is studied seriously by all members of the group, with the expectation being that every member will read through the entire Bible every twelve months. Regular and lengthy Bible studies are a feature of life in all the communes and other CCO living situations. These studies are nightly in nearly all communes and homes, led by "doctrinally sound" leaders or through the use of cassette tapes now manufactured and distributed by CCO.

CCO does not emphasize evil and Satantic forces as much as do some such groups and churches sharing similar beliefs. They focus instead on the experience of salvation, on love, joy, and celebration, making the Christian experience very appealing to the population of dropout youth and others as well. At the same time, however, there is a strong belief in the imminent second coming of Christ, which will signal the end of the world and the ushering in of his reign on Earth, something to which most members claimed in 1971 and 1972 (when our large surveys were done) to look forward to with great anticipation.

The beliefs of the group also include an emphasis on "experiencing the Holy Spirit," and his manifestations, although behavioral manifestations of the Holy Spirit such as speaking in tongues (glossolalia), healing, prophecy, and such are closely controlled. For instance, although most CCO members are led quite early into what for the group (and most other Jesus movement groups) is the important experience of "tongues," their subsequent practice of this "gift" is only in private prayer and devotional times. CCO leaders believe that allowing the uncontrolled manifestation of the "gifts" would disrupt and divide the group, so their use is carefully monitored in group settings.

CCO ideology includes a belief in an omnipotent God of history who regularly intervenes in human history to accomplish certain purposes. All things that happen (even the arrival of a group of researchers, see Appendix A for more discussion of this) are viewed as being at least within God's "permissive will." Coupled with this idea is faith in the efficacy of prayer. This omnipotent God can, according to group believers, be persuaded to intervene in history on behalf of certain causes, such as the success of CCO or the healing of an ill person. Predictably, therefore, CCO ideology contains a strong belief in miracles, and is, in fact, quite magical in orientation, although apparently this tendency had diminished some over time. Their "miracles" are now much more organized. We have heard many accounts of the miraculous appearance of needed food, goods, or jobs, and there are tales of healings of members of physical ailments—some quite serious. There also tends to be a general acceptance of "God's will" in the area of birth control, where the use of contraceptives "that emulate the action of an abortion" is discouraged, as are vasectomies and hysterectomies (unless the woman's health is threatened).

CCO beliefs are definitely *not* Calvinistic, and they have regularly suppressed the "antinomian heresy" [10] with strong defenses of the role of the individual in working out and maintaining "his or her own salvation." This belief is based on the definition of the nature of human beings espoused by the group—a belief that persons are by nature sinful and depraved, requiring rescue and salvation by God through the person of Christ. This anti-Calvinist stance is carried further by also rejecting the appealing notion referred to in religious parlance as "eternal security" or "once saved, always saved." For CCO, such an interpretation, although quite popular in certain circles (twelve million Southern Baptists in America swear by the idea), is just another way of avoiding Christian responsibility. Thus CCO ideology holds that a person can "fall from grace" by refusing to maintain beliefs and practices that are defined by them as Christian. The written history of CCO, referred to earlier, mentions several prominent cases (to the group) of early leaders "falling by the wayside," seduced by "false doctrines." Such instances clearly indicate the falling from grace motif, while also demonstrating developing boundaries of belief and behavior for the group.

Related Ideas and Practices

There are some ideas and practices that are sometimes associated with fundamentalist and conservative Christianity that need to be discussed, albeit briefly. The individualistic and voluntaristic emphases logically lead, especially in the American context, to evangelism and attempts to convert nonbelievers. CCO fits into the American revivalist tradition with its experiential thrust, with the major difference between the CCO and traditional revivalism being the population of potential converts addressed by its efforts. The focus on individual sins leads in this case (as in some previous ones) to an extreme form of asceticism. The use of alcohol, drugs, tobacco, and extramarital sex is strongly discouraged, and behavior is monitored to insure that group norms are adhered to in these areas of life. It also leads to a certain lack of social concern by members, an attitude supported also by the apocalyptic beliefs of the group. This lack of attention to social issues gives the group a not atypical implicit conservative stance toward political issues, a position that we will examine in more depth in a later chapter. The group ideology is also sexist in nature, a point to which we will also return (see especially chapter 5).

Other general characterizations of the beliefs and practices of the group worth presenting include their rather intolerant and elitist perspective with reference to other groups and especially nonbelievers. Some tolerance of other groups that share their beliefs has been noted, but in general, the group thinks that it has "the Truth," and that others are somehow off the mark (and some are "way off"). The group is also rather authoritarian, a not unexpected finding given their ideas about absolute truth and who possesses it. This intolerance stems in part from the extreme dualism of fundamentalism, a dualism that generally relegates all aspects of life into simplistic categories. Everything is black or white, and a person is either saved or not saved. (See Robbins, Anthony, & Curtis, 1975, for a discussion of the dualistic tendencies of the Jesus movement.) We have referred in an earlier paper (Richardson, Simmonds, & Harder, 1972) to the general ideology of the Jesus movement as a form of "religious totalism," which includes, among other things, the idea of "doctrine over person" (Lifton, 1963). While this group's beliefs do not seem to be quite so extreme as those of some groups (and the earlier paper of ours erred in lumping most Jesus movement groups together), they do fall within the bailiwick of fundamentalism, which can be generally characterized in such terms.

One could also characterize CCO ideology as relatively anti-intellectual and even simple-minded in its approach to life. Having the one answer—Jesus—and the one inerrant source of direction—the Bible—leads to a negative evaluation of other alternative answers. It should be stated, however, that CCO sees no conflict in using *technical* knowledge in its operations, even including evangelism. Any use of modern technology and expertise is deemed acceptable if it aids in accomplishing the overall goals of the group.

As Ellwood (1973) and Richardson (1979a) have noted, some of the attributes of fundamentalism are shared by the counterculture from which the Jesus movement came. But they also note that there are some aspects of the counterculture that have been kept by the Jesus movement groups which are not accepted by the theological tradition of which they are a part. Such is the case with CCO. They allow an appearance in terms of dress and hair length that is thought of as "hippie" by many in the society, and they are more tolerant in this area (and some others, such as racial differences) than many traditional fundamentalists. They justify their position scripturally, of course, as they do another major difference—that being their communal life-style. To many people who have beliefs similar to the members of CCO, communes mean, ipso facto, free love and sex orgies, a belief that is far from the truth in the case of this organization. The communal living is justified as being what the early Christians practiced, and primitive communism has been practiced (with some very interesting "revisionism").

Other points could be made about specific beliefs and practices of CCO, but hopefully, this brief discussion will at least give the reader a flavor for the beliefs of the group. Now we want to present a delineation of the present major operations and functions of CCO, along with some filling in of important happenings in their history from May 1970 (when they moved to The Land) until late 1977.

ORGANIZATIONAL DIFFERENTIATION AND FUNCTIONS

Christ Communal Organization, which had such an inauspicious beginning about nine years ago, has now grown into a nationwide organization which may be the largest—in terms of number of houses, size of membership, and geographic scope—Jesus-movement group in America (the only possible competitor is the Children of God, which is larger in terms of their worldwide scope, see Davis & Richardson, 1976). CCO has grown to include nearly fifty communes and "fellowship halls" across the country, located in almost twenty-five states, as of summer 1977. (It has been in more states during its history, but some consolidation has occurred in recent years.) It also includes several other major elements, all in one Western state, which serve organization-wide functions. The following separate facilities and operations, most of which are (or were) located within twenty-five miles of each other in and around a medium-sized city in a Western state, are important enough to CCO life and history to be described briefly.

The Land

The Land, which is a ninety-acre plot about twenty miles from the city that is the center of CCO activities, was the first real property purchased by CCO, and it has served a multitude of important functions in the group's history since it was obtained. It was here that CCO members got their first thorough experience in agricultural work and livestock raising, and their first experience in developing skills in constructing buildings. The Land has served as the established head-quarters of CCO's far-flung operations, and it was here that their schools for new members and evangelism teams (to be described in chapter 2) were started and still operate. The Land has become something of an organizational mecca, with most members thinking of it as the center of organization life and a place to go for retreat and rejuvenation. This strong feeling shared by most members is understandable in terms of the unique place that The Land has had in CCO history, the tremendous importance for individuals of visits to The Land in terms of resocialization into the group, and simply by virtue of the setting—beautiful fir-tree-covered land interspersed with open meadows, and watered by a beautiful stream.

When purchased in 1970, The Land was virtually untouched, accessible only by a muddy road for four-wheel drive vehicles and having no electricity. Two wooden sheds were present on the property. Now the entire scene has been transformed, although careful planning has generally allowed the unspoiled appearance of the property to be retained. Members formed work teams and began clearing some of the property, and plans were made for building a number of cabins and a central dining facility, which was to double as a meeting place for Bible studies and organization schools. About a dozen rustic cabins were built among the trees, and these continue to serve as dwellings for married couples stationed there, with one being converted to a nursery and child-care building several years ago and another becoming a "candy store" in 1977. The dining hall, also in rustic style, was remodeled and air-conditioned in 1974. It has a big fireplace, a public address system, some sofas and easy chairs, enough tables and chairs to accomodate about two hundred people for a meal, a completely modernized stainless-steel kitchen, a piano for use in group singing, and machines for dispersing coffee, tea, and juices. The interior is natural wood finish, and there is a large porch or balcony off one end of it where people congregate for casual conversation. A wrecked refrigerated truck served for a few years as the deep freeze for the facility, but this has now been replaced with a more modern refrigeration unit.

Other buildings have also been constructed on The Land. One building that served as the central office for several years shows signs of having been expanded several times as the functions accomplished at The Land increased in number and scope. A full-time secretary (a member) had quarters in this building in a well-equipped office (electric typewriters, dictaphones, copying machine, etc.). This person, whose office is now in the school building, finished in 1976, operates the communications system, which includes a phone system with several extensions in other offices and buildings, and an intercom system that links many of the more than twenty buildings now on The Land and has outdoor speakers as well. This intercom system is used to page people and allows people in all buildings to talk to the receptionist. The intercom system is tied to the speaker systems in the dining hall and in the newer school building, which allows the recording of sermons and lessons for future reference and inclusion in the growing tape library of the organization. The "tapes ministry" was first housed in the original office building at The Land, but has been moved with its sophisticated tape-copying equipment to a different location in the nearby city. This building also originally contained the print and photography shop, but this too has been relocated. Still located in this complex are offices for a nurse and doctor (both of whom are members), their equipment, a small medical laboratory, and two examining rooms. Also, the schools operating at The Land were coordinated here until the newer school was finished, and school supplies and equipment have been kept in some rooms. The CCO architect, who is also head of a construction team working from The Land, has an office in this rambling complex as well.

Two large two-story, rustic-style dormitories built by members serve as accommodations for "brothers and sisters" in the schools operated at The Land. Both these dormitories, one for males and one for females, are situated in a rather dense forest, and they are linked to each other and the rest of the camp by gravel paths clearly marked to discourage walking about that would harm the natural beauty of the area. The natural-wood finish dormitory for males has seventy beds, a large modern shower and toilet facility (tiled, well-lighted, with plugs for electric razors, etc.), a prayer and reading room, and a room about 15 feet by 25 feet for use as a classroom or for recreation. The beds are arranged in groups of four, two each (bunk-style) on either side of a curtained window in an alcove that is thus a three-sided small room with the fourth side open and facing toward the center of the large rectangular shaped room. Each person has a comfortable bed, a built-in chest/dresser for personal possessions, a small bookshelf (always containing a Bible), a small closet, and a high-intensity lamp attached to the bed so that occupants can read without disturbing others. The dormitory for females is nearly identical to that for the males but will accomodate only fifty persons. We have stayed in these dorms and have found them very comfortable indeed. Members stated that they were certainly a great improvement over the "tent city" that new members attending the school had to live in before the dorms were constructed.

Two large combination toilet, wash, and shower rooms, equipped with institutional-size clothes washers and dryers, were built early to serve the tent city, but now they serve general use. There are now several mobile homes located on the property, a definite switch from the original policy to use only buildings that blended with the surroundings. These mobile homes, some of which are "double-wide," are well-appointed, with carpeting, modern kitchens, air-conditioning, and so on. They serve as homes for some of the permanent staff and their families.

The agricultural activities on The Land involved several buildings and plots of land. There is a two-acre vegetable garden that furnished much of the produce for The Land kitchen and some other segments of CCO as well. There is a large woodshed and sawing facility for cutting the large amount of firewood required. (Some of the older cabins have only wood stoves.) There is a carpentry shop for building furniture and other small items, and a supply house (located in one of the original sheds) containing all sorts of tools and materials for use in agriculture and construction. A prefabricated steel building houses a well-equipped mechanic shop for working on the over two dozen automobiles, trucks, and farming equipment located at The Land. One barn contained a few horses, another housed pedigreed German short-hair dogs and some goats. At one time, a large pig operation with nearly two hundred pigs at a time fattened for sale and table use, and a large rabbitry, also to furnish meat for CCO communes, were located at The Land. A bee operation was also located there for a while.

Newer construction at The Land includes a beautifully designed five-room school and central office complex, a facility which allows much more flexibility in the schools for resocialization of new members. Also, a four-plex apartment for Land staff members has recently been completed. A large combination basketball-volleyball court was just built, and plans call for building an auditorium and gymnasium as well. (A decision was made to use timber harvested from The Land stand of trees in building new facilities. Students in the schools labored part of the day cutting timber, as directed by state forestry officials who said that selective harvesting of available timber would result in a better stand of timber remaining for future use or sale). More mobile homes are being located on The Land, mainly to serve the needs of permanent staff members (both single and married), and possibly to house families that might join and go through the schooling offered to new members. In recent years, all construction on The Land has been done by members, and the new projects are totally the responsibility of The Land construction crew that has been in charge of construction since soon after The Land was obtained.

University House

Several years ago, CCO purchased a large multistory colonial style house near a university in the city around which many members and most of their organization-wide facilities are now located. This facility too has had multiple functions for the group, serving first as an "in-town" office and commune for single males. (In 1971, the organization was renting office space in a downtown office building but moved the business functions to University House in 1972.) The development of CCO's nationwide accounting service, headed by the Vice-President of Financial Affairs, took place here, although this activity is now located on one entire floor of a modern downtown office building. At one time, nearly a dozen rooms of University House were dedicated to the financial operation, including one room to house their modern computer equipment. Members are trained at local junior colleges to learn the techniques of this important function. At the time of one visit to the University House, we were given a tour of the accounting operation and met some of the more than dozen men who regularly put in six-day weeks keeping up with the large flow of CCO financial transactions. We were also shown the new NCR 399 computer that is the heart of the system. When we saw it, this computer (with its 16K of storage capacity) costing about $25,000, was printing checks to be sent to creditors in all parts of the country.

The building, which was once a fraternity house, has a large resident capacity. Now that the accounting operations have been moved out, over one hundred people can be housed there, and it is being used mainly for a residence for single male members. There is a large, well-equipped kitchen, and a dining area as large as that at The Land. The setting is very pleasant, as the grounds are well-cared for and spacious, and the neighborhood itself is quite commodious. A new asphalt parking lot has been added in the back, and several CCO vehicles can be found there. Across the street is a commune for thirty to forty female members who regularly come to University House to take meals, as the kitchen there is better equipped to handle large numbers.

A point of interest is that even though University House is close to a major university campus, little direct effort has been made to minister to campus students there. This house is not a typical "campus ministry" operation by any stretch of the imagination, and nearly all occupants of the house are former itinerants from other parts of the country. If members of the local community express an interest in CCO, they are welcomed but are treated just like any other new member. There has been little systematic attention given toward developing a campus ministry-type program to attract campus youth here on a part-time basis, although such interest has developed within CCO operations in one or two areas of the country, as the itinerant youth "target population" becomes smaller. One such program has been quite successful recently at a large Midwestern university.

Financial Center

In 1974, CCO decided to move its financial operation from University House to an independent location. A historical house was selected in a nearby suburb of the larger city containing University House and other group facilities, and plans were made to purchase this house, in spite of protests by some local residents who did not want the historical building, which was already in poor condition, to fall into the hands of a "bunch of hippies." CCO leaders made a special effort to placate the local residents, and a great deal of time and effort was expended to refurbish the large two-story house in grand style. CCO's carpenters, electricians, plumbers, and others worked long and hard to make the house into a showpiece. They succeeded. The house was redone from top to bottom, with new light fixtures, wallpaper, wood paneling, paint job inside and out, carpeting, and other accoutrements. On our visit there that year, we observed the installation of a panel of telephone wiring at least three-feet square. This was a part of a special statewide CCO telephone system that allows most CCO facilities within the state to be phoned using a special two-digit code. An open house for local residents was a success, and area residents became more positively disposed toward the new owners of the historic building. However, this building burned shortly thereafter, forcing a move into rented but very pleasant office quarters in a downtown office building, where twenty-five to thirty CCO members now work full-time.

County Farm

The County Farm was a leased piece of property about ten miles from the headquarter's city that was at one time a home for the elderly operated by the state. CCO operated this property for several years but eventually gave up their lease on it as part of a long-range consolidation effort. The property had one large building that was the dormitory for former occupants, several out-buildings, a brick house of probably six to eight rooms, and a 1,000-gallon bulk gasoline storage tank truck for member use. The house was used as a married couple's commune, although it and the dormitory first housed single women with children and was referred to as the "Widow's House" within CCO. Some of the sheds contained livestock operations (the now discontinued rabbitry was here for a while after being moved from The Land) and served as storage sheds for equipment used in a large truck garden developed there. One area about fifty yards square was covered with logs for use in the CCO commercial firewood business. (On days when bad weather kept the men from working in the fields and forests, they cut the logs into split firewood for sale in the large city close by.) The dormitory was converted to a nursery, day care, and kindergarten facility for the increasing number of CCO children. This school was here for a while but was moved in 1974 to Fellowship Hall (to be described). This nursery school was developed according to state specifications and fully complied with state laws governing the operation of such schools. This meant that some members had to obtain special training, which was accomplished using secular education institutions in the area. About thirty CCO children were in the school while it was located at the County Farm.

Perhaps the most unique thing about the County Farm operation was the cannery. When CCO first began its agricultural activities, no thought was given to preserving food which was used, sold, or even given away when it was harvested. But CCO leaders quickly realized that this was a wasteful approach, and that some method had to be devised to make more efficient use of the foodstuffs that were being raised on CCO's farms, orchards, and truck gardens. A decision was made to build a cannery, although no CCO member had any previous experience with such an operation. The older man who had earlier ordained the leader and given them the nonprofit corporation had remained in contact with the group and came into CCO just to head up the cannery—although he had had no prior experience at such work. He and several of the men in the group took special courses offered by the state and became licensed canners. Used equipment was purchased and built into a small operational system by members, who learned as they worked. The cannery originally was located in a small town close by, but was soon enlarged and moved to County Farm. Extremely rigid requirements had to be met in terms of sanitation and health, but these posed no insurmountable obstacles to CCO. In 1973, an initial run of 170 *tons* of fruits and vegetables was canned using a system entirely built and staffed by CCO members. Food canned included tomatoes, carrots, beets, pears, plums, corn, beans, pickles, bell peppers, chard, brussels sprouts, cabbage, and squash. The largest single crop canned was peaches, as illustrated by a claim in the CCO journal that the printing staff (then located at The Land) had just printed twenty-one *miles* of peach can labels. The entire cannery operation prided itself on speed and efficiency. A recent journal article stated that, in 1974, a record had been set, with the cannery processing 1,540 two-pound cans of Royal Anne cherries in one shift, staffed by six full-time canners and a few "volunteers" from among the "married sisters."

We have toured the cannery facility, being required first to put on hair nets (required by state regulations), and we came away impressed with the efficiency of the operation. We can also testify to the quality of the products, as we have eaten canned fruits and vegetables on some of our visits to CCO communes, and they were also kind enough to give us a few cans of peaches to take home with us.

At the time of our 1973 visit to the cannery, all the canning was of CCO-raised fruits and vegetables. However, a shift of emphasis (to be discussed in chapter 2) resulted in the cannery being used the next year mainly to can quantities of food not grown at CCO farms and gardens, but instead purchased from local farmers using money earned by work teams. Whatever the source of the food processed, it is plain to us that this facility to preserve foods was an asset to the organization. We can attest to the improved diet of members, and the operation of the cannery was for two years a factor in this improvement (the general increased level of affluence being perhaps the major reason, however). Cases of canned goods were stored in a large building rented for just this purpose. The foodstuffs were used a great deal locally and were even shipped, via CCO vehicles, all over the country to help feed members of the many houses operating elsewhere. Plans were to relocate the cannery at The Land, possibly to have better access to laborers (students in the schools) and to allow the eventual phasing out of the County Farm operation. However, mainly because of a continuing shift away from agricultural enterprises taking place in CCO, a decision was made in 1975 not to operate the cannery again. The equipment was sold to another smaller JM group in the area.

Fellowship Hall

An important new facility was rented in 1974 and refurbished to house several important organization-wide functions of CCO, as well as to serve as a center of activities for the large number of CCO married couples living in the headquarters city. The building was an unused church building, centrally located in terms of other CCO operations in this area. The child-care facilities and nursery were moved from County Farm to this location and expanded. The "communications ministry," involving eight to ten people full-time, was also located here for a while (it has since been moved to yet another CCO property and is now being curtailed somewhat). This "ministry," which was originally at The Land, has two major functions. One is the "tapes ministry," and the other is the print shop. The tapes ministry is a growing aspect of CCO, and a great deal of sophisticated recording and tape-duplicating equipment is involved. The tapes are sent to CCO communes in other states and outside the country to be used in Bible studies and evangelism activities. Also, the tapes are used by married couples in CCO who no longer live in communes (more on this development in chapter 2).

The communications ministry print shop contains photography equipment, including an enlarger, a darkroom, and a Multilith 1850 printing machine (purchased new in 1974 for $18,000) with impressive capabilities. The photography arm of the communications ministry has movie equipment, which is used primarily in internal education. For example, in 1973 a film was made showing how to plant trees (an important activity which involves many members and brings in considerable money). This machinery is used to produce materials used in the CCO's evangelism efforts, in the internal operation of the "business," and in the schools. One of the first jobs done on the new machine was a printing of 200,000 gospel tracts to distribute throughout the country. Up until mid-1975, the print shop also produced the bimonthly CCO journal, a multicolor, slick-paper publication that might be described as a "religious whole earth catalogue."[11] This journal began in 1973, replacing a dittoed newsletter, and it was an impressive piece of work of value in communicating to members thorughout the country. The journal regularly contained a column on CCO history (to acquaint new members and to "set the record straight"), and columns by "regional overseers" describing how the work was progressing in various parts of the country. The journal also contained feature articles on various aspects of CCO life, along with very practical articles giving detailed information on all types of activities. A sample of titles of a few articles, some of them quite lengthy and with detailed drawings and photographs, will illustrate the scope of the journal and its orientation:

"Agricultural Report"; "(CCO) Building Projects"; "Keeping Food Safe"; "First Aid for Heat Related Illnesses"; "Gardens"; "Home Improvement: Painting"; "Education and Child Evangelism: Children—A Heritage of the Lord"; "The Year of the Famine" (a discussion of the worldwide food shortage, seen as a sign of the "second coming"); "Crochet for the Cold"; "Down on the Farm: Livestock"; "(CCO) Cannery"; "Fixing up for Winter"; "Job Finding"; "Fire Safety"; "(CCO) Teams Apple Picking Campaign '73"; "Aviation Report"; "Christian Communal Culinary Crafts"; "How to Have a Gas (on Pennies a Day)" (an article on useful techniques to get better gas mileage); "Practical Applications to Communal Housing Problems"; "Tree Planting '74"; "Teams School" (presenting functioning of the evangelism teams schooling); "Married Couples Fellowship" (explaining new arrangements for married couples); "Goats and Their Milk"; "(CCO) in Slow Pitch" (describing the efforts of an organizational softball team which participated in a local league); "Weekly Bible Reading Schedule"; "(CCO) Medical Clinic"; "Television Coverage"; "The Sheep Farm."

A new CCO journal is now being produced with a somewhat different focus on highlighting group life and telling "life stories" of selected CCO members. It is less directly instrumentally-oriented than the earlier journal.

Fellowship Hall has had other important uses. One of these was as a place of rehearsal and storage for expensive lighting and sound equipment for the growing CCO drama troupe. During a 1974 visit to this facility, we were allowed to watch the rehearsal of a dramatization of the entire book of Job, a "drama" with some 20-minute uninterrupted speeches by some characters. We were very impressed with what we saw, and apparently our evaluation was shared by others, for this play has had several live performances in the area. All actors and other personnel, some of whom work virtually full-time when a production is being readied, are CCO members, few of whom have had any previous experience in such activities. This play is the second done by the troupe, as the year before, selected psalms were presented locally in drama form, live, and on television.

The major reason for obtaining the Fellowship Hall property, however, was for use as a gathering place for CCO married couples and single members no longer living communally. Many activities of these members are now centered here, and a program similar to a typical church has developed (Sunday services, visitation, Sunday school classes, etc.). The facility is in use nearly every evening with various activities of those associated with it. The need for this type of a facility especially for married members will be more fully discussed in chapter 2, but suffice it to say at this point that there has been a very rapid increase in the number and proportion of married people within CCO in recent years. Renting Fellowship Hall is one attempt to minister to this growing subgroup within "the body." CCO now has fellowship halls in a half dozen cities across America and a way of working with the increasing number of married couples in CCO.

Peach Orchard

For several years, CCO owned an eighty-acre peach, pear, and cherry orchard about an hour's drive away from the headquarter's town. The orchard was completely cared for by members, and the cannery preserved a great deal of its produce for group use. The remainder was sold for cash. A note of interest concerns a tie between the bee operation at The Land, and the peach orchard. The bee hives (and occupants) were regularly moved to the orchard and other CCO fruit and vegetable operations to aid in pollination of the crops, a method that apparently paid off in terms of bigger yields of fruits and vegetables. (It also resulted in many different kinds of honey being available for internal use and for cash sales.)

Goat Dairy

In 1971, a goat dairy was purchased by CCO, and it was operated until 1976, when it was sold. This facility was used to furnish both milk and cheese to members and communes. Before the purchase of the dairy, goats were already being raised at The Land, with milk being sold to health food stores and used "in the body." A decision was made shortly after the purchase of the dairy to use the milk only for pig food while the dairy was refurbished and members got better trained to operate such a facility. In 1974, the milk was again being used for drinking at several area communes, The Land, and University House. Plans were for a cheese plant to be opened as well, as this was thought to be one way that the produce of the dairy could be transported around the country to other CCO houses.

The dairy itself was located on five acres of land, occupied by a

several-room house with a good-sized lawn and a smaller house closer
to the animal barns. A concrete-block building housed the dairy,
which had a newly-automated milking parlor, a bulk milk tank and
bottling room, and a walk-in cooler. A milk truck was purchased to
use in distributing the milk locally, and an application was made for a
state license so that milk from the dairy could also be sold commer-
cially again.

The herd was quite large and included pedigreed animals of several
types. In 1974, nearly fifty kids were born at the dairy, and plans
included keeping some of the doe kids to add to the herd. Artificial
insemination and other techniques are used to improve the herd
quality, which is already high, as demonstrated by ribbons won by
CCO goats in statewide livestock shows (such showing of stock was
viewed as a form of indirect evangelism and witnessing, and was so
justified). In a feature article in the CCO journal, pride was expressed
in the grand championship won by the main herd buck at a statewide
goat show in 1974. Many other good show placements were garnered
by the herd during the operation of the dairy.

This involvement with the professional commercial goat industry of
the state was a good example of the general orientation of the CCO
toward its enterprises. Those in charge were well-trained, having taken
courses offered by state agencies and colleges. They regularly participated in professional activities such as shows, conferences, and such.
The organization subscribed to professional journals, which were studied by goat herd "stewards" in an attempt to improve the operation of
the herd. "Goat stewards" also worked for other dairies in the area to
gain experience, and one member even worked for the state as a goat
farm and dairy inspector for the area. In short, this was a respectable
operation in every sense of the word, and it seemed destined to continue to improve. Our visit to this facility, during which we shared a
meal (complete with goat's milk) with the herd tenders and their families, resulted in the strong opinion that this was a sound enterprise,
making a contribution to the organization and to the industry itself.
However, the top-level CCO decision to move out of agricultural operations and into work teams and small businesses (more on this later)
resulted in a decision to sell the dairy, and this was done.

Sheep Farm

For several years, CCO was trying to obtain more property near
The Land, an effort that, in 1974, resulted in the purchase of a nearby
seventy-acre sheep farm (thirty acres of timber, forty of pasture). This

operation was part of a deliberate shift away from crop agriculture and toward the production of livestock. Again the emphasis was on a sound commercial and professional operation. A new large aluminum barn was built, and quality stock was purchased (including a recent state champion ram). The flock numbered about fifty sheep in 1975, with about that many lambs being born this first year of operation. Plans were to have eventually a flock of three hundred sheep, furnishing meat for the organization's tables, and wool and breeding stock to sell. Most of the sheep born in the flock were sold as quality and pedigreed breeding stock, with some of the proceeds being used to purchase feeder stock (nonpedigreed) to raise for CCO meat needs. The operation of the sheep farm also included the rotation of some cattle and goats on the pasturage to make better use of the land, while a new baler was used to bale extra hay for sale to other local stock raisers. The few cattle kept here were the start of what was originally hoped by CCO agriculture ministry staff members to be the beginnings of a larger herd of beef cattle, an operation that was planned to start as soon as more property could be obtained. The original leader of the organization lives in a commodious house on the sheep farm, although he spends most of his time in the teaching function and does not work directly with the sheep operation. The plans for the sheep farm have also recently changed, however. This (plus the hay operation) was to have been the only agricultural enterprise retained by CCO in its "new approach." However, in 1977 a decision was made to sell it, although this had not been done as of fall 1977.

The Farm

There should be some discussion of a rather important operation that CCO was involved with for three years, even though this operation was phased out in 1973.[12] This was a 110-acre leased farm on which berries and vegetables were raised. This facility was the one that we have used for our most intensive research on individual members and some aspects of group life. In the summers of 1971 and 1972, we went with interview teams to The Farm and interviewed nearly all persons there, gathering much data of different types (see Appendix A for more detail on our research experience, and chapters 6 through 9 for presentation of some of this data). The Farm operated with a skeleton crew of ten or twelve people during the winter, but in the summer up to one hundred members (mostly new ones) from throughout the country were brought there to work with the crops. The Farm furnished food and money from cash crops for CCO, and it also served as a sort of "boot camp" for new members. The work was hard and the hours long, and those who survived the summer (a large majority) were more committed members for having had the experience. During our visits to The Farm, we became acquainted with a number of group members and leaders with whom we still have contact.

The Farm itself was on a gravel road about five miles from a small town, which was itself about two hours drive from the headquarter's city. This isolation was functional in that it allowed, even forced, the members to build their own community and not depend very much on outsiders for support. Contact with the outside world was kept to a minimum and monitored, especially for newer members. The property had a main building which was used by the previous owner as a home, but was used by CCO as a dwelling by the families of several CCO pastors and other leaders staying at The Farm. All the single members were housed in sex-segregrated "labor barracks" which had the barest of essentials—bunk beds with sleeping bags or a piece of foam rubber for a mattress, no heat, and two community shower facilities (one for males and one for females). Toilet facilities were outhouses (except in the main house). Some tents were also used to house overflow from the barracks, and one was designated as a medical tent (anyone who became ill was isolated and given medical attention). One large building served as a kitchen, mess hall, and nightly Bible-study center, and another was a garage for storing and working on farm and other vehicles. Attached to the back of the garage was a large walk-in cooler about twenty feet by thirty feet in diameter for use in storing the fruits and vegetables raised. This cooler was, we were told, "provided by the Lord" as an "answer to prayer" shortly after The Farm was obtained.

The Farm, part of which was located on high ground with a beautiful view of the surrounding area, was mostly dedicated to the raising of berries of various kinds. A small amount of the acreage was used for vegetables, and about twenty acres was in wheat (about twenty acres were wooded). Our visits there were very enjoyable, as we liked the area, and we regularly participated in the life of the group living there. Our interview teams stayed in the labor accomodations, ate with the members, and even worked in the fields with them. This latter task was made more enjoyable by the side benefit of getting to eat all the berries we wanted. (When we prepared to return home, we were encouraged to take with us large containers of berries for eating on the way).

The Farm was very important in CCO history, as most of its present leaders and a great many members received some of their resocialization there. The Farm was the first large agricultural operation in which CCO was involved, and a great deal was gained from the experience. They proved that they could indeed successfully handle an operation of this type. The crops furnished money for group needs, and the work furnished a real test of member dedication (see chapter 4 for more detail on life on The Farm). The decision to phase out of the operation was made in late 1973, partially based on some difficulties in operating The Farm caused by a continuing problem with its sewerage system, and partially (mostly, we think) because of a shift in emphasis within CCO. The shift involved less emphasis on producing crops to sell, and more on working for money, which was then used to purchase needed food and other goods. This shift from producer to consumer in terms of certain crops is of import and will be discussed in greater detail in chapter 2. An interesting outcome of the decision to phase out The Farm was the immediate negotiation of a contract to furnish the owner with workers for his own operation of The Farm, a dramatic example of the shift in emphasis within CCO.

Other Property

CCO controls a great deal more property than has been described. Most of the other property serves as quarters for the various types of communes, as living quarters for members that live separately, or as other fellowship halls. Around the country, there are a number of "gathering" or "outreach houses" in operation, and most of these are rented or leased, as are a few "shepherding houses" for training new members converted in the more fruitful gathering houses. The same situation applies with the several dozen apartments and houses owned and rented by married families and single females with children living noncommunally, mostly in the area of the headquarters city. The renting or leasing of all but some of the most permanent facilities such as The Land is justified theologically. CCO leaders claim that renting keeps them relatively unfettered so that they can respond quickly if they think that God is leading them to move in new directions. This approach builds in a great deal of flexibility (and requires less capital), although it is not taken legalistically, as demonstrated by a willingness to purchase certain types of real property. In short, CCO takes a pragmatic approach to property ownership and use.

Transportation Facilities

Special attention should be called to the large cadre of vehicles of all kinds that are used by CCO in its many activities. The group owns dozens of cars, pickups, trucks, vans, and buses which are located throughout the country, although most are in the area of the headquarters. These vehicles are used for transportation of evangelism teams, work teams, and for everyday kinds of activities (such as shopping by members in the noncommunal family situations). As far as we know, all these vehicles are owned by CCO and allocated to members who need them. Some of them are "clunkers," but many are very comfortable new vehicles. In the summer of 1974, just before a visit we made to the area, seven new Dodge vans had been purchased to add to the already large fleet of such vehicles. A network of such vehicles is maintained around the country, so that goods and people can be transported to any CCO outposts. One use of the vans we observed involved the distribution of canned goods prepared in the CCO cannery to houses all the way across the country on the East coast. The returning vehicles picked up new members at various "gathering" or "shepherding houses," and brought them back to participate in the resocialization schools at The Land.

A large amount of specialized farming equipment has been owned by CCO, although most of this equipment has been sold off in recent years. This included tractors, road graders, hay balers, spraying equipment, trucks for transporting livestock, and a large dump truck. Some years ago, CCO experimented with fishing and bought two small oceangoing craft, one of which was parked at The Land during one visit. (These boats have since been sold.) A number of people work full-time in keeping all this equipment in working order, and there are mechanic facilities at several of CCO's operations.

Perhaps the most striking CCO vehicle is a twin-engine airplane, used to transport people around the country and allow closer supervision of and encouragement to the nationwide operations. Several members work full-time in this part of CCO work as pilots and ground mechanics. At one time, CCO owned another plane, but this was sold. The larger and newer of the two planes was kept as a permanent part of what the group calls its "aviation ministry." The plane is used to fly needed personnel to various houses, to take leaders around to exhort the members and "to find out what is happening," and even to fly members around the country in times of personal difficulty (such as a death in their family). A medium-sized motor home is also a part of this ministry of nationwide supervision, with CCO leaders embarking on tours of all the operations in a certain area of the country to help establish new work and encourage the membership.

NOTES

1. These disagreements were over matters such as points of doctrine and interpretation of the Bible, and control of new Christian converts. The Teen Challenge (TC) disagreement developed when a TC leader stated that one could not be a Christian without getting a haircut and "dressing right," a claim that was rejected by the leader of CCO and others from his group. Apparently, good relations eventually developed between TC and the group, as a later segment of the group history contained an apology to TC for earlier comments that might have been interpreted wrongly, an apology that noted that TC had since abandoned the earlier-held ideas about dress and hair length. Such a reconciliation does not seem in the offing with the COG, however, as the strongest language used by the CCO leader in his writing is reserved for the Children (who are called a "false cult") and especially their leader Moses David Berg, who is called a "sick and evil man," a "ravening wolf" whose writings are "an atrocity," "unfit to be held by human eyes." One interesting facet of this debate is that one segment of the history involves a claim for primacy in terms of starting the Jesus movement. In refuting a claim made by Berg to be father of the movement, the CCO leader stated, "I happened to be present when he showed up on the scene and it was much after the beginning of this member, and other members of the Lord's body."

2. This history is written using many interviews with members during several years of research, along with the history of the organization as written by the leader and published in the organization's journal. Another useful source is *The Reproducers: New Life for Thousands,* a book written by Rev. Charles Smith, with Hugh Steven (1972), about the development of the Calvary Chapel's unusual ministry among youth. (Only a part of this book is germane, as CCO ties with Calvary Chapel have become more tenuous over time.) The quotations in this chapter are from the written history included in CCO's journal or from interviews with members.

3. As a stipulation of our agreement with CCO that allowed this research, anonymity of the organization and the individuals will be maintained throughout this book, as in our other writings from the research. This agreement makes writing (and reading) about the group somewhat awkward, as we are forced constantly to use phrases like "the initial leader," along with a pseudonym for the organization name. However, we are committed to honor our agreement and trust that readers will not be put off by our euphemistic style. It should be noted that while this particular organization is not nearly as well-known as the COG or the Christian Foundation they are mentioned by name and location in several publications about the movement and its groups. Because of our agreement, however, we will not list the sources that do identify the group. We realize that some well-informed individuals will be able to identify the

organization, but we hope that such persons will aid us by maintaining anonymity in any discussions of our work.

4. These ties with Calvary Chapel may surprise some readers who have been overly impressed with the antiestablishment rhetoric of some groups in the movement. We would suggest that all such claims be taken with a grain of salt, as our experience had led us to the conclusion that there are many ties between most segments of the movement and the "greater society," including the much-maligned "institutional church." In the case of CCO, the ties have continued to exist, although the specific ties with Calvary Chapel have loosened considerably over the years, partially as a result of the move of the group several hundred miles away from Southern California, but also because of the growing strength of the organization. Other kinds of ties with society have developed over time, many of which will be mentioned in the following discussion.

5. It must be stated that such naturalistic explanations of the success of the group are nearly totally ruled out by group members and leaders, who claim that their actions have always been completely guided by God, and that God should get the credit. We do not think their perspective and ours necessarily are in conflict, but personally we prefer to address the matter of the functioning of the group in a naturalistic manner, a view more in keeping with the dictates of the sociological approach.

6. The pattern of rather rapid opening and closing of houses continues, although the number of houses in operation at any one time has shown a general gradual increase over time. This pattern is not appreciated by some commentators on the movement and by some commune theorists, who assume that because a commune has closed its door it has failed. Such an interpretation is invalid and overlooks the great flexibility and overall perseverance of this organization (and some others, also). More on this in the theoretical discussion of chapter 2 and in Richardson (1976 a).

7. This intelligent young man, who has been a very important contact for us, is a Yale University dropout who stated that he was "turned off" to university life by taking a sociology course that attempted to explain human behavior using math models. Sociology's loss was obviously a gain for CCO.

8. A number of publications have discussed, in general terms, the beliefs and practices of various Jesus movement groups. We will not attempt here to discuss the ideology of the broader movement, of which this group is a part, but would suggest books by Enroth, Ericson, and Peters (1972); Ellwood (1973); Ward (1972); and McPherson (1973) as being the best such discussions, along with our own earlier paper (Richardson, Simmonds & Harder, 1972) and the informative work of Robbins, Anthony, and Curtis (1973, 1975). Articles by Adams and Fox (1972), Mauss and Peterson (1973, 1974), R.K. Jacobson and Pilarzyk (1972), C. Jacobsen and Pilarzyk (1974), and Gordon (1974), all of which discuss in part the beliefs of specific groups within the movement, are also quite informative. The Adams and Fox paper focuses on Calvary Chapel, which makes it of special interest to this study.

9. We would suggest that the same comment can be made about other characterizations of Jesus movement *and* non-Jesus movement groups as

fundamentalist. Such simple characterizations should always be accompanied by some type of "intensity analysis" and by investigation to see if the beliefs claimed are put into any form of action.

10. By this, simply put, we mean the belief that all sins have been "washed away," and that it is not therefore possible to commit sin now, thus allowing for any all types of behavior to be practiced with "spiritual impunity."

11. A leader informed us by letter that the decision to cease publishing the CCO journal "had mainly to do with our dissatisfaction with the content of the magazine. The magazine itself was not serving the initial purpose for which it was created. We hope to replace it with a new magazine in the next three to six months that will be more reflective of our purposes ... the discontinuance of the publication does not manifest any peculiar, special or extraordinary financial difficulties."

12. Our first publication from this research focused on The Farm and may have left the impression that The Farm was the major focus of CCO (see Harder, Richardson, & Simmonds, 1972). Subsequent events demonstrated that such was not the case and we hope publication of this book will correct any misunderstandings caused by the 1972 paper. We are cognizant, of course, of the fact that the rapidly changing CCO will have "moved on" again by the time this book appears in print. Hopefully, however, we have stressed enough in this report CCO's flexibility and proneness to change to disallow tendencies to reify the structure of CCO as it appeared to us as of late 1977.

2

Organizational Evolution

Occasions to study closely the development of a new social entity are relatively rare, and we are pleased to have been privy to the early history of CCO, as outlined in the previous chapter. The way in which the organization carved a tenuous niche in the institutional structure of this society has been fascinating to observe and quite informative. In this chapter, we will become more analytical and sociological in our presentation, focusing on crucial ways in which CCO has managed to maintain itself by allowing changes to occur in certain areas of group life. There have been some classic studies of changes in new social movements and groups (see Gusfield, 1963; Messinger, 1955; Zald & Denton, 1963; Zurcher & Curtis, 1973, among others), and we hope to contribute to this important thread of sociological research in this chapter, in chapter 3, and in Appendix B.

In any organization, there are key segments that must be involved directly in any changes that occur. The distinctions between such segments may seem more analytic than real, but nonetheless we will discuss specific changes that have occurred in (1) the goals or aims of CCO, (2) the leadership structure of CCO, (3) CCO support methods, (4) living arrangements, (5) methods of resocialization or member training, and (6) evangelistic methods. Many other changes have taken place, but they seem less central to the basic nature of the organization. Some of the changes that have occurred in one area have had definite effects on other areas, and these instances will be noted. However, it should be understood that in most instances this type of specific causality will be impossible to establish, mainly because of the complexities of CCO, and because of rapid changes occurring in many areas of its life. Another caveat is that we seldom cite a specific date when a dramatic change occurred. (Indeed, most changes were not dramatic but relatively gradual.) Since at this point we are primarily interested in describing the changes and not necessarily in ascertaining specific reasons for the changes, this lack of date specificity will not unduly hamper analysis.

Before discussing changes in each of the six areas mentioned, one other important consideration should be mentioned. *Not all facets of CCO are changing.* In fact, some areas—notably those dealing with basic values and beliefs—have remained relatively stable, although there has been much elaboration and specification. This ideological continuity has contributed greatly to CCO's success in maintaining itself. The singleness of purpose of the fundamentalist-like belief system has furnished a reason for existence and even a justification for flexibility in nearly every other area of group life. The unstated motto might be said to be, "Try anything and if it works, God is glorified." Certain ideological limits, such as basic tenets of conservative Christian morality are defined as inviolate, but the generally pragmatic approach allows for a flexible and utilitarian life-style which has been extremely functional for group maintenance.

EVOLUTION OF GROUP GOALS

As has been noted in Zablocki (1972), many communal groups developing in the past few years have originated without a formal constitution or charter. Most such groups have simply grown "like topsy" in response to strongly felt needs. CCO is no exception, and thus they have no document that has, over the ensuing years, been amended to take into account new needs and goals, although they do have documents referring to some specific areas (such as finances), and they have written in group publications rather definitive explanations of certain facets of group life. Based on these sources and on our coutinuing observation, it is possible to discern shifts in emphasis and changes in overarching goals.

Note should be taken that CCO does claim to have a document on which all areas of group life are based. This "document" is the Bible, which is constantly referred to as a guide to follow in organizing the group and in answering specific questions that arise. The method of use involves prayerful discussion among leaders and "searching the Scripture" for answers and direction. The interpretation applied to the Bible, as was noted in chapter 1, is generally fundamentalist in orientation, with the Scriptures being taken quite literally in most cases.

When CCO first began to distill out of the chaotic "cultic milieu" from whence it came (see Richardson, 1979b), a major goal involved *individual rescue* and *maintenance,* as was the case with most such groups. The individuals involved were concerned about food, shelter, safety, and "meaning." The amorphous but rapidly solidifying "Christian houses" that were a part of the group's early history furnished these personal needs. If the developing group had not furnished "a way out of chaos" for many, CCO would never have started. As the organization began to achieve some stability of membership, the goal of individual maintenance developed into at least two individual-level goals. One involved the continuance of the individual rescue and maintenance function for incoming members, but another crucial goal became *member service* or *welfare.* As individuals came into the group, they required counseling, guidance, and continual support, at least until they found their place, and periodically afterward as special problems developed.

These goals, although continuing as major interests of CCO, were almost immediately joined or complemented by requirements of the "new" ideology of the group (a modified form of fundamentalism). The fundamentalist ideology of the group carried with it a heavy focus on *evangelism,* by which is meant the "winning" of new converts and inculcating them with group belief.

This quickly became a major goal of the group and a way in which CCO members spent a great deal of their time. (It was the major "instrument" of individual rescue.) This goal had as a direct consequence the recruiting of many new members (who were also quickly put to evangelizing). However, it also has several more indirect consequences which have been noted by students of fundamentalism before. Evangelism reinforces the beliefs of the evangelizers. Such "work" also keeps members busy and gives them a purpose ("the idle mind is the devil's workshop"), and it attracts the attention of potential supporters in the greater society (the media, churches, individuals).

Evangelism has continued to be a major thrust of CCO and might well be considered a dominant goal. Changes concerning evangelism are deemed important enough to develop in a separate section. However, other group-level goals quickly developed and must be discussed. One obvious goal that became important early on was *group survival* and *maintenance*. This goal seems a natural enough area of concern, but it should be noted that, in one sense, this goal is antithetical to an important ideological element espoused by the group, that of the rapidly approaching "second coming." As documented in our research, nearly all members claimed to expect the "second coming of Christ" imminently, and most expressed pleasure at the prospect of such a glorious end to worldly problems. Such beliefs might be taken to imply a lack of concern for group maintenance. Assuming the veracity of the reports given to us about such apocalyptic beliefs, apparently the emphasis on evangelism overwhelmed the pessimism of their apocalyptic views. In a classic pattern, CCO justified its existence and the goal of group maintenance on the need to do as much evangelizing as possible *before* the second coming.

We will also devote a separate section to further discussion of how some specific methods of maintaining and supporting CCO and its members have changed over the years. However, at this point we would emphasize that the twin goals of evangelism and group maintenance have interacted within CCO, as they have done in many other groups throughout the history of Christendom. And in their interaction, they have resulted in at least one important "hybrid goal." This goal might be termed building a Christian *utopia*, by which is meant the establishment and maintenance of a fellowship of believers who share beliefs, values, and most other significant aspects of human existence (even if they do not all live in a commune together or in a set of communes). CCO has tried to organize itself using its interpretation of principles from the Bible. This has been carried to the extreme in some instances, as when a modern computerized financial accounting system, centralized for the entire nationwide group operation, is rigorously justified using Scripture. Group leaders make these justifications on very practical grounds, saying that God has given adequate information in the Bible to guide all human activities. Also, however, it is plain from some of their comments that they think that setting up CCO on strictly Scriptural grounds will result in a demonstration to the world that there is validity to their message. The very success of their way of life is taken as evidence that God is blessing them, and this is thought of as witnessing on a large scale. This is analogous on the level of the collectivity to the Calvinistic claim on the individual level that the successful person must be one of the elect, or God would not be blessing so.

This goal of building a Christian utopia as a major CCO emphasis can be viewed as a logical or not unexpected development, given the success of the group in gaining and keeping new members (nationwide full-time membership of well over 1,000) and in achieving relative financial security. (We estimated capital net worth at nearly $2 million). In terms of evangelizing and "rescuing" individuals, there has been a shift from a strong, singular emphasis on street witnessing for all, to a multipronged approach (to be discussed in depth) that certainly includes the notion of "witnessing by example." The success of the group is a group-level "good example." In terms of group maintenance, there was a time when CCO was literally fighting for its existence. Maintaining the existence of the group at all was problematic. Developing economic security enabled CCO to give some thought to the *type* of lifestyle they desired, instead of giving all energy to concerns about whether or not the group would survive at all. During one visit in which we were allowed to watch the rehearsal of a lengthy play, *Job* (with dialogue memorized verbatim from the King James Bible), being readied by the CCO drama troupe for local television and live performances, a group leader explained why they were doing this type of activity. He said that now that a degree of economic security had been achieved, they could give attention to the arts and to other forms of witnessing. Presentation of the play was considered a major effort in CCO evangelistic activities, and also a way in which group members' talents could be used and developed in a manner "glorifying to God."

The development of the different goals is outlined in Figure 1 using an analytical distinction between individual-level and group-level goals. Both the "initial goals" have been partially supplanted by the "later goals." The maintenance of the group and its members allows more "individual rescue" through various direct and indirect evangelistic and "witnessing" activities. Member maintenance also furnishes members to do tasks necessary for organization survival and utopia building.

Note that, while group goals have changed markedly, there has not been as dramatic a shift in major goal as was described in Zald and Denton's (1963) discussion of the YMCA, which started as an evangelistic organization and is now completely service-oriented. Zald and Denton credit this shift to (1) the relatively decentralized and autonomous decision structure of the YMCA, (2) the Y's broadly defined goals, (3) the "low professionalization" of ideology (a way of discussing commitment), and (4) the "enrollment economy" of the YMCA. Since CCO is so new in comparison to the YMCA, it is difficult to compare the two groups' goal changes. However, we think the high level of commitment to the group ideology, coupled with operation of the centralized decision structure and fairly narrowly defined goals,

FIGURE 1
Evolution and Relationship of Organization Goals

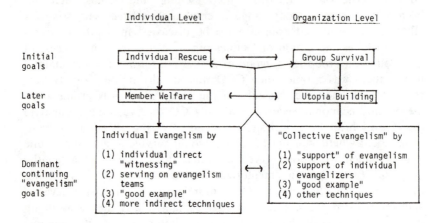

will work to preclude any change in goals as dramatic as occurred with the YMCA.

EVOLUTION OF GROUP LEADERSHIP STRUCTURE

CCO has developed an elaborate leadership structure in the process of trying to acomplish its major organizational goals. The structure logically breaks into two analytically distinct structures, which are sometimes overlapping in terms of personnel and function. These two structures are designated by us as the "formal authority structure" and the "steward structure." The formal structure has as its major function accomplishing the "member service" goals. The steward structure focuses more on group maintenance. This distinction is somewhat analytical, however, and, as has been stated, all segments of CCO have an overall goal of witnessing and evangelism (which includes resocialization of new members).

Formal Authority Structure

Initially this structure was not very differentiated, and its original impetus was simply young people, with no particular status vis-à-vis any group, witnessing to other young people. However, structure developed very rapidly as membership increased, and some systematization of leadership seemed needed. Certain persons in the individual Christian houses that were part of the early history of CCO became leaders and teachers, apparently because of their willingness to exert themselves and because of their relative length of time in the group, a result of a relatively early conversion to the group and its beliefs. Thus a two-level structure came into being quickly involving *pastors and members* (differentiated into *brothers* and *sisters*).[1]

This two-level structure was elaborated in two ways at least, including developing of layers of structure *within* a group. This would involve persons (males) being designated as *assistant pastors,* or more commonly, as *deacons* (some groups had both), making the structure within a given commune have up to four levels (pastor, assistant pastor, deacons, brothers and sisters). Within each group there could also be a partial vertical division, in that some relatively "older in the Lord" females would be designated as *deaconesses* (roughly the equivalent of an assistant pastor) with authority over other females, but not over any males.

A second type of elaboration of the initial two-level structure that was quite important in terms of group development involved the exerting of leadership by one individual—the leader—over several of the Christian houses, as was discussed in chapter 1. This person, who is still the legal and spiritual leader of the group, asked members of several communes that were a part of the early Southern California experience of the group to accept him as their leader and to follow his direction. After some discussion, prayer, and old-fashioned leadership struggles, an affiliation of several of the houses was accomplished. This movement into a federation of houses, in conjunction with the internal differentiation of some of the houses, brought about a structure that was five levels deep, and partially divided in terms of sex.

When CCO moved from the Southern California area to their present location and began to expand into a nationwide organization, other elaborations of the formal structure occurred. One additional level that was quickly added was *regional pastor* or *overseer* (there are now five of these), who supervise the house pastors in assigned areas across the United States and exercise considerable authority in terms of the allocation of resources and personnel.

Also, a board of directors called the Pastors' Council was developed in the headquarters area, made up of some of the especially talented, "spiritual," and energetic early members who had joined CCO in the first months of its existence. This important group of about ten people, made up of most of the leaders of houses and functions that were geographically located around the headquarters, has been meeting weekly for some years.[2] In these meetings, major decisions are after much prayer and discussion. Recently this group has begun using subcommittees to examine more complex problems and make recommendations back to the council. This subcommittee approach shows again how CCO has integrated rationality with its religion.

The legal leadership structure is a part of this group of leaders. Since CCO is a legally constituted nationwide nonprofit organization (we have a copy of their "articles of incorporation" and "bylaws") it has to have a minimum of three legal officers—a president, a secretary, and a treasurer (called within CCO Vice-President of Financial Affairs). The original leader serves as president and the two other officers are men who affiliated early with the group. The Vice-President of Financial Affairs has been briefly discussed earlier in the history section as being a key person in the CCO development.

One other differentiation that evolved was a new status for females— the position of *patroness*—which was a superior position to that of deaconess and is thought within CCO as being roughly equal to the position of house pastor. This position is reserved for a select few females of seniority and demonstrated ability who are assigned certain tasks in a specific large commune or in the organization as a whole. Since some of the tasks of the patronesses involved the goals of evangelism and member service, the position has been included in the formal authority structure. Note that *no female, not even a patroness, has formal authority over any male,* a crucial part of CCO beliefs on "the place of women." Generally the patronesses head all-female communes or all-female work teams. Care is taken to avoid conflicts in authority with males of any rank.

Thus we see that a complex and functional structure involving at least seven levels was developed in a relatively short time. The structure is further differentiated according to sex, a differentiation resulting directly from an acceptance by the group of the general fundamentalist position on the issue of sex roles (male superiority). This formal authority structure is presented in Figure 2. Note that the positions or roles are not necessarily exclusive of one another. Common "double-occupancy" examples would be where a regional pastor was also a specific house pastor, or where a member of the board would also be a house or regional pastor. Also note that the newer fellowship hall motif is not precisely represented in this discussion, even though the positions in a given fellowship hall are somewhat analogous to those presented.

Steward Structure

The other way of viewing the structure of CCO we call the steward structure, which refers to the division of labor developed to aid group

FIGURE 2
Outline of Positions and Lines of Authority in Formal Authority Structure *

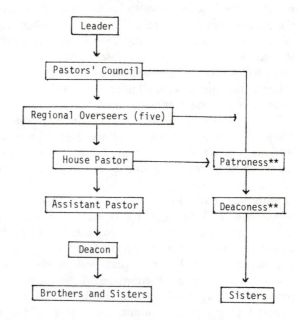

*Does not fully represent structure of newer "fellowship houses" for married couples, which have developed in about six cities across the U.S. recently.

**A patroness or deaconess can be head of a work team of women, with an organization-wide function, head of a women's commune, or head of a task group (of women) within a commune. The pattern is not set, and appears quite ideosyncratic up to now. Only if the task assigned a patroness is within a commune would the house pastor have authority over her. This situation is rare, as it leaves room for conflict, since the relationship between males within the commune and the apparently higher ranking female are problematic.

maintenance and the building of the CCO version of a Christian utopia. The structure is at once more simple and more complex than the fairly easily differentiated formal authority structure. Its simplicity derives from its functionality. By this we mean that this structure attempts to accomplish the necessary functions of CCO in a way that will allow the group to continue and to prosper (and, as members say, "to glorify God").

In simple terms, any time something needs to be done in a specific commune or in the organization, someone is designated the steward of the activity. This designation is not treated lightly by the group or its members. It is in effect a *calling*, in the sense talked about in Weber's discussion of the Calvinistic Protestant ethic (1958). A CCO leader (or leaders) would, after discussion and prayer, explain to a member that they felt led to designate that member as being in charge of or responsible for a necessary function of the group. In short, the task designated by the leader(s) was to become the "God-given" stewardship of the person until he was relieved of it by another "message from God." A member, because of having a personal, very Protestant-like relationship to God, can, of course, refuse a given "anointing," but apparently this seldom occurs. The member usually accepts the guidance of CCO leaders, and the task, no matter how arduous, is accomplished with great intensity and meticulousness.

Early in the CCO history, maintenance tasks were relatively simple. They might involve cleaning the house or washing clothes or dishes, or working outside the commune for money.[3] However, as the group grew and its activities became more complex, a more stratified division of labor developed.

Within an individual commune, sometimes the tasks became more complicated and differentiated because some of the communes grew to a large size and sometimes were actually large task forces brought together to accomplish a specific function of the entire organization. For example, at The Farm, which was the focus of much of our early research (see Harder, Richardson, & Simmonds, 1972), there was a steward in charge of washing clothes for the approximate by one hundred people there, another in charge of the garden, another in charge of the kitchen, another handling repairs on vehicles, another managing the planting, another the harvesting, and on and on. And some (most) of these had assistants to help with the task. Some, like the one in charge of planting or harvesting, had dozens of workers with what were in effect small staffs of assistants to take charge of smaller tasks within the overall task of harvesting or of planting.

At The Land, the same type of differentiation and stratification has occurred. There was a garden steward (who even slept in a tent in the garden to keep deer away); a hog steward who supervised the large hog operation that was located there at one time; a recreation steward; a nursery steward who cared for the children of couples located at The Land; a kitchen steward (referred to as head chef) who supervised several kitchen workers;[4] a steward of the vehicles who supervised the well-equipped repair shop; and literally dozens of other stewardships for necessary tasks.

Both the examples of The Land and The Farm also illustrate the development of an *organization-wide type of division of labor among communes*, as well as showing the developing differentiation within a specific commune. Some communes, such as these two, existed mainly to serve essential functions for CCO *as a whole*. While The Farm operated, it furnished money from the sale of cash crops and also served as a "training camp" for new member resocialization. Its existence was based on these group needs. (When such needs were found to be accomplished better in other ways, The Farm was abandoned.) The Land has served as a major training center for CCO, and its functions continue to be elaborated. (It will probably not be phased out as long as CCO continues to exist.)

The fact that some communes are engaged in organization-wide tasks means that there may be a distinguishing between tasks necessary for the upkeep of the specific commune, and those tasks that are more organization-wide in scope. Especially on The Land, an analytical distinction can be made between such tasks, although the personnel overlaps and it is sometimes quite difficult to designate a task as only local or only nationwide in scope. Examples of tasks hard to designate as local or nationwide are the steward of architecture and construction, whose task it is to design new buildings and supervise their construction, and the stewardships that involve the teaching and training of members who come to The Land for resocialization (newer members) and further education ("older" members).

Other stewardships located originally at The Land, such as those involving photography, printing, and tape recording plainly have a broader scope. These and other group-wide tasks have been designated as "ministries," a term that is an explicit recognition by the group that there is a great deal of difference between a steward of a small specific task and a supervision of a large and organization-wide task. Examples of such ministries operating in 1974 and 1975, each of which has a *head* (overseer) and possibly several *assistants* (who are effectively foremen), were the communications ministry, the financial ministry, the agriculture ministry, the forestry ministry, the cannery ministry, the jobs ministry, the school ministry, the construction ministry, and other such large-scale tasks. Each of these can involve dozens of people, some of whom often do not live together in the same commune (or in a commune at all). An example of the forestry ministry will suffice to illustrate the complex nature of such operations.

In the summer of 1974, a contract was being negotiated by the jobs ministry to furnish fifty full-time workers to a large lumber and paper company in the area. This contract was just one of several being negotiated by the jobs minister at that time, but it probably was the largest in terms of number of people and cash realization (each worker was to receive $5 an hour, with the proceeds, some $10,000 per week, going into the organization's central treasury). This contract was concluded, and then a separate person, the forestry minister, selected the crews for the various tasks (planting, pruning, etc.). The head of the forestry ministry then supervised the various aspects of this endeavor and put people in charge of the crews. The selection of workers and foremen was done in close consultation with the jobs overseer, who has been with CCO in many capacities since the early years, and knew most of the members very well. Some members of the crews were from the same commune, but some were not. And many married men were not from communes at all, but were living separately (a relatively new development that will be discussed in more depth).

Thus, the steward structure is quite complex. It overlaps within it-self, since overseers or assistants of organization-wide functions might well be expected to have more local responsibility in terms of their own commune (if they live in one). Also, there is a great deal of overlap between the more formal authority structure and the steward structure in that persons can occupy a position in each simultaneously, and, as just indicated, can even occupy multiple positions in each structure. An example of such a person would be the jobs overseer, who was also serving as regional pastor for the western region for a while. A more general example of overlap between the two structures is that nearly every deacon or deaconess (or patroness) has a specific stewardship for which he or she is responsible. How well they accomplish their task determines in large measure whether or not they will be "promoted," and if so, in which structure (some are "mobile" in both, of course).

A last layer of stratification in the steward structure involves the position of some (but not all) ministry heads on the Pastors' Council, some of whose functions we have already described. With the addition of this layer, and that of the original singular leader, who also exercises authority over the stewardship structure, we have a well-differentiated division of labor, which is outlined in Figure 3. Note the attempt to schematically present the somewhat analytical but still important distinction between local and organization-wide functions.

It should be understood that this structure is task-oriented, and that this orientation dictates much flexibility and autonomy of operation. For instance, when a task needs doing, someone is assigned the task by the person whose general area of responsibility includes this new specific need. In our observation of how CCO operates, we see them use efficiency as a key factor in such decisions. We have not seen, for example, instances where a task went undone because no one would accept it, nor have we seen examples of the authoritarian nature of the

FIGURE 3

**Outline and Lines of Authority in Task-Oriented "Steward Structure,"
with Differentiation between Local and Organization-Wide Tasks** *

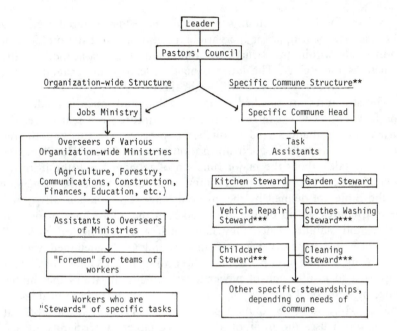

*Nearly all positions are at least theoretically open to females as long as the cardinal rule that no female have authority over any male is adhered to. This, of course, effectively prohibits females from holding most important positions.

**There is, of course, the intermediary of the regional overseer between the specific commune and the Council and sometimes this person does get directly involved in the internal functioning of a commune, especially if the commune is new, or if it is having some difficulty. Note that this structure is similar in approach to that of the newer "fellowship hall" structure involving married couples living noncommunally.

***These are only "typical examples," and vary greatly from commune to commune, and from fellowship hall to fellowship hall.

organization being carried to the dysfunctional extreme of the leader having to approve every minute appointment within an individual commune or on a specific task. Those occupying various positions have considerable autonomy, and it is used, always (as far as we can tell) with the primary goals of the organization serving as the "guiding principles" of decision making. Note also again that the newer fellowship hall structure is not completely represented by this discussion, although the general approach taken in such is similar.

Justification of Structures and Selection of Position Occupants

Before closing this section, some comment seems required regarding the selection of people for the various positions, about the mobility of individuals within the structures, and about the justification of the structures themselves. The latter issue is crucial to understanding the other two, so our discussion will begin there.

The structures are justified using the Bible, and much is made over the fact that CCO organizes itself using Scripture. In a real sense, the structures are made sacred through this process, and this "apotheosis process" seems to be a good illustration of what Berger (1967) means when he talks about the major function of religion being the justification of structure to give order to human existence. Since the principles of the Bible are defined by the group as "age-less," the actually-quite-new structures set up by the group take on the appearance of permanence and stability, since they have such a long "Biblical history." They are just a new version of an old and God-sanctioned way of organizing human groups, at least according to CCO ideology. This approach to justification of power arrangements illustrates the importance of traditional authority to some types of apparently radical social change. Hill's term "revolution by tradition" (1973) seems to aptly fit CCO, which uses the tradition of New Testament Christianity to justify its "revolution." While it is important to note that charismatic leadership has been important to CCO, the essential nature of the tradition to which the charismatic leaders pointed must be understood as well. The complexities of the CCO authority patterns force an appreciation that, indeed, all three of Weber's types of justifications for authority—charismatic, traditional, and rational-legal—have been important aspects of CCO leadership.

A key element of CCO ideology is that the leaders are somehow (through their better "spirituality" or simply through the "choice of God") in better communication with God, and thus their judgments are usually not to be questioned. Such judgments and decisions are usually made by the Pastors' Council, a method that allows much discussion and feedback concerning decisions and disallows an individual leader making a major decision that could be "misguided." When two or more pastors or other leaders reach a prayerful decision, this is interpreted as being a "sign from the Lord" that the decision is sound and should be followed. In really major decisions, the Pastors' Council operates on a consensus model, and when consensus is reached, the decision is accepted as God's will. In short, the leadership structure itself is defined as "sacred." This authoritarian element has been extremely functional from the point of view of group maintenance, and it has succeeded, even though the "priesthood of believers" idea, with its inherent schismatic potentiality, is also a part of CCO ideology.

One way that this authoritarianism is manifested is the selection of people for the various positions. There is little democracy in CCO, and people are placed in positions because leaders, after prayer and discussion (among themselves and with the individual) decide that a person's skills and the needs of the group combine in a certain task, a method of job allocation sometimes found in other "successful" communes (Kanter, 1972). The description of the negotiations concerning job assignments is a bit idealistic, since many of the tasks are unskilled labor jobs and can be done by just about anyone. However, in recent times, as jobs have become more specialized, there has been more of a serious attempt at occupational counseling as a part of the general socialization process. Also, as CCO has become stronger and more differentiated, more flexibility in terms of individual choice is being allowed. Nonetheless, the sytem is still a theocracy of sorts and is basically authoritarian in nature.[5]

CCO's relatively rapid expansion has assured a high degree of *vertical mobility* in terms of people being able to be placed as leaders of new houses, fellowships, or other functions. The multilevel stratification of the organization allows individuals to move through many successive layers, and thus experience some upward mobility. If the rapid expansion of the group slows down (we have little evidence on this point), or if the number of activities of the group actually decrease (this may be the case, as is discussed in the section on changes in group support methods), then chances for vertical mobility may decrease. The many different branches and functions of CCO also give the opportunity for *horizontal mobility*, and unless the group sharply contracts (which we doubt), this opportunity will remain. Thus, even if vertical mobility is slowed down, horizontal mobility may continue. Examples of horizontal mobility would be the reassigning of a person to a similar task in another commune, or in another work team. A combining of horizontal and vertical mobility is illustrated in the practice of making an assistant pastor in one commune pastor in another, or in assigning an assistant in a work team to be head of a new work team. Another example (and one of increasing import) is the movement of a person from a staff position and/or a position in a specific commune to a position of leadership in one of the fellowship hall operations that are rapidly developing in several locations around the country.

EVOLUTION OF SUPPORT METHODS AND LEVELS OF SUPPORT

Group Maintenance

When CCO began, there was little in the way of organized methods of group support. The continued existence of the several early CCO houses was, for a time, an open question. Essential support in terms of places to live and bare necessities were furnished by a large youth-oriented church in Southern California, by concerned individuals who donated unused buildings, food, clothes, and such to the group, and by some contributions from the participants (although these were usually small). Members were not expected to make regular financial contributions to the houses, and only those with something to contribute did so.

This pattern of depending on others for most support continued for some time, and was not drastically modified until the newly formed organization moved from Southern California and began to establish itself in its present headquarters area. Even then the acceptance of gratuities from interested persons and agencies continued to be an established pattern. For instance, the Salvation Army and a Goodwill store made important contributions of food, furniture, clothes, and so on to the first independent commune that was established in the new area to which CCO had migrated. Donations from interested individuals continue, including parents of members, sympathetic businessmen, and others. A great deal of the early possessions collected by the group came from such sources.

Governmental agencies also have made major contributions to CCO, although this has declined in importance as the group has grown stronger. Initially, the group benefited from federal commodity foods programs (all bread served at The Farm during our 1971 and 1972 visits there was made from "commodity foods" flour). Also, since The Farm was considered a labor camp by the county in which it was located, this meant that free medical and dental care could be obtained for residents at The Farm. CCO members have availed themselves of public education facilities in the area as well. They have received much advice on agricultural matters from representatives of governmental agencies too. Perhaps the most important continuing support by a governmental agency is the tax exempt status that CCO has enjoyed for several years. This indirect support has, we think, been essential to the level of success achieved by CCO.

Another source of funds is the members themselves. When they join, they are expected to turn over to CCO all possessions and money, and they are expected to work to support CCO activities. This pattern of working falls into two categories. One important category, which has been discussed in terms of the steward structure, is work *within* the group. But funds are essential to purchase needed services and supplies. This need for funds led rather quickly to the development of a pattern of individuals, particularly males, working *outside* the group to bring in money for group support.[6] This work, usually at unskilled types of jobs, was initially done on an individual basis, with each male expected to try to find a way to contribute to the support of the group. This pattern apparently still continues in some of the individual houses around the country. However, before long the group realized the social-psychological truth that such individual work situations often resulted in members being placed under great pressure to renounce their new-found beliefs. Therefore, a different pattern emerged where members would try to find work only as teams. Thus the jobs ministry quickly emerged, with a few individuals having the responsibility to locate jobs in which member teams could work together, unbothered by the presence of nonbelievers. The type of work done was still usually relatively unskilled, with teams being engaged to help landscape roadside parks, plant trees, pick apples, and other agriculture-related jobs.

Examples of this work motif are numerous in CCO. We have already discussed the "forestry ministry," which is a good example. CCO furnished for a time virtually all the laborers for planting and pruning trees for the large lumber and paper company mentioned. They successfully supplanted the usual type of migrant laborers, partially because the young Jesus people are such hard workers. Forestry work is still a major source of CCO income.

We observed regular requests by local farmers who wanted to hire the entire work force of The Farm for use on farms in the surrounding area. On days when there was little to do at The Farm, many workers would be hired out in response to these requests. The money from this work went into the CCO treasury, a usual practice of the group. Another regular work situation of this type has been the apple-pruning and picking teams that even traveled into adjoining states to engage in work that brought in needed funds. Such large work teams have been used less in the last year or so.

Note that the example of The Farm work crews is something of a "borderline" case between the "internal" and the "external" work of the group. What occurred was the evolution of a disciplined work force, based on experience gained within the organization. This pattern has been repeated in other areas of CCO life. A particularly important example of this is what has happened in the area of building construction. When CCO purchased The Land, they immediately began to construct new facilities there. Initially CCO hired skilled craftsmen to do the carpentry, electrical, and plumbing work, but CCO members worked with them, studying their techniques. Soon some members became proficient enough at these tasks that they could do them themselves and still meet the state and local building codes. They organized their own construction company headed by one of the original members (who is also the group architect, having finished his degree, at group expense, at a school in the East). Since then they have constructed several buildings at The Land, and have been involved in other remodeling and construction work at other CCO holdings. This construction company has now "gone external" and is licensed by the state. So far, they have not undertaken major jobs from the general public, focusing instead on remodeling and other relatively small tasks. However, the company may get more involved in the construction industry in the area as a way of earning funds for the CCO and for supporting individual members.

This example of the changes in the construction company illustrates a marked and fairly recent shift in the way in which the individual CCO members are used in group and individual support methods. We have seen them move from an initial situation of nearly total dependence on others, to one of obtaining partial support from the work of individual members working outside the group for funds for group support. This "work motif" was quickly altered so that *teams* of workers would hire out at unskilled, usually agricultural-related work, in order to gain money and retain their members. At the same time, large numbers of members would be employed in CCO farming and livestock-raising operations, although some of these teams would sometimes be hired out when they were not busy. This mixed approach, with a heavy emphasis on growing all of the food needed in the organization, continued for two or three years, and led to the rapid expansion of CCO agricultural holdings and the building of the cannery in order to make better use of the crops. Within the past few years, however, there have been further marked shifts of major importance. First, the emphasis changed from one of growing most of the food used and selling any surpluses as cash crops, to one where the major manpower use is in working for others as teams of workers hired out as a result of contracts negotiated between the CCO representatives and representatives of firms and agencies in the area. This approach has been partially supplanted by a trend toward small service-oriented businesses, such as janitorial services, which are now a major income source. Large work teams are still used but not as much as in the past, and they tend to be smaller when they are used (no more than about twenty workers).

Kanter (1973, p. 223) has furnished a valuable three-part typology of orientations of communes toward economic concerns. Some communes are economic *generalists*, which refers to attempted self-sufficiency that is inclusive of all group needs. Some are economic *specialists*, which means they specialize in some area, with the products of such specialization being sold of exchanged to meet needs of the group and its members. A third type are *dependents*, which refers to a dependence on external sources of sustenance (including earned income). CCO was originally totally dependent, but then made strong efforts at economic self-sufficiency, moving toward a more *generalist* position. The organizational focus for a time on producing livestock and foodstuffs for cash sales indicated a movement toward the *specialist* orientation. However, shifts toward contract labor by work teams were indicative of a move back toward a different kind of *dependent* status, albeit via a much more socially acceptable method—working for others. CCO specialized in furnishing workers for business and public concerns in the area. Now it is specializing more in furnishing services to the general public, via small companies such as janitorial services, house remodeling, and such.

The modification in the use of the labor of CCO members was partially responsible for decisions to phase out The Farm, which was very important in early CCO development, and to sell off the peach orchard, the large hog operation, the rabbitry, the goat dairy, and some vegetable gardens. The two fishing boats had been discontinued earlier as well. These decisions were explained to us purely in terms of financial considerations.[7] We were told in 1974 that CCO would continue to produce some food and livestock, but only that which was *maximally profitable.* Much food and other things would be purchased using funds gained through working for others. This even included, in 1975, the purchase of fruits and vegetables to be canned in the CCO cannery. The shift involved a recognition that many members had developed valuable skills, and that these skills were worth more on the open market than they were just being used internally. The later shift toward small service-oriented businesses is simply an economically-based logical extension of such thinking. In this sense, the experience of working in the group has made the group and its members socially mobile, and they are now, as a group, moving back into the middle-class existence from which most of them came when they joined the "counter-culture" (which, of course, made them temporarily downwardly mobile.) The shifts toward contract labor and, more recently, to the service industries also are implicit admissions that CCO does not now mind being more dependent on the society from which it initially withdrew.

Support for Individual Members

The ideas just described on how to use individual members' talents and skills are something relatively new for CCO. The "new approach" has implications for financial support for individual members, an important concern not often discussed in much detail by commune theorists (see Stein, 1973, for a general discussion of some aspects). Most organizational theory takes into account the need to reward participants in any organization (see March & Simon, 1969), and CCO is no exception. The way in which individual support methods have changed can be viewed as a gradual increase in inducements to members to remain CCO members.

In CCO there was little initial differentiation between group support and individual support. All energies were directed toward getting enough food to eat and clothes to wear. As the organization achieved a degree of stability, especially after the relocation, some bifurcation of the maintenance function evolved, and a pattern emerged whereby individual members who were without some supply of money (for example, from parents) were given an allotment of spending money whenever there was money available. This was especially true in the case of married couples with children. They were furnished with pocket money to avoid the problems caused by requiring parents to ask for money for things needed in child care. Individual needs for food, shelter, transportation, clothes, medical care, and the like were furnished by the group directly, with no money usually being handled by the individual members, except for funds for emergencies and for the allotments just mentioned.

This allotment system seems to have worked well, as long as everyone was living together in communes. However, an evolution in living patterns (to be discussed) led to a major change in the way in which CCO supported its members. Now there are two major methods whereby members receive financial support. One is the initial method, referred to by the group as being "in the pot." This means that everything the individual earns is given over to the group, and all the needs of the individual are taken care of. Some single members are still in the pot and live in a manner not unlike members of many communes, both past and present. Most married couples were initially in the pot, but now the only married members remaining are married pastors, who receive support from the organization.

The new method of support is much more unique in the history of the Jesus movement and of communes in general. This involves a member, initially usually a married male, *drawing a salary from the organization*. This salary is not overly large (and was initially generally equal for all) but was intended to cover the basic living costs of a man and his family. This would include normal living costs, with some increments being given for larger families and/or handicapped children, and (more recently) for seniority and job responsibility, among other things.

The separation between the two methods of individual support is not total, and the new method is not legalistically administered. For example, we understand that all the rental units, including the newer individual family dwellings, were, for tax reasons, initially rented in the name of CCO. (This method has been supplanted now, with members paying rents from salary, except for some leaders who receive a designated and traditional "parsonage allowance.") All medical and dental care which cannot be furnished by CCO medical personnel is paid directly by CCO, which has developed a sophisticated group insurance plan that combines self-insurance (by CCO) with an externally purchased group major medical coverage. Nonetheless, this new mode of individual (and family) support is a marked change from the initial "in the pot" way of supporting CCO members and families. Now all members except house pastors, patronesses, house staff, and other single staff and members are supported using the salary method.

One result of the increased affluence of members, and of the fact that some now have their own money to manage, was an internal savings bank, called "Kionopia Bank," which lasted over three years. Application was made to the Federal Credit Union system for affiliation, but such was refused because of some unusual operating procedures of the bank. This bank was unique in that it paid no interest to savers, charged no interest, and required no collateral for borrowing. This bank, like all other aspects of CCO life, was justified using Scripture, with over forty scriptural references given in the three page description of operating procedures of the bank. But, the negative decision of the Federal Credit Union system was the deathknell for this unusual experiment.

An interesting comment apropos to the new mode of individual and family support, and also to the discussion of organization goals, was made by the head of the jobs ministry in a conversation held in the summer of 1974. He said that CCO considered that *one of its major functions is to furnish jobs for members.* By this he was referring to the jobs for members on organization work teams, jobs that furnished the members with a salary paid by CCO. This statement seems to indicate some evolution of group goals from evangelism to member welfare. Such changes suggest a growing desire of many members, especially those with children, for more amenities of "the good life," and at least for a more "normal" existence in terms of the broader culture. Thus we can see what appears to be an implicit appreciation by CCO leadership of the value of inducements to members, although the leaders would state that jobs were being furnished out of love and concern for the members.

One other facet of individual and family support that requires mention is the development of what is, in effect, a full-time staff of CCO. Many of the original members are now involved full-time in such things as the education and training of new members, and other functions such as organizational finances. Most of these people are supported through the newer salary method, and many live on their own, coming to the group headquarters during work hours and for other specific functions only. This withdrawal is partially a function of the fact that nearly all of them have families. However, we are interested in whether or not the new method of individual and family support was designed especially for this class of "older" members. Whatever the situation, these leaders made up a good portion of the over fifty families that were living under the new method shortly after its inception in summer 1974. (In early 1975, correspondence with one leader revealed that seventy-five families were under the new plan, which was approximately one-half of all CCO married couples at that time.)

A very new but possibly significant development in individual support methods is the open encouragement to some longer-term full-time staff to accept "secular" employment. This new development only involves to date (late 1977) about a dozen males in the headquarters area. The reasons reported to us for this dramatic change, which is diametrically opposed to the work team approach used for several years, include two factors. One, upward mobility for newer members is increased and new blood is brought into leadership positions. Two, such a move means that the individual leaves communal living and becomes a part of a fellowship hall group, usually in a leadership position. The few individuals who have been encouraged and allowed to seek secular employment are "strong in the Lord," and thus deemed less susceptible to worldly influences working alone. Also, some obviously have developed valuable skills during their time in CCO, and moving them to secular employment seems to be viewed as a way of maximizing their earning power and thereby decreasing the financial drain on CCO.

Most of the changes in group and individual support methods, outlined in Figure 4, have been facilitated by the growing affluence of the organization. Without the wherewithal furnished by others and by the dedicated work of members, CCO would probably not still be in exis-

FIGURE 4

Evolution of Methods of Organizational and Member Support, and Levels of Such Support

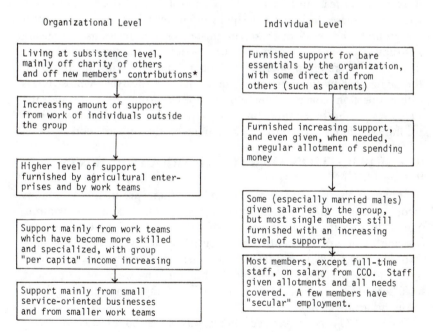

Organizational Level

Individual Level

| Living at subsistence level, mainly off charity of others and off new members' contributions* | Furnished support for bare essentials by the organization, with some direct aid from others (such as parents) |

| Increasing amount of support from work of individuals outside the group | Furnished increasing support, and even given, when needed, a regular allotment of spending money |

| Higher level of support furnished by agricultural enterprises and by work teams | Some (especially married males) given salaries by the group, but most single members still furnished with an increasing level of support |

| Support mainly from work teams which have become more skilled and specialized, with group "per capita" income increasing | Most members, except full-time staff, on salary from CCO. Staff given allotments and all needs covered. A few members have "secular" employment. |

| Support mainly from small service-oriented businesses and from smaller work teams | |

*The organization still expects new members to turn over money and possessions upon joining, but this seems to have more value in terms of individual commitment than it does in terms of a source of funds. Also, charity is still accepted, in the form of material goods and/or money, but we are convinced that this type of support, while essential in the early stages, has lessened considerably in importance (and in percent of organization "GNP").

tence. A situational set of circumstances also contributed greatly to the success of the group. By this we mean that, particularly because of their migration from Southern California, they found a ready market for their initially relatively unskilled labor pool that developed as a result of their evangelism methods having struck a resonant chord with large numbers of young people. Their move into agricultural enterprises that lasted several years was extremely important because it furnished them foodstuffs, cash crops, a place to train their unskilled labor pool, and the necessary isolation to resocialize members and to give the organization a chance to get started. As the level of member skills rose, the teams of skilled and semiskilled workers (in things as varied as apple picking, forestry, and construction) were also able to find work in the generally prosperous economy of the headquarters area. And the increasing skill levels and management experience allowed the formation and successful operation of the many small businesses that now furnish the major financial support for CCO members and functions. Thus we see a situation in which some wise decisions were made, at least in terms of the circumstances in which CCO found itself. And these decisions have paid off in terms of the prosperity of the group.[8] The result of these circumstances and decisions is a strong and upwardly mobile group of young people and a streamlined organization, with fewer properties and operations but with an improved (larger) cash flow that supports a more affluent lifestyle. A most interesting question concerns the ability of the group to withstand the pressures of the new-found prosperity—pressures that might well lead to dramatic but as yet unforeseen changes in the organization.

EVOLUTION OF LIVING ARRANGEMENTS

When communes and communal organizations are mentioned, many people assume that "a commune is a commune," and that communards all live the same. Such is not the case at all in CCO, as the specific living arrangements have been many and varied over its short existence. A much more detailed discussion of family life and courtship will be presented in Chapter 5, but for now we want to present, in a somewhat abstract fashion, important changes that have occurred in living arrangements.

When CCO first organized, there was a period of flux in living arrangements. Males and females lived together under the same roof, but in separate rooms, with segregation of the sexes. The few married couples were allowed to cohabit. They usually had a room to themselves and often served as leaders of the commune. The problem of keeping the sexes separate (an important element of group beliefs) was made easier by the rather low number of females involved in early CCO experience, a fact partially due to the high proportion of males in the countercultural milieu from whence came most members, but also probably a result of the rather subservient position of females within the group.

As the group grew, and as increasing numbers of females joined, a new living arrangement evolved. When CCO relocated in the new state after migrating, it began some communes where members of only one sex resided. The communes were referred to as brothers houses and sister's houses. Such single sex communes were usually close together, and there was considerable interaction between members of the separate houses, but such interaction was task-oriented and was closely supervised to insure that no "problems of the flesh" arose. On other communal operations such as The Farm, the sexes were strictly segregated as well, although they did work, eat, have fellowship, and attend Bible study together.

Another innovation was communal facilities known as widows' houses. These communes were composed of unmarried women with children, and *never,* so we were told, contained any real widows. These communes were simply an attempt to minister to the needs of many young, unmarried women with children, and the term widows' house was selected as a somewhat scriptural, euphemistic term to designate such communes. These communes were initially supported by the work of members of the single-male communes. No widows' houses have existed in CCO for over a year, as the "single mothers" (CCO term) have been integrated into other communes or have married. (In 1977 there is still a significant number of "single mothers" in CCO, as such people seem to be disproportionately attracted to CCO.)

Thus there was, over the course of the first two years of the group's existence, a communal living situation with three major types of communes—the brother's houses, the sister's houses, and the widows' houses. Another pattern that soon developed as the proportion of married couples increased was that of married couples' communes. It was thought unwise to mix marrieds and unmarrieds very much, thinking that such would lead to many "temptations of the flesh" for the unmarried members, many of whom had had an active sex life before joining CCO. Thus when couples married, they were either sent to another commune of single members with the male as a leader, or they joined a married couples' commune. Initially, most married couples were leaders in the other types of communes, with separate living quarters that afforded some privacy in the commune. Also, some couples lived in separate dwellings at The Land and worked in a staff capacity there. However, given CCO views about mixing couples with singles, a rapid increase in marriages between members forced the operation of separate houses for married couples, especially in the area of the headquarters city. In married couples' communes, couples often lived with little autonomy and privacy, a situation which apparently caused problems in some of the marriages. Sometimes single members' and married couples' communes existed at the same location, as at The Farm, where the original owner's house was used for married couples (the males of whom were leaders at The Farm), and the migrant laborer shacks were used for single members, who were segregated by sex. Other facilities such as the goat dairy, and the Country Farm at one time involved only married couples living communally.

During 1974, a new and somewhat radical departure from the communal life-style developed. A number of CCO married couples started living in single-family dwellings, often somewhat geographically isolated from other group members. This new living arrangement has obviously been made possible by the increased prosperity of CCO, since it is much more expensive to maintain separate dwellings for families than it would be to support them in groups of several families per dwelling. Two reasons were given to us for this new arrangement. One was the fact that children of members were having difficulty in knowing to whom they belonged and who had authority over them, and this was leading to problems of discipline. The other reason, which was emphasized, was explained in terms of the ideology of the group. We were told that it was difficult for males to maintain authority over their own households in the communal living situation with several other couples. This problem was crucial since CCO ideology contains the belief that the male is superior to the female, and that he should govern his home. CCO leaders had decided, based on several years of communal experience, that a man could only be master of his home when that home did not include other adult nonfamily members.

We have not been able to discern if there were other problems (such as marriages dissolving because a member of the couple grew attached to other commune members, or a general desire for more privacy), and so are left with the apparent fact that, at least in part for ideological reasons, CCO has drastically altered its usual living style in a way that severely limits control of the individual families by the group. The problems of male superiority and mastery, and the identity problems of children must have been severe. The group must have felt very strongly about such matters for it to give up the close supervision and continual contact of communal living, usually thought important to maintaining doctrinal and behavioral norms. Whether or not this "loss of surveillance" of members, and the encouragement given to family (as opposed to organizational) ties will result in the eventual loss of some members and a weakening of the group remains to be seen. Such outcomes plainly are possibilities, however, if the work of Kanter (1973) and Talmon (1973) on familism/collectivism tensions in communes has any credence at all.

It should be said that CCO leaders realized some of the problems with the new living arrangements, and sometimes deliberately rented several houses in the same area so that the members could maintain a close fellowship. Also the new Fellowship Hall in the headquarters' city was rented in 1974 mainly to afford a place where married couples could maintain fellowship with each other. (There are, as of 1977, fellowship halls in several other cities as well.) The couples (and a few nonmarried members) are organized, using the Old Testament example of the Israelities under Moses, into "groups of ten" (cadres of four to six couples), each with a "shepherd" of its own (one of the males) who leads the unit in Bible study once a week at night. Many of the men from a group of ten will work at the same task, and the women will often work at organizational tasks (such as sewing) together at their homes, or at the fellowship hall.

This new living arrangement, as of 1977, involved virtually all married (and some single) CCO members. It is thought of as a new way of evangelizing. as married couples are expected to witness to their friends and neighbors. But this form of evangelizing itself raises potential problems. Recall Bryan Wilson's point (1969, p. 234) that the greatest problem of new religious sects is not caused by the growing up of the children of members, but is more immediately caused by recruiting members whose experience has been greatly different from that of most members.

CCO does allow new married members to join without going through the same lengthy and vigorous resocialization process required of single members who come into CCO through the "normal" evangelistic methods. Not allowing the "lower" membership requirements would limit the effectiveness of the new living arrangements as an evangelism tool, but allowing married couples to affiliate with the fellowship hall group without going through the entire usual resocialization process potentially includes a set of members in the group who do not have as important a stake in the group. This could lead to schisms, as the new, relatively untrained members participate in group activities, especially if the singles complain about the development of a relatively privileged class within the organization.

Only time will yield the answer to these important questions, and we will be watching intently for signs of the answers. In one issue of CCO's bimonthly journal, we were interested to note what may be an implicit recognition of the special problems afforded by the new living arrangements, and a direct attempt to deal with the potential (or real?) problems. There was a small mention of a new proposal to build a community of single family dwellings in what was to be a self-contained and self-sufficient community in the general geographic area of The Land. We know none of the details (or causes) of this new plan for living arrangements for the group's increasing number of married couples, and we are unaware of the proposal being acted upon. But perhaps CCO leaders have already decided that having married couples living separately and isolated from other members is not necessarily good for the organization. We also know that special resocialization methods are being used with these newer married converts in an effort to deal with problems arising from their recruitment. Such methods include home Bible study courses on tapes, regular seminars and activities at Fellowship Hall, and a regular program of visitation in the homes of new member couples by CCO "older" leaders. Also, a night school at The Land has been started within the past year just for new married couples who have joined via the fellowship hall outreach. Some women among these new married converts also are participating in the normal day school activities at The Land (more on CCO schools in the next section of this chapter).

Thus, there have now been several important modifications of living arrangements within CCO. They are schematically presented in Figure 5. Note that all forms except widows' houses still exist, but a larger proportion than formerly was the case are involved in the married couples' arrangements, which are growing in numbers of people involved as members marry and leave the single-member communes. Presently about half of all CCO members are married.

METHODS OF MEMBER TRAINING AND RESOCIALIZATION

Bible Studies and Doctrinal Purity

The methods used by CCO to train and resocialize new members have undergone much rationalization and elaboration, and easily compare in their thoroughness to those of the Bruderhof much publicized by Zablocki's (1971) treatment. The CCO approach to the crucial concern of resocialization was initially very unorganized and even haphaz-

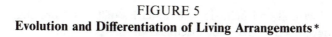

FIGURE 5

Evolution and Differentiation of Living Arrangements *

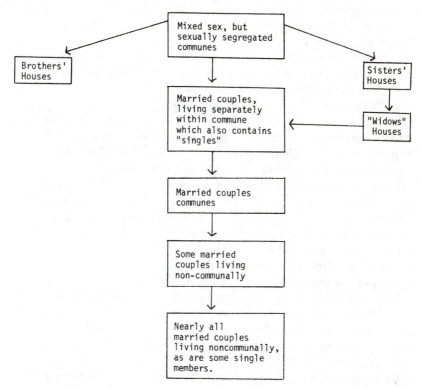

*All types of communes except "widows"' houses continue to exist in the organization, with a gradual movement of more members into the married couples' living arrangements.

ard. People coming into CCO during its formative time in Southern California were expected to read and study their Bible themselves (still a primary expectation) and to participate in the occasional Bible studies that early leaders would provide. The studies were sometimes sporadic and seldom occurred more than every few days in most of the early houses, partially as a result of there being more houses than leaders for a time, or more correctly, there were more houses than there were "acceptable" leaders, with "proper" training in the Scriptures. The situation was ripe for doctrinally-based arguments, and a few did occur.

When, as described in chapter 1, the person desiring to be the original leader exerted himself and was accepted by the several early houses in Southern California, this started a long process of delineating the doctrinal and behavioral boundaries of CCO more clearly. The leader developed a group of disciples who agreed with him on points of doctrine and on other matters, and successfully thwarted attempts by some who disagreed with him to assume the leadership of some of the first houses. As more leaders developed who were "doctrinally pure," they were designated house pastors and began regular, daily Bible studies. As these leaders were placed, the Bible studies evolved from a situation where members simply took turns reading the Bible to each other, to a situation where a single leader, "certified" by the original leader of the group, led lengthy studies that were in fact informal sermons or homilies. These sermons explained the CCO interpretation of the various verses of the Bible and also afforded ample opportunity to comment on behaviors and other matters.

These sessions have been extremely important in the resocialization process for new members. The frequency, length, and intensity of these studies allowed ample opportunity to fully elaborate the all-encompassing fundamentalist-oriented CCO "world view." These sessions, along with the individual Bible study and prayer times, expanded to fill nearly all available free time, thus also effectively disallowing time for competitive alternative world views to be presented.

This pattern of regular Bible studies led by house pastors, and individual Bible study, continues to this day in the various CCO communes and homes of CCO members around the country. It has become much more systematic as a result of a decision made several years ago to have all houses across the country study the same Bible passages during a designated time period. There is a "unified plan of Bible study," whereby house pastors teach from the same passages, and individuals read the same passages at each CCO outpost. This program is designed to have the entire membership read the entire Bible in a year. Daily reading assignments are heavy, and the group Bible studies themselves sometimes last over two hours.

The unified Bible study plan does not in itself guarantee doctrinal purity, of course, and CCO has devised some subtle, but quite rational procedures to help maintain consensus. We have described in an article on the application of a "thought reform" model to the Jesus movement as a whole (Richardson, Simmonds & Harder, 1972) some of these mechanisms that operated on individual members on the movement in general. Here we will focus on newer structures specific to CCO, developed to cope with the increased membership size and national scope of the organization.

We have already presented information on the nationwide communications ministry, which includes a journal and, more importantly for purposes of maintaining doctrinal purity, the tapes ministry. This ministry records acceptable Bible studies and makes multiple copies for nationwide distribution. CCO presently has a library of over one hundred such tapes, and more are being developed. These tapes are sometimes used in lieu of a study led by a local leader, and they are listened to by leaders and members alike in their individual studies. They have been especially useful in new married couples fellowships as a tool of evangelism among neighbors of CCO couples living communally, and, of course, as a way of helping insure that these new groups teach and live the group's beliefs and practices.

Another method which helps maintain doctrinal purity is a system of "recycling" leaders. Leaders of the various units around the country are, in a somewhat irregular but definite way, brought back to CCO's headquarters for further study. This may take the form of having them come back to teach in the schools developed for members (which wll be described in full). Such guest teaching is subtly monitored by the full-time teaching staff (now five), and the guest teachers are counseled as they teach. These visits to the headquarters area also have the effect of rejuvenating leaders and increasing their level of commitment to the organization. Such pilgrimages are anticipated with high interest by CCO leaders, who may have had an assignment several hundred (or even thousand) miles from most of the rest of "the body" (a term members use to refer to CCO). These leaders get to come back to the beautiful headquarters area and meet new people, see how CCO has prospered, and enjoy fellowship with old friends, thus reestablishing affective ties that the "call of duty" may have temporarily severed.

Organizational Schools

The most dramatic method whereby members are resocialized and trained (and whereby doctrinal purity is maintained) involves CCO's "in house" schools that have been developed. We will describe the schools as of 1974, and then discuss modifications of this basic resocialization structure that have been made since (through fall 1977). Three major types of schools had evolved as of 1974 as the organization grappled with the problem of developing and maintaining agreement on what CCO's leaders considered crucial issues, and these structures lasted several years before being modified. These were the Children's School, the Lambs' School, and the Teams' (or Sheep) School. The Teams' School developed first, but it operated for several years in tandem with the Lambs' School, so the two will be discussed together. The development of the Teams' School will be covered in more depth in the section on evolution of evangelism methods.

Taken together, the Lambs' and Teams' Schools formed an extremely effective resocialization and commitment mechanism that virtually guaranteed a high level of member retention and a strong commitment to CCO and its ideology of those going through the process. When the "recycling" of leaders, the regular Bible studies (with a new twist in 1977 of correspondence courses), especially for new married converts, and the Children's School (to be described) are considered as well, it is obvious that by 1974 CCO had organized a nearly never-ending education process which inculcated new members with the group culture and continually reinforced the values of group culture in all CCO members. This education function has been (and still is) viewed as so central to accomplishing the goals of the organization that nearly one entire major facility—The Land—has been dedicated to this task, as have other CCO resources as well. The Land is financially supported mostly by the work of other segments of CCO, although "pupils" in the schools do sometimes get involved in labor that directly realizes funds for support of The Land.[9] The two dormitories on The Land were built to serve as domiciles for those attending the schools. The "single family dwellings" on The Land (mobile homes, rustic cabins, and new apartments) serve as residences for full-time staff members and their families. The large dining hall served as the central location of the classes for several years, and each dorm has classrooms as well. The building of a five-room school complex of The Land was completed in 1976, indicating a strong and continuing commitment by CCO to the education (resocialization) of its members. This new modern, and beautifully designed building allows simultaneous classes for a total of 105, students, and also contains office space for school administration. The staff stationed at The Land teaches in the schools, and more recently, also grades correspondence lessons from the taped "Home Bible Study" courses completed by members from all over the country.

When a new member joins CCO, usually through one of its houses, the convert is assigned to a commune for a short time. The assignment is usually to the same house to which the member became a convert, and the length of this initial stay is usually around three or six months. Some variation is expected, as for instance when workers are needed at some task, leading to the immediate assignment of the new member for various lengths of time to a new commune because of manpower needs. During this early period, the member is observed to see if he or she is truly a "believer in Christ" and is committed to CCO, and to get some idea about the skills of the person. After this initial trial period, if the member is adjudged to be serious about a commitment to Christ and the organization, then he or she is reassigned to The Land, the headquarters training commune earlier described.

Lambs' School

This reassignment until recently made the new member a part of a Lambs' School (a "lamb" is a new member) class which spent three months in intensive study at The Land. We were present at The Land when classes were taking place and had the opportunity to observe an orientation session for a new class in summer 1974. The classes typically included about forty individuals from all over the country. (the orientation session we observed had over forty people from over twenty different states.) They were usually nearly equally divided between the sexes, with slightly more males.

The Lambs' School had several major functions. One was to get the lambs "into the Word," and during the three months spent there, all class members were expected to read through the Bible. This was done under the guidance of staff members, most of whom were full-time permanent staff members at The Land, but which also included some "recycled" leaders from other areas. Several hours a day were spent in systematic group Bible study, and the spare time of each member was also to be taken up in Bible study and prayer.

Another major function of the Lambs' School was to acquaint the new members with the full extent of CCO's activities, and to get the individuals fully integrated into the life and culture of CCO. An important way of doing this is through what the organization called "culture class" which, according to an article in the bimonthly CCO magazine: "explains and presents to the lambs a vision of this ministry as a people unto God, living together, serving together, loving one another. The discussions cover a whole range of whys—why we have all things in common, why we live as we do within the surrounding community, why we work, why we have chaperones, why we even want to be a people unto God."

The experience of Lambs' School was deliberately designed to be enjoyable, the rigorous study and work notwithstanding. The setting was idyllic, the fellowship genuine, and eligible members of the opposite sex were present. Life was strictly supervised, as evidenced by the lengthy set of rules read and commented on by group leaders in the orientation session we attended. But this supervision was apparently fully accepted by these new members, many of whom were completely rootless with no place to call their own before joining.

Yet another major function of Lambs' School was to teach the members a useful skill. Most of the converts knew "next to nothing" about practical matters such as carpentry, auto mechanic work, cooking, farming, tree planting, and other tasks important to CCO. This Lambs' School time was designed to allow the member to learn a skill and thereby to find a place in the task (steward) structure of the group. A strong effort was made for each new member to receive vocational counseling. One of the early leaders of the group who was full-time staff at The Land and who served on the Pastors' Council was the CCO vocational counselor. He discussed group needs and individual skills and interests with each member, and helped them select an area of work on which to concentrate. He also maintained a file of individual skills and requests to work at certain tasks to use in selecting individuals to do necessary jobs. This should not be interpreted to mean that each new member got a free choice at a chosen occupation. Such was not the case, as organization-wide needs (and also those of The Land commune) had to be met. Therefore, from one point of view, the counseling was an attempt to get necessary work at The Land done. Members' preferences could only work within the bounds of available and needed tasks. The assignments to various tasks required that the person "called" to a task spend time each day with the task, learning, in an apprenticeship fashion, how to accomplish the task. Thus each day in the life of a member of a Lambs' School class was divided between Bible study and working at a skill, but with the major emphasis being the Bible study and other direct resocialization mechanisms.

Until 1976, after the three months in the Lambs' School, new members were graduated into what was called the helps' ministry, which means that they became a part of the CCO labor pool. Thus they were subject to decisions made by group leaders (about necessary tasks) and especially to decisions made by the jobs ministry, which put together large specific work teams and assigned them to tasks that had been taken on by the organization. The demise of really large work teams in CCO life was a major cause for phasing out the helps' ministry.

Lambs' School graduates were made to feel a special responsibility by being told that their labors would support the next Lambs' School (the class immediately after their own), just as their own class had been supported by the work of the previous Lambs' School class after it graduated. This justification (which was true) served well to get the new members integrated into CCO life and into the CCO labor force.

Service in the helps' ministry was indefinite in length, but for most it usually lasted about nine months. During this time, the members were observed to see how they functioned within their group, and to see how they developed "spiritually" and in terms of practical skills. This observation was not without specific purpose, for CCO was continually forming evangelism teams to send out to open new "gathering houses" in areas not yet having CCO outposts. Also, as has been described, new work crews were organized somewhat sporadically as new jobs were taken on by CCO, through work-seeking efforts of the overseer of the jobs' ministry.

Teams' School

Teams' School (or Sheep School) for evangelism teams, which was the first organized school developed by CCO, has not been discussed, so some detail will be given about how the teams were structured and trained, even though there has been some recent change in this approach to evangelism.

Each evangelism team was composed of from seven to ten people, with the ideal being about ten members. Team members were selected by CCO leaders, based on recommendations of those directly supervising the newer members. Each team (which usually included both males and females) was formed around one person who was designated the pastor of the new group and also most likely head of a commune in a new target area. Most teams were predominantly male, but in 1974 the first all-female team was organized, under a patroness, to work in child evangelism in a large city. Each team was deliberately structured so that skills essential to organizing a new commune would be available. For example, if the team was to form a new separate commune, it required a cook, a carpenter, an auto mechanic, someone who knew something about growing food, and so on. Each team was rather carefully preselected, with attention paid to interpersonal relations. By this we mean that each team was composed not just of people having necessary skills, but it was also composed of people who were thought to be able to get along with each other. After a team was selected, an attempt was made to have them live together in one of the larger CCO communes for a period of about four months in order to see if they could function as a unit. During this period, the group worked at a joint task and was observed to determine if it would "make," or if some members would have to be replaced.

Once the team membership was set, the team was sent to Teams' School at The Land with four other teams. Teams' School lasted for three months, during which time serious attention was given to a differentiated curriculum, which included Bible study, classes on evangelism methods, and continuing the development of personal, practical skills. Over half the work day was spent in study (five separate classes, five days a week), with the other being spent working at the chosen and/or assigned jobs. During one visit to The Land, we observed some Teams' School classes, including a child evangelism class (for female team members, but taught by a male) with multilithed handouts on techniques that would have "done any fundamentalist church proud." [10] The entire approach was quite sophisticated and the schedule rigorous, possibilities allowed for by the relatively high levels of education of members (an average of over twelve years apiece), and by their high motivation.

During our summer 1974 visit to The Land, we observed the final session of a Teams' School. It was handled differently from the typical session and involved the imaginative use of sociodrama. Full-time staff who had been involved in teaching in the school arbitrarily selected members of the class and assigned them parts to play in several selected sociodramas. Some full-time staff were also assigned parts in the sociodramas in an obvious attempt to make sure that certain points were made in the process of acting out the hypothetical situation of the drama. One sociodrama setting was the visit to a hypothetical commune by some irate parents (played by some full-time staff members) who were accusing the commune "leaders" and "members" (about eight class members) of brainwashig their children, stealing them away from their homes, and all kinds of immoral behaviors. This "drama with a message" was plainly chosen because of the many media discussions at that time of just such accusations by parents of members of some Jesus movement groups (especially the Children of God and the Christian Foundation organizations). The class members were expected to develop a way to handle, as a team, such difficulties, and they went about it in a deliberate, even if somewhat disorganized, way. Another sociodrama situation involved an attempt to witness to a recalcitrant hippie type (played by a talented full-time staff person) who was obviously "totally spaced." Again, the approach to the problem was team-oriented and thoughtful. We were impressed by the use of the technique, and by the ability of some (obviously group leaders and usually males) in handling the situations as they were given to them with little if any preparation time.

When a team finished Teams' School, they were usually sent directly to a general area or city which had been selected by CCO leaders during the time of the school. The news of where each team was going was withheld until the last of the three-month-long term, and great anticipation built up among team members. In the early summer of 1974, one set of teams (five) was assigned to New York state, and we were told that the teams leaving later that summer would go into the South, although the specific locations had not yet been selected.

The entire flow of members through the process which began when they joined CCO and continued at least until they were placed on an evangelism (or work) team is outlined in Figure 6. The figure is derived from a drawing in a 1974 issue of CCO's own magazine, which had an article briefly describing the process as it was at that time. As we said, it represented a very rational and functional approach to the problems of new member socialization, continual reinforcement of

FIGURE 6
Flow of a New Member through the "Schools" for Resocialization, with Approximate Time Spent in Each

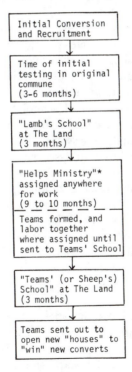

*"Helps' ministry," phased out in 1976, and Lambs' School and Teams' School juxtaposed in time and renamed "Bible Survey" and "Bible Analysis," respectively. Also, those in Bible Analysis will not automatically be sent out as a missionary, as was the case with Teams' School graduates.

group cultural values, and recruitment of new members and evangelism.

The newer modifications to the process have also been developed quite rationally. Now, since large work teams are a thing of the past in CCO, there is less need for large numbers of relatively unskilled workers. Thus the helps' ministry has been phased out, and new members attend six consecutive months of intensive school at The Land. The school is broken into a two-month session and a juxtaposed four-month session called, respectively, Bible survey and Bible analysis. The format for these two sections is quite similar to the earlier Lambs' and Teams' School and represents a combining of the two with no helps' ministry in between. The goals are similar as well—teaching people to be good CCO-style Christians and focusing on evangelism. Facilities at The Land allow 105 people per term, and these facilities continue to be filled (in fact, there is a need for more dorm space for women because of the increasing proportion of new female members). Every six months a new term starts.

Simultaneous to the Bible survey and Bible analysis sessions is a night school of around forty-five people. This group is made up largely of new married converts who have joined through the area fellowship house. They use the school facilities in the evening, returning to their individual homes afterwards, instead of living permanently at The Land for six months. Night school takes a year to complete, since only the evenings are used. The format is quite similar to that of Bible survey and Bible analysis sessions.

Not all who complete Bible analysis will eventually be sent out to open a new gathering house. This represents an important difference between the old and new resocialization approaches. We were told that CCO is being more selective in who is sent out to open a new evangelism outpost, and that CCO has come to accept the fact that some Christians should not be missionaries in the direct sense. This new thinking probably indicates some loss of evangelistic fervor, but we cannot yet tell its effects for certain.

Children's Schools

One other CCO school that has been developed is the Children's School. When CCO began, there were no children involved, except for an occasional child of one of the few married couples. However, several years have passed since this start, and a number of married couples now exist within the organization, and many of them have children. Also, the children from the widows' houses described earlier contributed to the developing problems of how to take care of the children while parents worked at group tasks, and how to educate the children.

An early solution of the care problem for individual married couples' communes was the assigning of one person (or several, taking turns) in a commune to mind the children. This assignment of a nursery steward has worked very well and continues to be used, especially for younger-age children and especially in the larger communes. For example, on The Land, one of the original cabins has been developed into a nursery, day care, and pre-school facility, and a female member has this as nearly her entire stewardship. She educated herself in the area of child care and development by reading materials and by taking courses at a junior college nearby.

As the first children grew older, it became imperative to decide whether or not to organize a more systematic separate school system. CCO leadership chose to do this, at least on an experimental and small scale, and started preparing to open a day care/nursery school/kindergarden facility in the general area of the headquarters city, so that more member parents in that area could avail themselves of the opportunity to have their youngsters in a Christian school. They chose the site of the County Farm described earlier, which had been a home for the aged prior to being leased by CCO. Much time and effort was put into remodeling several rooms of this facility, and several members spent time training themselves through junior college classes and in self-education in order to be prepared to teach in the school. The school had to meet rather rigorous state requirements before it could be licensed, and this was done. The school opened in 1973 and had about thirty children. The first head of the school, interestingly, was a male. The selection of him over several women with previous training in child-care methods may illustrate sexual discrimination deriving from the fundamentalist ideology of CCO. However, females have headed the child-care operations since that first year.

After its beginning at the County Farm, the Children's School was moved to the building referred to as Fellowship Hall where it was incorporated, along with the "single mothers' (widows) program" into the new married couples ministry, which is centered at Fellowship Hall. This building, which is much more centrally located than the County Farm, seemed a logical choice for the Children's School, since most of the married couples in the area of the headquarters used this building as a center of activities, and some of the wives worked in the school as well. The establishment of this school did not, of course, supplant other such schools developed more informally at communes too distant from Fellowship Hall to use those facilities, nor has it replaced the facility at The Land, which serves mainly full-time staff who are permanent residents there. However, in 1977 this school was phased out, and it appears that CCO is now rethinking its decision to maintain alternative schools. The Land Children's School and some others still operate, but are usually found now only in situations where sound alternative educational and child-care facilities do not exist.

It will be interesting to see how comprehensive a school system CCO will try to establish in their attempts to see that their children get a "good Christian education," an interest which has as an obvious goal the continuance of the children in CCO when they get older. So far, CCO leaders have decided against an alternative primary school, mainly, they say, because of financial reasons. Some consideration is being given at the time of this writing to planning for an alternative middle or junior high school, on the grounds that during those years many youngsters are making important moral choices and need special attention. We were told also that CCO now has enough state-certified teachers as members to make such a plan feasible. The major proponent of the middle school idea is a CCO member with considerable educational experience, and who is presently serving as school superintendent of a small town in the area.

Although CCO is relatively young and is made up nearly entirely of adult converts, the growing number of children (and their continually increasing age) is posing a problem for the organization. That problem involves what to do about members born into the group. How are they to be trained? And what is to be expected of them in terms of commitment to the organization? Goldenberg and Wekerle (1972) have written insightfully about the severe test to which any utopian group that values human freedom is put regarding its children. They point out that two values often conflict—personal freedom of choice and group maintenance. They claim that in two well-known communal experiments—the Bruderhof and the Kibbutz—what is utopia for the first generation becomes a "total institution" for the second. This claim is based on the lack of true choice given to commune children, who are socialized in a very thorough and systematic way to choose to stay in the organization. Our observations of child-training practices in CCO, including the Children's School and the child evangelism methods, lead us to the conclusion that for several years the practices differed little in intent from those of the Kibbutz and Bruderhof described by Goldenberg and Wekerle. A strong attempt was being made to give the children "a good Christian education," and little attention was being paid to informing the children about viable alternative belief systems and life-styles so that they could make a more informed choice later in life. However, the decision not to develop an alternative primary school may indicate a profound change in the direction of integrating both CCO *and* its children back into society more so than has been the case heretofore.

More "Secular" Types of Education

CCO is by no means hesitant to avail itself of the educational opportunities in the greater society as a part of its overall resocialization and training effort. The only criterion that is used in such decisions is whether or not the organization needs certain skills which are unavailable within the group. There has developed in recent years a pattern of sending members to public education institutions, especially the more practically-oriented junior colleges in the area. Men have taken courses in financial accounting, mechanic work on vehicles of kinds (including airplanes), livestock raising, farming, and such. Women have taken sewing, cooking, and child-care classes, as well as studies in other traditional areas of female endeavor.

Some selected members were sent to a special school operated by the state to learn skills associated with operating a cannery and became state certified canners (who were required before the cannery could open). Other members have even attended professional meetings, for instance in the area of animal husbandry, to learn the most up-to-date methods of, for example, managing a goat dairy. Subscriptions to professional journals in certain areas are supported by the organization, and other practical literature, such as that available through agricultural extension agents, has been obtained and studied as well.

In special individual cases, CCO has even supported sending members away to finish partially completed educations. One such instance was the supporting of the head of the construction ministry in his last year or two at a university in the East, where he finished work on an engineering degree. They may have also supported some of the last of a new member's medical education, but we are not certain of this. And the Vice-President of Finance, a key CCO leader, is presently working full-time on a university degree in business at the local state university, while he and his family are being fully supported by CCO. Other longer-term members are also being allowed to take university courses, and we know several who are involved in seeking degrees. This development possibly raises some question about our earlier statement that they are antiintellectual, and also demonstrates again the rapidity with which CCO can and does change.

EVOLUTION OF EVANGELISM METHODS

A great deal has already been said concerning the emphasis on evangelism and member training that has dominated CCO life. However, this is such a crucial area of interest that it seems imperative to explore more systematically the evolution of evangelism methods that has occurred. While the specific methods discussed are points of focus in terms of accomplishing the goal of evangelism, it should be remembered that, as far as we can tell from our continued observations, virtually every individual and group activity has as its ultimate justification, however indirect and idealized, the general goal of evangelism. Thus, if we asked why a person was working as a gardener, we might well be told that the garden furnished food for individual members (and possibly cash from the sale of crops), so that "the body" could continue to be a witness to and for God. And the gardener might well add that his diligent work in the garden was itself a testimony to the power of God, and that the fruits of his labors were in fact gifts from God, with the ultimate purpose of glorifying God and drawing more people to Him.

This kind of virtually total permeation of group life with a singleness of purpose has been extremely functional from the point of view of group survival and maintenance. The strength with which this overriding goal is held, coupled with the strong affective ties within the group, clearly has helped CCO avoid schism, although this should not be taken to mean that no differences of opinion have ever developed within the group. However, even the important differences of opinion have usually tended to be about *specific methods* used to accomplish this overriding goal, rather than whether evangelism was the most important goal of the organization and its members.

The first "method" used was a kind of "catch-as-catch-can" approach with the few early converts operating out of the first rather disorganized Christian houses in Southern California. This continued for some time, with new converts being won either by street witnessing, or by being brought into one of the houses and witnessed to by a member individually, or through the Bible studies. Wherever they were won, they often ended up in one of the quickly overflowing houses. This was especially the case with the relatively rootless ones with few ties of import with the greater society. These new converts were immediately expected to begin evangelizing also, and their "fruits" added even more people to the first houses. Some of these early houses were so full of people that they slept on the floor (which was virtually covered with sleepers) and in the yards of the houses (mild weather made this possible). Pressure developed to open new houses simply to take care of the large number of people, but also to evangelize in new areas (and from some irate neighbors who did not like "hippies," however Christian, living and sleeping in the neighborhoods).

Originally, CCO opened new houses in a very haphazard way, opening one when there were too many people for a facility and when another facility and leaders were available. Leaders of the group, at the beginning of its history, were simply doing what they could to furnish basic needs for the people who were being attracted to CCO. As the organization continued to gain in numbers, self-confidence, and economic strength, CCO leaders began to be much more systematic about opening new houses. Small teams of people (sometimes just one couple) were sent out to pre-chosen general locations to open up recruitment centers in "new territory." Part of the push to do this was, of course, the push of numbers. New members were coming in and they needed to be put to work at some task. The primary goal of evangelism absorbed many of the new converts, and as they opened new houses in "fertile fields," even more converts were attracted, causing the process of growth to continue as long as there was a pool of potential converts to evangelize.

It became clear quite early to CCO leaders that care had to be exercised in putting evangelistic teams together and in training them for the often difficult task of opening and maintaining new houses in unknown territory. So the process was rationalized, and it worked for several years pretty much as has been described in the previous section on CCO schools. The method called for the formation and training of twenty teams a year (five per quarter), with the Teams' School at The Land operating continuously, keeping its full-time staff of teachers and support personnel very busy. The operation of the Teams' School (and the simultaneous Lambs' School) was a great drain on CCO finances. About ninety students at a time were continually at The Land, and they were nearly totally supported by the efforts of other segments of the organization.

The new organization of the CCO schools at The Land involves more students (105 day plus 45 night students, new approach, versus about 90 total, older approach), but apparently, fewer teams to open new communes are being sent out. Most graduates are simply integrated into the normal occupational and family life of CCO. Some teams are still formed and sent out, but not so automatically as before, and not in the same numbers.

The decisions about where teams should be sent and specifically what they should do is one of importance to CCO. The Pastors' Council, headed by the original leader, makes these decisions, and they are far from arbitrarily made. For example, early in 1974 a set of five teams was sent to New York state to open communes there. They were sent out to the same general area so that they could help one another get established, and this worked well, according to reports coming back on the new centers—reports published in the CCO journal. Apparently, a division of labor has been worked out among these five communes, with two of them serving as work houses whose main task it is to support the other house ministries in the area. Each house and/or each group of houses is expected to be self-sufficient (after an initial orientation time), and this seems to have been rapidly accomplished in the case of the new New York communes, as it has in other areas as well.

The operation of the Teams' School and the "production" of twenty teams a year did not mean that CCO was continually growing by twenty houses per year during that period, as there was an attrition of houses. Over CCO's relatively short history, there have been many closures of various reasons, including such things as police harassment, lack of potential recruits, the loss of a building (they usually rent and are thus subject to whims of landlords), and the needs of the organization which require the movement of members to other branches for work teams and other activities. Most closures were the result of rational decisions made by the Pastors' Council.

Two general processes operating at that time also contributed to the demise of some houses which were evangelical recruitment centers. One was the tendency for some communes to get large, as the group developed internal tasks that required large numbers of people (such as The Farm or The Land), or contracts were negotiated to furnish large numbers of workers to a concern in a specific area. This latter case is illustrated by the over 50 people involved in the forestry ministry for a time a few years ago, the over 100 sometimes involved in apple picking, and some other large jobs taken on to earn money for the organization.

Another internal process causing slower growth in the number of communes (that still continues today) was the marriage of members, and the movement of many of these couples out of communal life (but *not* out of the "fellowship"). One leader who is on the Pastors' Council estimated (in a personal correspondence) that there were, in fall 1974, 150 couples "in the body," and that about 75 of these couples were living noncommunally. By 1977, virtually all married couples lived noncommunally, and the number of married couples was around 200. From the standpoint of CCO, each of these families is now an evangelical outpost in its own right, and such thinking was part of the justification for the new living arrangement. Based on this logic, it could be said that the group has rapidly increased the number of evangelical houses in the past few years or so, but this would at least conceal the fact that a large number of the recent houses in fact have only one family whose major task is not direct evangelism, but is instead the maintenance of a fairly traditional family unit.

Also, such a rationale to justify the noncommunal motif would not recognize fully the notion of a possible saturation of an area by evangelizers, since most couples living apart are concentrated in a few geographical areas. The early new communes were made up predominantly of single members trained at The Land and sent to "prime targets." By this was meant large cities in which CCO did not have a house, or had one that had too many participants. Within the large cities, an attempt was made to locate a house where maximum exposure to itinerants would be gained. For example, in one 1974 bimonthly journal, a regional overseer expressed great pleasure that, in one town, a house had been secured which was close to two freeways, both of which were much used by hitchhikers. This philosophy of seeking "prime targets" is certainly not adhered to in the growing move to live noncommunally within CCO.

The previous points notwithstanding, it should be understood that CCO is growing in number of members, and that a large amount of its resources are continually being devoted to direct evangelism, vis-á-vis evangelism teams and other techniques. However, the previous examples also demonstrate an important differentiation of evangelical methods, in that attempts are being made to develop evangelism efforts among nonitinerant populations, especially in the general area of the headquarters city, but also in a special and specific way in the houses around the country. The latter technique will be discussed first.

Each evangelism team has always been given regular in-depth instructions in child evangelism, as this is considered by CCO leadership to be a very valuable recruitment tool. Those involved in this effort are usually females, and it certainly furnishes the many single CCO females something "important" to do. Nearly every "area report" by an area overseer in the first CCO bimonthly journal contained some mention of the success of the child evangelism efforts, both in terms of the numbers of children being reached, but also regarding the number of adults (especially young mothers) that have been won as a result of the child evangelism efforts. What these CCO women apparently do is operate something akin to vacation Bible schools for children in the neighborhood of their communes. They bring in small children and teach them some basic knowledge about their Christian views, accompanied by singing, "kool-aid and cookies." Such programs are well-attended, since they at least are furnishing free child care, and also apparently many parents do not mind (or even desire) that their children receive religious instruction. All over the country, "clubs" of children have been organized by the women of the various communes, and significant numbers of people are being recruited to CCO through this method.

Other modifications of the original "catch-as-catch can" evangelism methods have also been developed. One more important one, particularly for the large and relatively isolated communes (such as The Farm and The Land) has been the taking of everyone to town on organization buses at a set time of the week for a stint of street witnessing. During such efforts, potential converts are given tracts and are invited to "accept Christ" and join the group. This occurred while we were at The Farm on some of our research trips, and it was an activity that involved nearly every able-bodied resident. Most members looked forward to such campaigns with great enthusiasm, even though they were putting in very long hours in the fields during the days. The bus would be loaded up with people and driven to the central area of one of the towns or cities in the general area, where itinerant youth could usually be found. On the way, a leader would exhort the members to be diligent, coaching them about specific Bible verses to use in the street witnessing. Using this and other slightly less organized approaches by the small communes, the original street witnessing to itinerants continues to be practiced by the group. And it is an important source of new converts.

Other techniques that are embellishments on the original method used by individual communes include visiting prisons and juvenile wards in some areas. Sometimes permission is gained to allow preaching to (or at least conversation with) detainees in such institutions. And in at least one state (that of the headquarters), juveniles are sometimes remanded to CCO for custody. Leaders of CCO communes around the country also systematically accept speaking engagements from churches, youth groups, school classes, rotary-type clubs, and the media. Some successful campus ministry type work has developed recently in one Midwestern state, but this has not been the usual practice in CCO. And, of course, CCO members everywhere are encouraged to follow the traditional evangelical pattern of witnessing to anyone they come in contact with while they work or even during recreational activities. One recent method of witnessing that is particularly applicable to the fellowship halls is a very serious attempt at follow-up work with new couple converts. Special visits are made by CCO members and leaders to the homes of new members, just as is the case in many traditional churches around the country.

These techniques on the local level are augmented considerably by the development of some organization-wide means of witnessing. The development of the original CCO bimonthly journal, which was very well done (and available to just about anyone who cared to subscribe until its recent suspension), and the replacement journal (also available on subscription) can both be viewed as witnessing tools. The tapes' ministry, which is a key way of insuring "doctrinal purity," now has over one hundred tapes of various sermons and Bible studies, and the aim is to get the CCO's interpretation of the entire Bible taped so that it can be used anywhere. As has been stated, this tapes' ministry is seen as an especially important part of the new married couples' ministry, with the many home Bible study groups that have developed. Correspondence courses had been developed for use with some tapes. These are used mostly by new married converts around the country who cannot attend school at The Land.

Other methods include CCO efforts in the arts. The drama troupe has appeared on television in several of the larger cities in that area of the country, and it has also given many live presentations in churches and in "town squares." This effort has contributed an aura of success and professionalism to CCO, and has added to CCO self-confidence. This specific attempt at the arts is dormant as of late 1977, but it was operated for two or three years. A recent development in the arts area is the formation of a musical touring group that presents "Jesus rock and folk" music in churches, schools, and parks.

One other recent note in terms of CCO's evangelism techniques involves what are called "associate communes." These are communes that were not initiated by CCO, but ones which desired some ties with CCO after they were formed. Such groups are not tied into the CCO financial network, but might use some CCO materials and seek some help from CCO leaders. Some of these more informally attached groups have developed around a large Midwestern university at which CCO has had success at campus-ministry-like work. A few others have developed in jails, on ships, and even in some foreign countries. Obviously, allowing such affiliations can be viewed as a form of evangelism, even though such new forms blur the belief and behavioral "boundaries" of CCO.

We will close this section by discussing what some may consider the ultimate witness, but which others may consider the possible death knell of any evangelical organization. We refer here to the notion of witnessing by example, which can be practiced, of course, on an individual or a collective level, with individuals "being a living Christian example" and the organization demonstrating the efficacy of fundamentalist beliefs and practices in terms of building a "Christian utopian" organization. It appears to us that, all the specific efforts just described notwithstanding, there has been an evolution of methods of evangelism within CCO in the general direction of a less active effort in direct evangelism. Not all individual members and not all segments of CCO have moved in this direction, but there still appears to be such a tendency for those who care to see it.

The effects of maturation and differentiation within the organization can be viewed as "causes" of this shift toward indirect evangelism. The organizating of large work teams that work in isolated locations limited the opportunities of many to witness, and this has had to be justified in terms of maintaining the organization. Service-oriented small businesses also impede direct evangelism efforts. Attempts to overcome these problems are being made, but it remains to be seen whether they will be successful or not. Also, the marriage of so many members has resulted in many members, particularly women, being isolated in the communes or individual homes to care for their families. The husbands often have divided loyalties, desiring simultaneously to be with their families, but also realizing the need to witness. The involvement of many males, married and single, full-time in the work for CCO has also resulted in a limiting of the chance to witness directly to the itinerants that made up most of the early converts.[11] And the new single-family living arrangements, while being partially justified in terms of the evangelism goal, require much more of CCO's resources to support, diverting funds and energy from direct evangelism.

We are not trying to sound a note of pessimism here, for we have no way of discerning what is "good" for CCO (although we may have our opinions). Perhaps the shift to less direct evangelism (if it truly has occurred as we think) will not result in the loss of incoming recruits. Strong attempts are being made to continue direct evangelism, and the success of the organization may itself be enough to attract new converts. We do not even know if CCO needs new recruits, but it does seem that its ideology—an ideology that has contributed immeasureably to the group's success—would require continual new recruits as a "validity check" on the value of the organization and what it was doing. Perhaps a combination of old approaches and the new methods (including the home Bible studies and fellowships) outlined in Figure 7 will continue to furnish a steady supply of malleable recruits who can be fitted into the various CCO functions. Only time can tell.

PREDICTIONS OF FORESEEABLE CHANGES

During the late 1977 visit, two long-time leaders of the group were asked what kind of major changes they would predict for the foresee-

FIGURE 7
Evolution* and Differentiation of Evangelism and Resocialization Methods

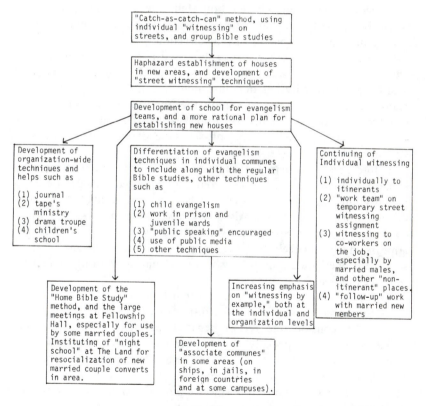

*The establishment of an exact pattern of evolution of evangelism methods is impossible, and unnecessary for our purposes. This figure should be treated as more a presentation of the differentiation itself, rather than a statement about exactly when the differentiation occurred, although some chronology is represented in movement from top to bottom of the figure.

able future. One of these people was the Vice President of Finance and the other has headed up the jobs ministry, been a regional overseer, and done many other important tasks in CCO life. Both are on the Pastors' Council. Asking them this question was an attempt to avoid having our material already dated at the time of publication, a possible occurrence given the propensity of CCO to change so rapidly.

They mentioned three major areas of focus and possible further change for CCO in the near future. Both agreed that there would be a continued effort in the area of the fellowship hall type of ministry. There are presently six of these operations, with the largest being the group of about 250 located in the headquarters city. The next largest has about half that number involved, and the other four are smaller. The leaders being interviewed both felt that more fellowship halls would be opened, and that the present ones would be strengthened by allocation of more resources in that direction.

Campus ministry work was also discussed as an area requiring more attention. The quite successful efforts along these lines at one large Midwestern university has demonstrated that this is a fertile field, and plans are being discussed to exploit the opportunity. A planned publicity push on the large campus in the headquarters city was discussed, a plan which involved a very soft-sell type of approach using some striking artwork as posters.

A third area of anticipated attention and growth is the international scene. CCO currently has a few communes located outside the continental United States (Canada, Virgin Islands) and is involved in direct mission work to Venezuala. Also, they have some informal ties with a communal group in Spain that was started by a previous member. It appears that CCO feels that the door is opening to the international scene, and they are going to very seriously consider putting more CCO resources into such efforts.

We also discussed one other aspect that the two leaders viewed as of crucial importance in affecting the future of CCO. At least partially as a result of considerable recent negative publicity about some new religious groups (especially the Unification Church, but also such groups as the Children of God), the IRS is reexamining its policies regarding tax-exempt status for religious groups. CCO leaders expect this review to result in stiffer rules about what kinds of groups and what kinds of activities within a group will be tax exempt. CCO is not concerned about the possibility of losing its tax-exempt status altogether, but they do fear that new rulings might force them to pay taxes on large portions of their total income. Because of this concern, the Pastors' Council has established a subcommittee made up of some people from the council and some other knowledgeable members to discuss possible alternatives for reorganization that would be better able to pass IRS muster. A number of alternatives have been developed and they are being examined in depth, with a decision planned for sometime in the next few months.

The leaders interviewed indicated that they and other CCO leaders realized that any restructuring, even if thought to be a mere paper rearrangement to satisfy the IRS, could well have long range implications. Also, apparently some of the alternatives being considered would have fairly overt implications for the structure and operation of CCO, and this is appreciated by those considering the problem. Thus in a certain sense, the future of CCO is clouded by this desire to protect their tax-exempt status, and the organization may have to change in ways that are not yet understood as a result. Here we see a classic illustration of the operation of social control on deviant groups, as CCO tries to respond to the fact that it has been caught up in the controversy between opinion makers and social control agents in the society and certain more "far out" deviant groups.

THEORETICAL COMMENTS ON ORGANIZATION'S CHANGES

Before closing this chapter, some application of a few relevant sociological concepts to the CCO organization seems appropriate. This group is not a fly-by-night group of young kids which will disappear as a social entity in the near future. It is a complex, growing, and widely dispersed multimillion dollar social organization, with a bureaucracy focused on realizing the goals of the organization. The bureaucracy works with an amazing amount of efficiency, functioning to service members, maintain the organization, and contribute to its growth. In the next chapter, as a way of discussing the possibilities for continued existence of and changes in the group, we will discuss the group in some depth from the perspective of a social movement organization, applying attendant theory from the work of Zald and Ash (1966) and others. For now, however, we want briefly to relate our research to three other obvious areas of sociological theory—those of commune theory (particularly commune typologies), sociology of religion theory (using "sect-church" theory), and the recent discussion of the so-called "reintegrative hypothesis." First, a look at CCO from the perspective of sociology of religion.

Church-Sect Theory

Church-sect theory generally includes four major terms—cult, sect, denomination, and church—each of which can be further differentiated. The cultic origins of the Jesus movement as a whole have been described (Richardson, 1979b), and CCO fits the general pattern well, although it rapidly became a sect in the usual sense of the term. CCO has also started to show some denominational tendencies (such as increased tolerance of other groups and social mobility of members—see Martin, 1965), but such are not overriding considerations at this time. The sociological concept of the church does not apply at all to this group. Thus we are left with the fact that the group rapidly became and still remains a sect, and it is to this concept that we now turn to aid our understanding [12] in a treatment that will ground our discussion of CCO goals more thoroughly in sociological theory.

Probably the best-known classification scheme for sects is that of Bryan Wilson (e.g., 1969a), who differentiates between seven types of sects on the basis of their *response to the world,* a view obviously related to our earlier analysis of changes in organization goals. His seven types are conversionist, revolutionary, introversionist, manipulationist, thaumaturgical (magical), utopian, and reformist. His scheme should not be viewed as static, and the types, although emphasizing the major goal of a group, are not mutually exclusive. These crucial considerations of change over time and of a possible multiplicity of important goals will be emphasized in our application of his scheme, since it is impossible to place CCO easily in one static category.[13]

Two of Wilson's types—*manipulationist* and *thaumaturgical*—refer to what most other theorists in the sociology of religion refer to as cults. The concepts thus have obvious application because of the cultic origins of CCO, but these two responses (or goals) seem to relate inversely to each other vis-á-vis CCO. Magical tendencies were much more pronounced in the early stages of the group's existence, when signs and miracles were regularly sought and found by leaders of the group. Now, however, there seems to be a pronounced deemphasis on such reliance on the mystical, and instead a much more rational approach is taken. We can even say, on the basis of our observation, that CCO appears to be making more of a manipulationist response to the world. Members make claims to having special knowledge, and they are willing to be very innovative in spreading that knowledge. The all-important goal of evangelism is used to justify a certain amount of manipulation of others and of situations.

Of the remaining five types of sects, only the *reformist* seems not to apply at present, but this may be just a result of the relative short life of the organization.[14] Plainly, the group is *conversionist,* as a great deal of group resources and individual effort is directed toward this goal. Wilson notes that such sects have a strong tendency to develop into denominations, mainly because of the effects of continual recruiting of new people without the stake in the group that older members have. Since the group has other goals, this tendency may be overcome, but at this time, we are not disposed to predict whether or not the logical outcome of a strong conversionist response to the world will prevail. We would reiterate, however, that there does seem to be a shift of emphasis from evangelism per se to other goals of the organization.

The major "replacement goal" or response has been that of developing a Christian utopia, an emphasis which corresponds to Wilson's *utopian* sect. The leaders of the organization have decided to attempt to build a utopian community, both as a "witness to the world" and to allow members and their children to live and grow up in an environment radically different from that usually experienced by people of their type of backgrounds. This latter consideration integrates with the especially strong *introversionist* thrust of CCO in its early history, a tendency that continues in muted form today, but in the more self-confident form of utopianism. At its inception, the group wanted to withdraw to allow a "time of healing" for its members, but now that the strength of members is returned and the organization is also strong, there comes an understandable desire to build, and in ways that are much less withdrawal-oriented.

The group is also *revolutionary,* at least in the sense of emphasizing their eschatology, which claims that the second coming of Christ is imminent. This claim helps give impetus to their evangelism efforts, but as will be discussed, from the point of view of traditional politics, members have been nearly totally apolitical. Thus the term revolutionary is not to be construed in the common use of the term. Also, even though the group stresses the end of the world, they go on "world-building" nonetheless, a sure sign that this goal is not a major one.

To sum up the application of Wilson's types, CCO has major goals (or responses to the world) that are conversionistic and utopian, with the former being preeminent in its early history and the latter gaining ascendency in recent times. Introversionist tendencies have always been present but seem to be on the wane, as indicated by the rapid movement of nearly all married couples into noncommunal living arrangements and by the degree of functional integration back into society CCO has achieved as a collectivity, via such things as its work teams and its small service businesses. Thaumaturgical tendencies were strong at the inception of the group, but they have largely disappeared, to be replaced by rational thinking that tends toward manipulation at times. Revolutionary tendencies are talked about but apparently not really accepted, although the fervor of evangelism activities might be taken to support the idea that group members really believe their claimed eschatology. Reformist tendencies are not yet present to any degree but might develop if CCO continues to gain strength and thus become more able to wield some power in the area of politics.

Commune Theory

Several theorists have developed typologies of communes, but most such classification schemes suffer from several difficulties, among them lack of agreement concerning criteria. Richardson (1976a), in a critique of such typologies, states that a major difficulty is that such schemes are rather static in orientation and also focus on one factor in classifying communal groups. Some schemes also use a "religious" category as somewhat residual, and not worthy of extensive analysis. None of the schemes of which we are aware take adequate account of the Jesus movement and similar contemporary communal groups; instead they tend to focus on the countercultural "hippie" type of commune. This singular focus has also obscured the significant fact that some communes are organized into federations of communes somewhat similar in form to CCO. For all these reasons, the schemes have difficulty in encompassing empirical phenomena that plainly should be a part of any effort to explain communes.

Some typologies that are plainly inadequate are those of Fairfield (1972) and Roberts (1971), while that of Rigby (1974), which will be used for illustration, offers some promise because of its slightly more general nature and some of his selected criteria. Rigby has six basic types, including (1) self-actualizing communes, (2) communes of mutual support, (3) activist communes, (4) practical communes, (5) therapeutic communes, and (6) religious communes, which are of two types—mystic and ascetic. Rigby uses a separate religious category, and we would guess that Rigby would classify CCO (overlooking temporarily the problem of classifying a *federation of communes* in the scheme) as an *ascetic religious commune*. Rigby appreciates that there is some inherent difficulty in having a residual religious category for he says (1974, p. 173) "it would be wrong to consider them as being of a completely different genus from the other [types] considered." We agree, for plainly this group is *therapeutic,* especially regarding new members, most of whom have had severe problems of one type or another. The group is very *practical,* especially in areas where the strict belief system does not impinge. Contrary to popular usage of the term, we would also make the claim that CCO is *activist,* especially in terms of its strong efforts at evangelizing and its energetic utopia building.[15] Whether or not the group is involved in *self-actualization* depends on one's definition of self-actualization. The personality assessment data presented later in this book evidence the "dependency-proneness" of most group members, but they would claim that they are self-actualized in terms of their understanding of human beings. (See Fromm, 1950, for a discussion of the effects of an authoritarian religion on personality that takes issue with prevalent views in CCO.) But even in terms of the traditional Maslow-like (see Maslow, 1962) use of the term self-actualization, we would suggest that a few members (and especially leaders) of the group are self-actualized.

No contemporary discussion of commune theory is complete without reference to the seminal work of Kanter (1972, 1973). We will return to her work, particularly regarding assessing the continued success changes of CCO (see chapter 10), but for now an examination of her classification scheme of communes is in order. Her 1972 scheme included utopian and nonutopian communes, with the latter being divided into two subtypes—retreat and service communes. The Kanter scheme does not seem to allow adequate discrimination regarding groups like CCO, and it is somewhat static in nature. Nonetheless, she probably would classify CCO, on the basis of her description (Kanter, 1972 pp. 191-93), as a *service nonutopian commune,* although to do so conceals a great deal of the utopian emphasis in the group and the fact that CCO as a whole contains individual communes that fit each of three types quite well. In later work (1973, p. 6), Kanter has presented a three-part typology of retreat, missionary, and domestic communes, although she does not give enough other information to fully apply this typology. Using these gross categories, CCO plainly is a *missionary commune,* although it was in its very early history perhaps more *retreat*-oriented. The *domestic* category is difficult to apply in the sense intended by Kanter (hippie type communes), although there is a growing emphasis on domestic groups (conjugal families) in CCO as more members marry fellow members, and as ideological considerations lead to more independence for family units.

Kanter is certainly to be credited with taking seriously communal organizations which are religious in thrust, and her scheme does allow for a valuable "principal goal" analysis of communes. But her two schemes are not without problems when applied to an organization like CCO, which is simply too complex and ever-changing to be easily forced into any simple classification scheme.

Another approach to commune analysis is illustrated by Zablocki's (1972) categorization of theoretical models used by commune researchers. He distinguishes between (1) the historical model, (2) the collective decision-making model, (3) the educational model, and (4) the kinship model. Two of these models are of particular interest in terms of classifying communes. The educational model, which we think is better termed the *transition model,* highlights a common contemporary tendency for communes to be viewed by members as not necessarily requiring a lifetime commitment. Instead the commitment is viewed as temporary, and the participants move on to some other group or life-style after a time. While this may be a popular approach in many counterculture-oriented communes (and in some other Jesus movement groups), it should be stated that such is *not* the case with CCO. A lifetime commitment is expected, and leaving is not encouraged (and is in fact actively discouraged). The overall attrition rate is quite low, although it is plain that for many members the time they spend in organizational communes for unmarried members is viewed as limited, since they plan to marry. Also, for many single members, the time spent in certain communes (such as the original commune of entry or The Land settlement) is viewed as limited by definition. Continuous membership in CCO is expected and encouraged, *but membership in any one specific commune within CCO is viewed as subject to rapid change.* This situation is another illustration of the problems of understanding caused by studying only one commune in a larger federation of communes. The transition model "works" in helping explain intra-organizational movement, but *not* in classifying the organization as a whole.

The tribal model, which we prefer to refer to as the *migratory model,* is somewhat useful in categorizing CCO as a whole. Some of the facilities (such as The Land settlement) are viewed as more-or-less permanent fixtures ("until the Lord comes"), and even some of these can be abandoned rapidly (evidence the decision to leave The Farm). However, most of the communes, especially the smaller segments that make up the nationwide network of "gathering houses," are viewed as temporary. They are maintained as long as it seems feasible to do so and are abandoned with dispatch and no regrets once the decision is made. The groups of people may stay together but will be moved to another location. Thus, some of these groups might even be classified as "traveling communes," and the entire operation of the organization can fruitfully be viewed as migratory, a situation that can be applied to several other of the more prominent Jesus movement groups (Children of God, Milwaukee Jesus People, etc.) as well (see Davis & Richardson, 1976; Jacobson & Pilarzyk, 1972; Jacobsen & Pilarzyk, 1974; Curl, 1975, for discussion of such other groups).

CCO and the "Integrative Hypothesis"

One of the most important issues deriving from the recent rapid growth of interest in the "new religions" is that of the so-called integrative hypothesis, which is derived in part from the earlier work of Johnson (1961), research which is of special emphasis because of similarities between CCO and the groups he studied. Robbins and Anthony (1972), in a widely-cited paper, claimed that involvement in the Meher Baba cult was an important way for many young people to "get straight," and live a "post-counter-cultural" existence much more integrated into American society. They followed this paper with another (Robbins, Anthony, & Curtis, 1975) that, in a much more thorough and theoretically profound manner, evaluated the integrative hypothesis. They claimed that the new religious movements among youth served pattern maintenance and tension management functions for the society, and that also the new movements reintegrated the members back into the social system. Their insightful discussion of the ways in which new religious movements reintegrate is probably applicable to most recent such movements.

The Robbins, et al. analysis makes some use of another paper, that of Mauss and Peterson (1974), which seems especially relevant to our work since it is based on research on two other considerably smaller Jesus movement organizations. In both the work of the Robbins and Anthony research group and that of the Mauss and Petersen team, there is an assumption of a fairly automatic movement of people back into society after they have been in one of the new religious groups for a while. And that movement is an *individual* movement. In other words, a person affiliates with one of the groups and after a certain amount of time, that person is expected to "leave" the group (figuratively if not literally) and go out into society to work and raise a family.

We consider these earlier analyses extremely useful in helping understand the experiences of many who have moved through some of the newer religious groups. However, the model developed and/or assumed in this earlier work does not fully explain what has occurred in the case of CCO, and perhaps some other groups as well. The model of reintegration may not apply nearly as well to CCO, and if it does apply, it needs one additional step added to the process in order to incorporate the CCO experience.

First, at least in the case of the groups studied by Mauss and Petersen, the organizations involved seem much less well-organized, stable, and long-lasting. They seem much closer to the migratory type of communal organization referred to in the previous section. Such organizations may not require or expect a permanent commitment from members. As has been noted, CCO differs in this regard, and its members are expected to give a lifetime commitment. Thus Mauss and Petersen may have been led to generalize from cases significantly different from CCO. Second, there are at least two ways that the reintegration hypothesis might work to reintegrate people back into society, and the work cited deals mainly with only one. The way that is described and analyzed at some length in this earlier literature might be called *direct individual reintegration.* Another way, which might be called the *indirect individual reintegration* or the *collective reintegration* seems exemplified by CCO.[16] CCO went through an initial stage of withdrawal from society (although not all ties were ever severed, as is discussed in chapter 1). Then it started to allow and even encourage contact with the dominant society, particularly as it tried to obtain enough money and other support for survival. But as has been stated, very quickly CCO leaders learned not to allow individual members to "go out into the world" by themselves to work. Thus the work team motif was developed and flourished for several years. The work teams effectively protected the members from many types of influences that CCO leaders viewed as harmful. Team members were isolated, even while they worked for non-Christians "in the world." They were encapsulated in nearly all activities. (See Lofland & Lofland, 1969, pp. 39-60; and Lofland, 1977, pp. 809-11 for a discussion of the encapsulation process.) The more recent CCO emphasis on small service-oriented businesses has continued this team motif, as groups of CCO members work together at remodeling, janitorial services, or other such tasks. Even the newer fellowship hall experience can be viewed as relatively encapsulating.

It can certainly be argued that CCO members are being reintegrated into society by virtue of being reinculcated (or maybe inculcated for the first time) with the work ethic and other elements of the dominant culture. They have learned many valuable skills, along with some other elements of the ethic such as punctuality and responsibility. And many are now involved in fairly traditional family situations. We agree with this thinking, but would note that there seem to be profound differences between the overt efforts of CCO to *disallow* total individual reintegration and the sometimes nearly as overt efforts of some groups to *encourage* individual reintegration. At least in the case of CCO, reintegration theorists must allow for a stage in which the integration is on the level of the collectivity, as the organization finds and develops a niche in the economic structure of the society, but at the same time tries to protect its members from being totally reintegrated. Also, reintegration theorists should perhaps admit that, at least in the case of CCO, the judgment is still out as to whether or not experience in CCO is fully reintegrative for most members (see note 16).

With that, we close this description and brief theoretical commentary of changes in CCO organizational structure. Now we will move into a more thorough analysis of the changes in CCO in a test of ideas in the movement organization literature given impetus by Zald and Ash (1966).

NOTES

1. All the terms used in this section are those used by CCO members in referring to themselves and positions in the group structure.
2. The importance of these weekly meetings is illustrated by their influencing the cycle of activities at The Farm during our 1972 summer visits. The meetings occurred on Monday, and they were some two hours drive from The Farm. Every Monday morning, some of the leaders from The Farm would drive to The Land for this meeting, returning late that evening. The fact that the meetings were on Monday and drew some of the key leaders of The Farm operation for the day, resulted in Monday being designated the "day of rest" for The Farm. It was on this day (instead of the traditional Sunday) that the members "took their sabbath," and had a day of relative relaxation and worship. (So as not to mislead, it should be stated that this day of rest did not involve members going to church in the traditional sense. They considered any attendance at specific churches to be a waste of time. Also, note that the day of rest was not total. The leaders were still working, and essential farming activities were also carried on with "volunteer labor.")
3. Evangelism or witnessing has always been considered such an important task that we, in an attempt to reflect the group's concern in this area, have treated it separately in our earlier presentation of the formal authority structure.
4. One somewhat dated description from an early CCO publication of The Land kitchen staff will illustrate the immense amount of differentiation that has occurred with some of the functions internal to specific communes:

> There are seven positions in the kitchen operation. One and two, dish washers whose jobs are to wash all pots and pans, operate the dish washer and clean spills, etc. The dishwashers do not handle any food. Three, cook's helper—this brother's job is to thaw vegetables and

meats, make sandwiches, granola, and all breads, but he does not actually "cook" anything. He is helper of the cooks.

Four and five. First and Second Cooks—these brothers' positions are to cook all foods such as vegetables, soups, eggs, roasts, meats. These brothers learn proper ways to use spices, different ways of cooking, preparation and serving food.

Six, Assistant Chef—this brother's job is the same as the first and second cooks', except that he works with the head chef in purchasing food and meal planning.

Seven, Head Chef—works as the head of the kitchen and works with the other brothers teaching them their duties. He is also in charge of all planning of meals and food allotment.

Note that the staff is entirely male, although the additional serving staff includes both males and females who now wait on tables (people used to line up cafeteria style, but now they are served at the tables). The same article, from a 1973 issue of the CCO journal, says that over 400 meals a day were served at this one facility, a total that has increased. We can also testify that the overall quality of the food has improved greatly, evidencing the increasing prosperity of the group and the increase in their culinary skills. An interesting anecdote concerning The Land kitchen staff was reported in a later issue of the CCO journal. One of the cooks had been flown on the CCO airplane in an "emergency" rescue mission to a commune in Florida, which is about three thousand miles from the headquarters. It seems that the commune had had a rapid growth, and the kitchen staff needed "shoring up a bit" to take care of feeding the over ninety people per day who were there. Thus we see that even in this type of organization, rapid and "done in style" transfer of trained personnel can occur.

5. Group leaders would argue perhaps with our "sterile" sociological analysis of this process of "promotion," claiming that God makes the choices *through them* or using them *as instruments.* We respect their right to that view, but note that we are simply trying to isolate factors that we think impinge on any such decision, no matter *who* makes it.

6. The decision was not entirely rational. In fact, it was made after a traumatic but Scripture-based decision to "totally depend on the Lord." All possessions of any value were sold, and the group quickly became destitute. A "vision" received by one of the leaders resulted in the group's members starting to seek jobs for money to support the group, and this somewhat mystically-derived orientation toward work continues to the date of this writing—a pattern not adhered to by all segments of the Jesus movement, some parts of which are notorious for their refusal to work for others in order to support themselves (see Davis & Richardson, 1976, for a description of the Children of God group). The present philosophy of work in CCO is presented in one of their documents dealing with details of their approach to work. This philosophy was written at least in part to insure that CCO had a defensible position in terms of tax-exempt status from income derived from the work of members. The statement, from page 234 of their "Labor Contract Negotiation Manual," dated April 26, 1977, is as follows:

WORK PHILOSOPHY

We believe that a church or charity should become involved with the whole man, including the spiritual, mental, physical, emotional and economical facets of man. Work fulfills this purpose for us by:

1. Providing an environment to teach honesty and giving (Ephesians 4:28);

2. Teaching evangelists in training how to pay their own way so as to preach the gospel for free (I Thessalonians 2:9 and I Corinthians 9:18);

3. Training in skills and work attitudes;

4. Offering a means of worshipping God, as our labors are conceived as being for Christ;

5. Providing a vehicle of fellowship through the sense of community that is developed in working together. This is an aid in establishing each new believer through a total Christian environment.

The purpose of this environment is to help remold the whole man—spirit, soul, body, emotions, hope, ambitions—into the image of Christ. Because a "church" to us is not a building, but those called out from the world as defined in the *Bible*, the church travels and goes with us to work. For us, work is an inseparable part of these functions because we believe and base our lives on the *Bible* which commands us to work (I Thessalonians 4:11-12).

7. There were other "reasons" or justifications for the decisions to phase out some of CCO's agricultural operations. For instance, the decision to give up The Farm was at least partly caused by serious difficulties in developing a sewage system that would meet county regulations. The third year of operation, in fact, had seen the major part of the workers housed several miles away in a small town. This problem could have been overcome but was not. Instead, a decision was made to give up the lease, although CCO continued to furnish—for a fee—workers to help operate The Farm for the owner. The decision to get out of the hog and rabbit businesses was justified on ideological grounds. A study of certain scriptures revealed to the satisfaction of CCO leaders that pigs and rabbits were "unclean," and that they should concentrate on raising "clean" animals (cattle, sheep, and chickens). So they sold their pigs and rabbits and planned for a time to get gradually into raising other types of livestock. They have also discussed a more gradual reentry into more farming but have taken no action we know of to replace The Farm. The peach orchard has been sold, and the large gardening operations have been curtailed.

8. CCO leaders and members, of course, do not view the set of decisions that have resulted in their success and relative affluence as being accidentally or arbitrarily made. They have consistently claimed the guidance of God in making all decisions and give God the credit for the results.

9. A favorite activity that sometimes involves CCO students at The Land is "chicken picking." Teams of "pickers" go to large broiler plants at night when the chickens are roosting and take them by hand off their roosts.

They are then crated and sent to processing plants. CCO gets a set amount per bird for this nocturnal activity, which is viewed as "half work, half fun" by participants.

10. CCO has developed much of its own materials, but it has no aversion to using materials developed by others, *if* the materials are "doctrinal." For example, they distribute tracts put out by fundamentalist organizations more associated with the "institutional church," and they use some "Moody Films" (put out by the Moody Bible Institute) in their schools, as a part of the curriculum and for a kind of recreational "religious movie night." A recent decision to curtail their printing ministry somewhat is but the latest indication of CCO's willingness to use materials developed by others.

11. A key problem is the size and distribution of the pool of potential converts. If potential converts are not available or are not where the organization's efforts can locate them, then obviously changes must occur within the organization. Such demographic macro-level considerations, while obviously crucial, are beyond the scope of this section (see Richardson, 1975, for more on this type of consideration).

12. There is general agreement among most scholars that a sect has the following characteristics. It is a voluntary association and a position in it is "achieved," rather than "ascribed." It has tests of membership and is usually exclusive, allowing as members only those who meet the criteria. It has clear group boundaries in terms of beliefs and behaviors. Members have a strong sense of self-identity and are somewhat elitist in orientation, thinking that they and they alone possess the "way to salvation," and "the Truth." A sect demands, on threat of expulsion, the total allegiance of its members, and its criteria for expulsion are established. It has certain ethical standards for its members which limit behavior, and it usually rejects traditional authority, especially that of institutional religious basis. See Wallis (1974) for a discussion that takes issue with some of these generally accepted criteria, and see Richardson (1979b) for a theory of cult to sect changes.

13. It is not obvious that Wilson intended his typology to be applied in a manner that intermingles the "responses to the world" in such a fashion, and emphasizes changes over time. His own tendency has been to use the principal goal or response at a given point in time to classify a sect, although he certainly emphasized change in sects. We prefer a dynamic use of the typology, as it allows us to focus on different, even conflicting joint goals, and the changes in goals that have occurred already in CCO's short history.

14. One CCO leader ran for Congress in 1976 and got a fairly impressive campaign going, even gaining, as an independent, the endorsement of one major area newspaper. However, his running seemed more of an individual decision which was allowed by CCO, rather than a well-thought out plan for CCO to become involved in politics. Nonetheless, this event seems of significance in CCO's evolution as an organization. At the time of this writing, several CCO members are considering running for local school board offices, with plans to try changing the public schools somewhat.

15. Most commune researchers exhibit a bias in their assumption that only

politically oriented communes can be "activist," and that the only "acceptable" form of activity is political. CCO's brand of activism may not appeal to some, but it is activism nonetheless.

16. In addition to the problem of not distinguishing between "direct" and "indirect" individual reintegration, there is an attendant difficulty of not specifying completely what is meant by integration. Obviously the reintegration process would operate differently for different types of people in different situations. Reintegration in one time/space environment may not be the same as reintegration in another.

3

Analysis as a
"Social Movement Organization"

So far we have presented the history of CCO and the evolution of the group as it has become a much-differentiated and complex organization. In this chapter, we want to examine CCO in more depth from an organization point of view. During the years in which we have been associated with CCO, we have noted growth of membership, expansion of financial support, and a broadening of the financial base of the group, and several important structural changes which have already been described. During its early existence, CCO overcame most of the problems associated with fledgling groups in new social movements, referred to by Stinchcombe (1971) as "liability of newness." Stinchcombe points out several sources of this liability of newness—first, new organizations, especially new types of organizations, must rely on the generalized skills provided outside the organization or must invest in education of members to new roles. In CCO, especially initially, members were untrained in the various occupational areas required for maintenance of the group—accounting, organization skills, child care, carpentry, crop planting, harvesting, animal husbandry, and so on. As members learned the requisite skills, they passed them on to new converts who were being integrated into the steward structure of the organization. Due to the emphasis on recruiting new members, there must be a continual investment in the education of members to new roles, both social and occupational.

Stinchcombe also points out that the process of inventing new roles, determining their relationship and the structuring of the rewards and sanctions has high cost for a new organization. Because CCO has been growing and is now including a larger target population base than the earlier population of street people (which itself has changed from the late 1960s), we still see some new roles developing, for example the incorporation of a slightly stronger leadership role for women. But the basic structure, based upon the group interpretation of Biblical teachings, has remained quite stable, even though it has been elaborated considerably. As a result these costs, which Stinchcombe sees as being expressed in terms of time expended, conflicts over structure, worry, and initial inefficiency, have decreased somewhat over time, and CCO appears to be relatively stable. Once the basic structure of leader and followers was fleshed out to the nationwide and differentiated structure that evolved several years ago, the initial "capital outlay" of "costs" was lessened considerably. A third point made by Stinchcombe is that new organizations must rely heavily on social relations among strangers, a situation which leads to interpersonal problems and strains. This concern remains for CCO, which continually converts the uninitiated. Leaders are now close and long-term friends and are familiar with the organization—their solidarity is no longer a problem, and they can enhance the rapid development of a feeling of "we-ness" and a common goal of bringing more people "to the Lord." There are enough "old-timers" in CCO now to greatly facilitate the transference of group culture to newcomers, who make up a smaller proportion of total membership than was the case earlier. Thus, it seems to us that CCO has overcome many of the problems associated with new organizations. It is presently well-organized, efficiently run, and provides rewards essential for the maintenance of membership.

On the basis of this brief analysis using Stinchcombe's ideas, we think CCO a relatively sound and potentially long-lasting new group. This conclusion means that CCO is a worthy vehicle for a more detailed analysis of the propositions and hypotheses developed in the "social movement organization" literature given impetus in Zald and Ash (1966), Zurcher and Curtis (1973) and Curtis and Zurcher (1974). The issue of long-term maintenance will itself be examined in more detail in the last chapter, where we apply Kanter's (1972) model of commitment to CCO.

"SOCIAL MOVEMENT ORGANIZATION" ANALYSIS

Zald and Ash (1966), in a seminal theoretical paper, developed a series of propositions about social movement organizations (MO's). Their work is an attempt to move beyond the Weber/Michels model that focuses on the supposedly "natural" processes of routinization of charisma, bureaucratization, and oligarchization, although the Weber and the Michels theoretical ideas are incorporated into the more general scheme Zald and Ash present. The effort is commendable and noteworthy in its scope and its attempt to integrate consideration of both internal *and* external factors that influence the history and structure of an MO, but it should be noted that their scheme is *not* a truly formal model, and some of their propositions are not well-justified or logically derived. They end the paper with a call (1966, p. 341) for "systematic testing of the propositions, using large numbers of historical and contemporary case studies—in short, a comparative analysis of social movement organizations," a call to which this chapter is a response.

This call was heeded earlier by the team of Zurcher and Curtis (1973), who accepted Zald/Ash's approach with its basic conceptualizations and applied it in their comparison of two antipornography organizations. In the process of their work, they formalized some of the propositions a bit more (see their Figure 1, 1973, p. 177), something that is in itself helpful and should be done in more detail. They were also able to test many of the propositions, although admitting that Zald and Ash intended their propositions to apply mainly to large-scale, national social movement organizations. Most of the Zald/Ash propositions were supported in the test (see Table 3.5), and those that were not were "explained" in terms of the operation of other crucial variables, some of which were not well-integrated into the original Zald/Ash scheme. Zurcher and Curtis said (1973, p. 186): "We conclude that in the small or emerging social movement organization, the variables leadership orientation, goal specificity, and incentive structure are significant and perhaps over-riding independent variables, accounting for much of the variance in other organizational characteristics. In the national and more firmly established social movement organizations which Zald and Ash considered in their propositions, these factors may be relatively less salient as antecedent variables."

They then closed their article with a set of hypotheses of their own, developed to fit certain kinds of small emergent social movement organizations. We will be looking at some of their hypotheses in the course of this chapter and in Appendix B, since CCO seems classifiable as a "small, emergent social movement organization." There is some difficulty in categorizing CCO as Zurcher and Curtis seem to think relevant and in accepting their conceptualization of some variables (which they took from Zald and Ash).

In a later theoretical paper (Curtis & Zurcher, 1974), the concluding hypotheses of the 1973 paper were incorporated into a typological scheme for such organizations. In this paper, the authors opted for two variables as being of most importance. These two variables were *organizational goals* and *conditions of membership,* which were dichotomized as "expressive and diffuse" or "instrumental and specific" and as "inclusive" or "exclusive," respectively. They elaborated upon these variables, allowing for mixed types, and added four more variables which they claim effect group structure, organization, and longevity. These four other variables, and their subcategories are: *membership incentives* for the attainment of goals (solidary or purposive); *leadership style* (persuading or directing); *contact with environment* (highly to loosely specified); and *type of membership* (homogeneous or heterogeneous). Mixed levels are also allowed for each of these four other variables. These six variables were related in a table, which was at once a typological scheme, a set of hypotheses, and a statement about the relative importance of the variables. The scheme is presented in Table 3.1.

Curtis and Zurcher thus have, on the basis of a literature review and their research, suggested in Table 3.1 nine unique types of social movement organizations. They also categorize the nine types according to "congruity," in what is admitted to be a somewhat arbitrary designation. They designate two polar types (on the two major variables)—types 1 and 9—as congruent, stating (1974, p. 360) that "congruent is used here as a hypothetical construct which identifies structural correspondence among organizational components." Noncongruent organizations, according to Curtis and Zurcher, are best exemplified by types 3 and 7, although they also include the mixed types (2, 4, 5, 6, and 8) in this noncongruent category.

We will examine the basic structure of the model presented by Curtis and Zurcher (1974), and then (as presented in some detail in Appendix B) try to test relevant hypotheses from this work and the 1973 paper they did (Zurcher & Curtis), along with hypotheses from the original Zald and Ash (1966) paper. In critiquing the earlier work and testing the hypotheses, we will, of course, attend particularly to CCO, but on occasion we will also, for comparison purposes, make reference to the Jesus movement as a whole and to some other specific groups within it. We will begin by discussing organizational goals and

TABLE 3.1
Goals, Membership Requirements, and Related Structural Characteristics of Social Movement Organizations

Conditions of Membership	Goal Orientations		
	Expressive (and Diffuse)	Mixed	Instrumental (and Specific)
Exclusive	(1) Solidary Incentives — Highly Specified Contact with Environment — Directing Leadership Style — Homogeneous Membership	(2) Solidary and Purposive Incentives — Highly Specified Contact with Environment — Directing Leadership Style — Homogeneous Membership	(3) Purposive Incentives — Highly Specified Contact with Environment — Directing Leadership Style — Homogeneous Membership
Mixed	(4) Solidary Incentives — Moderately Specified Contact with Environment — Directing and Persuading Leadership Style — Moderately Homogeneous Membership	(5) Solidary and Purposive Incentives — Moderately Specified Contact with Environment — Mixed Directing and Persuading Leadership Style — Heterogeneous Membership	(6) Purposive Incentives — Moderately Specified Contact with Environment — Mixed Leadership Style — Heterogeneous Membership
Inclusive	(7) Solidary Incentives — Broad Contact with Environment — Persuading Leadership Style — Moderately Heterogeneous Membership	(8) Solidary & Purposive Incentives — Broad Contact with Environment — Persuading Leadership Style — Heterogeneous Membership	(9) Purposive Incentives — Broad Contact with Environment — Persuading Leadership Style — Heterogeneous Membership

conditions of membership, the two "major variables" used by Curtis and Zurcher.

Conditions of Membership

Based on our study of CCO and of other such groups, we have some basic criticisms of the way in which the two major variables used by Zurcher and Curtis have been delineated. Both variables seem limited in possible application and somewhat idiosyncratically defined. The *conditions of membership* variable (taken from Zald & Ash) seems to confuse, in the Curtis and Zurcher paper, conditions of membership and the characterization of membership in an organization. Conditions of membership are not directly related to heterogeneity and homogeneity of membership, as is proposed by Curtis and Zurcher. The fact that a group has relatively easy membership requirements does *not* mean that it will automatically have a heterogeneous membership, just as having rigorous membership conditions does *not* mean that the membership will necessarily be homogeneous (except in the limited sense of all having shared similar requirements and experiences of affiliation, a case perhaps overdrawn by Curtis & Zurcher, 1974, p. 357). We prefer to think of conditions of membership in terms of rigorous versus easy, with a moderate *and/or* mixed possibility. Note the distinction between mixed and moderate. If an organization does have a more heterogeneous membership, then it is possible (and maybe even expected) that the various membership groups might vary in terms of conditions of membership. On the other hand, a more homogeneous membership might well have moderate membership requirements. This point is apparently appreciated by Curtis and Zurcher (1974, p. 357), who explicitly mention the possible presence of both components in some organizations.

Thus, the homogeneity or heterogeneity of membership will be considered separately, as indicated by the possibilities of Table 3.2. This change will be reflected in an adjustment of the major headings of Table 3.1, as demonstrated in Table 3.4 (which also incorporates a change to be discussed in the other major variable, organization goal orientations). To demonstrate the independence of the two variables, consider the case of CCO, which started in cell 7 of Table 3.2, quickly moved through cell 4 to cell 1, then moved through cell 2 to cell 3 (if having singles and marrieds is considered heterogeneous, something not clear from the earlier work of the Curtis/Zurcher team or of Zald and Ash). The newer tendencies to witness to some more "structurally inhibited" people (such as other noncommunal married couples who are neighbors) may result in a further "movement" to cell 6, with mixed conditions of membership. As has been said, this mixed situation may increase susceptibility to schisms.

Organization Goals

Organizations may, Curtis and Zurcher state, be distinguished according to whether their goals are primarily "inward" (oriented toward

TABLE 3.2
**Relationship of Characterization of Membership to Conditions of
Membership**

<table>
<tr><td colspan="2"></td><td colspan="3" align="center">Characterization of Membership</td></tr>
<tr><td colspan="2"></td><td align="center">Homogeneous</td><td align="center">Changing</td><td align="center">Heterogeneous</td></tr>
<tr><td></td><td>Rigorous</td><td align="center">(1)</td><td align="center">(2)</td><td align="center">(3)</td></tr>
<tr><td>Conditions
of
Membership</td><td>Mixed and/
or moderate</td><td align="center">(4)</td><td align="center">(5)</td><td align="center">(6)</td></tr>
<tr><td></td><td>Easy</td><td align="center">(7)</td><td align="center">(8)</td><td align="center">(9)</td></tr>
</table>

member satisfactions) or "external" (oriented outward toward non-members), which they claim is similar to the expressive versus instrumental distinction proposed by Gordon and Babchuk (1959). Zurcher and Curtis say (1974, p. 357): "The expressive organization manifests a goal-orientation towards satisfying the social and psychological needs of its members through acts of participation. The instrumental organization manifests a goal-orientation of accomplishing some specific task external to the organization."

As noted in Table 3.1, the authors do allow for a mixed type, which makes the distinction more valuable from our point of view since CCO plainly combines both emphases at this time and has *always* had a strong instrumental emphasis. However, there does seem to be a difficulty in positing the similarity between inward and expressive, and between outward and instrumental. This difficulty needs to be addressed before proceeding with any testing of specific hypotheses.[1] *Either an inward or outward focus could well be considered instrumental in nature.* If the (or a) major goal of an organization is the changing of people, then there must be "instruments" designed to accomplish such an aim. The organization itself may well be considered an "instrument to change people," and could include focusing on people inside *and* outside the group. A similar comment could well be made about Gordon and Babchuk's (1959) examples of instrumental groups—the NAACP and the League of Women Voters. Also, focusing on some task external to the organization—such as evangelizing or voting behavior—may (and often does) have a strong expressive component. Evangelism activities of all kinds plainly satisfy social and psychological needs of the evangelizers, who sometimes are at least trying to convince themselves, by repetition and by "fruits," that what they believe is true and important. In short, we are suggesting that the two variables expressive-instrumental and inward-outward may well be orthogonal to each other in certain groups and situations, as depicted in Table 3.3, and they may also be mixed. We are certainly suggesting, at least, that the expressive-instrumental distinction as conceptualized by Gordon and Babchuk (1959) and used by others has difficulties, and is not a "pure" dichotomy or continuum. The change of conceptualization of this variable is incorporated in Table 3.4.

CCO has, *as a group,* always occupied the lower right-hand portion of Table 3.3, starting in cell 9 (or perhaps 8), and then, we think, moving to cell 6 and then to 5 as the pressures of the increasing numbers of families and children, among other things, grew. Whether or not the movement toward the upper left portion of the table will continue remains to be seen. Any tendencies for certain subsets of membership to move further than others in such a direction would seem to increase the possibilities of schism greatly, since all subsets are competing for resources which may be (or become) somewhat limited.

From the outset, CCO has exemplified the complex relationship of these two variables, a complexity that is only partly explained by possible differences in orientation between the leadership cadre and the followers, as is suggested by Zald and Ash (1966, p. 332) and accepted by Curtis and Zurcher (1974, p. 357) as a partial explanation of mixed orientations. (This possible difference of orientation between leadership cadre and followers will be discussed in more depth later, but suffice it to say that we think such differences more crucial in more "democratic" organizations). As we tried to demonstrate in the earlier discussion of the evolution of group goals (chapter 2, see es-

TABLE 3.3

Relationship of "Expressive-Instrumental" Orientation to "Inward-Outward" Focus of Organization

| | | Orientation | | |
		Expressive	Both	Instrumental
	Inward	(1)	(2)	(3)
Focus	Both	(4)	(5)	(6)
	Outward	(7)	(8)	(9)

pecially Figure 1), CCO has been trying to do many different things at once, and it seems to have succeeded in its efforts reasonably well. Admittedly, some members have been more concerned with the "inward-expressive" kind of considerations, but others are working full-time at furnishing the "instruments" to assuage these "expressive" concerns. Other members (or subsets of members) have approached evangelism in a very outward-instrumental fashion, but some also exemplify the expressive orientation in their evangelism (this seems to be the case especially for newer converts). Also, we have indicated that CCO as a whole seems to have shifted gradually from a more outward to a more inward concern, with more attention being given to the needs of members. But this shift has been accompanied by no less of an instrumental approach. In fact, we have observed the proliferation of instruments to accomplish the "new" goals (or the differentiation of major goals) as the shift has taken place. Another point is that the leadership cadre is itself divided in terms of areas of concern and responsibility, with its primary focus being the development of instruments for taking care of both inward and outward goals. And also there plainly is an understandable strong expressive element in the way in which some leaders approach their assigned jobs.

Our criticism of Curtis and Zurcher's conceptualization of organizational goal orientations seems reasonable on the basis of our research and of other work on the Jesus movement (see Mauss & Peterson, 1974, for example). Also, however, the comments vis á vis goals seem applicable when considering other nonreligious organizations as well. In short, we think the instrumental-expressive distinction lacks clarity, since the two supposedly polar concepts are not universal opposites at all.

We must carry our critique a bit further by questioning Curtis and Zurcher's relating of diffuseness-specificity to their expressive-instrumental dimension.[2] Expressive goals can be very specific in their conceptualization and in their implementation, as in the case of furnishing food and shelter to members, or the development of schools for the children of members. Certainly the growing expressive needs of this group entail *more* specific goals, but *it is not clear that more means ipso facto more diffuse.* Instrumental (or outward in our terms) goals can also be quite diffuse. These comments illustrate our earlier point about the confusion brought about in attempting to treat expressive-inward and instrumental-outward as being congruent types. From our experience, we must suggest that they are not necessarily congruent types, but are *empirical possibilities only.*[3]

Because of these problems with the organizational goals variable, we are forced to restate that part of Curtis and Zurcher's typology also (see Table 3.4). For our purposes, the distinctions between expressive and instrumental will be discarded as a major variable in the typology, and we will also not attempt to relate diffuseness-specificity to the remaining inward-outward distinction. This is not to say that such considerations will not be spoken to in our analysis; it is only to say that they will be handled separately.

Another point of criticism seems germane to our interest here. Those doing research on religious groups have a continual problem (to which they sometimes contribute themselves) concerning the simplistic treatment often afforded such groups in more general analyses. We have already briefly illustrated this in our discussion of commune theory (see chapter 2), and here again is another example of such treatment. Zald and Ash (1966, p. 331) state that "Some MO's, especially those with religious affiliations, have as operative goals the changing of individuals." This may well be generally true, and the notion will certainly hold up under some conditions, as is demonstrated by Zurcher and Curtis (1973, p. 185). However, to treat this as a generalizable law of MO behavior seems questionable, *especially* when the assumption is made that "religious" MO's are thus automatically inward, expressive, and have diffuse goals. Our discussion has already, we hope, demonstrated the problematic nature of such assumed ties between variables. People-changing goals can be directed outward, in a very specific and instrumental fashion. *The assumption that most religious MO's are not so characterizable derives, we think, from the simple fact that most such groups are relatively small and "weak" in terms of members, financial strength, and "self-confidence."* [4] When an organization gains numerical

TABLE 3.4

Relationship of "Focus" of Organization to Conditions of Membership *

		Inward	Mixed	Outward
	Rigorous	(1)	(2)	(3)
Conditions of Membership	Mixed <u>and</u>/ <u>or</u> Moderate	(4)	(5)	(6)
	Easy	(7)	(8)	(9)

*This table is based on a critique of Table 3.1, which should be examined for information on other independent variables Curtis and Zurcher (1974) think important, and which are listed in each cell of Table 3.1.

and financial strength, and self-confidence, it may well become a very outward-looking and acting group. It gets progressively more difficult to treat groups like the Jehovah's Witnesses (see Beckford, 1975), the Mormon Church, and CCO, among other "successful" religious groups, as inward and expressive, and as paying little attention to changing their external environment. The distinction between individualistic and collectivistic orientations seems quite germane to this point, and this will be discussed in greater depth in a later chapter. The fact that groups have an individualistic orientation does *not* mean ipso facto that they are inward turning and expressive. Depending on the strength of the organization, it seems just as logical to think that such groups might well be directing their major efforts toward changing the greater society, but *in an individualistic mode.* This general problem leads, we think, to weakness in Zald and Ash's original treatment, and in the subsequent analysis of the Curtis and Zurcher team.[5]

One other point of criticism of the earlier MO literature that is directly related to the way in which religious groups are treated concerns the notion of successful accomplishment of goals. There seems to be an assumption that religious groups do not need to concern themselves with successful accomplishment of goals if they are not milleniastic (Zald & Ash, 1966, pp. 331-32), and that if they are religious and/or people-changing, their goals can never be accomplished successfully, since every potential convert is not "won" (Zald & Ash, 1966, p. 337; Zurcher & Curtis, 1973, pp. 184-85). We would suggest that individualistically-oriented evangelical religious groups can be successful, even if their goal of people-changing evangelism does not result in the conversion of everyone. Using objective criteria, it is difficult, for instance, to say that CCO is not successful at what it is trying to accomplish. In a few short years, the group has grown to over 1,000 full-time members, and a capital net worth of nearly $2 million—and they are *not* resting on their laurels. Even though direct evangelism efforts have slackened somewhat, *this has occurred, we think, because of, among other things, their relative success, not because of their failure to convert everyone.* We must add a further note as well; success is an amorphous and very subjective quality, and such must be considered by anyone assessing success or failure of MO goal accomplishments. Beyond a doubt, members of CCO define the group as successful, and this assessment has had many direct effects on group life. For social scientists to claim, because their goals might be "never-ending" (a better term than diffuse), that the group has not been successful would be viewed by most CCO members as ludicrous (and as more evidence for their view that social scientific research is meaningless).

Having said all of that, we will now proceed with a more systematic characterizing of the group we studied in terms of the apropos concepts just discussed. For a more detailed "test" of relevant hypotheses from the MO literature, turn to Appendix B.

CHARACTERIZING CCO USING MO CONCEPTS

We have already characterized CCO somewhat in our illustrations of Tables 3.2 and 3.3, and in other ways. Now we want to go into more detail and describe the group using all the independent variables suggested by Curtis and Zurcher and presented in our Table 3.1. CCO definitely exemplifies an organization interested in people-changing. The organization considers itself to be "in but not of the world," focuses on an afterlife, and devotes considerable resources to "bringing people to the Lord." The society as a whole is seen as relatively immutable (more on this later), and hence much effort is directed at changing the hearts and minds of individual potential Christians (and resocializing new converts), rather than attempting to alter the structure of the society through political activity, legislation, and so on. The way to solve the problems of the world, according to group beliefs, is to "change men's hearts," not to change the political or economic structure, or alter participation therein. This orientation toward people-changing does not mean that the group would not like to change society (and that it is not trying to do so), but that the method they are implementing is *more indirect,* with their focus on individual evangelism and on a corporate witnessing by example. This comment notwithstanding, it is still correct to consider the group as focusing predominantly on changing individuals.

Such a focus on witnessing means, we think, that CCO is best thought of as more outward than is often assumed to be the case with religious groups, even though the emphasis now being given to utopia building indicates a shift that seems to require considering the group a mixed type on the variable of inward-outward (which, recall, is our substitution for Curtis and Zurcher's expressive-instrumental dimension). Also, CCO seems to have become, at the same time, *more* instrumental (using our definition), a situation which seems to demonstrate the problems of treating the expressive-instrumental dimension as inward-outward. A multiplicity of instruments and techniques have been developed both to service members and to reach out toward the greater society. And this growth of instruments has been *accompanied and partially caused by* a growth in expressive interests by members. The diffuse-specificity dimension also shows an interesting change. The overriding goal of evangelism can be considered quite specific in terms of singleness of purpose, but the way in which it can be accomplished has a diffuse character, and we have seen a growth of diffuseness in terms of specific methods. As new populations have been addressed (nonitinerant youth and other groups, married couples, children of members and nonmembers), the specific goal of evangelism has become more diffuse or differentiated in implementation. Note that, as already has been said, we assess CCO as relatively successful at accomplishing all its major goals outlined in chapter 2.

In terms of membership conditions, CCO was originally relatively easy, but quickly evolved into a more rigorous organization, as demonstrated by the rigor of the resocialization methods employed. But the attention being given to new target populations, such as married couples who are relatively settled in society, indicates a possible shift toward the mixed category in terms of membership conditions.

The classification of CCO in terms of the two major variables means, we think, that the movement of the organization within the modified Table 3.4 derived from Curtis and Zurcher (1974; Table 3.1 here) can be traced quite accurately. Originally, CCO was easy-outward (type 9), or possibly easy-mixed (type 8). It shifted rapidly through type 6 (mixed-outward) and/or type 5 (mixed-mixed), and ended up in categories 3 and/or 2 (rigorous-outward and mixed-outward). Presently, after some nine years of existence, we note what seems to be a shift back toward more easy membership conditions, forced by the differentiation of target populations, and the organization seems headed for type 5 (mixed-mixed) again, although it certainly is not there yet.

Note that in all this movement, CCO has *never,* according to our best judgement, occupied the strictly inward column of the table. It is and has been mixed on this dimension, but our observation of the persistent outward thrust of CCO does not allow us to treat it as a solely or even predominantly inward group. Such a classification would do an injustice to the facts and to CCO. It appears to us that the group is simply normal in that a reasonable amount of inwardness has been noted, but that its predominant focus has been outward. This may not be the case always as internal (i.e., familistic considerations) and external conditions (such as general economic conditions) may force changes, leading CCO to occupy cell 4 or even 7 in Table 3.4.

Also note that the movements of CCO in Table 3.4, if we have assessed them properly, indicate a rapid change from Curtis and Zurcher's congruent category (which included only types 1 and 9 to the incongruent category, where the group has since remained. The rather rapid shift from one of the "pure" congruent types of Curtis and Zurcher (type 9) to one of the "pure" incongruent types (type 3) seems to call into question their basic distinction between incongruent and congruent types. It seems certain that the distinction has limited application, and that outwardly focused groups with strongly held beliefs which they try to propagate and enforce in members are just as "congruent" as any other type of group.

The movements of CCO parallel, we think, those of some other Jesus movement groups, the Children of God being a good example of such an outward-turning rigorous group which has changed much like the group described herein (see Davis & Richardson, 1976). Other Jesus movement groups, however, differ considerably, which may help explain why some such groups have disappeared (or not gained strength). More attention to expressive considerations (as contrasted to an inward orientation) and less rigorous membership requirements have led some such groups to become (or stay) types 4, 5, 7, and 8 in terms of Table 3.4. Looking at available information on various JM groups suggests that the key variable is *leadership style* or degree of authoritarianism, coupled with the values and ideology of the leaders of specific groups.

Our placing CCO in Table 3.4 and tracing its movements therein does not mean that we agree with the way in which the other four variables included by Curtis and Zurcher operate, and some comment seems called for in this regard. The most obvious comment concerns the *characterization of membership*. The fact that this group and most other Jesus movement-derived organizations all had easy membership requirements at first (and some retained them), did not cause a great amount of heterogeneity in the membership of such groups. All research has indicated a very clearly delimited social category that flowed into the movement groups (see Adams & Fox, 1972; Mauss & Peterson, 1974, and later sections of this book). Granted that the developed rigor of resocialization efforts soon separated the "sheep from the goats," and made the group even more homogeneous; nevertheless, there appears to be little empirical justification in the case of organizations such as CCO for claiming a tie between ease of membership requirements and heterogeneity of membership. The latest movement of CCO back toward the easy end of the spectrum does probably indicate the effects of a developing heterogeneity as the organization "divides" into single and married members, but the original movement toward the rigorous end of the scale was as much *caused by* the homogeneity of membership as anything.

The variable of *leadership style* seems to operate in CCO generally as Curtis and Zurcher indicated, but the style did shift to a more directing and authoritarian type *before* the group developed its rigorous membership categories, thus suggesting a causal relationship between those two variables which seems quite feasible. The change in degree and specification of *contact with the environment* seemed to occur at about the same time as the rigorous membership conditions, and was in fact *a part of* the rigorous requirements directed by leaders. This comment implies that perhaps leadership style is a variable of more importance than conditions of membership, at least for this type of organization. This notion seems more congruent with the Zurcher and Curtis conclusions, which were quoted (1973, p. 186), than with the Curtis and Zurcher paper. This difference (partially "explained" in a footnote in the 1974 paper), between the two papers by the Zurcher/ Curtis team is intriguing, especially given the fact that the two sets of hypotheses offered by Zurcher and Curtis were couched in terms of differences in leadership orientation (see 1973, pp.186-87, and our note 2). This point will be discussed further.

The way in which Curtis and Zurcher integrate incentives into their typology seems also characteristic of CCO, although, as we have indicated (note 1) we see some difficulty in assuming certain relationships between inward-outward considerations and type of incentives. Also, we are puzzled about the omission of Clark and Wilson's (1961) material incentives from the Curtis/Zurcher scheme. In CCO, attention to such considerations, especially by married couples, contributed to some of the changes that have occurred in the organization. We would suggest that material incentives could well be an important way to characterize an independent incentive variable for more inward-oriented organizations. But we would also reiterate that purposive incentives would seem to operate in just about any MO, for all such groups are trying in various ways to implement the values they share. The fact that some MO's might well have more inward-oriented values does not mean that they are not purposive. No group is valueless, which is a criticism of Clark and Wilson's (1961) original attempt to differentiate types of incentives, not just a criticism of how the MO literature since has used their ideas.

Thus, on the basis of our attempt to apply Curtis and Zurcher's typology to CCO and to other Jesus movement groups, serious modifications of the model are suggested. We have earlier suggested a clarification in their use of the terms exclusive and inclusive, substituting rigorous and easy, along with an important middle category, moderate and/or mixed. And we discarded their attempt to tie diffuseness-specificity and expressive-instrumental together, and to the notion of inward-outward focus. We would go further and suggest that the variable of leadership style should be elevated past conditions of membership into a position of more prominence as a (and possibly *the)* major independent variable with small and new MO's. Stated in statistical terms, we think that more of the variance in changes in MO's can probably be explained by use of the variable leadership style, *including* variability in the conditions of membership. In CCO and many other groups with more authoritarian structures, the decision of whether to press for many "converts" by being more easy or fewer "converts" by being more rigorous is strictly tactical and depends on the situation, as assessed by leaders, who are engaged as leaders in implementing certain values they hold dear. We also do not agree that there is a necessary relationship between incentive types and other variables, a criticism based on a possibly faulty conceptualization of the original distinction. Further, it seems evident that some qualification is needed concerning the effects of easy membership requirements on heterogeneity, at least in terms of the early history of MO's, many of which (especially in the Jesus movement) have a relatively homogeneous membership at their inception, simply because they appeal to a limited segment of the greater population. One of the variables—contact with environment—seems to operate fairly well as Curtis and Zurcher claim.

Concluding Comment on "Movement Organization" Literature

While we may have appeared quite critical at times here and in Appendix B in discussing the social movement organization literature, we are very appreciative of the efforts of the four theorists involved in this "new" area. The work of Zald and Ash was a quantum step past most of what had gone before in this area, and the Curtis/Zurcher work was another such quantum step beyond the Zald/Ash work. Curtis and Zurcher were greatly aided in their efforts by the more moderate step of testing the Zald/Ash scheme in their 1973 paper. It is hoped that our test of the several schemes taken together (see Appendix B), along with the theoretical development included, will contribute to yet another quantum step forward in this important area of sociology. We plan to attempt to produce such a contribution, and we hope that others will also try, and that they will find our work useful in such an effort.

NOTES

1. This forced confluence of two possible independent elements may have derived from a statement in the Zald and Ash paper that links the two variables. Zald and Ash say (1966, p. 331) in their discussion of goals that focus on changing the individual, "the commitment of members in (the "people-changing") type of movement organization is less dependent on the external success of the organization. Commitment is based to a greater extent on solidary and/or expressive incentives than on purposive incentives." It appears that, on the basis of their own research experience (see Zurcher & Curtis, 1973, p. 183), Curtis and Zurcher chose to omit the *or* and emphasize the *and*. However, we would suggest that the *and/or* is the most fruitful way to view the relationship between solidary and expressive, although it should be said that Zald and Ash may have misapplied concepts derived from Clark and Wilson (1961), who distinguished between three major types of incentives that can be used by organizations to harness individuals to organizational tasks. These are, to quote Zald and Ash (1966, p. 329), "material (money and goods) incentives, solidary incentives (prestige, respect, friendship), and purposive incentives (value fulfillment)." We would suggest that "solidary" and "expressive" should not be treated as synonyms, as expressive seems a broader term capable of incorporating *all three types* of incentives presented by Clark and Wilson. Also, various incentives can under-gird more outward and/or instrumental-type efforts, not just purposive ones, as Zald and Ash, and Zurcher and Curtis seem to imply.

2. This linkage apparently derives directly from the research described in Zurcher and Curtis (1973), which revealed a positive relationship between diffuseness and expressiveness in one of the two organzations they studied, and of "instrumentalness" (by which they mean attending mainly to external goals, a view we have already criticized) with specificity. We take no issue with this finding, but would suggest that this one-time occurrence does not establish the ties between the two variables as being easily generalizable to other MO's. Zurcher and Curtis are careful not to overstate their case, as is indicated when they state their own set of hypotheses in the conclusions of their paper. They state two sets of hypotheses (1973, pp. 186-87) for "small or emergent" MO's—one for MO's "when the leadership is oriented toward goal specificity and purposive incentives," and another set for MO's "when the leadership is oriented toward goal diffuseness and solidary incentives." As we have said (note 1), we do not agree with this use of Clark and Wilson's terms, but nonetheless, we are pleased to note the qualifications of Zurcher and Curtis. It is noteworthy that in the Gordon and Babchuk (1959) paper the *only* use of the term "diffuse" is in conjunction with their discussion of what they call an instrumental organization—the League of Women Voters (1959, p. 26), an example that also illustrates the problems with the use of the term "instrumental" that we have tried to delineate.

3. Note that this is not what Curtis and Zurcher mean when they use congruent (see 1974, p. 360). We are simply employing a general notion of

congruency ourselves to a part of their scheme. More will be said later about their specific use of the terms congruent and noncongruent.

4. This characterization of religious MO's exhibited in the papers being discussed may also derive in part from what Zald and Ash (1966, p. 340) refer to as the "metaphysical pathos" of scholars writing in the area. Individual preferences may have blinded some to the immense complexities, strength, and effectiveness of certain types of religious groups. There may well be a tendency to put certain religious groups into a separate residual category deemed of little further interest, as seemed to be the case with the commune literature alluded to in chapter 2.

5. We stated earlier that some of Zald and Ash's propositions are not so easily derivable as others. We have a good example of this in terms of the point just being made. Zald and Ash (1966, pp. 331-32) make some questionable statements about religious sects, including a claim that non-millenastic sects are "not subject to the problems of success and failure in the environment," and that "the organization that attempts to change individuals, especially its own members, is less constrained by the definitions of reality of the broader society." On the basis of such claims, they then offer a complex proposition that seems on face value highly questionable, apparently contradictory to other of their propositions (6 and 7), and not particularly related to other things they have said (1966, p. 332):

> Proposition 2: The more insulated an organization is by exclusive membership requirements and goals aimed at changing individuals, the less susceptible it is to pressures for organizational maintenance or general goal transformation.

We were certainly not surprised to note that Zurcher and Curtis did not find support for the part of the hypothesis dealing with people-changing goals.

PART B

GROUP LIFE AND CULTURE

We have presented in Part A a thorough-going analysis of Christ Communal Organization from an organizational point of view, focusing first on a historical account of the group, and then on a more analytical treatment of changes that have taken place in CCO in its relatively short history. To some readers the account and analysis may have seemed a bit abstract and too analytical. We agree that to treat a vibrant and changing organization like CCO in such an objective fashion leaves out some of the real meaning of the organization for participants. In this relatively short section, we want to present a more full description of what life in CCO is like and by so doing make the organization somewhat more real from the viewpoint of our readers.

In chapter 4, we will briefly describe the everyday life and existence that CCO members lead in some of the living situations that have been or still are important to CCO. This includes life at The Farm, The Land, and in a typical gathering house (which is the CCO term for communes located around the nation whose major purpose is the "winning" of new converts). We hope, in these descriptions, to convey some feeling for the kind of life experience of CCO members.

Chapter 5 will be a longer discussion of some quite crucial aspects of CCO life and culture. We will discuss sex roles in the groups, in an expansion of our comments on the sexism inherent in CCO ideology (chapter 1). Also, the entire configuration of norms of belief and behavior surrounding the regulation of sex and the rearing of children will be examined in some depth. By looking at the interesting courtship patterns developed in CCO and the way in which CCO families are organized and function, we hope to add to reader understanding about what life in CCO is and has been like.

The chapter on sex roles, marriage, and the family will close with an analysis of what has happened concerning those aspects of CCO life and culture. We will apply the insightful work of Kanter (1973) on the familism-collectivism conflict, along with a brief comparison of CCO life and culture to that of the kibbutz, using the work of Talmon (1973). Farber's work (1964) on general family theory and that of Berger and Hackett (1974) dealing with child-rearing patterns in modern communes will also be used in our analysis.

4

Daily Life in CCO

The discussion of the organization and structure of CCO gains flavor when supplemented by an understanding of the typical daily activities of its members. In this short chapter, we will try to furnish more information about what life in CCO is like from an individual member's point of view. We will focus on typical situations at the risk of glossing over the continual personal drama of being in a group that is growing and which can and does make dramatic changes of structure and activities.

Group members have generally predictable lives, but their routines can be (and are) interrupted at any moment by an assignment to another activity or another location, or both. At times, the life of the entire collectivity, or large segments of it, may be changed, as when large work forces are gathered for special tasks. For instance, two hundred or so have been engaged yearly on apple-picking crews that literally involve large migrations to and within an adjoining state. (This was not done in 1977, however.) Other large task forces have also been involved in the forestry industry in the region, in CCO's own agricultural activities, and other things. With this qualification about the "emergency" nature of CCO life (which we think is actually functional for the group), we will proceed with our discussion of "typical" daily life.

Our first encounter with CCO was at one of the communal houses. However, after this house was closed (see Appendix A), our research efforts concentrated on The Farm and its residents. During subsequent trips, we visited The Land, spent more time at CCO headquarters, and were also able to visit with some members in their new individual homes. Although The Farm, upon which so much of our attention was focused initially, has been phased out, during the early history of the group it served as a training and testing ground for persons who were "new in the Lord." In addition, The Farm seems to have played an important role in the personal histories of many members who now occupy leadership positions. Because of the import of this phase of CCO history, our discussion will turn first to life at The Farm.

THE FARM

The Farm was nestled in a valley in the rich agricultural area of America's Northwest. It was about an hour's drive from a large Northwestern city, set in an area of productive farm land, surrounded by orchards of trees heavy with peaches and apples, and fields of berries. After driving over winding hilly roads, the rough cabins and meeting hall of the settlement could be seen from the crest of a hill.

Five long cabins were located on the edge of the small settlement. The dining hall, which was also a meeting hall, was in the center. A large grassy area between the cabins provided space for games and fellowship, and a sloping hill, ending in a natural amphitheater, was a comfortable and peaceful spot for large prayer gatherings, singing, and group fellowship. A farm house on a hill above the "labor camp" served as the residence for The Farm pastor, his wife, and several members who were year-round residents of The Farm, including other married couples. The cabins provided sleeping room for brothers and sisters who came from CCO's other houses for the summer to pick berries and other fruit, and to "get closer to the Lord." The cabins were furnished sparingly, each having several bunk beds and shelves for clothes and the few personal belongings members brought with them. Two shower rooms were located between the men's and the women's cabins, and outhouses built by the brothers were nearby.

The settlement was shaded by fruit trees and evergreens. The large quiet trees provided isolated spots for small groups to engage in fellowship or for individuals to pray in solitude. A small earthen and wood structure built for the purpose of prayer assured isolation and privacy for those young Christians who needed its special solace.

During the week, the day began for most brothers and sisters at about 4:30 A.M. Before dawn, the "wake-up steward" came to each cabin to wake its sleeping residents. He tapped on the window of the sisters' cabins, entered the brothers' cabins and woke them with a Scripture reading. The brothers and sisters responded with "God bless you brother" or "praise the Lord" and their day began. For several hours, a few sisters had been preparing a simple but hearty breakfast for the young Christians. Breakfast was served in the dining hall in two shifts, at 5:00 A.M. and at 5:30 A.M. during the week. Group prayers were said and sung before each meal, with the brothers and sisters holding hands in a circle, asking the Lord to bless their food, and praying for his help with the day's work. The brothers and sisters stood in line to be served a breakfast of hot cereal, pancakes, or eggs and biscuits. Nothing was left on the plates—the simplest meal was considered a blessing.[1] By 6:30, the old yellow school bus, used to take the brothers (and some sisters) to the fields, was loaded. A few brothers remained at The Farm to do chores and repairs; most sisters remained behind to wash clothes, clean, and prepare the noon meal. Upon arrival in the fields, prayers were shared, and the workers teamed up to begin the day's work.

As a rule, members picked the fruit and berries on land owned or leased by CCO, but when workers could be spared, teams were hired out to other growers in the area. These young Christians were hard and steady workers, "working for the Lord," and were in great demand by other growers.[2] As the members worked, they shared stories of their path to conversion and sang spirituals. Picking berries was hard, hot work, as pickers literally crawled or "duck-walked" down the rows, pushing a container (called a flat) along the row with them. Most members of our research team did some picking and can testify to its rigor. We can also testify to the powerful dedication and fervor of the work crews, and the strange and moving experience of hearing a large work crew break out spontaneously into a song of praise while engaged in such an arduous task.

Sometimes a deacon would walk up and down the berry rows reading from the Bible. Sounds of "praise the Lord," "God bless You brother," and "thank you Jesus" often interrupted the readings. The noon meal was very simple and sparse, usually consisting of peanut butter sandwiches (with fresh strawberries) and water. During the half-hour meal break, Bible study by individuals was commonplace, and a prayer preceded the return to the fields. After lunch, the brothers and sisters returned to the fields and worked until mid or late afternoon.

Upon returning to the settlement, brothers and sisters had an hour or more of free time before dinner. This time was usually used for cleaning up, tending to individual ministries, fellowship, or prayer. The first horn for dinner sounded about 5:00 P.M., with another at 5:30. Prayers were said or sung, and individual members contributed their own prayers—asking Jesus to bless newcomers, to help a brother or sister with his or her trial, or thanking God for a productive day (or asking his help so that certain researchers would "see the light"). During the second major research visit to The Farm, spirituals were sung inside the dining hall and members were then led in prayer by one of the pastors before eating. Brothers and sisters mingled at meal time, talking quietly of the day's activities or plans for tomorrow. Conversation seldom centered on events or concerns "of the world."

After supper, there was generally about an hour between the meal and the evening prayer and Bible study meeting. During the evening prayer meeting, the entire body gathered on the grassy slope (or in the dining hall if weather was bad) to listen to Bible readings and Scriptural interpretations given by The Farm pastor or visiting CCO pastors, and sometimes to enjoy the commune's singing group doing Scriptural religious songs set to rock music, and to sing and pray together as a group. Announcements were made and organizational business was taken care of. The evening prayer meeting might last until 11:00 P.M. or later, by which time most residents were more than ready for rest. Some lingered in small groups and discussed the Bible, some remained to pray, and some talked over their trials with a fellow Christian. By midnight the camp was quiet, and only the light in the communal kitchen remained on, indicating that a sister was already preparing breakfast for the next morning.

During the summer of 1971, Sundays on The Farm were not usually work days, unless picking of a crop could not be postponed. On Sundays, breakfast was served later, and if possible, a favorite food was prepared. A more elaborate, hot meal was shared in midafternoon. Usually on the weekend, one evening (or perhaps afternoon) would be spent evangelizing in nearby towns. The residents would load into any available vehicle and go "witnessing." Great rejoicing would ensue if some new converts returned to The Farm with the members. During the second summer visit, Mondays were taken as the day of rest because pastors from throughout the state had a staff meeting at The Land on that day. On rest days, members did only the necessary chores and spent most of the day praying or engaging in fellowship. The men might play games, such as frisbee or softball, but for the most part, members talked in quiet groups of three and four, wrote letters, read the Bible, and rested.[3]

Since The Land has replaced The Farm in many of its functions and reflects the increasing differentiation and complexity of the group, a consideration of life at The Land will add to our discussion of the organization and changes it has undergone.

THE LAND

The Land, as described more in chapters 1 and 2, is a ninety-acre plot located about fifteen to twenty miles from the large city that contains CCO's headquarters. In order to accurately describe life at The Land, it is necessary to discuss the various categories of persons who have lived there, since the different categories of members have somewhat different experiences. For several years, one major group to live at The Land was the lambs (brothers and sisters "new in the Lord") who had been brought to The Land from CCO houses all over the country. The lambs had spent several months in a communal house before being brought to The Land for a period of extensive Bible study and training. They spent much of their time together in formal Bible classes, in informal Bible study and fellowship, and even in compulsory physical education classes. The pastors viewed this period as one of significance for the new brothers and sisters, for here they learned the rules of living in the group, the Scriptures, and the expectations the organization had for them, and finally decided whether to remain in the group or leave. Pastors recognized the problems of isolation and doubt that new members might have, and encouraged them to question themselves and to come to a decision about their commitment to life in the group. Pastors indicated that the new members would be put through tests and experience many difficulties. Their days would be long, their schedule rigidly structured. They would be up by 6:30 every morning and have lights out by 10:30 each night. During the day, they attended a series of classes on different subjects, from Bible study to occupational training. The lambs would be separated from parents and friends, and would be governed by an authoritarian leadership structure. They would spend their free time in a Bible study, rather than reading books or magazines, listening to radio or stereo, or watching television.

Upon arrival, lambs had an orientation session during which they were briefed on the daily schedules, given the rules and regulations, and introduced to one another and to the pastors who would direct them during their stay. Lambs were encouraged to develop strong in-group ties, to experience a feeling of shared trials and growth, and to this end engaged in many activities as a group. Often other brothers and sisters "older in the Lord" were excluded from their meetings.

However, lambs and those older in the Lord (sheep) did have their meals together and shared sleeping quarters in the dormitories. This partial division of lambs from sheep, in a manner analogous to different classes in the classic Dornbush (1955) study of the Coast Guard Academy, provided an opportunity for the development of cohesiveness among new members and a sense of sharing in progress and trials, while at the same time it provided role models and the opportunity for a good deal of informal socialization. The sheep were anxious to help the new Christians by answering any questions they had and by being "good examples."

The sheep had usually returned to The Land after spending four or five months in the helps' ministry, which has been described. During their months away from The Land, the sheep had been working at jobs such as fruit picking or tree planting, usually with other commune members, which provided money for CCO's operation. Helps' ministry participation was required for all persons wishing to remain in CCO after the initial training period. Before returning to The Land for sheep (or teams') school, the members were formed into teams, the organization and structure of which have been discussed (chapter 2), in preparation for establishing new houses in new cities.

While at The Land, the sheep also followed a rigorous class schedule, and were often seen studying or carrying notebooks (and their ever-present Bible) around with them. The school had evolved by that time into a rather structured educational experience with set periods, homework, and even required physical education. But both sheep and lambs seemed to respond positively to this type of experience, even though many had fled similar experiences in the recent past.

As noted in chapter 2, the school has now been modified to combine the lambs' and teams' schools without the interim help's ministry and without the assumption that all would be involved directly in mission activities. Life is similar for participants in the new arrangements, however.

In addition to students at The Land, several pastors and their families live there year around. One male is pastor of The Land, and his main function is to oversee the physical operation of The Land. Another person is pastor for the students, and his main function is to answer questions for new members, help them work through personal adjustment problems, and provide counseling. These top level leaders, along with several other pastors and their families who are teachers and permanent staff at The Land, live in several trailers, twelve cabins, and new apartments on The Land. Although most of the married brothers and sisters have separate cooking facilities, they eat most of their meals in the dining hall a half-hour earlier than the students, except for breakfast, which they have after everyone else has finished.

We have been impressed in recent years with the growing independence of the older married couples in CCO and with the privileges that seem to accrue to such leaders and their families. One prime indicator of the growing differentiation and stratification within CCO is that the two groups (married people and single people) live somewhat separate lives, with there being an apparent decreasing amount of contact between the two groups. On The Land, as elsewhere in the organization, many married couples live lives that appear closer to a typical existence outside the group than they do to the communal experience most of them had when they affiliated with CCO, and which most single people in the group still have.

We will not describe in detail the type of life of many married couples who now live in separate dwellings. Suffice it to say that usually the women stay home and care for the children, preparing meals and such, while the husbands get up each morning and leave to work the day at some task assigned by CCO leaders, often having to travel miles to work. On The Land, there is some qualitative difference in life experience for the pastors who lead the schools and the now-typical CCO married couple's experience, since the married leaders are responsible twenty-four hours of the day for their charges. Perhaps the best analogy to life for Land staff members who work in the schools would be to the typical life of a pastor and his family in the "outside world," except that some activities (such as eating) are done communally, and both pastors and students live in the same small rural community.

LIFE IN INDIVIDUAL COMMUNES

Life at the gathering houses has changed somewhat with the establishment of separate domiciles for most married couples. However, a large number of single members (several hundred) and a few married couples (typically house pastors) still live communally. In the communal houses located throughout the country, single brothers and sisters share eating and living areas but sleep in strictly sexually-segregated quarters. Married couples have private rooms. In nearly all communes, the pastor is married, so few communes are now made up of all single people.

Old houses, usually located in fringe or transition areas close to main transportation arteries, are rented and transformed into multioccupant houses by the team which has been sent to the city. These houses vary in size and condition, but on the average will house about twenty people and have enough area for Bible studies involving larger numbers of people. The communes are each directed by a pastor, aided by members of his team. Sisters usually do the sewing, cleaning, food preparation, and serving of meals, and usually work at child evangelism in the neighborhood. Brothers work usually at low-skill jobs in the city or make improvements on the house, repair machinery or other belongings. They also spend much spare time evangelizing, and as has been described, a division of labor may develop within a commune or among a set of communes to maximize the evangelism effort. Certain brothers (or even an entire commune) may work for money to support the entire commune (or group of communes), freeing others to spend full-time at street witnessing and related activities.

Since their stay at a given gathering house may be relatively short, brothers and sisters who work in the community don't usually seek long-term employment or job-training programs. In many ways, the houses act as "feeders" into organization headquarters. Potential converts may usually remain at a house for about three days without making a commitment to the commune or to seeking the Lord.[4] They are treated very cordially, encouraged to read the Bible, given food and a place to sleep during the period, but are then asked to leave if they do not show enough interest in what CCO stands for. This rule governing transients not only eliminates the possible disruptive effects of having a nonbeliever continually present, but also limits the financial drain of providing for persons who will make no "contribution" to the group.

Life at the houses is peaceful—there is no "secular" music, no television, and little reading material other than the Bible. Members are admonished to speak quietly, not to smoke, drink, or use drugs, and not to behave in a boisterous manner. Both brothers and sisters typically spend some time each day proselytizing, usually in pairs or groups, and all members take part in an evening Bible study to which any interested person is invited. Members then usually go to bed shortly after Bible study is over to rest for another exciting day of serving their God.

NOTES

1. Food at The Farm was quite unexciting by normal middle-class standards, and during our research trips, we supplemented our diets by eating food brought with us. Particularly the breakfasts were difficult to eat, as they were commonly made from government surplus oatmeal or such. The only really enjoyable thing about such food was the homemade

bread used at all meals—bread made from surplus flour furnished by the federal government. Any special liquid with a meal was unusual, and water was the typical fare. One day during our second major visit, the research team chipped in personal funds to purchase enough milk for one meal for the entire camp, an action not done from any desire to ingratiate, but which was greatly appreciated by residents. As has been noted elsewhere, the diet of CCO members has improved markedly in recent times, as a direct function of increased group prosperity.

2. During the second major visit, we had an opportunity to observe the situation in which for about the first time that season the work crew of The Farm was being hired out to a neighborhood farmer. The Farm crops were still a few days from being ready to pick, so most of the crew was available for reassignment on a temporary basis. Particularly interesting was the justification given by CCO leaders to the work crew for hiring them out, at an obvious financial advantage to organization coffers. Workers were told that God had furnished them with an opportunity to practice picking, so that a better job could be done when the crops of The Farm were ready. Also, it was pointed out that by working hard for the neighboring farmer, the group could witness to him about the truth of their beliefs. With that as an explanation, the crew then rode several miles on a flatbed trailer pulled by a pickup over dusty roads and worked for several hot days eight to ten hours a day. And from every appearance, the workers, many of whom had never done such hard physical labor before, enjoyed their work immensely.

3. This account of "life on The Farm" is typical of what we encountered on our visits there on two separate summers. During the next (and last) year of operation at The Farm, the situation was changed somewhat as problems with the sewage system forced the group living there to reside in tents and to cook and eat all food outside. They were divided into "tribes" of ten each for work, cooking, and sleeping, and all cooking was done by the "tribe cook" for the day on small iron charcoal stoves called habachis. The only other difference was that, because of the lack of lighting in the tents, the schedule for the entire day's activities was moved up by an hour or so. This meant that people would be awakened by about 3:30 A.M. and finally get back to bed by about 9:00 P.M.

4. This rule is flexible depending on circumstances. Our very presence as researchers for longer periods of time than three days demonstrates that the rule can be bent. However, the rule can also be made more rigorous. One account in the CCO journal about the San Francisco situation described a situation where the "overnighters" were allowed to sleep there, and were fed a "continental breakfast" before being asked to leave at midmorning. After the visitors left, a hearty meal was served to the "working brethren." At night the procedure is similar: commune members eat early, and at 6:00 guests are allowed in for a Bible study, after which soup, coffee, and tea is served. This rescue mission motif was developed out of necessity, as the commune was, we were told, being overrun with people who wanted "food instead of the Lord." The San Francisco situation has also contributed to yet another variation, in that there are two houses there—one a typical gathering house for evangelism purposes, and the other a commune where serious new converts are placed for a time of "seasoning" before being sent back to The Land for school.

5

Sex Roles, Courtship, Marriage, Family Life, and Children

The institutions of marriage, and family and the courtship process leading to participation in these institutions, are intricately linked with sex roles in CCO, as they are in the larger society. Role distinctions based on age, race, and sex are perhaps the most important distinctions among individuals and categories of people made in Western society. Brown (1952, p. 588) indicates that "sex roles are emphatically discriminated, the category of sex being more durable, more pervasive and more universal than any other, even age and race." In CCO, which is quite homogeneous in terms of race and age categories, there is considerable sexual differentiation, in part because there is little else which can be used for internal differentiation.

In the larger society, some role positions are available to members of both sexes. In addition, "role expectations" held by various "role partners" within a "role set" are not always consistent or compatible, allowing for the possibility of conflict. Not only may expectations conflict, but role positions filled by the same individual may be in conflict. Frequently, rigid requirements for entrance into certain roles require rejection of earlier roles for various reasons, such as the possibility of interference with performance of the current role, or because role demands would be inconsistent. Such diversity of role positions and role expectations is not surprising in the complex, highly differentiated society of the latter part of this century. In preindustrial societies and in other less industrialized, less heterogeneous, and less highly differentiated societies, the role structure is not so complex.

CCO, along with other communal groups, has self-consciously attempted to establish a more simple and initially more pastoral society, whose structure and goals differ markedly from those of the greater society. Some groups such as CCO have sought to establish self-sufficient organizations, especially stressing the virtues of "living the Christian life." In CCO, the simplicity of the role structure reflects the comparatively simple organization of the group and its uncomplex view of the world as an orderly place in which God and the Devil carry out a battle for souls. Competition, material gain, professional or educational achievement, and almost all other success criteria of the wider society are ostensibly rejected. The differentiation among positions in the organization is, as a result, not yet very extensive, and the division of labor is not overly complex, although marked differentiation is occurring, as described in chapter 2. Theoretically, all jobs done by the brothers and sisters supposedly have equal status according to the fundamentalist theology of the group, even though they are rigidly separated on the basis of sex and in reality are accorded quite different statuses. Even though all work is "equal in the eyes of the Lord," the position of pastor, which is available only to males, carries more prestige and authority than the position of patroness, and the position of deacon carries more prestige and authority than that of deaconess (see Figures 2 and 3).

The sex roles within CCO are clearly defined and easily differentiated. Role expectations are outlined clearly and simply, and most members seem to hold the same general expectations for each role position. Even when members have extreme difficulty in conforming to their sex role expectations, they "seek the Lord's help" or the counsel of a brother or sister, rather than challenging the appropriateness of the expectations. This consensus on appropriate role behavior and the clarity of role definitions should enhance adjustment to roles (Cottrell, 1942). The rules of conduct applying to individuals who occupy particular positions in the social structure of CCO are largely distinguished by sex, and in most ways, the roles available to males and females are consistent with those available generally in society. The number and variety of available roles are, however, more limited.

ROLE EXPECTATIONS FOR WOMEN

Women may fill several major roles—those of "sister, wife, and mother. They also occupy other role positions in the occupational (steward) and organizational (formal authority) structures of CCO, although the decision-making positions available to women are limited to deaconess or patroness, both of which carry limited authority extending only to other sisters and limited primarily to household maintenance tasks. Women leaders are selected by the male leadership. The exclusion of women from leadership positions is characteristic of many early and contemporary communal movements, such as the Bruderhof discussed by Zablocki (1971), the Hutterites (Peters, 1966), and others (Nordhoff, 1966). Scriptural justifications cited by group leaders for the exclusion of women from authority are several, including Timothy 2:11-12. "Let a woman learn in silence with all submissiveness. I permit no woman to teach or to have authority over men; she is to keep silent."

In the occupational or steward structure, certain positions are expressly provided for women, although there is some fluidity defining these roles. During our first visit to The Farm (in 1971), sisters were responsible for preparing meals, cleaning the cabins and the dining hall, washing and mending clothes, caring for children, and gardening. Sisters also worked in the fields and orchards during planting and harvest times. By 1973 at The Land, men had assumed primary responsibilities for cooking and were now called chefs, rather than cooks, and more women were involved in agricultural activities. There was, for example, a team of sisters who planted trees, a team of sisters who thinned and picked apples, and sisters who were directly involved with maintaining the goat dairy. Sisters were also an important part of the proselytizing efforts of the group. Work in which sisters engage, however, is usually defined as "women's work" and is as much a part of being a Christian wife and mother as it is of being an unmarried sister. When women work in areas dominated by men, it is made clear that they are not nearly as efficient or productive. For example, we were told that males on tree-planting teams averaged about a thousand trees a day, whereas women planting trees averaged less than four hundred. A leader pointed out that if a male could not average eight hundred trees a day by the third day of planting, he would usually be dismissed by his employer.

Although the roles of sisters and brothers have changed some during the period of study, women living with their husbands in separate quarters usually engage only in traditional female activities. Women are responsible for child care, cooking and serving meals, cleaning, and sewing. Some such activities are done in groups, such as groups of women having a sewing group to make clothes. Brothers and sisters share responsibility for work in the gardens.

Females in any position are expected to be submissive; as sisters they are to be submissive to males in the commune, before marriage they are to bow to the wishes of their fiancés, and as wives they are to be submissive to their husbands (unless said male directs them to "sin"). Just as God is the head of man and man the head of woman, woman is the head of her children, according to the CCO philosophy. A woman is given primary responsibility for raising their children, but her authority is implicitly granted by her husband. The behavioral expectation of submissiveness is perhaps the dominant expectation for all role positions filled by females in this religious communal organization. Other expectations, similarly, are consistent with the dominant one for females, no matter which of the available roles they may fill. In any role position, the female is expected to be nonaggressive, nurturing, self-effacing, and to engage in what is traditionally considered women's work.

Within CCO, there exists a clear pattern of definite, distinct "places" or positions to be filled by sisters. However, most male and female members assert that women are not inferior to men, although they are seen as "weaker vessels" and "in subservience to men just as men are in subservience to God." Sixty-six percent of the members interviewed during our first visit to The Farm said that men and women were equal, while 31 percent said women were not equal to men. Members seemed to see no contradiction between their statements that men and women were equal and the fact that women were not allowed to hold the same positions of authority or to have the same responsibilities as men. Members explained that all Christians are "equal in the eyes of the Lord," but that he has established unique places for males and females, and the place of the female is in subjection to the male. "And Adam said, This is now bone of my bones, and flesh of my flesh. She shall be called woman because she was taken out of man" (Genesis 2:23).

Women are viewed as being weaker vessels than men, more emotional, nurturant and docile, but to a degree, they are simultaneously viewed as sensuous beings and as temptresses. Their bodies may cause men to have fleshly desires, so women must dress and conduct themselves in a manner which will not arouse males and which will not show vanity or pride. Women are given the responsibility of avoiding sexually charged situations and must take care not to "stumble" (sexually arouse) the brothers. During our visits of 1972 to The Farm, a sister was publicly chastised after inadvertently exposing a breast while working in the fields, thus "stumbling" a brother (who complained to a pastor). Women are placed in the position of agreeing that their bodies can cause sin, because such ideas are a part of the basic belief structure of the group. Men are absolved of much responsibility for sexual encounters or stimulation, since, according to CCO beliefs, it is their God-given nature to become automatically aroused at the sight of certain parts of the female body, or by any other indication, however implicit, of sexual availability.

As indicated, there have been some changes in the women's place in CCO during our several years of association with them. During our first visit, women were not only expected to be subservient to men, they were expected to be rather servile. They dressed in very nondescript, formless clothes, waited on males, and queued at the end of the food line. At that time, less than 20 percent of the members at The Farm were women. By the time of our second visit to The Farm a year later, we noted some changes in the expectations placed on women *and* an increase in the number of women in the group—up to about 35 percent were female. In the interim between our visits, CCO leaders had met to discuss the place of women and perhaps as a result of dissatisfaction among women with their "place," had come to the conclusion that, although women were "weaker vessels" and were not, according to Scripture, to supervise men, neither were they to be accorded the status of servants. CCO leaders felt that they needed to bring the behavior of group members "into line with the Scriptures." Hence, we noted some changes in interaction between the males and females and changes in the definition of a woman's place. No longer were brothers altogether free from household chores; for example, men were expected to volunteer to work in the kitchen, and more women were being allowed to work in the fields. We view these changes as indications of organization attempts to gain more female members and to retain the sisters already in the commune, even though such attempts were always couched in Scriptural terms. Plainly the group would have problems in maintaining itself if too few females became members to furnish wives for all the males. Thus, in this age of more liberal ideas concerning sex roles, the move toward liberalization of the female role can be viewed, we think, as an action in support of group maintenance. Also, as Kanter (1973, p. 300) points out, the very act of living communally "may potentially reduce the differentiation between men and women," as such a life-style makes status distinctions harder to maintain.

By 1973, other changes in sex roles had occurred. More women are now included on missionary teams, and women no longer wait in line to eat after all the men have been served. Dress norms had also liberalized some, with at least one female at The Land seen wearing cutoffs (shorts). During our 1974 visit, we noted the behavioral changes mentioned above as well as other changes in appearance of the sisters. Although they still avoid tight-fitting, revealing clothes, most sisters wore jeans and blouses, their long hair was usually loose, sometimes in braids, some wore earrings, rings, and bracelets. Their appearance was similar to that of many of their more hippie-oriented peers in colleges and high schools. One leader reported that, as of 1977, the dress code for females had changed even more. He said, "You may be amazed to learn that we allow tasteful bikinis and other 'tempting' attire. As a matter of fact, we are generally disgusted with dress codes, formal and informal, and feel it is a part of the clothesline gospel Christianity that we earnestly reject as hypocritical."

Leaders now state that the proportions of males and females are closer to equal than ever before. Because of our lack of access to organization membership records (they claim that very few records are kept, and this seems to be true), the proportion of females must be estimated. There do appear to be more females than previously, with females probably comprising about 40 percent of the total membership. In 1974 a new class for the Lamb's School had about 35 percent females, and this level has been maintained and even raised since then.

More changes could occur related to the role of women in CCO, especially given the authority of the leaders to revise their interpretations of Scripture to justify needs and behavioral expectations. So far, however, CCO leaders have steadfastly refused to allow any women to hold authority over any male CCO members, although in 1977, a nonvoting female was added to the Pastors' Council as a representative of the unmarried female members. The increasing differentiation and stratification of the group, coupled with the new move to single-family dwellings (which counteracts the tendency Kanter noted for communal living to break down sex role differentiation), may work together to stop further evolution in this important area of group life. Thus, although there has been an attempt to bring behavior in line with group theology and to provide a less repressive role for women, the basic role structure of CCO remains the same. A functional analysis of the role structure of this group and the expectations associated with these roles would indicate many system-maintaining characteristics, but the members and leaders would claim that women engage in certain activities because "it's the Lord's will." And so far, at least, their fundamentalist view of the "Lord's will" has prevailed.

In closing this section, we would like to present a direct quote from one key informant, who disagrees somewhat with our interpretation of the inherent sexism in CCO. This brief account will add balance and also bring in some additional information. The written statement was given to us after this leader read early drafts of some of the chapters of the book in summer 1977.

The male is NOT superior to the female in our ideology. They are equal. However, we believe certain social roles are prescribed—namely that the husband is head over the wife and the wife over the children. This does not mean that every man is head over every woman. One man is head over one woman, his wife. In the context of the whole church, women are not to hold line authority over men nor teach doctrine to other believers. I know this sounds absurd in the light of the women's movement. But I think it is important to see through the intellectual climate of the day to what we are saying and not saying. We are not saying that women can't have a career. They can. Some hold advisory authority in the organization, are department heads over other women, edit our magazine, run our medical program, preschools, Sunday schools, etc. We encourage women to teach "unbelievers" and be evangelists recognizing that the first evangelist was the woman at the well in the Gospel of John and that Mary Magdalene was the first to see Jesus after his resurrection. We see no limits imposed by the scripture on secular careers for women. In our minds, the scriptural social role taboos are very specific:

(1) The wife must submit to her husband (with the exception that she not submit to instruction to sin, such as murder, etc.). In exchange, the husband is to love her as described in I Corinthians 13.

(2) The woman is not to hold "line" authority over men in the church. (Men do not have automatic authority over women. Indeed the scripture says to submit one to another in love. This clearly implies to me that men also "submit" to women.)

(3) A woman is not to teach "doctrine" to the entire church. It is acceptable for her to teach women, children, or unbelievers (male or female) or "secular" subjects.

Please note, in our theology, *wives* are to be "subservient" to husbands as their leaders. Reciprocally, husbands are to "lay down their lives" for their wives. The supreme example of laying down your life, is Christ himself on the cross, and is the example a husband is to follow in loving his wife. This is not the same as women subservient to all or any men.

ROLE EXPECTATIONS FOR BROTHERS

Role categories available to males are also relatively few in number, although more numerous than those available to females (see Figures 2.2 and 2.3). Roles available to males are those of brother, husband, worker, and the several leadership positions, including deacon and more important leadership positions such as minister for agriculture or regional overseer and, of course, the top leadership positions in the Pastors' Council. Behavior expected of males in any of these positions is fairly similar, so that we would not expect great difficulty in role transition, nor would we expect significant role conflict. In all positions, males are generally expected to have authority over females and other males who are below them in the leadership hierarchy. (Recall also that, virtually by definition, no female can ever be *above* a male in the hierarchy). Males are expected to "work hard for the Lord," to be nonquestioning and noncritical of decisions made by persons who are "older in the Lord" (longer-term members occupying superior role positions). As brothers, they are expected to accept the authority of group leaders without question, and as workers, to accept the authority of foremen. Leaders have more flexibility in their role performances, and this flexibility is always justified by reference to the authority of God, to whom all leaders give allegiance.

The position of leader or house pastor receives the highest status in each individual commune. Persons who fill this position may also be selected to fill leadership positions in the larger organization. Males are encouraged to strive for these positions through demonstrating their closeness to the Lord, and an understanding of Scripture. Other leadership positions are achieved in a similar fashion, with brothers being selected to fill open positions by incumbents or other CCO leaders.

We have not found many changes in the male role positions or expectations, except continued differentiation and some stratification. Males retain leadership positions, decision-making prerogatives, and the authority over their households and its members. There have been some important changes in living arrangements for married couples which appear to relate to male role expectations, as has been noted in chapter 2. In the role of husband, males are expected to conform to many traditional expectations. However, several important considerations need to be discussed. There are some Christian couples that are a part of the organization and engage in continuous fellowship with communes and are thus considered part of "the body." This includes most CCO leaders or staff members who are married and who now live relatively independently, now usually in separate rented houses or apartments. This living arrangement is a change from what we first encountered in 1971. We were told that problems in fulfilling a major sex role expectation—male dominance of home—contributed greatly to a basic restructuring of the life-style of the organization. Families are now allowed, even encouraged, to live independently so that the male can be head of his household. This triumph of familistic considerations over collectivistic concerns evidenced by this shift of living arrangements seems of great import. The strong familistic bias forebodes ill for the organization, unless strong measures are taken to counteract this trend. Kanter's (1973, pp. 279-86) analysis would seem to support such a conclusion. Talmon's (1973) work on the Kibbutz mentions specific methods devised to overcome schismatic familistic tendencies, but the attempts being made by CCO seem rather meager by comparison (more on this later). The strong emphasis on male dominance, thus, seems potentially significant, with its latent familistic bent.

Families that did not live independently were defined as being "in the pot." [1] In such cases, the expectation adhered to by the greater society that males provide for their families did not directly apply, which probably contributed to the aforementioned problems by undermining male's basis of authority within the family. In this "in the pot" situation, a male was not the sole provider for his family, and earnings were turned over to group leaders, a method much more collectivistic in orientation. Kanter (1972) notes that in such a situation, the obligation to provide for individual families is diffused among the members in many contemporary communes. The husband's authority in these "in the pot" families must be based on a structure legitimated by a suprahuman being, rather than merely upon the husband's assumed decision-making abilities, physical strength, ability to provide, or any of the more usual bases. The husband is in a position of authority and responsibility over his wife and she over their children and both are "under God," *only* because "the Lord has established such an authority structure and outlined it in the Bible," and not because of the provider status traditionally occupied by males. Thus males must try to retain authority within the family despite an economic situation which seems to weaken their basis of authority. The move toward providing salary for married males seems interpretable as a direct attempt to support traditional male superiority and is thus another indication of growing familistic tendencies in CCO. As noted, by 1977 virtually all married males (except full-time staff) were on salary, thus taking their families "out of the pot."

The CCO Scripturally-based ideology concerning sex roles leads to a quite striking family structure. The different sex roles are very complementary and indicate a task-oriented family structure reiminiscent of frontier times (Parsons & Bales, 1955). The marriages, while plainly encouraged by desire for sex, children, and companionship, are not the common "companionship" model so prevalent in parts of contemporary American society. As might be expected in such a situation of functionality and complementarity of sex roles, divorce is a rare phenomenon in CCO. The family is supported both by the functional complementary role structure and by the group ideology as well. In such a situation, we would certainly expect marriages to last longer than in "normal" society. However, *there is a possible question about the longevity of the organization, given the emphasis on familistic considerations.* Some commune theorists (i.e., Kanter, 1973) seem to think that "imbalance," such as may be the case now in CCO, means that the collectivity itself may eventually suffer. Her theorizing would suggest that such a dominance-subservient complementary role structure may possibly be inimicable to the development of a strong and continuing collectivity. The fact that CCO gained such momentum in its early years may, then, have been directly related to the initial heavy preponderance of single males without family ties to detract them from their "world building." The increasing proportion of married members, coupled with the familistically-oriented changes in life style, brought on or encouraged in part by the traditional emphasis on male dominance, certainly suggests that a slowing down of organizational momentum could occur. The effects of such a change are interesting to contemplate.

COURTSHIP

Most members interviewed in 1971 were socially and sexually active before joining CCO, and many had had serious romantic involvements. Most of the young people had experienced premarital sexual intercourse and were, in sum, not socially repressed or naive. They had participated in a society which values sexual availability, physical attractiveness, and popularity.

Upon affiliating, the "young Christians" had to be resocialized. The value system, roles, and norms within CCO were generally quite disparate from those of contemporary society, and in some important ways were in conflict with them. Members entered a world which disapproved of vanity, self-pride, and attempts by members to enhance their physical attractiveness through the use of cosmetics, stylish clothes, or seductive behavior. Members were not to differentiate themselves on the basis of physical attractiveness; rather the distinction was to be made on the basis of "closeness to the Lord." Bodily pleasures were to be forsaken for spiritual pleasures, hence little thought should be given to the Lord's "vessel" other than keeping it "pure for the Lord." Smoking, alcohol, and drugs were prohibited, a prohibition contradictory to most members' previous life-style, which for most included an emphasis on drug and alcohol usage (more on this in chapter 6). Members came from a society which emphasized physical attractiveness and pleasure, and from an age group courted by advertisers and manufacturers of clothes, jewelry, cars, and other items. They were from a consumption-oriented segment of the society and had chosen to join a group that appeared antithetical to such a view. The fact that CCO has in recent years become more "consumer-oriented" does not detract from the initial affiliation experience of many CCO members in this regard.

The behaviors learned in the greater society for attracting or indicating an interest in a member of the opposite sex were considered inappropriate in CCO. Dating per se was prohibited until the past year or so because it led to temptations and sometimes to "transgressions," or so was the philosophy of CCO leaders. Young Christians are still warned of the pitfalls of spending too much time in each other's company and are admonished to love all brothers and sisters equally. Premarital and extramarital sexual intercourse are defined as sinful, members are instructed not to allow their thoughts or actions to wander toward "bodily pleasures," and are reminded of the "weakness of the flesh." To guard against sins of the flesh, the organization established explicit rules to govern interaction between brothers and sisters, rules that have been relaxed somewhat in recent years. Interaction between lambs (new converts) is more carefully monitored and more clearly delineated than is that between persons who are "older in the Lord," although for all members permissible behavior is much more narrowly defined than it is for most of their peers in the "outside world." When new students come to The Land for their training period, for example, the pastor reads them very specific instructions during their orientation meeting which govern male-female interaction. Brothers and sisters are not to go for walks as a couple alone; they must be accompanied by a chaperone. There must be no holding of hands, touching, or exclusiveness. They cannot leave the lighted area of the community together after dark. As members "grow older in the Lord" they are allowed to interact more freely, have dinner at each other's houses, and spend more time together alone, but the prohibition against touching or kissing persists.

Thus newer members are placed in a situation which renders customary male-female interactions inappropriate, and their expectations about male-female interaction must change. Yet the group has developed ways to legitimize some sexual relationships, and to provide channels through which members may enter such legitimate relationships. Without some such measures, the group could probably not maintain itself, a fact realized by leaders. It was possible, at least theoretically, that the leaders could have chosen just about any method of regulating sex, from celibacy to "free love." They selected a moderate and somewhat traditional approach, one that involved legal marriage and sex only within marriage. And, of course, CCO has had to develop (or co-opt) norms that allow movement from the initially preponderant status of being single to the status of being legally married.

In the larger society, there are various methods which an individual can use to indicate a romantic or sexual interest in another. In CCO, male-female relationships are viewed as good only when it seems that "the Lord has selected the partners," and that their major shared interest is not each other, but their "love of the Lord." Members, to attract one another, use techniques which are also used in the "outside world," but their range of such possible behaviors is more limited. At The Farm in 1972, we noted the following techniques of initial courtship. Members showed their interest in another by their tone of voice, when they said "Good morning, Brother," or by displaying a special smile or a lingering glance. A more direct method of initiating a relationship would be for members to engage in fellowship with each other, to pray together, or to discuss the Scriptures. Sisters might give brothers in whom they were interested extra helpings of food when they went through the food line or might offer them extra dessert or "seconds". Sisters and brothers might also try to work as partners in the fields, which gave them time to be together and to talk. Members could eat their meals together, and evangelize together, but in all cases, their relationship had to be placed within the framework of Christian fellowship and love of the Lord delineated by the group. Their behavior had to always be open to surveillance by other members and leaders, and they were prohibited from being alone together.

Given the restrictions of developing relationships, how has the courtship process been structured, and how has this been functional for the group? There are several characteristics of CCO which are of significance here. First, although the male-female sex ratio is now closer to equal than ever before in the group, males have always outnumbered females. In-group jealousies or tensions which would disrupt the group might occur if the general development of romantic involvements was positively sanctioned and unregulated, simply because there have never been enough females for all the males. This imbalanced sex ratio was particularly the case in the first years or organization life and probably contributed to the early adoption of ideas strictly regulating interaction between the sexes. If persons spent their energies attracting each other or engaging in behaviors which were not directly related to the needs of the group, this was thought to damage both in-group solidarity and the financial status of the group. CCO leaders were faced with the problem of maintaining commitment to the group, while at the same time denying behavior which had been part of these young people's lives and which had apparently been somewhat rewarding, if our data are correct. Hence, in order to prevent divisiveness, romantic relationships were (and still are to a lesser extent) restricted. Members were asked to place their love "in the Lord" and to be devoted to him. Relationships would develop when and if "the Lord willed." As earlier discussed, the members define their relationship to the Lord as a personal one in which they place their lives in his hands and are merely vessels through which he works. Reliance upon God as the active agent and definition of self as a passive being doing his work reduce efforts to actively develop romantic relationships. "The Lord loves His children and will care for them—when the Lord chooses He will bring two people together." This view implies that active attempts to attract another would be fruitless. "The Lord provides" in romantic relationships, as he does in all other areas of a Christian's life.

When members are "drawn together," others appear happy for them—they define their relationship as a "blessing," and as "the work of the Lord." Members are encouraged to search their hearts, to take their feelings to the Lord, and to discuss their feelings immediately with their pastor, who counsels them about their relationship. If two persons agree that they are in love, they usually decide to become engaged. Engagement is a formal status in CCO, and the decision to become engaged is viewed as a serious commitment. At The Farm during our earlier visit, when a brother and sister wished to become engaged, they were required to "counsel with" a pastor, either the pastor of their house or a regional pastor. The pastor discussed with them the seriousness of their decision and helped them, through prayer and discussions, to "seek the Lord's blessing" for their union. The engagement period brought with it new freedoms as well as new problems. Engaged couples were allowed to spend more time together alone, although they are admonished not to spend too many hours alone, due to the "weakness of the flesh." Since, according to the CCO interpretation of the Scriptures, men are more easily tempted by bodily pleasures, responsibility for avoiding compromising situations fell most heavily on the female. Engaged couples, however, could hold hands, touch, and sit close together at group meetings. They were looked upon by others as sharing a special, blessed state. The engagement period lasted for six months, and brothers and sisters were usually required to be separated for three consecutive months during this period of trial. Engaged members were often sent to separate communes and encouraged to spend these months of separation "seeking in their hearts" and praying for guidance. This requirement of separation was applied more loosely in the few years after our visits to The Farm. This occurred, we were told, mainly because the size of CCO means that the chances of becoming attracted to members not in the same house have increased. Since two people living in separate houses are already physically separated, further complete separation is usually not required. Recently, the requirement of separation has been deleted, and other rules of courtship have been liberalized.

On one recent visit, members indicated that brothers and sisters are not so eager to become engaged as they were when the group was new, due to some relaxation of the rules which govern brother-sister interaction. This has apparently led to a rise in the average age at which marriage takes place.[2] The lambs are still discouraged from directing their attention "away from the Lord" and his Word and giving it to another brother or sister. However, those "older in the Lord," more strongly based in His teachings, and more committed to a

Christian life no longer have to be engaged before they interact with a member of the opposite sex. Several brothers and sisters can get together for dinner or to talk, or for group activities which provide an opportunity for interaction, though not directly for intimacy. Even the limited forms of physical contact allowed engaged couples, however, are prohibited to those not engaged. Several members indicated that there was less pressure to become engaged now that it was possible to be with another person without the establishment of a formal relationship.

Members at The Farm, recognizing the engagement period as one of trials and seeming to expect some depression or unhappiness from the separated couple, attempted to help them through. It was assumed that by the end of this period the couple would know whether the Lord wished their relationship to end in marriage. If the couple decided not to get married, the engagement could be broken, apparently with neither member suffering humiliation or losing face, because the trial period is established with the Lord as the ultimate judge of the viability of the relationship. According to CCO beliefs, if the engagement is broken, it is because the Lord has deemed it necessary.[3]

In addition to the trials of separation, the engagement period presented other difficulties for the young couple. Most had loose ties with their parents, and although their parents might be happy to have their children living "a Christian life" instead of being on drugs, for many parents the thought of their child marrying a "Jesus freak" was not pleasant. Some parents thought that marriage ties were even more likely to bind their children to what may be viewed as a deviant or nonproductive life. Because of this, many young couples seemed to spend some energy considering the consequences of their marriage on future family relationships. In some cases, members have been under considerable pressure from parents to leave CCO and return home rather than marry a CCO member.

This engagement period seemed to be especially difficult for the young woman. Although she had a subordinate position in the group as a whole, she was even more directly subservient to her fiancé. Frequent conversations at The Farm among women centered on the "trials of knowing your place," and it was apparent that for several young women, accepting the instructions and authority of their fiancés was a difficult task. However, during this process the young couple was being prepared for the roles which would be more formally demanded after marriage. Older sisters or married sisters often served as advisors for the engaged woman, reminding her that these were heavy burdens, and that the Lord was testing her love for Him. Older sisters, in talking with the newly engaged woman at The Farm, asserted "what a blessing to know your place."

The engagement period, then, even with the more recent liberalization of norms, allows for anticipatory socialization into marriage roles and provides both persons an opportunity to reflect on the requirements and responsibilities of marriage. The period of engagement is a formally institutionalized period during which potential mates test their love for each other, grapple with problems of dominance and subservience, and test their relationship, as partners, with the rest of the group. In addition to the role models available within the group, members are encouraged to turn to the pastors or other CCO leaders for more direct counseling and advice about their trials. They are admonished to know their hearts and to place their faith "in the Lord," to take their problems and hopes "to Him in prayer." The pastors serve much the same function in this case as they do in the established denominations, except that in, these instances, the CCO pastors are usually much closer emotionally to the couple, and also the counseling pastor has more authority over the actions of the couple.

One final comment seems appropriate when summarizing the thrust of all the norms and expectations involved in courtship. Gans (1962), in his discussion of West End peer group life, makes an important distinction between object-oriented and person-oriented individualism and says that the former "involves striving for the achievement of an object" (pp. 89-90). Such an object can be anything, including an ideological one. We would suggest that the stringent courtship rules evidence the general object orientation of CCO. The commitment that members have to Christ, via their fundamentalist-oriented ideology, overrides all considerations, including even the personal needs and desires of members. Such an object orientation—"doctrine over person" in Lifton's (1963) terms—may be essential to group maintenance, but some observers will be impressed with its ostensible coldness and rigidity and will think such a perspective costly in terms of humanistic considerations.

MARRIAGE

Unlike some communes which encourage celibacy, free love, or otherwise prohibit monogamous marriage, CCO incorporates a rather traditional marriage pattern. Thus the organization does not require members to reject marriage roles with which they are accustomed or to disregard the formal and informal socialization concerning marriage provided by their parents. Our data indicate that most members came from middle and upper-middle class families, and the marriages of their parents were usually fairly traditional. When mothers worked, for example, it was usually to earn a supplementary income. In addition, the majority of members came from families which were unbroken by death or divorce, so that most had both male and female role models available. After participating in the "normal" society for approximately twenty years, being exposed to its values, norms, roles, and participating in its major institutions, members' familiarity with traditional sex role behavior and expectations was probably thorough. The encounter with CCO, with its sexist ideology, served to reinforce these traditional views (even if they were latent), and to squelch contemporary tendencies towards such things as women's liberation.

It is apparent that the institution of marriage within CCO differs little from the ideal espoused in the "outside world." CCO members may seem deviant only in their rigid adherence to roles and norms which are not usually taken so seriously in the culture from which they came and in the degree to which marriage is theologically justified. The institution of marriage in the group then is an important, traditionally-structured institution, justified by such Bible verses as this: "Nevertheless, to avoid fornication let every man have his own wife, and let every woman have her own husband" (Corinthians 7:2). The division of labor and the appropriate sex roles within marriage are carefully defined, as they are for group singles prior to marriage. After marriage, as before, men engage in physical labor, working initially in the fields and forests, and now often in small service businesses. Some take part in CCO decision making. Married women clean, cook, care for children, and a minority may work in the fields or at other CCO tasks. An individual's behavior, duties, and demeanor are not expected to change drastically upon marriage, except for sex being allowed. As indicated earlier, movement from one role to another does not usually lead to role conflict because of the high internal consistency of the entire set of CCO roles. The expectation of a woman as a sister and as a wife and mother are quite similar—major breaks with prior behavior are not required. This protection against conflict is seen as generally functioning to maintain the group.

Scriptures from the New Testament are cited to elucidate or justify the relationship between the Christian husband and wife. One example cited was: "Even as Sarah obeyed Abraham, calling him Lord: whose daughters ye are, as long as ye do well, and are not afraid with any amazement. Likewise ye husbands, dwell with them according to knowledge, giving honor into the wife, as unto the weaker vessel, and as being heirs, together of the grace of life; that your prayers be not hindered" (I Peter 3:6-7).

Married women are expected to be subservient to their husbands, and this is a position with which they have gained familiarity through their experiences in the group prior to marriage. As sisters they are to be subdued, to not question and challenge, and to not seek involvement in group decision making. During engagement, a sister learns more direct submissiveness to her fiancé—which prepares her for her role of wife, in which the husband is the figure of authority and decision making.

Marriage is considered a state of blessedness, and members who are engaged are allowed some special privileges because of their closeness to marriage. Couples who are married seem to receive prestige from their situation. CCO leaders encourage marriage because they believe this relationship is sanctioned by God. Of course, it also adds stability to CCO by allowing intimacy, regulating sex (a more immediate concern), and insuring reproduction and eventual orderly replacement and hence continuance of the group, considerations of which group leaders are aware. For some individual members, the possibility of sexual activity is one of the major motivations for marriage. As one young brother told us—"I'm anxious for the Lord to provide me with a wife so we can have sex."

FAMILY LIFE

During the early period of CCO's history, provision of separate quarters for married couples appeared to be functional in various ways. First, especially for the newly married couples, there was time to get to know each other, to be alone and away from the surveillance of others. Even though members may show affection in public, frequent or intense displays are seen as tasteless and offering temptation to unmarried brothers and sisters that might lead to desire for "pleasures of the flesh." So romantic or sexual desires of married couples generally had to be expressed privately. Privacy also increased the satisfaction of married couples with CCO because the group was not acting as a frustrating or prohibiting agent. Thus privacy enhanced the enjoyment of the married couple, and it also sheltered other CCO members from temptation. The development of married couples' communes helped alleviate some of the problems associated with mixing singles and marrieds, but as noted in chapter 2, other problems arose that brought that living arrangement under pressure for modification.

Most married couples' communes have now been replaced by a living pattern more characteristic of normal society, a new structure that has been described (chapter 2). It involves a renewed emphasis on the nuclear family, or neo-local residence, bilateral descent, and, of course, the continued emphasis on monogamy. This "new" (for CCO) structure now involves nearly all CCO married couples (which constitute as of 1977 nearly half of all CCO members). In each such family, the man is the head of the household; his decisions are complied with and his wife is directly responsible to him.

CCO has also expanded to the point of accepting married couples who are not members "of the body," but who are considered Christians and who engage in fellowship with other married brothers and sisters. The living arrangements for married couples now in existence seem less foreign to most couples who may be interested in joining CCO, but who are not accustomed to communal living. Thus a new channel is provided for gathering converts.

Although the married couples' living arrangements are now more similar to those of the greater society than they were previously, there are, as has been stated, still some significant differences. The family is defined as part of something bigger and even more important than itself—that being the CCO organization and God's work through CCO. Members are expected to marry fellow group members, (and to stay married to them). This somewhat endogamous motif contributes, we think, to group maintenance, helping counteract some of the familistic tendencies mentioned earlier. Both members of the marriage are expected to give their main allegiance to CCO and its beliefs.

These types of considerations notwithstanding, in CCO, the nuclear family is recognized as a significant separate unit, although it differs in some ways from the typical nuclear family unit. It is closer to the historical model of the American family as a unit of production than it is to the more recent view of the family as primarily a unit of consumption (see Bell, 1971a), although it is not the extended family which some mistakenly assume is characteristic of early families in this country (Skolnick, 1973). In contrast to CCO, some contemporary communes have prohibited the development of separate families within the larger family of the commune—for example the Lynch family and a group called The Family do not allow marriage of couples—the entire membership is seen as married to each other with sexual access. Some contemporary non-Jesus movement communes have established group marriages in which all members take the same last name, but some do not use last names at all in order to decrease differentiation of members (Kanter, 1973). In CCO, the traditional pattern of the wife and children carrying the male's last name is followed, which according to Kanter (1973, p. 288), indicates an increased familistic emphasis. The somewhat fundamentalist Christian doctrine upon which this group is built and which is used for its justification, necessitates the development of separate family units, units which consist of husband, wife, and children, and in which married partners have exclusive sexual rights. Exclusive sexual access within marriage is yet another of the important ways of emphasizing the family, as also noted by Kanter.

Married couples are expected to have children, and the arrival of a baby is met with rejoicing. Married women who remain childless are considered unfortunate, because "God has not blessed them with children," since CCO beliefs define women's true fulfillment in bearing and raising children. These processes are considered to be the most important and most fulfilling aspects of a woman's life, which is centered around her husband and children, even though she is not expected to neglect her responsibilities to the group, nor to isolate herself completely from her sisters. Her major commitment is "to the Lord," and she attempts to carry out His will in being a good Christian wife and mother. Women we interviewed indicated that, although they loved and honored their husbands, their major commitment was to the Lord, and that if their husband were to "fall away from the Lord" they would not follow him "down the path to sin and Hell." So the "love, honor, obey" dictum apparently applies only as long as the husband remains a CCO-type Christian, another evidence of object-orientation and of "doctrine over person."

There have been very few divorces within CCO. (Only three have been reported to us.) One of the reasons is that the only acceptable ground for divorce is adultery.[4] The commission of adultery, we were told, only leads to divorce when the wronged partner has "hardened his or her heart," and cannot forgive and love the one who commits adultery. Other factors may also contribute to the number of stable marriages, including the careful anticipatory socialization period through which members go; the thorough consideration of marriage and the counseling received during the engagement period; the "separation motif" (when practiced); the participation of the couple in a strong supportive environment; as well as the view that it is sinful to "burst asunder" a unit established and blessed by God.

HAVING CHILDREN

Despite the belief that children are a blessing and are loved, women members have helped convince CCO leaders of the need for some method of birth control. In the first years of CCO, the only approved form of birth control was "trusting in the Lord." The leaders, while still prohibiting birth control pills, "morning after" pills, intrauterine devices, and especially abortion, now allow contraceptive foam and the condom, both less effective means of birth control. The relative ineffectiveness of allowable birth control methods are recognized, as birth control practices and prohibitions are discussed very candidly. As usual, a religious justification for their decision on birth control is provided. According to one leader, the less effective means of birth control still allow for the intervention of God, so that if a sister becomes pregnant, it is the Lord's will. (Of course, someone might proffer the argument that if God is all-powerful, his will would be done no matter how effective the birth control method being used.)

In any case, the change in birth control practices seems to indicate another recognition by CCO leaders of the need to gain more female members and to prevent dissatisfaction of present women members in order to make membership more attractive to females. The liberalization of contraceptive practices probably also contributes to marital stability, not to mention the probable increase in sexual gratification for married individuals. In addition, leaders may have considered the youthfulness of most members and recognized that many of the young women did not feel prepared for the responsibilities of parenthood. And they may have been encouraged to liberalize by the knowledge that a large and rapid increase in the number of children would require a drastic reallocation of people and other resources into child care and education. Our earlier discussion of the role of women illustrated other attempts to gain and/or retain female members which are consistent with their more lenient view of birth control (i.e., having men do volunteer work in the kitchen, altering the dress requirements for women, and taking women out of a position of total subjection, while still maintaining a belief that men were meant to be dominant).

Even though there has been the growing interest in birth control, CCO is still committed to the idea of children, and pregnancies and childbirth are viewed as important, even sacred events.

It may seem inconsistent for this group to simultaneously proclaim the end of the world and encourage procreation. When asked why they wanted to have children if they expected the world to end, members said that the children would share the wonders of the next world—they were pure vessels and would live eternally blissful lives "in Heaven."

Responsibility for children rests primarily with the mother, although the father is the ultimate figure of authority within the family. Children are expected to be submissive to their parents (their mother during the everyday course of events), just as the wife is in subservience to the husband, and he is subservient to God. Children live with their parents and take the surname of their parents. (They are often given Biblical first names such as Michael, Ruth, or Rachael.) The mother is expected to devote most of her energy to her children, although there are many sisters available and ready to assume her child-care responsibilities if she wishes to engage in some other activity. Also, as described earlier, CCO has organized some preschool, kindergarten schools for use by married and unmarried mothers with work responsibilities that take them out of the communes or homes. These schools illustrate the general instrumental perspective taken by group members. Women are helped in their efforts to work outside the home by having the free in-group child-care service.

Although children are expected to conform to the wishes of parents and are not to be "spoiled," they receive a great deal of attention, especially from the sisters. They are pampered and seem to be adored as babies and are sung to, jostled about playfully, and admired. Parents take special pride in their children and delight in their achievements just as most parents would. To date, few CCO children are old enough for us to be able to tell if there will be a decline in age grading within this organization. Berger and Hackett (1974) have documented a dramatic shift in age-grading patterns in a number of rural "hippie" communes, with children being treated simply as "small adults," instead of being forced to occupy such roles as childhood and adolescence. In the communes they examined, children of very young age were allowed to use drugs, participate in sex, and generally have autonomy in settling disputes. Frankly, we do not expect such a dramatic shift of children's role expectations in CCO, which seems to approach child rearing in a rather traditional fashion and which now raises most of them in traditional nuclear-family situations (a few, ages 14 to 16, who are children of older converts to CCO, are allowed to join a singles commune). The father is "boss" not only of his spouse, but of his children as well. Certainly the idea of allowing children to participate in sexual activity and drug usage is anathema to CCO parents. Possible counters to traditional child rearing that might contribute to some shift in children's roles include the self-sufficient emphasis and the initial rural-oriented nature of CCO. Also, the strong Biblical base for CCO culture might have some long-term effects on CCO young children.

THEORETICAL CONSIDERATIONS: FAMILISM VERSUS COLLECTIVISM

The family in CCO is generally developing in the direction of being a more autonomous social and economic unit. Some might even think it is fast becoming a unit for consumption of goods and leisure strikingly like many families in America. Our most recent visits to the group have impressed us with their growing materialism; kitchens of some single-family dwellings (admittedly of leaders) are well-equipped with modern conveniences, the homes are commodiously furnished, and garages are filled with newer cars. Plainly, the increasing economic strength of CCO is indirectly aiding the growth of family independence. Also, there is a growing "social independence," illustrated both by decreasing social contact within the married couples of CCO and by the reduced amount of interaction between most married couples and most single members. A number of married couples have some contact with single members (who still live communally), but many couples have little such interaction. When a couple lives separately with the man working with other married men and with the woman working in the home and/or with other married women, such contact is minimized. This differentiation into a married group and a single group represents a structural change with potentially profound implications.

Some of these implications involve individual considerations, while others deal with organizational interests. The individual "gains" include the ability of the male to maintain a place of dominance in the family and the ability of the female to be the "second in command" in a single household unit. Some might suggest that the costs involved for the female were relatively high in the neolocal residence situation as she is plainly subservient to her husband. Most household duties, including those of mother, fall on her, whereas in the married couple communes, more sharing of duties and division of responsibility was usually the case. The children, under the new living arrangements, possibly stand to gain in terms of self-identity, but only of course, if the point made to us about this being a problem in the communal living situation was of substance.

From the organizational viewpoint, the gains of the new system *appear* immense, at least at first glance. CCO leaders have allowed its definitions of a family and of sex roles in general to evolve to the point where member satisfaction is high. Both males and females appear to like the slightly more relaxed approach to sex roles. We were told by several married leaders (and their wives) that most, if not nearly all, married couples prefer the new living arrangements to the old communal model. Considerations of privacy, desire for materialist possessions, a better feeling of being in the proper role for both males and females, and the socialization of children were all cited to us as considerations. All taken together, the problems of the communal living (including one that might be suspected but for which we have no data—increased sexual attraction between individuals married to others) represented what Farber (1964) would certainly call a *crisis*. In this instance, from the group perspective and from the view of individual families, a process model such as that discussed by Farber worked well to facilitate maintenance of the group. A "new" approach to the family and sex roles was worked out which seemed to meet most of the major problems. The changes involved a movement away from what we first thought was going to be a kibbutz-like situation such as described by Spiro (1958) and Talmon (1973). For whatever reason, the movement away from such a communal family style with its more collectivistic emphasis was rather rapid, occurring in just a few years.

It must be admitted that this rapid change is *potentially* disastrous from the point of view of group maintenance. While it can certainly be argued that the shift in sex roles was virtually essential to group maintenance (otherwise, not enough females would have been attracted to CCO), a similar position regarding the growing emphasis on familism cannot be so easily supported. This conclusion is based on relevant literature on communal life, particularly that of Talmon (1973) and Kanter (1973). Because such considerations are so crucial to the continued existence of CCO, we will present some of the work of these two theorists and contrast our own finding apropos CCO to the conclusions of Talmon and of Kanter.

Kanter (1973) has presented perhaps the best available general statement concerning familism-collectivism tensions of communal life. She presents six analytically different ways in which that tension can be resolved in favor of "minimal differentiation of nuclear families"—a situation where collectivism gains primacy. First she mentions the abolishment of individual and family last *name usage,* pointing out that allowing individual families to retain last names (of the male) is counter to collectivism because it allows families to be clearly distinguished within the group. We found that last names of people were well-known by all, and that females took the last name of their husband, as did any children resulting from the union. This is in sharp contrast to groups such as the Children of God, whose members are not allowed to retain first names, and whose last names are not well-known by most members and are seldom used (see Davis & Richardson, 1976).

A second consideration is the disallowance of the development of *erotic* and *emotional bonds* between individuals. Kanter makes the interesting point that attempts to stop such pair-bonding can go to either extreme, and have, as illustrated by the Shakers who practiced celibacy, and the Oneida community which practiced a form of complex marriage involving open sexual access to all other members. We found a situation in CCO in which such pair-bonding was actually strongly encouraged, with negative sanctions attaching to any attempts to detract from such bonding or to form multibonded relationships. The new living arrangements also obviously contribute to the development of emotional ties between couples. And a possible (even probable) result of allowing nuclear families is development of emotional ties between parents and children that rival ties the children might develop with the collectivity.

The area of *power* is a third area discussed by Kanter, who says (1973, p. 291), "Nuclear families can also be differentiated by the fact that as a unit they have legal or legitimate control over certain areas of life and the right to make autonomous decisions over those areas binding for their own members." In communes, group policies develop that infringe on the autonomy of nuclear families, and the pervasiveness of such collectivistic policies is a measure of the group's emphasis of collectivism. In CCO, the situation as regards power and autonomy is mixed. Certainly there is a growing autonomy for families living apart, but group policies still impinge on such families to a considerable extent. For instance, group policy on contraception is supposedly binding, and we are unaware of any refusals to abide by the group decision to disallow oral contraceptives. Also, group decisions on where to live and what the male household heads will do for an occupation seem compulsory, as are general rules governing family life and child rearing. Thus, unlike the first two considerations mentioned by Kanter, this point seems ambiguous at present. Close scrutiny of familial autonomy over the next few years will be very revealing in terms of the issue at hand, and we will observe any shifts with great interest.[5]

A closely related consideration to autonomy is that of *property ownership,* another issue discussed by Kanter (1973). Communes generally try to develop some sort of system of joint ownership of needed material goods, with control of them vested in the group decision-making apparatus. Such a system has the consequence of diminishing the influence of the nuclear family, which has to depend on the group to allow it to use needed items. Again we find an ambiguous, but possibly changing situation in CCO. On The Farm during our first visit, we noted that about all that members owned were a few clothes and a toothbrush. Everything else was considered to be jointly owned, and needs were met, through a request system in which members would tell their pastor when they needed something or when they wanted to use community property (such as a car). This antimaterialistic bent has been modified somewhat under the joint pressures of increased prosperity and family life. There are now more material goods to be had, and members may actually have even an automobile or separate dwelling assigned to them for family use. Both will probably be in the name of the organization (since tax laws are taken full advantage of by CCO), but it seems to us that there is the growing feeling in CCO that such assignments just formalize an ownership process. Certainly such things as equipment for child rearing are passed on to others when not needed, but this generally happens in the greater society among friends. The legal boundary of tax laws makes any drastic and formal shift in the direction of maximizing familistic considerations unlikely. However, within the boundaries of law, a shift has occurred, we think, and we will be watching for other signs that property ownership is being redefined.

Spatial and *territorial considerations* are important to minimizing familial tendencies as well. Some communal groups mentioned by Kanter disallow the idea of a private family dwelling-place altogether, and others have private bedrooms, but require eating and other activities to be done with other commune members. Certainly for the married couples that are living separately, we find a strong familistic emphasis. Such families have their own territory that is defined as their home. Permission must be asked and granted for others to come into the home, and the home is cared for by a member of the nuclear household. Such privacy, which was deliberately sought, allows for the growth of intimacy between members of the inviolate home. For the very few married couples still living communally, the situation differs somewhat, but even there the couples generally have a private room, although they may eat with other group members and share commune chores.

A last important consideration presented by Kanter concerns *social and organizational ties*. She notes that communal life serves to furnish an all-emcompassing set of social and organization ties for members, while at the same time discouraging, at least implicitly, ties with non-members. Members become "insiders," and all nonmembers, even family of orientation members, are "outsiders." CCO is predominantly collectivistic on this variable, although they do allow or even encourage reestablishing ties with parents, and we have seen quite a few parents visiting CCO facilities during our own trips there.[6] They certainly do not have the reputation that some groups (such as the Children of God) have for trying to sever relationships with family members. Nonetheless, most of the social life of CCO members is with other members. There is a great deal of visiting back and forth between communes with some groups traveling long distances to spend holidays with members of other communes. Employment is sought that allows members to work together. Even the social life of married couples living separately is dominated by organizational activities. For example, we have been told that Fellowship Hall is in use nearly every night with some form of activity involving married couples. Such reports remind us of the apparently quite functional family-oriented but church-centered system developed by Mormons.[7] It is worth reiterating that, although there are few social and organizational ties with outsiders, there are two relatively separate spheres of activity *within* CCO. The single members have little contact with most married members, whereas some married couples have little contact with singles (or even with many other married couples). This latter point about the marrieds is especially true for many of the married women, who are nearly as cut off from the rest of society as their counterparts in the greater society.

Kanter's theorizing has afforded us some general idea of the thrust of CCO, and we are forced to conclude that this emphasis is predominantly familistic, especially if one allows, as we do, for the greater import of allowing affective ties to develop between family members, which seem to suggest competition for loyalties at the very least. The integration of such a strong familistic tendency with concerns for group maintenance will probably be the most important challenge facing CCO in the next few years.

Before leaving this type of consideration, however, we thought it might be useful to make some specific comparison with another communal experience, that of the kibbutz. We can make this brief comparison because such a thorough account of this aspect of life in a kibbutz is available by Talmon (1973), who directly addressed the issue of family versus collectivity and presented some specific methods whereby the collectivism was supported. We earlier mentioned that, by comparison, the attempts to support the collectivity by this group were meager, and now we will mention enough specifics to give the reader a sense of what was done.

Initially, kibbutz husbands and wives were assigned to different jobs in different locations, and there was little sexual differentiation of available jobs. All meals were taken in a common dining hall, and nearly all goods and money were distributed equally. Having children was discouraged, and this had the effect of lessening the need for those to do traditional "women's work." Care of children was the responsibility of the kibbutz and most children did not even stay with their parents at night, although strong emotional bonds sometimes still developed between parents and children. Direct efforts were made to overcome conventional norms concerning sexual behavior. Chastity and lifelong fidelity were discouraged, as was any "double standard" for males and females. Premarital sex was considered acceptable, and a sexual union did not require a marriage ceremony. A formal wedding was usually not had until the first child, and then only to legitimate the child. Housing problems led to a lack of privacy for cohabiting couples, and even when separate quarters were obtained, the male was expected to help with housework, as being married did not change the status of the wife nearly as much as in conventional marriages. She was still a worker and defender, and had her own responsibilities as a member of the collectivity. Within the "home," private radios and teakettles were banned for a time, because they tended to make the home more attractive and encouraged couples to withdraw into themselves. Nearly all rituals were collective in nature, and even weddings were short and informal.

We could go on with other specific illustrations, but hopefully, the point has been made that the kibbutz situation differed markedly at its inception with what we found in CCO. Even the considerably "normalized" contemporary situation in the kibbutz, with its increased familistic emphasis described by Talmon (1973) and by Rabkin and Rabkin (1969), seems collectivistic when compared to group life in CCO. Talmon (1973, p. 331) makes an important point that helps explain the developing détente between familism and collectivism in the kibbutz situation. She says: "The attenuation of the collectivistic ideology [helps] ease the tension between family and community but the basic rivalry does not disappear. Inasmuch as the family accepts the primacy of collective consideration, it may become a valuable ally. Inasmuch as it resents a subordinate position and disputes the authority of collective institutions, it is still a potential source of conflict and competition" (p. 331).

Her point is well-taken, and what remains to be seen is whether the family in CCO will be a good ally of the collectivity, or whether instead it will compete for personal loyalties and thus possibly divide the group.

One final comment: Farber (1964) makes the point that we should examine the family from the perspective of an independent variable. He talks about the necessity of accepting the functional autonomy of the family. We tend to accept this view, but with some qualification. Recall that in our discussion of the male sex role, the point was made that consideration of problems in the way this role was allowed to operate may have been the major impetus to the rather drastic or far-reaching change in family life. As we said, this change was based on (or perhaps just justified by) an ideology that is plainly sexist in nature, that of fundamentalism. To this extent, we might characterize CCO as idealist, in that its structure was greatly influenced by certain ideas to the extent of being profoundly modified. This is just another way of saying that, at least at that time in the history of CCO, the family was not a strong independent variable but may have been a "poor second" to ideological considerations. We admit the obvious point that there must be families before the family can have an independent effect, and that CCO was relatively "familyless" in its early history. Thus the changes over which we have labored so long were more like simply getting organized, instead of being modifications of long-term and viable structural arrangements. However, now that the changes have been made and the approach to family life has developed as it has, we expect that Farber's admonishment will hold true. We expect that familial considerations will have a major effect on the future life of CCO. How certain new problems, such as isolation from the community of believers, developing exclusive affective ties among family members, increased contact with nonmembers, and higher financial costs are handled will, to a large extent, determine whether or not CCO will continue as a viable organization (more on this point in chapter 9).

NOTES

1. There is some overlap between living separately and being "in the pot." Most families live separately and are "out of the pot" and drawing salaries now, although we understand that a few (pastors) are not. Also, not all families who live communally are "in the pot," although most seem to be.
2. This conclusion is based in part on unverified information. We have been told that the average age of the membership is still twenty-one years (which is what we found on our first visit). If such is the case, then some

recruits must actually be younger than most recruits in the initial organizing stage, if the effect of the older members' increasing age is to be
counterbalanced. We have not yet been able to check this claim.

3. We generally are bothered by the tendency of this group's ideology to
"credit" God with all that happens, since such ideas, we think, detract
from the achievement of "personhood" by absolving individuals of
human responsibility while also detracting from human potentiality.
However, in the case of "blame" for breaking an engagement, we recognize that there may be some value in shifting responsibility from either
partner in the engagement.

4. We are unaware of any divorces directly based on a spouse "falling
away" from group beliefs, although it should be noted that perhaps a
likely way that a person could indicate his or her having "fallen away"
would be through extramarital sexual activity.

5. We think it is especially intriguing to consider adherence to contraception
policy, given the great amount of literature on this issue that has arisen
from the similar, but even more limiting situation in the Catholic church
regarding contraception.

6. Reestablishing ties with parents is encouraged, but not to the extent of
leaving the group. We think that this emphasis on parental ties, which is
justified on Biblical grounds and often directly for evangelistic reasons,
has been important to group maintenance. Most parents seem to be won
over to a position of support for CCO once they have visited and found
out that their son or daughter was getting along all right. This neutraliz-
ing of a possibly strong alternative for members has been important, for
apparently, most parents think members can and should remain as members, and some parents even give money in support of CCO.

7. We intend to examine literature on Mormons in an attempt to come to an
understanding of how such a strong familistic system can be, at the same
time, a strong collectivity. The Mormon situation seems to run counter to
some of the notions in the familism versus collectivism literature and may
well furnish some hints for us in understanding what CCO does to maintain itself (assuming that it does maintain itself).

PART C

INDIVIDUAL CHARACTERISTICS

So far we have discussed Christ Communal Organization from the perspective of organizational analysis (Part A), and we have presented some material about the life and culture of the group (Part B). Now we want to examine in some depth the background characteristics of CCO members. We want to show the "social locations" from which they came, and thus we will present demographic data on members. We also want to present information on the personal histories of members, indicating what kind of family ties and previous experiences they had. Special attention will be given to the drug history of members, since so much has been made of this aspect of the new religious groups forming in the late 1960s. And we will attend to the political and religious experiences of these youth before they came into CCO. That kind of material will be presented in chapter 6. In chapter 7, we present part of what may be the only personality assessment data available on members of a Jesus-movement organization. These data are presented in conjunction with commentary on the relationship of religiosity and personality, and with a discussion of methodological problems of such research. In chapter 8, we go into more depth concerning the political experiences of these young people, both before and after affiliation with CCO. Special attention is given to the concept of alienation, as that idea has been developed by Peter Berger in *The Sacred Canopy* (1967). We extend Berger's theorizing on the concept and attempt to operationalize some of the relevant notions.

169

6

The Sisters and Brothers: A Profile

Two of the most frequently asked questions about the Jesus movement, or for that matter any social movement, are "What kind of people join?" and "Why do they join?" These questions intrigue social scientists, theologians, politicians, and journalists, as well as the curious public. In this chapter, we will provide information on the backgrounds of persons who joined this particular religious sect. This will hopefully illuminate the more illusive "why" (dealt with at length in chapter 9), as well as provide material for comparisons with other social movements and religious organizations.

There have been many popular treatments of the Jesus movement presenting various views of participants in the movement. Such protagonists as Plowman (1971) and Vachon (1972), and early leaders Duane Pederson (1971) and Arthur Blessit (1971) describe the Jesus movement or particular segments of it as bringing salvation to sinners groveling in their own hells on earth. Converts are viewed as making a transition from wretched, drug-addicted, hippie radical thieves to loving, peaceful, Christians. Others less enamored with the movement offer scathing criticisms of the movement and its members. Among the better-known articles presenting the more negative view are Nolan (1971) and Cahill (1973a, 1973b), which are sarcastic, scathing attacks on the Jesus people, who they see as at least apolitical, if not the result of a right-wing conspiracy. Almost all persons who have written on the movement, including those who write from a more sociological perspective such as Enroth, Ericson, and Peters (1972), Adams and Fox (1972), Jacobson and Pilarzyk (1974), and Mauss and Peterson (1973) agree that some significant changes, either temporary or permanent, take place among converts. Little systematic information, however, has been gathered on the characteristics and life-styles of members before they joined the movement, so that tracing these changes has been primarily conjectural.

One of our initial interests was to discover whether there were any characteristics that participants held in common. We turned our attention to the various social, economic, and experiential characteristics of these young Christians prior to affiliation. Several areas were of special sociological interest to us, including religious socialization, past political orientation and involvement, drug use, relationship of the member with parents, siblings, and peers, and member's perceptions of their lives prior to joining.

DEMOGRAPHIC CHARACTERISTICS

A brief discussion of the demographic characteristics of members will provide a framework for the material related to social, political, and experiential background characteristics of members, Most of the information reported is based on our extensive interviewing of eighty-eight members in 1971, but this material is supplemented and validated by data from other visits to CCO operations.

One of the characteristics of the Jesus movement most obvious to even the casual observer is the young age of most members. Seldom in the television coverage of the groups within the movement did one see a face that looked over 25—the few exceptions almost always were leaders, such as Tony and Sue Alamo of the Christian Foundation; "Daddy" Jack Sparks, a former statistics professor at Pennsylvania State University who headed the Christian World Liberation Front; Arthur Blessit, "the minister of Sunset Strip"; or Duane Pederson, who brought people to salvation through the *Hollywood Free Paper* which he founded.

CCO adheres to this youthful picture with most of the members ranging in age from 18 to 24, the average age in both 1971 and 1972 being 21. During our first visit, the youngest person was a 15-year-old "sister" and the oldest a 31-year-old "brother." The make-up of the organization is changing somewhat as members remain in the group and have children, and as proselytizing begins to focus on Christian couples and families in the various communities in which CCO has facilities and outposts. However, most converts still come primarily from the 18- to 24-year-old age group. Thus the recruitment base has been similar to that of other Jesus movement organizations throughout the country. The Children of God, for example, made early claims that 70 to 90 percent of their members come from a dropout youth culture (Enroth, Ericson, & Peters, 1972, p. 33). Streiker (1971) also reports that most communal Christians are young people who have been participating in a street culture.

Dramatic changes which CCO has experienced during the last few years may well lead to an increase in the average age of members, if the growing number of children of members are not included in the averaging. As the number of street people has declined (partially because of a basic demographic fact of there being fewer people in that age category than was the case in the 1960s), the organization has refocused its recruitment efforts on persons who are participants in the dominant culture. This refocused evangelism, coupled with the twin facts of all members getting older and some (many) now having children, means that the age span of members has increased rapidly and will continue to increase. In the years ahead, the age structure in this group will probably come to resemble other "alternative" religious communities, such as the Bruderhof, so well described by Zablocki (1971).

Another characteristic of the Jesus movement which is frequently mentioned (and of which the leaders of CCO are aware) is the almost exclusively Caucasian membership. During our first visit to The Farm there was only one black member, a male (who was, incidentally, the only person who refused our interview). Several more blacks have joined since our first visit, mostly males. Leaders have been concerned about not reaching minority populations with "the Word" and have attempted to rectify the situation through the development of black and Indian evangelism teams, which they feel would be better able to communicate with minority prospective members than would white teams. Several of the black members have held leadership positions with CCO, and at least two have married white "sisters." This intermarriage has been an interesting development, given the implicit conservatism and fundamentalism of the sect and the potential Biblical justification for prohibiting racial intermarriage, a prohibition which has traditionally been enforced by some fundamentalist religious denominations.

It may well be that the racial homogeneity of the group only reflects the predominance of whites among the street population and the selective appeal of a life-style which ostensibly rejects middle-class values. It may in addition be that a retreatist, communal, fundamentalist life-style was viewed as a viable alternative only by white youth going through the strains of the 1960s but was not so viewed by black youth. The number of black and other minority converts has increased slightly in CCO during the last several years, perhaps as a result of energetic recruitment efforts, but does not yet reflect the proportion of blacks and minorities in the general population. In contrast, Zablocki (1971) found that the Bruderhof experienced considerable ethnic and national diversity, and that the community enjoyed a rich cultural mix, characteristics not yet found to any extent in the Jesus movement and in CCO.

The members' educational backgrounds were much like those of their peers in the dominant culture, with the average educational attainment being 12.1 years. Both males and females reported an interest in higher education before joining. Fifty-three (60%) of the members interviewed indicated that they had considered going on to get a higher degree. In addition, career aspirations had been fairly high, with 50% indicating an interest in a career, this interest being proportionally greater among females (64%) than among males (47%), an interesting finding given the sexism of the group. The educational and career interests of these young people were sharply curtailed upon entering CCO. A common response, for example, to the question "Do you have any career plans?" was "Just working for the Lord," a response which often came from young persons who had career aspirations prior to joining. CCO, however, does encourage selected persons to gain skills and education which will be of direct benefit to the organization, and a number of members are regularly taking higher education courses in areas such as child care, accounting, business administration, and so on.

Much of the popular literature on the Jesus movement presents the members as coming from diversified social and economic backgrounds, sharing only their salvation by the Lord. Streiker (1971), for example, in describing who these young people were and where they came from says the range of backgrounds and life experiences was great, from the major urban ghettos to the wealthy suburbs. We found in contrast that most members of CCO we interviewed had middle- to upper-middle class backgrounds. Although 32 of the members interviewed said they did not know their parents' income, the average reported income was $17,000. Sixteen members reported that their parents made $20,000 a year or more. In addition to reported income, the parent's education and occupational status indicated a middle-class background. The average educational attainment for fathers was 12.6 years and that for mothers was 12.3 years. Thirty-nine respondents (48%) said that their father was a professional, manager, official, or self-employed business-man. Members came from fairly large families, with 13 saying there were 6 or more children in their family and only 2 reporting that they were only children.

CCO is peopled with individuals who have been voluntarily down-wardly mobile (for a time) from a middle- or upper-middle class exis-tence. The profile of members prior to affiliation is quite similar to the category "college youth" in the Yankelovich (1974) study. We found that CCO members came from families with relatively high levels of educational and occupational achievement (and income), and that they were predominantly white, a pattern clearly evident in Yankelovich's college youth sample. Whether or not this pattern of downward mobil-ity is permanent remains to be seen, but the fact that it was entered into voluntarily is striking.

BACKGROUND CHARACTERISTICS

These demographic characteristics provide a picture of the educa-tional, economic, and family backgrounds of members and offer a description upon which to base our discussion of a more detailed investigation of the social, experiential, and religious backgrounds of these young converts. Because CCO is a fundametalist-oriented re-ligious organization, requiring a rigorous life-style, and demanding rigid adherence to religious tenets, the backgrounds of members are of special interest.

Let us first look at the relationships that members had with mem-bers of their family and friends before joining. Most (61%) of the members' parents were still married, while 25 (26%) came from fami-lies which were broken by divorce or separation. Comparing the di-vorce pattern of the parents of members of CCO with national figures, we see that there may be a slight tendency for more members to come from broken homes, especially if we attempt to include desertion in the national figures. Reiss (1971, p. 282) reports a current divorce rate of about 14 per 1,000 couples as of 1970, cautioning that the divorce rate has been rising slowly since the peak year of 1946 immediately following World War II and should be leveling off in the 1970s. He indicates that because slightly over one in every one hundred mar-riages ends in divorce in any particular year, if this rate continues, one in every four couples will eventually experience divorce.

The relationship which members had with their parents while they were living at home were not especially poor, although they had improved for some since joining CCO. Given the literature on the adolescent phase, we would not really expect the members of CCO to report especially warm, engrossing, encompassing, easy relationships with their parents. Adolescence is viewed by many family theorists as being a period of strain and conflict. Winch (1971) sees the conflict as stemming from middle-class goals of success or upward mobility and achievement of a gender-appropriate repertory of behaviors which are imposed upon the adolescent. Bell (1971b) stresses role confusion, the nonexistence of a clear status for the adolescent, the dilemma of being neither fish nor fowl which is characteristic of this period as largely responsible for the difficulty of adolescence. He suggests that, because the interaction of parent and adolescent in many middle-class families is based upon such different values and ends, conflict in the family is inevitable. Keniston (1962) portrays the adolescent pattern as one which, while not explicitly antiadult, is belligerently nonadult. He sees the discontinuity between specific generations, the clear separation between parent and child as leading to chronic intrafamily conflict. This conflict is characteristic of societies with a high rate of social change, alternatives of career, moral codes, and life-styles. Streiker (1971) writing specifically about members of the Jesus movement, portrays their parents as "middle Americans" who, above all, believe in the American Way of Life and who stress the necessity of working hard to obtain the good life. He says that, in addition to the stresses of adolescence and the search for identity, the young find themselves alienated from their parents' value system. This separation results in a paucity of emotional support from parents coupled with mounting pressure to make choices, decisions reflecting adult status. All of these authors recognize adolescence as a difficult time for the individual and as being one of conflict with parental standards and values.

Such reasoning notwithstanding, in CCO both males and females were likely to report good relationships, especially with their mothers. Seventy-nine percent of the females and 62% of the males reported good relationships with their mothers while 15 (20%) of the males and none of the females reported bad relationships with their mother. Thirty-one percent of the members reported a good relationship with their father, another 31% said it was neutral or vacillating and 34% characterized their relationship with their father as bad. Respondents were more likely to describe their mother as warm (78% for mothers, 45% for fathers), and females were more likely than males to view their mother as warm and less likely to describe her as cold. The relationship the members had with their father was fairly distant, with

42 (48%) of the members saying that their father spent very little or no time at all with them when they were growing up, and 49 (56%) saying that they never talked with their father about things that were important to them. Forty-one (47%) of the members said that their mother spent a lot of time with them when they were growing up, and 43 (50%) in addition said that they talked with their mother about things that were important to them. Still, 34 (38%) said that their mother spent very little time with them. Bronfenbrenner (1971) reports a slight trend, at least with young children, toward both parents being warm toward the child, but these CCO young people apparently had a warmer and closer relationship with their mother than with their father.

We also found that a large minority of parents were seen by their children as having a bad marital relationship. Thirty-three (38%) of the members reported that their parents' relationship was bad, 43 (49%) reported a good relationship between their parents. Only 8 (9%) described the relationship as "average." CCO members interviewed said that they got along fairly well with their siblings, with only 13 (15%) reporting poor or very poor sibling relationships. Most members said that their relationships with their families had improved since they joined CCO, a finding of note in light of the debate about such new groups "stealing" children. Those that had been members for two or more years did not report any greater improvement in their relationship with parents than did new converts. The improvement in this relationship may be related to the feeling by many of the members (58%) that their parents approved more of the way they were now living than they did of their lives prior to joining. Many of these young people were on the streets, engaged in drug use, extramarital sex, and other activities that may have been upsetting to their parents. In addition, CCO encourages its members to "honor thy mother and thy father," a lesson which members attempt to follow and which they are encouraged to follow, unless the parents attempt to pull their children away from CCO. Leaders evidence concern over the feelings parents have about their children joining such an organization and caution their members not to push their beliefs on their parents.

Members did not appear to have been friendless or social isolates before joining. Only 15 of the members, all males, said that they had no close friends before joining. The majority said they had at least one good friend in whom they could confide. It is of course possible that the friends were social isolates and that the convert interacted primarily with persons who were not well-integrated with society. Characterization of high school years may give some indication of the individual's perception of self as a meaningful part of his/her world or as an isolate. Thirty-one (35%) of the respondents characterized their high school years as happy, 22 (25%) said they were about average, and 34 (38%) said they were unhappy years. More males (41%) than females (29%) described their high school years as unhappy. One possible indication that social ties outside of CCO may have been lacking in warmth or strength is the statement by 31 (35%) of the members that the warmth, closeness, and love were the characteristics of CCO which first attracted them.

Altogether, the childhood and adolescent years of members of CCO did not appear to have been overwhelmingly unsatisfactory, and their relationships with parents did not seem especially bad. Many members did come from homes which were disrupted, and a sizable minority reported poor relationships between their parents, however. Respondents' relationships with their parents and siblings were not particularly poor, and most respondents had not been social isolates; they had friends, even romantic involvements, and participated in school activities.

The period immediately preceding contact with CCO did, however, seem to be characterized by unhappiness and disruption. Over half of the respondents said that their lives before joining were unhappy. A majority said that their lives were in some ways difficult or upsetting during the last six months before they joined CCO. General unhappiness and depression and what were described as bad drug experiences were frequently reported during this period. Many had left home as a result of problems with their families and were involved with drugs, alcohol, or merely wandering. Although their unhappiness was nonspecific, we cannot assume it was less real than unhappiness emerging from a specifiable source. Gouldner (1970) Frankl (1963), Fromm (1941), and Maslow (1962) all recognize the impact of the problem of finding meaning and self-fulfillment in an industrialized mass society, and the particular social disruptions of the 1960s in America only exacerbated the situation for many young people.

The separation of members from their families may have been one source of unhappiness. Many CCO members had left home under duress. Often their parents did not approve of their lives, and information gathered during informal discussion leads us to believe that few were receiving financial support from their families. The broken family ties and the appparent lack of close relationships on the streets may have led to unhappiness for these young people from fairly affluent, traditional homes. This period immediately preceding contact with the group will be more fully discussed in chapter 9, in which we discuss the various conversion models and attempt to develop one which incorporates our data.

Most of the literature on the Jesus movement suggests that heavy drug involvement was a preconversion characteristic of the young Christians. Drakeford (1972), in his study of the early Children of God history, notes that many converts to religious communal sects had drug experiences. In discussing the Children of God, he reasserts the view held by leaders, members, and the public that a communal Christian lifestyle is an alternative to addiction. The popular slogan, "getting high on Jesus," reflects the significance of drugs for these converts in their pre-Christian days and lends some credence to the view that the Jesus movement is a drug replacement. Enroth, Ericson & Peters (1972) also emphasize the drug culture as an important factor, as do Plowman (1971) and Streiker (1971).

Because so much has been written on the relationship between drug use and commitment to the Jesus movement, and because heavy involvement with drugs and experiences growing out of this involvement may have presented problems to members, many of our interview questions were related to drug use. Our data on drug use indicated that most members used drugs of some kind, and most used them frequently. Seventy-nine (90%) had used drugs. Thirty-three (42%) had used drugs all the time or every day, while 26 (33%) used them fairly often, two or four times a week. Not only were most members users of marijuana (not uncommon among persons of this age), but 64 (72%) of those who used drugs had been involved with harder drugs such as opiates and hallucinogenics. We rated the drugs in terms of "hardest drugs used by the respondent." Information on the types of drugs used by respondents who used drugs in terms of the hardest drug used is presented in Table 6.1. Nine persons said they had not used drugs at all before joining.

Fifty-seven (72%) of those who used drugs said they had bad experiences with drugs, 27 (47%) of whom had had several bad experiences. Few descriptions of bad or good drug experiences made reference to religious experiences. Nine (16%) persons reported experiencing Satan or hell while 3 (5%) reported experiencing God during a bad drug experience. Two reported that their good experiences involved an experience with God. The majority, 41 (51%), reported a mood change, a pleasant or happy experience.

There was a high association between the time of the respondent's last bad drug experience and the time he/she joined CCO. If we look

TABLE 6.1

Hardest Drugs Used by Drug Users of CCO

Hardest Drug Used	No. Using	Percent of those who used drugs
Opiates, heroin, cocaine	21	27%
Hallucinogenics, NDA, acid	43	54
Uppers, speed, downers	7	9
Marijuana, hashish	7	9
	—	—
	78	99%

at the 54 persons who reported bad drug experiences, we find a tendency for this experience to have occurred shortly before joining.

Fifty-two (66%) of the respondents who used drugs and 59% of all the respondents who used drugs and 59% of all the respondents reported that using drugs was an important part of their lives. Twenty-two (27%) of the users said it was not very important, although none said it was not at all important. Sixty-five (73%) persons said that most of their friends used drugs, and of these 62 (95%) said that they did not now approve of this, which is predictable from their present religious tenets. Twenty-nine (36%) of the respondents first started using drugs because their friends did, or to be "in," while thirty were curious or expected some pleasurable experience. No respondents reported using drugs at the time of interview. Fifty-six (71%) reported that they stopped for a period of time *before* coming to CCO, which is inconsistent with the usual explanation of the Jesus movement as directly rescuing people from drugs. Twenty-six (46%) of these had stopped less than one month before, while another 16 (28%) stopped less than six months before. Fifteen (19%) said they stopped at the same time they joined, while 7 (9%) stopped after joining, all but one within one month. Fifty-one (65%) gave religious reasons for stopping (Bible commands or found Jesus) while 24 (30%) gave responses such as "nothing in it anymore" or "knew it was wrong," which in the perspective of the respondents could be taken as a religious response, since many persons elaborated that there was "nothing in drugs since they came to the Lord."

Only rather passing attention will be given here to the political activities and involvements of the people of CCO since we will discuss their political involvements in some detail in chapter 8 when we give consideration to Berger's theoretical analysis of the relationship between religion and alienation. But for now we will look at the political involvement of the friends and family of the group members.

Twenty-two (25%) of the respondents had close friends who were involved in political activities. Of these, 17 (77%) of the friends were involved in radical groups, such as SDS and Weathermen. The respondents came from families which, for the most part, were fairly uninvolved politically. Only 11 persons (12%) said that their mother was active in political activities or organizations. Thirty persons (34%) described their mother as politically moderate, and 17 (19%) indicated that they had politically liberal mothers. Only 7 (8%) of the respondents indicated that their father was active in political organizations or activities. Forty-three (49%) described their father as conservative, 19 (22%) described him as moderate, and 11 (12%) as liberal or radical.

Not unexpectedly, given national figures on party registrations, more parents belonged to the Democratic party than any other. Of the mothers, 34 (39%) were reported to be Democrats, 17 (19%) Republicans, 10 (11%) Independent, and another 10 had no party affiliation. Thirty-two (36%) of the fathers were reported to be Democrats, 28 (32%) Republicans, 8 (9%) Independent, and 5 had no party affiliation.

Because of our theoretical interests and because the organization which we studied was a religious one, much of our focus fell upon prior religious experiences and socialization of members. Although members now reject the established denominations as hypocritical and condemn "Sunday Christians" and such groups as Campus Crusade as "plastic Christians," the information we gathered from our interviews indicates that most members of CCO had, to a large extent, experienced religious socialization before joining. The majority of respondents reported coming from homes in which both parents or parent figures attended church. Seventy (80%) of the mothers and 58 (65%) of the fathers were church attenders. More fathers than mothers did not attend church at all. Of those who did attend, most mothers and fathers attended church frequently, once a week or more. Seventy-three (83%) of the respondents claimed to have attended church while they were growing up, the majority frequently.

Parents attended theologically moderate churches predominantly, with 35 of the mothers (50% of the attenders) and 33 of the fathers (58% of attenders) attending such churches as Presbyterian, Lutheran, and Disciples of Christ.

An equal number of CCO members interviewed in 1971 had attended Catholic and moderate Protestant churches. Twenty-three

(31%) had attended moderate Protestant churches such as Presbyterian, Lutheran, or American Baptist. Seven (10%) had attended conservative Protestant churches such as Southern Baptist, Missouri Lutheran, or pentecostal churches. Eleven persons (25%) had attended liberal churches, including Congregation, Methodist, and Episcopalian. Two persons had attended the Mormon church, one a synagogue, one the Greek Orthodox church, and one the Grace Mennonite church. Classification of religions as conservative, moderate, or liberal is based upon the criteria and classification system presented by Glock and Stark (1968).

Table 6.2 shows a comparison of the self-reported prior religious affiliation of CCO members with data showing the religious composition of the United States, based on data reported by Broom and Selznick (1968).

The table indicates that a larger percentage of the population of CCO reported no religion prior to joining than did those of the general population. Seventeen percent of the members, compared with less than 3% of the general population, reported no religion. The 17% figure for CCO members may be somewhat suspect, however, since it was obtained in answer to the question, "Did you attend church when you were growing up?" Thus the figure is not directly comparable to the Broom and Selznick "none" category. Also, of course, that comment means that the other CCO figures reported in Table 6.2 may not be directly comparable as well.

Most members attended only one denomination while they were growing up. Only 12 attended churches other than their primary church of attendance. For the most part, religious participation was a family activity. Only 12 respondents report that they went to church

TABLE 6.2

Comparison of CCO Prior Religious Affiliation with Religious Composition of U.S.

Religious Category	Religious Composition of U.S.	Prior Religious Affiliation of CCO
Protestant	66.2%	46.7%
Catholic	26.1	26.1
Jewish	3.0	1.0
Other	1.2	4.0
None	2.8	17.0

alone or only with their brothers and sisters. Forty-nine (56%) attended with their parents or entire family. Forty-five (51%) of the respondents considered their mothers to be religious or very religious, but only 21 (24%) of the fathers were considered religious or very religious. Thirty-seven (42%) of the mothers were described as not very religious, while 58 (66%) of the fathers were seen as not very religious or not at all religious.

A minority of the respondents and their siblings were involved with other religious organizations before they joined CCO. Twenty persons (22%) said that at least one sibling had belonged to a religious organization or group, most of them belonging to school-related or Campus Crusade types of organizations. Seventeen (20%) of the respondents belonged to religious organizations before joining CCO, but their affiliation had frequently been with other communal religious groups similar to CCO, or with youth-oriented churches, such as Calvary Chapel or Church of the Living Waters.

Respondents were familiar with prayer and religious values while they were growing up. Thirty-six (40%) persons indicated that prayers were customarily said before meals in their homes while 53 (60%) indicated that they prayed privately at home. Nineteen of these (36%) prayed at least once a day and 27 (31%) prayed only when they had special needs or problems. A minority of the respondents, 11, said that their family engaged in religious observances other than Christmas or Easter, and a large majority (91%) said that their family did not read the Bible at home. Almost half, 37, said that their family sometimes turned to God in times of a crisis.

Our data indicate that the majority of the members of CCO attended church while growing up and attended frequently. They were familiar with religious values and activities before leaving home. Among Protestants, members were more likely to be moderate than conservative. There were, however, a large number of Catholics in the group, and they are sometimes considered as more conservative. When Catholic and Protestant conservatives are combined, they constitute almost 40% of the population of CCO.

CONCLUSIONS

The results which have been presented provide preliminary descriptive information on members of a communal religious group which originated as part of a widely publicized but little understood social movement. Our general impression from these data is that most converts were relatively "normal," white, middle and upper-middle class kids, but that many had been heavily into drugs and a good proportion had experienced bad drug trips close to the time they affiliated with CCO.

The data on religious socialization indicate that most members of CCO had experienced considerable religious socialization, although a substantial minority apparently had not. Most of the respondents attended church while growing up, and their attendance was relatively frequent. Parents, in addition, were church-goers for the most part and they also attended frequently. Members did not indicate that their backgrounds were dominated by religious values and activities, but most were certainly familiar with these values and explanations of the world. Members of CCO attended church as part of a family unit, for the most part, but claimed to be more frequent attenders than either of their parents. Prayers were said in the respondents' homes, especially before meals, religious holidays were celebrated, and the respondents prayed privately while living at home. Their families, however, did not usually engage in such activities as reading the Bible aloud or other religious ceremonies. Many families viewed God as a suprahuman being upon whom they could rely in times of crisis or stress. This information indicates that members of CCO were familiar with religious explanations of the world, with religious language, and the Christian system of beliefs, a finding with implications for models of conversion (see chapter 9). The world view of CCO and its reliance upon Jesus as "personal savior" was not alien to them, although it may have placed more stress on Christianity as an all-consuming way of life than they had previously felt it to be.

7

Personality Assessment

The major thrust of our research has been sociological and social psychological. The sociological focus has involved study of CCO as a developing and changing organization, as a commune and as a cult and sect, while the social psychological foci have been on conversion and commitment models and on assessing selected attitudes and changes that occurred in the members' attitudes. However, as a complementary aspect of the research, we have done personality assessment as well. This chapter will present results from our first such effort to characterize individual CCO members.[1] These results will, we think, contribute to an understanding of CCO, and they will also be a provocative entree to the following chapters on alienation and political attitudes (chapter 8) and on conversion models (chapter 9), an area on which we have concentrated much effort. But first, some brief introduction to the general area of the relationship between religion and personality seems in order.

RELIGIOSITY AND PERSONALITY

Much previous research on personality attributes characteristics of members of religious groups has generally revealed tendencies toward pathology, deficiency, and low intelligence (Dittes, 1969). Religious conversion is usually seen in terms of an attempt to compensate for frustrations and inadequacies, of providing an "inheritance for the meek." Use of the religion scale of the Allport-Vernon Inventory has revealed negative correlations with more desirable personality attributes (e.g., Cowen, 1954; Prothro & Jensen, 1950). Measures of intelligence and religious affiliation have also yielded negative correlations (e.g., Brown & Lowe, 1951; Stark, 1963). Wood's (1965) study utilized a Rorschach technique to compare members of a Pentecostal group with non-Pentecostals. He found that the former displayed an "inadequately structured value-attitude system." Other research on Pentecostals has led to differing interpretations (see especially the work of Gerlach & Hine, 1970; Hine, 1969), but most work of either view can be faulted on methodological grounds (see Richardson, 1973), thus leaving the question open. This research on Pentecostalism is of special interest since most members of CCO regularly practice glossolalia, a finding corroborated by other research on the Jesus movement.[2]

The relationship of conventional forms of religious commitment and personality has been addressed in a provocative review and research article by Stark (1971), who claims that the relationship between commitment to conventional religion and various levels of psychopathology is *negative*. He criticizes a number of previous studies mostly on methodological grounds and presents evidence to support his own theoretical contention. The research he reports is valuable, but because of its own "one-shot" study design approach, it does not refute the alternative explanation that some of the negative correlations between his measures of religiosity and various indices of psychopathology could derive from *changes* that occur in the individuals *as a result of* joining a religious group. Many religionists would not be surprised at such an idea, but it is not fully appreciated by Stark. He says (1971, p. 170), "the widespread belief that psychopathology is a source of religious commitment requires a positive association between the two," a statement that requires some qualifications to take into account the much-heralded healing function claimed for religion by many religionists (and even some others). As has been noted in Richardson (1973), only some sort of time series or panel design that apprehends subjects prior to affiliation can even begin to adequately address the question of the relationship between religiosity and personality. Such methodology is difficult to apply in studies of religiosity, of course.

Furthermore, Stark bases his conclusions on samples of more mainstream or conventional religious persons who should perhaps not be expected to differ in any marked degree from the population of non-churchgoers. The Jesus movement, in general, and CCO in particular,

condems traditional religious groups and exhibits many of the behaviors that Stark labels as "extremist or pathological forms of commitment"—for example, "convictions that one has received a new
revelation for mankind, or obsessions with personal holiness" (Stark
1971, p. 167). Stark's point is well-taken, however, that findings concerning these more extreme groups should not be generalized to followers of more conventional religions. However, he is not clear on
how to distinguish between "conventional groups," some of which
certainly would seem extremist by Stark's criterion.

The personality assessment research reported here was only meant
to be descriptive and exploratory. The purpose of this personality
assessment portion of our study was to discover something about the
self-perceived personal characteristics of CCO members, and to find
out whether the results based on CCO's members would agree with
previously published research results in the area of religiosity and
personality.

METHODOLOGY

The Adjective Check List (Gough & Heilbrun, 1965) was administered in the summer of 1971 to 83 group members who were in
attendance at a nightly prayer meeting and Bible study session at The
Farm. Sixty-six male and 17 female members, which provides an adequate representation of the sex ratio within the group at The Farm at
that time, completed and returned the anonymous test forms. There
were indications that, in completing this task, members adhered to a
group norm which encourages candor and honesty. A few members
were not present at the time of the administration, mainly because of
involvement with chores, but we have no reason to suspect that any
bias was introduced by the absence of these members, since most
members systematically took turns at nightly chore assignments. Most
of those taking the test had been CCO members for several months,
although almost all had only recently arrived at The Farm for the
summer from other CCO branches. During the week that the Adjective Check List was administered, most subjects were also being interviewed individually to obtain other information. Since as directed no
names were placed on the forms, it was impossible to correlate ACL
results with other data gathered from the same subject (later research
allowed such correlations, cf. Simmonds, 1977a; 1977b).

The instrument selected for initial use was the Adjective Check List
(ACL), which is composed of a series of 300 adjectives which may be
used for self-description, for the description of an ideal person, for

descriptions of others, or in other ways. Twenty-four standardized personality variables are assessed through the self-description format, fifteen of which are variables utilizing concepts first described in Murray's (1938) need-press system, a typology of individual needs which are influenced by situational pressures. Raw scores are converted to standard scores, taking into account the total number of adjectives checked. Standard scores for a sample of 800 male and female college students have a mean of 50 and a standard deviation of 10.[3]

RESULTS

Self-Descriptions

Raw scores were converted to standard form utilizing norms established for college students. The student sample on which the ACL was standardized was chosen for comparison purposes since the mean age (21.0), educational level (12.2 years), and parental income, occupational, and educational classifications of CCO members approximate the norms for college students.[4] Significant differences between CCO members and the college student sample *at the .001 level* were assessed through *t*-tests.[5] The findings are summarized in Table 7.1 and described below.

1. Total number of adjectives checked (Tot Ckd): While males did not check significantly more adjectives than did the normative sample, females checked significantly fewer. Gough and Heilbrun (1965) describe the low scorer "to be quiet and reserved, more tentative and cautious in his approach to problems, and perhaps at times unduly taciturn and aloof." [6]

2. Number of favorable adjectives checked (Fav): Males checked significantly fewer favorable adjectives than did the normative sample, and there was a trend for the females to check fewer also. The common interpretation of a low score on this variable is defined in terms of individualism and accessibility of emotions.

3. Number of unfavorable adjectives checked (Unf): Males checked significantly more unfavorable items than did the comparison samples and females tended also to check more. The failure to reach statistical significance for the female group can probably be attributed to their checking significantly fewer adjectives altogether (as well as to the small size of the female group).

4. Defensiveness (DF): Both male and female CCO members tended to score low on the defensiveness scale with the combined sample

TABLE 7.1

Mean Standard ACL Scores for CCO Males (n = 66), Females (n = 17), and for the Combined Sample (n = 83)

Scale

	Tot Ckd	Fav	Unf	Df	S-Cfd	S-Cn	Lab	PA	Ach	Dom	End	Ord
Males: $\bar{X}$ =	50.59	39.55	57.14	44.74	40.47	43.02	49.99	39.83	43.86	40.33	44.65	42.23
t =	.35	-5.90	4.21	-3.25	-9.36	-4.30	-.02	-6.67	-4.47	-8.93	-3.27	-5.50
Females: $\bar{X}$ =	32.12	41.82	54.24	38.18	44.53	43.00	49.18	43.35	41.59	39.71	44.35	43.94
t =	-5.76	-2.59	1.27	-3.42	-2.76	-3.25	-.31	-2.43	-3.82	-4.89	-2.22	-3.28
Combined: $\bar{X}$ =	46.81	40.01	55.54	43.40	41.30	43.01	49.81	40.55	43.40	40.20	44.59	42.58
t =	-1.85	-6.41	4.30	-4.40	-9.25	-5.16	-.15	-6.38	-5.51	-10.01	-3.93	-6.18

TABLE 7.1
(cont'd.)

Scale

	Int	Nur	Aff	Het	Exh	Aut	Agg	Cha	Suc	Aba	Def	Crs
Males: $\overline{X}$ =	44.52	45.39	44.15	42.20	47.92	48.05	50.14	42.62	58.86	54.50	52.71	58.32
t =	-2.98	-2.27	-3.30	-5.77	-1.70	-1.30	.08	-6.04	7.33	5.40	1.86	8.04
Females: $\overline{X}$ =	45.35	45.00	41.71	45.76	47.18	50.29	50.24	46.29	60.29	53.94	51.29	43.82
t =	-1.63	-1.98	-3.48	-1.91	-1.52	.12	.12	-1.46	3.90	1.05	.76	-2.20
Combined: $\overline{X}$ =	44.69	45.31	43.65	42.93	47.77	48.51	50.16	43.37	59.16	54.39	52.42	55.35
t =	-3.36	-2.76	-4.22	-5.94	-2.10	-1.14	.11	-5.89	8.21	4.36	1.97	4.45

Note: Italicized values are significant at $p < .001$.

attaining significance. Gough and Heilbrun (1965) advance the interpretive suggestion that, "The lower-scoring subject tends to be anxious and apprehensive, critical of himself and others, and given to complaints about his circumstances. He not only has more problems than his peers, but tends to dwell on them and put them at the center of his attention."

5. Self-confidence (S-Cfd): The male sample attained a high level of significance in scoring low on this variable, while the female sample came close to significance, also scoring low. The low scorer is viewed "as unassuming, forgetful, mild, preoccupied, reserved, and retiring."

6. Self-control (S-Cn): Again, the males scored significantly lower on self-control, while females showed a strong tendency to score lower. Descriptions of low scorers include such terms as inadequately socialized, irresponsible, complaining, and impulsive.

7. Lability (Lab): This variable refers to characteristics such as "spontaneity, flexibility, need for change, rejection of convention, and assertive individuality." No significant differences between CCO members and the normative sample were found.

8. Personal Adjustment (PA): Males scored significantly lower on the personal adjustment scale and females showed a strong tendency in this direction. Gough and Heilbrun describe the low scorer as one who "sees himself as at odds with other people and as moody and dissatisfied." Words used to describe such a person include "aloof, defensive, anxious, inhibited, worrying, withdrawn, and unfriendly."

The next fifteen variables are the need scales which are based on Murray's (1938) need-press system. The descriptions and definitions of each variable are taken from Gough and Heilbrun (1965).

9. Achievement (Ach): Male CCO members scored significantly lower than did the normative sample on this variable. The definition of achievement, from which this scale was originally constructed, stresses the "socially recognized significance" of achievement-oriented pursuits. In endeavors of this nature, the low scorer is described as "more skeptical, more dubious about the rewards which might come from effort and involvement, and uncertain about risking his labors. He tends also to be somewhat withdrawn and dissatisfied with his current status."

10. Dominance (Dom): Both males and females scored significantly lower than the normative sample. The low-scoring person is described as being "unsure of himself, and indifferent to both the demands and the challenges of interpersonal life. He . . . avoids situations calling for choice and decision-making."

11. Endurance (End): The combined sample scored low on en-

durance. The typical low-scoring subject is characterized as "erratic and impatient, intolerant of prolonged effort or attention, and apt to change in an abrupt and quixotic manner."

12. Order (ord): Male CCO members reached a significantly low score, and the female sample was near significance. Persons low on the order scale are described in terms of quickness of temperament and reaction or impulsiveness.

13. Intraception (Int): Although no significant differences were observed for male or female CCO members, the combined sample attained significance in scoring low on intraception. The description of the low scorer states that in the use of intellectual talents, "he tends toward profligacy and intemperateness. . . . He is aggressive in manner, and quickly becomes bored and impatient where direct action is not possible."

14. Nurturance (Nur): "To engage in behaviors which extend material or emotional benefits to others." No significant differences were observed between the normative sample and CCO members.

15. Affiliation (Aff): Males scored signficantly lower on affiliation, while females tended to score low. "The low scorer is more individualistic and strong-willed, though perhaps not out of inner resourcefulness and independence. He tends to be less trusting, more pessimistic about life, and restless in any situation which intensifies or prolongs his contacts with others."

16. Heterosexuality (Het): Males scored significantly lower on this variable, while females did not. "The low scorer tends to be dispirited, inhibited, shrewd and calculating in his interpersonal relationships."

17. Exhibition (Exh): "To behave in such a way as to elicit the immediate attention of others." No differences were found.

18. Autonomy (Aut): "To act independently of other or of social values and expectations." No differences were found.

19. Aggression (Agg): "To engage in behaviors which attack or hurt others." No differences were found.

20. Change (Cha): Males scored significantly lower on this scale. The low-scoring person is defined as one who "seeks stability and continuity in his environment, and is apprehensive of ill-defined and risk-involving situations. In temperament he is patient and obliging, concerned about others, but lacking in verve and energy."

21. Succorance (Suc): The male sample scored higher than did the comparison group. The high scorer is one who is trusting, even naively so, in his faith concerning the integrity and benevolence of others; he is "dependent on others, seeks support, and expects to find it."

22. Abasement (Aba): Males scored significantly higher than did the

comparison group. Higher scorers are described as "not only submissive and self-effacing, but also appear to have problems of self-acceptance. They see themselves as weak and undeserving, and face the world with anxiety and foreboding. Their behavior is often self-punishing, perhaps in the hope of forestalling criticism and rejection from without."

23. Deference (Def): "To seek and sustain subordinate roles in relationships with others." No differences were observed.

24. Counseling readiness (Crs): A final scale (counseling readiness) was developed by Heilburn and Sullivan (1962) "to help in identifying counseling patients who are ready for help and who seem likely to profit from it. In this case the males scored significantly higher than the comparison group while the females tended to score lower, but not significantly so. The high scorer "is predominantly worried about himself and ambivalent about his status. He feels left out of things, unable to enjoy life to the full, and unduly anxious. He tends to be preoccupied with his problems and pessimistic about his ability to resolve them constructively." The low scorer is characterized by freedom from these concerns and "enjoys life in an uncomplicated way."

Ideal Descriptions

Since the purpose of asking subjects to describe the ideal group member was to gain normative information on the group's values, no attempt was made to score ideal descriptions and to contrast them with either group self-descriptions or self-descriptions from the college students comparison sample. Since the male and female portions of the sample had virtually identical descriptions of the ideal member, results from the combined male-female sample are presented. Adjectives which were checked significantly ($p \leq .05$) more often by members in describing the ideal group member, as compared with non-checked adjectives, were: calm, capable, clear-thinking, dependable, forgiving, friendly, gentle, honest, kind, meek, patient, peaceable, reliable, stable, understanding, warm, and wise.

DISCUSSION

Meaning of Self-Characterization ACL Data

The interpretation of results described above is not intended to imply rigorous analysis of the "personality" of CCO members. This would be impossible because of the "one-shot" research design we were forced to use, because of the flexibility inherent in the ACL as an analytical device, and because the device only measures a person's view of self. Rather, the purpose of the descriptions is to present a general characterization of members of CCO (as of 1971), in comparison with a normative sample of college students. These comments notwithstanding, it seems useful to discuss a kind of "modal personality" for females and for males separately (in contrast to normative sample data) before discussing the population of study as a whole and drawing conclusions.

Females viewed themselves, as reported, as somewhat reserved, tentative, and cautious in their approach to the problem. This would, of course, fit in with the sex-role definition given to CCO females (see chapter 5). Females also tended to check fewer favorable adjectives and more unfavorable adjectives. We are prone to take a fairly straightforward view concerning these two variables. The self-definition of female members of fundamentalist-oriented religious groups such as CCO may well tend to be negative, as indicated by the numbers of adjectives checked on both favorable and unfavorable scales.

All three variables just discussed may be subject to a type of response set. It is possible that norms of the group dictated the individuals filling out the ACL form according to certain definitions shared by the group. It is impossible at this point to ascertain whether this is the case or whether there is a true representation of "personality" given by the use of this instrument. We would suggest, however, that the dichotomy between what one says about one's self and what one "really is" may be more apparent than real. Stark (1971, p. 173) discusses this problem in his reference to the conflict in social science between cognitive and emotive theories of behavior. He says, "Cognitive theories are inclined to take seriously the role played by beliefs people hold and to regard beliefs as in large measure *learned* by the individual in interaction with others." We tend to share this perspective and think that something akin to the notion of self-fulfilling prophecy may function when people define themselves in a certain way.[7] The rather large literature on conversion, resocialization, "brainwashing," and related phenomena (see chapter 9) indicates at least that rapid and profound changes can occur, for instance, when individuals, made responsive for various reasons, encounter pervasive, open, and loving social situations.

Often, interpretations of number of favorable adjectives checked include the notion of modesty. Most CCO members are generally quite self-effacing. Perhaps checking fewer favorable adjectives is just another one of the indicators of this kind of self-definition. In terms of unfavorable adjectives, perhaps the less candid group is the normative sample. Many of our subjects, in their very supportive environment of the group, seemed to feel that they had nothing to lose by being honest and candid, and this should be taken into account in interpreting results.

That female CCO members tended to score lower on defensiveness and on self-confidence, self-control, and personal adjustment would be viewed by many as disturbing. The descriptions associated with low scores on these variables suggest that perhaps the pattern of personality being fostered in CCO is somewhat maladaptive (when compared with the normative sample), at least for females.

In terms of Murray's need-press system, females again reported what appears to be a somewhat "maladaptive" self perception. They scored lower on dominance, indicating a certain lack of surety (and possibly their sex role). They tended to score low on endurance, indicating an erratic and impatient nature, and low scoring on order is another indication of a possibly maladaptive syndrome.

With reference to male CCO members, we see a similar situation with some changes probably related to the culture of the group. We found a pattern in which males, compared with the normative sample, tended to check fewer favorable adjectives and more unfavorable ones. We also found males low on defensiveness, low on self-confidence, low on self-control, and low on personal adjustment, just as was the case with the females. On the fifteen variables involved in the Murray need-press system, the males had a slightly different pattern than did females. For instance, males scored low on achievement, dominance, endurance, order, intraception, affiliation, and heterosexuality. These low scores seem to cohere in a pattern thought by many to indicate maladaptivity in terms of a "normal" existence. Of particular interest may be the heterosexuality variable. Males are negatively reinforced for engaging in most kinds of sexual behavior except inside the bounds of marriage. Thus we appear to see a group of males acting in a somewhat nonmasculine manner, especially as masculinity is defined in the broader culture. Males also scored lower than the normative sample on change, higher on succorance and higher on abasement. Another difference between males and females was the fact that males scored higher on counseling readiness. This scale derives from the clinical concept of "available anxiety," which implies that the person is motivated to change and to improve. It does not indicate so much an overriding need for counseling as it does an openness for counseling in conjunction with a negative self-concept. In view of this, the higher score for males might be attributable to the possibility and expectation that males would move up the male-dominated status hierarchy in the group. This expectation does not apply to females, of course, who are encouraged to "know their place," and to pursue a simple, quiet, and unchanging life.

What might be said about the general pattern of personality that one defines in this group? The results remind one of Fromm's (1950) discussion about the differences between authoritarian and humanistic religions. Fromm, in this classic differentiation, pointed out that authoritarian religions have a deleterious effect on personality, rather than fostering growth and development. The authoritarianism inherent in fundamentalism is prevalent in CCO, and these data may indicate some negative effects of it. Whether or not CCO simply attracts such individuals or helps develop them into this type of personality after converting them appears to be something of a moot question. The fact is that individual group members do reveal the kind of self descriptions just described, so such patterns are fostered in one way or another.

Individual CCO members obviously have personality patterns that differ from a normative sample of college students to which they were compared. However, it is very difficult to say which group is "better off" than the other. Perhaps CCO has accomplished an end that many claim to seek—that is, to develop a viable alternative life-style with its attendant alternative personality patterns. The ideal descriptions data seem to illustrate a desire on the part of members to become a kind of person contrasted to the "normal, hard-driving" American, bent on achieving the Horatio Alger myth. The modal personality patterns also exhibit this tendency. This basic difference between "normal culture" and CCO culture should be kept in mind in any evaluation of this group.

One way to illustrate the problems of making hasty judgments about the ultimate value of the Jesus movement experience is to discuss further the concept of maladaptivity which we have employed in describing results. Our data do not necessarily mean that responses which might be interpreted as maladaptive in relation to those of a normal sample of college students are maladaptive *within the social context of this group*. This point is made in appreciation of the fact that "personality" is in large part dependent on situational contingencies. What might appear maladaptive to "objective observers" might be totally adaptive and functional, and that which would usually be designated acceptable, good, adaptive, and so on could be totally useless or even destructive in certain contexts. What should be understood, however, is the possible incongruity *between* social contexts.

People resocialized into the culture of this group may not "fit" easily in "normal" society again. This reasoning suggests an important qualification to any statement about the maladaptivity of personality patterns fostered by (or attracted to) such groups. Perhaps all we should say is that such personalities are maladaptive only *if* they involve people who are going into a context in which such personalities are demonstrably dysfunctional. (See Richardson & Simmonds, 1977, for more discussion on problems of interpreting personality assessment data.)

CCO does not explicitly serve a therapeutic purpose for resocializng members with reference to social demands *outside* of the group context (recall the chapter 2 discussion of the "integrative hypothesis"). Thus, it could be said that the experience in CCO would not generally be transferable to other contexts. There is disagreement, however, on this point (see Mauss & Peterson, 1973, who talk of the "half-way house" function of one movement group). Some would suggest that many movement members are at least being taught how to work, a propensity lacking in some modern youth. Others would go further and suggest that the personality pattern found in this group is quite functional for workers on an assembly line or in other similar tasks necessary in an industrialized society. (See Anthony, Robbins & Curtis, 1974, for a particularly thoughtful discussion of these issues.) We have also noted that many members are marrying and getting established in comparatively permanent social relationships, an occurrence that would possibly contribute to any future integration into "mainstream life" in society.

This type of consideration raises at least two additional points. One concerns delineating a good or optimum personality, and how it can best be achieved. Maslow (1962), Fromm (1950), and many others who have addressed this issue at length stress the value of personal autonomy to personality integration. Our tendency at this juncture in our research is to avoid making a final evaluation. More data have yet to be analyzed, and also certain types of important data about what happens to those who drop out of CCO (approximately 10 to 15 percent) are not yet accessible. We do tend to agree with Maslow and with Fromm, however, which implies our opposition to authoritarian structures—be they religious or otherwise. However, we must again point out that, according to the ideology of the group, the members *are* "self-actualized" in that they are "in God's will." Most readers would not accpet such a use of self-actualization, but even the usual meaning of the term has, we think, some application in describing those in leadership positions within CCO. (Our data include a few

198 Organized Miracles

leaders, but because of the anonymity of instrument administration we cannot isolate them to check this notion.)

There is also a related question of defining dysfunctionality. Do we mean dysfunction for the individual (and using what criteria) or do we mean dysfunctional for the greater society (again using what criteria)?

As an illustration of this problem, would it be that perhaps a totally "broken" or subservient individual would make the best type of worker in some job situations? A related question is whether or not the "fully developed" personality (in Maslow's terms) is a "poor fit" in some social contexts. We have no pat answer for these questions, but hope that our efforts in this chapter contribute some information of value to their resolution.

NOTES

1. The data in this chapter are discussed in some detail in Simmonds, Richardson, and Harder (1976). Simmonds (1977a) has also used a longitudinal comparison of scores across a two-and-one-half month resocialization period to postulate that an "addictive personality" might be present in this group. Because one form of analysis showed that there was no substantial personality change across time in the group, and because converts to this group had revealed patterns of dependency prior to conversion in their responses to questionnaire items, it was suggested that perhaps "conversion" might be a misnomer in describing affiliation with this group; in other words, affiliation might represent an attempt to perpetuate dependencies on external sources of gratification, this time within a religious context. In a nonparametric analysis of these longitudinal data, Simmonds (1977b) detected a slight pattern which suggests that perhaps resocialization might lead to the possible intensification of a "maladaptive" personality profile, at least in comparison with scores obtained from the normative population.
2. CCO (and virtually the entire Jesus movement) is a part of a much larger and growing interest in "tongue speaking," as evidenced by the neo-Pentecostal movement in many mainline Protestant denominations, the "Charismatic Renewal" in the Catholic church, and the rapid growth of classic Pentecostal groups around the world. See especially the works of Meredith McGuire (1974; 1975), Fichter (1975), and Harrison (1975) among others on the Catholic Charismatic Renewal, and the work by Reidy and Richardson (1975; 1978), Richardson and Reidy (1976; 1977), and Richardson (1973).
3. Personal communication with Dr. Harrison G. Gough, October 27, 1971.
4. It might seem more justifiable to compare the scores with results from a sample of *nonreligious* "hippies." However, normative data on such a population are neither available nor easily attainable. Therefore, the rough matching on age, educational level, and socioeconomic class characteristics was used to allow some comparison. The comparison group was obtained by Gough several years ago, and this too presents some prob-

lems of interpretation. However, even with these problems, the comparison still yields, we think, valuable information.

5. The .001 level was used in order to call attention to only the most substantial differences. Please note that using such a stringent significance level will lead to very few of the comparisons of females attaining statistical significance, because of the small n involved, although there are definite "trends" (e.g., at the .05 level of significance) within the female sample. Note that t-tests were used instead of a generally preferred analysis of variance because of the small number of females in the sample which would have called into question the interpretations of significant F scores and because original scores on the college student normative sample were no longer available from the Institute of Personality Assessment and Research in Berkeley. We do, however, know the n of the original sample (1600) and the standard deviation (10) and mean (50) for the standard distribution, and this lent itself to t-test analysis.

6. Other quotations in the results section are also from Gough and Heilbrun (1965).

7. We realize, of course, that one implication of adopting such a position means that we must accept the idea that the research situation, which involved a great deal of intense interaction between subjects and researcher, may have contributed to the self-definition process in a way that would have respondents changing in the direction of their own group's norms, even as they filled out the instruments and responded to interviewer questions. Such a result, however distasteful, seems unavoidable if such research is to be done at all. See Appendix A for more on this and related issues.

8

Alienation and Political Orientation

Throughout the 1960s and 1970s, there has been much concern both in the popular media and the scholarly literature with the multifaceted concept *alienation*. Parents, teachers, politicians, and employers evidence alarm over the "alienation" of youth, of workers, of voters, of individuals in general. Unfortunately, much as with the wide acceptance and limited understanding of Freudian concepts during the 1950s, the explanation during the last decade of widely varying behavior in terms of alienation has made the concept almost meaningless. Prison authorities may see their inmates as alienated people "striking out against the world." Youth workers explain delinquency, drug use, sexual misbehavior among young people as resulting from alienation. Political analysts blame lack of citizen participation in the political process on alienation of the people from their government and their society. Faulty workmanship and inefficiency are viewed as resulting from alienation. Students in high schools and universities often describe themselves as alienated and warmly embrace a dropout subculture which provides antihero role models. Radicals, especially those on the left such as the Weathermen or SDS are described in the media as alienated, as were members of the Symbionese Liberation Army. Just as neurotics, psychotics, and anal retentives dominated the 1950s, alienation seems to be the all-encompassing byword of more

201

recent times. Due to its easy and loose applicability, the concept of alienation has almost achieved the "wastebasket status" that the term neurotic has occupied for so long.

The immense literature on alienation within sociology evidences little agreement on the concept and on the best way to use the concept in empirical research. We will not attempt a thorough analysis and critiue of this literature here, but we will make some brief comments on some of that work and delineate our own views of how fruitfully to define the concept and use it in research such as that reported here. One way to proceed with such an analysis is to categorize approaches to alienation in some general, but theoretically important manner. Peter Berger (1967, p. 198) does this by implication in his seminal discussion of alienation when he comments that work on alienation and anomy has been confused "by the psychologization of both concepts." By this he seems to mean the tendency in the literature to treat alienation from a subjective and individual point of view. Some classic examples of this approach are the works of Seeman (1959) and of Keniston (1968), both of whose much-cited work is based on a methodology that requires asking subjects their feelings and thoughts about their life and work situations. This approach has yielded some interesting results, but its lack of conceptual clarity, criticized by Berger (1967) and Rigby (1974), among others, has made the term difficult to define and has contributed to the vulgarization of the term *alienation* in some scholarly and much popular writing.

Berger takes a more structural approach, using an importantly-modified Marxian perspective which is basically structural in its orientation.[1] Instead of relying on what people say about their personal condition, Berger seems much more willing to admit that *sometimes people do not understand their situation,* and that their views cannot be used as a sole criterion for any meaningful analysis. Indeed, the implication of his work is that a singular reliance on a subjective approach will mislead. Berger is particularly upset by those who confuse the concepts anomy and alienation (i.e., Clinard, 1957, and many others as well who follow the Seeman, 1959, tradition), and fail to see that the concepts are related, but in an inverse sort of relationship. Berger defines alienation (1967, p. 85) as a situation

> in which the social world and socialized self confront the individual as inexorable facticities analogous to the facticities of nature.
>
> Put differently, alienation is the process whereby the dialectical relationship between the individual and his world is lost to con-

sciousness. The individual "forgets" that his world was and continues to be co-produced by him. . . . The essential difference between the socio-cultural world and the world of nature is obscured—namely, the difference that men have made the first, but not the second.

The alienated state is sharply contrasted to a situation in which the individual does not feel normative constraints of the society of which he is a part. Such a "normless" situation has been talked of, since the time of Durkheim's *Suicide,* as *anomy.* Berger points out that alienation and anomy are contrasting tendencies, as he says (1967, p. 87), "the apprehension of the socio-cultural world in alienated terms serves to maintain its nomic structures with particular efficacy, precisely because it seemingly immunizes them against the innumerable contingencies of the human enterprise of world-building."

Rigby (1974) has also grappled with the problem of the conceptual clarity of alienation in a treatment similar to Berger's analysis. He criticizes (1974, pp. 50-51) such theorists as Seeman (1959), Nettler (1957), and Nisbet (1962) for focusing on the "subjective experience of estrangement from the social world," and contrasts this with the, "essentially Marxian perspective . . . of the alienated individual as one who is unaware that one possesses any control over life, for whom the ways of the world stem from the natural and inevitable order of things that individuals cannot choose but to follow."

Rigby then develops a fourfold typology, relating the two dichotomies "alienated-unalienated" to "estranged-unestranged," which may be viewed as an attempt to extend Berger's ideas. The attempt is noteworthy in the context of our study, although Rigby's basic idealism about the contemporary commune movement and his lack of appreciation of one crucial distinction made by Berger detract from his analytical treatment. Rigby defines each of his types as follows (1974, p. 50):

Alienated-estranged
> Alienated individuals, estranged from existing social order but unable to conceive of the possibility of social change.

Alienated-unestranged
> Alienated individuals but feeling at one with the existing order of things. They are unable to conceive of any alternative social order.

Unalienated-estranged

The utopians at odds with society but able to conceive of the possibility and desirability of social change.

Unalienated-unestranged

Those who are aware of man's ability to control his social environment but who are attached to the status quo and who do not seek radical social change.

Those familiar with Berger's writings, and with the Marxian tradition from which they derive in part, will question the designation of the last category (unalienated-unestranged) as "unalienated." Rigby has chosen not to adopt an objective position that makes a structural analysis of a person's position and has relied more on *what the occupants of a category say* in placing them in said categorization scheme. The fact that individuals do not perceive themselves as alienated is only an evidence of the effects of "complete" systems of thought, with their "double theodicies" (Berger, 1967, p. 194) that not only justify the position of the poor, but of the rich as well. Richardson (1971) has pointed out that representatives of this latter class are often indeed alienated, but their lack of "estrangement" (in Rigby's language) often makes them very active defenders of the status quo or supporters of reactionary-oriented movements. *Such individuals may be alienated, but they are certainly not withdrawn and inactive.* They differ considerably from Keniston's alienated youth (1968), who were nearly totally "estranged." Instead, such "unestranged" individuals epitomize the non-anomic but alienated state and are perhaps only slightly more well-dressed "happy robots," which is Rigby's term for the "alienated-unestranged" category.

Those slightly less enamored than Rigby with the commune movement will also take some issue with the "mantle of salvation" pressed upon the perhaps equally disillusioned members of the commune movement. Apparently Rigby sees certain parts of the commune movement as one of the sole possessors of truth and light, trying desperately to awaken an otherwise alienated and "unestranged" world.[2] Only Rigby's personal preference, we think, is used to establish the participants in the commune movements as being, by definition, less alienated than others. While we readily admit that some volition is usually involved in participating in something like the commune movement, we would suggest that such volition usually operates within structural boundaries, and would note that most of the participants entered the movement at a time and "place" when they were much less "structurally inhibited" than many others in society (most communards were from relatively young and well-to-do social positions). No matter what one thinks of the idealism of some in the commune movement and of the effects of that idealism, recognition must be given to the fact that those ideas may well be, for some (even many), nothing more than an ex post facto justification of a somewhat arbitrary decision. In short, the approach to an intolerable situation may well be the resignation that Rigby talks about with reference to his "alienated-estranged" category, but that resignation may well take the form of joining a commune. No one class of people has a corner on the idealism market.

Rigby seems to be aware of some problem in his thought, for he delimits his "chosen category" to include left-oriented groups of a Marxian bent in an attempt not to include certain communal groups that are "obviously" alienated. He says (1974, p. 56): "Marx differed from the religious utopians of an earlier age who legitimated their millennial claims by reference to some supernatural, sacred realm. Such people could be viewed as constituting a fifth social type—that of alienated utopian—according to the degree to which they denied man his world-creating ability and located this power in some superhuman entity or power." [3]

THE ALIENATING PROPENSITY OF RELIGION

We have already (chapter 2) criticized Rigby's relegation of "religious" communes to something of a residual status and will not critique his problematic typology of alienation further in that vein. However we were, at the outset of our research, interested in whether or not the members of the group we were studying were "alienated" in a more classical use of the term, and using the work of Berger, we developed an admittedly tentative and exploratory empirical approach to some of Berger's ideas relating religion to alienation. Before proceeding with a presentation of how we "operationalized" and even perhaps extended Berger's ideas, some explanation should be given about how Berger relates religion to his notions about alienation and anomy. His approach is certainly worth investigating in some depth, if for no other reason than that his work has seldom been made use of in empirical research.[4]

For Berger, society is possible because of three closely interrelated dialectic processes—those of *externalization, objectivation,* and *internalization.* Man is compelled, due to his biological makeup, to "externalize" himself, and as individuals externalize themselves in common activity they collectively produce their "world." This world becomes an objective reality through the process of objectivation. Then, as it is internalized through socialization, it becomes part of the subjective consciousness. Society is a product of human activity, and it confronts man as an objective reality. When man forgets that his social world is constructed by him and other men, this is alienation, as the quotes in the introductory portions of this chapter evidence. What is of special interest to us here is the part played in this alienation (which Berger seems to treat as a "natural" and "original" state of man) by religion.

Berger refers to the world constructed by human beings as a *nomos,* and discusses the "co-extensive" nature of the nomos and the cosmos, by which he means the tendency of man to project externalized meanings onto the entire universe. He says (1967, p. 25), "Religion is the human enterprise by which a sacred cosmos is established," and gives numerous examples of the designation of things as sacred, as he focuses on how religion functions to make sacred things that would perhaps otherwise not be sacred. In his discussion, he produces the profound insight (1967, pp. 26-27) that the most important opposed category to that of the sacred is not that of "profane," but, "that of chaos. The sacred cosmos emerges out of chaos and continues to confront the latter as its terrible contrary.... The sacred cosmos, which transcends and includes man in its ordering of reality, thus provides man's ultimate shield against the terror of anomy.... All the nomic constructions ... are designed to keep this terror at bay. In the sacred cosmos, however, these constructions achieve their ultimate culmination—literally, their apotheosis."

While admitting that it is possible to have a "nonsacred cosmos," Berger points out that it is a historical fact that most cosmoi in human history have been "sacred." This fact supports his claim that religion has played an important part in "the human enterprise of worldbuilding." Proceeding logically from *world construction,* Berger then discusses the function of religion in *maintaining* the nomoi arrived at through man's insatiable world-building propensities. He says (1967, pp. 32-33):

> Religion has been the historically most widespread and effective instrumentality of legitimation.... Religion legitmates so effectively because it relates the precarious reality constructions of empirical societies with ultimate reality.
>
> Religion legitimates social institutions by bestowing upon them an ultimately valid ontological status, that is, by *locating* them within a sacred and cosmic frame of reference.

Berger then presents a thorough and somewhat compelling discussion of "the alienating propensity of religion" (1967, p. 87). He says,

"Religion has been so powerful an agency of nomization precisely because it has also been a powerful, agency of alienation." His admittedly Feurbachian argument reaches a controversial crescendo with the following passage (1967, p. 90):

> Religion posits the presence in reality of beings and forces that are alien to the human world. Be this as it may, the assertion, in all its forms, is not amenable to empirical inquiry. What is so amenable, though, is the very strong tendency of religion to alienate the human world in the process. In other words, in positing the alien over against the human, religion tends to alienate the human from itself.
>
> It is in *this* sense (and *not* in the sense of regarding the religious assertion as such as epistemologically valid) that we feel entitled to associate religion with false consciousness. . . . Whatever may be the merits of religious explanations of the universe at large, their empirical tendency has been to falsify man's consciousness of that part of the universe shaped by his own activity, namely the socio-cultural world. This falsification can also be described as mystification. The socio-cultural world, which is an edifice of human meanings, is overlaid with mysteries posited as non-human in their origins. All human productions are, at least potentially, comprehensible in human terms. The veil of mystification thrown over them by religion prevents such comprehension. The objectivated expressions of the human become dark symbols of the divine.

There is much more to what Berger has to say on the alienating propensity of religion, but that lengthy quote will suffice for now as a demonstration of his position at the time of his writing.[5] We thought his ideas provocative and also potentially testable, although we would be the first to admit that our efforts are meager when compared with the scope of Berger's theorizing, as we only address a small part of his thought. Now we will indicate the way in which we made Berger's ideas more specific and translated them into research questions.

THEORETICAL SPECIFICATIONS
AND OPERATIONALIZATIONS

Berger's analysis is quite general in nature, and nowhere (of which we are aware) in his discussion of alienation does he make any theoretical differentiations concerning the relationship of alienation to *types of religion,* different *levels of commitment* and *amount of exposure* to certain religions. He seems to be talking about religion (a certain kind, that is) as a monolithic phenomenon that is ipso facto all-pervasive in its effects. Such an idea about religion seems potentially quite limiting. It seemed to us that, especially given the increasing pluralism in American society (and much of the rest of the world as well), the type of religion to which one was exposed and socialized, and to which one has developed a commitment, would perhaps be very crucial in terms of the theorizing of Berger. In short, it seemed possible to develop a set of hypotheses about the relationship of alienation to various types of religion, to various amounts (and even kinds) of exposure, and to levels of commitment.

For a start, it seemed that the alienation of which Berger talked would occur most in situations where people were thoroughly exposed and committed to a religion that was, as a part of its basic tenets, directly and overtly *supportive* of the social order in a given society. The polar opposite case would be a situation in which people were exposed and committed to a religion that was directly and overtly *nonsupportive* of the social order. In between these two polar cases are varying "shades of grey," as the three variables—type of religion, "amount" of exposure, and degree of commitment—vary, sometimes together and sometimes not. We do not claim that this specification is the last word on how Berger's ideas might be better understood and used in research. Indeed, for our own research such specifications may be somewhat superfluous, if only because of the particular type of religion and kinds of individuals (with certain background characteristics) included. However, we think that our attempt at expanding Berger's idea somewhat will help place in context the bit of research that we did in this area. To this end the following table is presented, indicating various levels of the three variables, all of which have been treated in a somewhat arbitrary manner in terms of grossness of measurement.

Even though we were not, in this research, involved directly in a comparative study on this issue, perhaps our ideas will be applied by others. With this possibility in mind, we will give a bit more information about why we chose the three variables we selected, how we interpreted them, and why we decided on the divisions within each one. First, type of religion seems easy to understand, even though to propose such a distinction is at once a criticism of Berger, who, we think, paints his masterful canvas with strokes too broad. It seems quite logical that the type of religion believed and lived by a person would be extremely important in assessing the contribution. Here we are obviously not concerned with the differences between, say, most

TABLE 8.1
Relationship of Amount of Exposure, Level of Commitment, and Type of Religion

"Amount" of Exposure	Supportive of Social Order				Not-Supportive of Social Order			
	Overt		Covert		Covert		Overt	
	High Com.	Low Com.	High Com.	Low Com.	High Com.	Low Com.	High Com.	Low Com.
High								
Medium								
Low								

Methodists and most Baptists. The differences between those two groups are probably inconsequential in terms of the theorizing of Berger. Plainly most basically Christian groups would gather at one end of a continuum with the underlying variable being support for the social order. Some might be slightly more covert in their support (and might even disguise it with critical rhetoric, an important point within the context of this research), but in the main they are supportive. In point of fact, one might have to abandon substantive definitions of religion in order to "allow" anything to appear on the nonsupportive end of the continuum.

In terms of the segmentation of the continuum into four parts, we can only state that we were trying to make the important qualitative distinction of supportive-nonsupportive and, within each of these, to focus on the overt-covert (direct-indirect or latent) distinction. A given group might well shift in terms of its emphasis from covert to overt, but seldom would there be a group that moved from one end of the continuum to the other. One might possibly cite the English Quaker history as an example of such a shift, but it should be kept in mind that the shift was perhaps dealing with only a relatively few issues, that it occurred gradually, and that during the time of the change the greater society itself was also "moving."

The other two variables might well be considered together; however, we prefer to think of them as variables that can have independent effects. If there is any credence to the "socialization hypothesis," then the "amount" of exposure, particularly at certain times in one's life, seems important to consider by itself (see chapter 9 for more on this). Certainly, lengthy religious socialization as a child would be expected to have an effect, even if it only inculcates "religious need," as discussed by Yinger (1974). But, we mean even more by "amount," for we think that what might be called the "quality" of the religious socialization is also important. For some individuals, the socialization might be lengthy but not very "intense," while for others the length might be shorter but the "intensity" greater. Persons low on both "intensity" and length of time would be classified by us as "low" on amount. All others would fit in the other two gross categories, depending on the assessment of individual cases.

By "intensity" we mean that those responsible for a person's religious socialization make determined attempts to inculcate the person (or allow others to) with certain specific beliefs and values. An example of such an extremely intense situation would be the new child-care approach of the Children of God group. Children in this organization **are** started at a very early age in a rigorous Montessori-based educational program, a program which is quite disciplined and has high expectations in terms of performance for the children. And the content of the experience is nearly totally fundamentalist-oriented and Biblically-based. Children of two and three are reciting Bible verses; all stories read to them are Bible stories; their games and drama experiences are centered around the Bible; and they even have Biblical names. CCO is perhaps not so extreme, but its children (and the children in many a conservative and fundamentalist church) receive something only slightly less intense, as a part of their religious socialization. A contrasting case would be in a situation where children were given much more freedom in their religious training and not forced to absorb only certain ideas and values.

Concerning level of commitment (or perhaps "saliency"), the focus is on the *present*. No matter what the early socialization experience of the individuals, what do they claim to believe now? And how strongly do they hold their beliefs? We fully realize that this variable interacts with religious socialization and with type of religion, since some religious groups expect members to hold beliefs very strongly, in something of a "do-or-die" attitude, and members are taught this. However, we expect that, if ways could be found to measure each of these variables with any precision, there would be some independent effects of level of commitment (or saliency). (See Bahr, Bartel, & Chadwick, 1971, for one sound attempt.) Aside from that consideration though, it must be noted that this variable does "measure" the present situation, whereas "amount" of exposure refers to the past.

Given that brief theoretical excursus, where would we expect members of CCO to "locate" in Table 8.1 and what can we say about their "position?" We thought that the ideology of CCO (see chapter 1) would place them in the "supportive-covert" category, and that within that class we expected a high or medium "amount" of exposure, coupled with a high level of "commitment." We accept the fact that the rhetoric of the group has in the past been rather "nonsupportive" and even "overt," but in this instance we thought it more fruitful to look at the *latent* consequences of their life-style, while realizing that some aspects of that life-style could be viewed as somewhat nonsupportive (communal living, for instance). We now think that time has vindicated our original assessment, and that few CCO members would argue with our earlier assessment. In terms of the "meaning" of this assessment of the group for the purpose at hand—"testing" some of Berger's notions (and our extensions) dealing with the alienating propensity of religion—we think CCO offers a good test of what Berger says because they are fairly close to the "supportive" end of the continuum of support for the social order. If there are any effects of joining and being in such a group in terms of alienation (as Berger defines it), then they should show up in this kind of group, with its high level of commitment, and with the anticipated propensity for most to have had relatively "intense" religious socialization (which was found generally to be the case, as reported in chapter 6).

There is at least one theoretical "sticky wicket" in terms of our extension and specification of Berger's thought. In the latter part of the discussion on religion and alienation, he issues an important qualifier when he says (in contrast, he claims, to Marx) that religion can also furnish the impetus for *de-alienation*. He points out that religious legitimations can be withdrawn from social institutions, because any religion that posits a transcendent god must at the same time grant autonomy to that transcendent deity, and that deity's autonomy is sometimes (though rarely) used to critique the social order. This "religiously induced skepticism about commonsense verities" (1967, p. 97) is illustrated, for instance, by mystical religions (or religions with a mystical possibility) which seem prone to this, according to Berger, who says (1967, p. 98), "Mystical religion, with its radical depreciation not only of the value but the reality status of the empirical world, has a similar de-alienating potential. To the mystic this world and all its works, including those of 'ordinary' religious practice, are relativized."

Thus Berger seems to let himself off the hook by saying that the same monolithic and undifferentiated variable "religion" can cause both alienation and de-alienation. His only comment that helps extract him (and us) from this "box" concerns the relative rarity of the latter event. He certainly does not give enough information to be credited with developing a "theory of de-alienation," and only offers a hint with his reference to mysticism. We are not dissuaded by the comments on de-alienation from our view that groups such as CCO offer something of an ideal case for testing his major idea, for we do agree that such de-alienating episodes are extremely rare on the collective level (the individual level might well be another matter, however), if only because of the logical and psychological difficulties such efforts entail. Early in our research project we became firm in our conviction that CCO was *not* such a historically unique group in this respect (even if they are somewhat unique in some other important ways). Our assessment was based in part on our observance of a nearly systematic suppression of some tendencies toward mystical experiences (such as only allowing glossolalia during private devotion and prayer times), as well as on other information. Because of this assessment, we decided to proceed with what is only an exploratory and tenative approach to research on alienation and religion, as based on Berger's theorizing.

For the sake of clarity, before proceeding with details of our research, we will reiterate the distinction between the approach of Berger which we have generally adopted for this study, and that of theorists of the other major tradition in alienation exemplified by Seeman or Nettler, for example. Nettler or Seeman would probably, like Berger, consider CCO members to be alienated. The reasoning behind the apparent similarity of expectations would, however, be quite disparate. For Nettler, members of CCO would probably reflect alienation through their separation from the world, their refusal to support directly its major institutions, and their claim to reject society's cultural values and norms—they would therefore be viewed as estranged from, or unfriendly toward their society. They may, in addition, be described by the press and others either friendly and hostile to them as alienated because of their rejection of and removal from society, their failure to participate in its processes and structures, and their attempt to build a separate viable life-style. But for Berger, their alienation would be reflected in their implicit or latent support of the structures of society, their view of the society as given, as objective, by the "taken-for-grantedness" of society's structures and institutions, and their view of them as immutable, extant, created by God rather than man-made and thus challengeable. In Nettler's terms, persons involved in the student movement, the antiwar movement, SDS, as well as members of the Jesus movement could be viewed as alienated. In Berger's terms however, the alienated would *not* be rioting in the streets, calling for an end to American imperialism, protesting the decisions of the administration, or demanding civil rights. Rather, they would be those who do *not* perceive societal structures as particularly challengeable—and this group would, we thought, include most members of CCO and the greater Jesus movement. Now for a look at exatly what we did, and the results.

METHODS

Our efforts took two forms. One was to develop a few questions for an "alienation scale" that seemed to access the domain of substance addressed by Berger and by us, although it should be understood that the questions were developed by the authors with very little aid from others or with little pretesting.[6] The questions, which are presented below, were asked of a group, as reported in chapter 6, predominantly made up of males who were, on the average, twenty-one years of age. Common sense might cause one to expect that this group of eminently draftable subjects would, in 1971, overwhelmingly disagree with all the questions. However, *if* we have correctly tapped the domain Berger talks about (and if we and Berger are correct in our theorizing), the modal response category should be agreement with the statements.

Alienation Scale Questions

1. Do you think that God has a hand in the nomination and election of our country's leaders?
2. Do you think that the leaders of our country are guided by God in making decisions?
3. Do you think it is a sin to break a law of the land?
4. Do you think that the United States generally is an instrument of God in the area of world politics?

We also asked a number of related questions about attitudes toward authority and about politics in general. Although hampered by a limitation of data—only retrospective data was gathered (see discussion of this problem in Appendix A)—we attempted to assess what changes had occurred as a result of joining the group (or of conversion, as CCO members prefer to say). And we tried to assess the implications of the group's ideology, which all members are expected to accept heartily, for our ideas about alienation. Some information relevant to the concerns of this chapter has already been presented in chapter 1 (on group ideology) and in chapter 6 (background characteristics of members).

ALIENATION RESULTS

First, we will examine the responses to the four questions deliberately designed to tap alienation as Berger conceptualized it. Table 8.2 includes a summary of the responses to the four major questions. Note that the questions were "open-ended" and allowed the respondents to discuss the issues raised. Some of these comments are quite interesting, but in the main nearly all were codable as either "agree" or "disagree," although we had to allow for qualified responses in some cases. When responses were not codable as an "agree" or "disagree," we have, for the purposes of this presentation, disallowed them. Such cases, when the comments were self-contradictory and no main line of thought could be discerned, were relatively rare, involving only as much as 10% of the cases with one question (number 2).

We do not want to read too much into these results, but it does seem to us that there is some support given for Berger's general notion, and for some of our own ideas. The general response to the questions, as a set, was positive, with only number 4 (U.S. as an instrument of God in world politics) not achieving an agreement response from a majority of the subjects. To be honest, we were somewhat surprised to see the percentage of agreement with that question as high as it was, given the population of study and the "events of the times" (this was asked in 1971, at the height of the Vietnam conflict). It is not surprising to see less of a tendency to agree, the more the questions were potentially relatable to the Vietnam conflict and other more domestic ills. Thus, the lower agreement responses to questions 2 and 4 seem understandable.

A closer look at the data reveals even some indirect support in the negative responses. For instance, the twenty-seven who disagreed with question 2 (leaders guided by God in decision-making) generally were nearly unanimous in their explanation that although God knows what

TABLE 8.2
Responses to Alienation Questions

Question	Agree[a]	Disagree[a]	Total[b]
1	77 (95%)[c]	5 (6%)[c]	82
2	50 (65%)	27 (35%)	77
3	75 (91%)	7 (9%)	82
4	38 (47%)	43 (53%)	81

1. Do you think that God has a hand in the nomination and election of our country's leaders?

2. Do you think that the leaders of our country are guided by God in making decisions?

3. Do you think it is a sin to break a law of the land?

4. Do you think that the United States generally is an instrument of God in the area of world politics?

[a] Includes some qualified responses
[b] Totals differ because some questions were not responded to in codable fashion
[c] Percentages are based on the number of codable responses for the specific question.

man does, he does not intervene in man's decisions because "he has given his children free will." In explaining their negative responses to question 4 (U.S. instrument of God in world politics), many members said that God was no more involved in the politics of this country than he was in the politics of any other country, a response that might be interpreted as supportive of the theorizing being tested. A check of these data controlling for previous religious affiliation showed no dramatic effects of this variable, possibly indicating that the socialization experiences did not have a presently discernible differential effect, or that the immediate experience was of much greater import, with its requirement of high commitment.

Other related data also support the general picture of alienated people being attracted to or formed by this group. One illustration is our finding that 98% (87) of the persons interviewed felt that established laws must be upheld whether or not they personally agreed with them. (This compares to the 13% who, in the Yankelovich, 1968 survey, affirmed that people should "(abide) by laws you do not agree with," p. 69). Approximately half of the CCO members justified their response in religious terms, with 43 persons saying that the Bible or the Lord says to "obey man's ordinances," Another 22 gave more general responses to the effect that order must be maintained. We found no differences by previous denomination affiliation. In response to our question "Do you think that the elected officials know what is better for the country than the average person does?" 28 persons (32%) said no and 9 said they didn't know, while 44, or half of the 88 respondents, answered this question positively. The most frequent explanation for this response, however, was in terms of the job requirements and the amount of information held by these officials, not in terms of direct religious reasoning. Another illustration of their lack of political interest was the finding that 67 of the members (76%) said that nothing can be accomplished by being politically active, the main reason given being that "the Lord has control" over what occurs. Sixty (68%) stated that the only way for man to change his own life was to come to the Lord or to rely on God.

One of the most difficult questions in this vein involved the military draft and military involvement. Almost all CCO members interviewed had indicated that it was a sin to break a law of the land. Yet when asked, "If a person is drafted, is it his personal duty to serve in his country's armed services?", not quite half were willing to say yes. Thirty percent said it was not a duty and 17 said "it depends on the situation" or "it is up to the individual." Members seemed to have difficulty resolving the contradictions between the group view that the laws of the land must be supported and their belief that it is a sin to kill, a likely eventuality if one were serving in Vietnam. Members attempted to resolve this contradiction through religious explanations. They were likely to respond that if God allowed them to be drafted, they would probably be doing his work among the other soldiers. Others felt that "the Lord wouldn't allow them to be placed in such a situation." Almost all of the respondents indicated that they would refuse to kill under any circumstances, even if instructed to do so by their commanding officer, possibly indicating a contradiction between God's law and man's law in this case, and that they would prefer to break man's law than to commit the sin of killing, which might be viewed as a "more important, God-given law." [7] Six persons who said they would kill if instructed to do so responded that the Lord would not allow them to unless it was his will—the Lord had control over it.

To further investigate Berger's ideas, information on the respondents' evaluation of this society and their attitude about involvement in it was gathered. It is one thing to conform to and support the institutions of a society which one positively evaluates, and quite another to accept or conform to the institutions of a society of which one disapproves. Implicit in Berger is the idea that no matter what an individual's evaluation of his society, if he is alienated, he will accept its structures and institutions. The institutional structure will not be viewed as alternative man-made forms but as unchallengable reality. Most of the members (83%) felt that overall this society was bad, usually giving the explanation that it was not following the "ways of the Lord," or that it was corrupt and sinful. (This may be compared to the 35% positive response rate to, "We are a sick society," in Yankelovich's, 1968 survey, p. 121.) Only 22 (25%) of the respondents gave more "secular" explanations for their evaluation of society, saying such things as everyone is out for himself or that the world is filled with violence, hatred, drugs, and fornication, and even these responses are relatable to the ideology espoused by the group. Despite these negative evaluations, the great majority of members felt that the society must be supported, with as we have said, 91% agreeing that it is a sin to break a law and 98% feeling laws must be upheld whether or not they agreed with them. They seemed caught up in a deep "love-hate" conflict relationship with their society that is resolved only by an acquiescing withdrawal from it.

POLITICAL SELF-CHARACTERIZATIONS AND INVOLVEMENT

Closely related to the previous results are data dealing with political self-characterizations, and with previous and present levels of political involvement. The data on "before" (retrospective data) and "after" self-characterizations are presented in Table 8.3, along with the percentage of change in such self-characterizations.

Even granting that there may be special problems of interpretation associated with these self-reported data (see Appendix A discussion), we still note a striking pattern in the table. Although a relatively large number of members (27) indicated that they were totally disinterested in politics before affiliation, the majority were at least willing to self-characterize themselves retrospectively using one of the categories offered. Radical and liberal were the most prevalent responses of those who so chose, although care should be taken in interpreting the import of this information. For example, 72% of those interviewed said they had not participated in any political activities or groups before affiliation.

The "before" retrospective characterizations do indicate that CCO members may have been somewhat different than "normal" people their age. The Yankelovich (1968, p. 121) survey indicates a smaller

TABLE 8.3

Political Self-Characterization Before and After Affiliation

Characterize self as:	Before joining	After joining	Change
Conservative	8	6	-25%
Moderate	6	5	-17%
Liberal	19	1	-95%
Radical	23	3	-87%
Nothing, don't care	27	71	+163%
Total	83*	86	

*Totals differ because some information was not ascertained. Eighty-eight were interviewed.

percent claiming to be radicals (4-5%), but on the other hand, the "forced choice" Yankelovich survey apparently did not allow a "nothing," or "don't care" category, which may have inflated the numbers in the conservative to moderate categories in that survey. Our own research revealed 32% in the "nothing" category, which helps balance the 27% claiming to have been radical. In short, CCO members were from all over the political map, with perhaps a tendency to have been more radical than those in the Yankelovich survey.

Although we expected, on the basis of work such as that of Johnson (1966), that persons from conservative religious backgrounds would be more likely to characterize themselves as politically conservative prior to affiliation, we found that controlling for denomination did have an effect on the members' description of themselves as politically conservative, moderate, liberal, or radical. Neither did denomination affect the individual's participation in political activities. For the most part then, members came from families that were relatively politically inactive and which were politically moderate or conservative. When asked, members would characterize themselves according to general political orientation, but they were nevertheless primarily politically uninvolved, as had been their parents. Since the press and many authors have stressed the prior political involvement to members of the Jesus movement, we examined more closely those who were politically involved. Of these who claimed a general political orientation prior to affiliation, 28% claimed to have participated in political activities or organizations. Consistent with popular notions, of those who participated, radicals were most likely to be involved politically, with conservatives least likely. Of the 23 persons who characterized themselves as radical before joining, over half (13) indicated that they had participated in political activities or groups. Of the 24 persons who indicated that they had participated in political groups or activities, none were conservatives, 2 were moderates, 6 were liberals and 13 were radicals. Thus, a relatively small segment of CCO members did come from somewhat politically active backgrounds. These persons reported that they had friends who were involved in radical groups such as SDS and Weathermen, and that they too were involved in such groups. However, this segment comprised less than 15% of the total number of members interviewed, and in addition, *only 2* said that they were "very active" in political groups or activities. These figures are comparable with the estimate by Yankelovich (1974, p. 8), who says 10-15% of the college population comprises a small core of "political radicals (who) took the lead in interpreting the war...." The CCO figure is slightly higher than Keniston's (1968, p. 340) estimate that the active protesters' number was "extremely small—zero per cent on most American campuses, and probably nowhere more than ten per cent." This slight tendency for CCO members to *claim* a more active political history could be an artifact of the research situation (see Appendix A), but even if not, we are convinced that CCO members as a whole were not greatly different from others of their age, class, and educational background. Consistent with the work of such authors as Flacks (1967) on political involvement across generations, we would expect that persons coming from fairly religious, upper middle-class homes, in which parents generally were not politically active, would themselves generally be politically disinterested and uninvolved. This is in general what we found, contrary to views of some commentators who seemed to think most Jesus movement participants were exradicals.

If prior to joining, a general pattern of political uninvolvement among converts prevailed, we would expect, based on theorizing of Berger, that such involvement would be even less after joining. As we have already said, members view themselves as "in the world but not of the world," as physically a part of society, but having little interest in it nor commitment to it except as it represents a pool of potential converts. Members have limited and structured contact with persons of the greater society and its institutions. The group discourages the view of the world as alterable by structural changes and encourages change through individual transformation. New members, then, would be expected to decrease their political contacts with society and to further disassociate themselves from a position of any political involvement. (This does *not* mean all contact with society ceases—evangelical activity may actually result in *more* contact, but of a more "people-changing" variety).

We found that political involvement and interest changed dramatically after persons joined, as indicated in Table 8.3. Whereas prior to joining, 27 persons responded "nothing, or don't care" to our question of political affiliation, this number increased to 71, or 82% of those interviewed after joining. Furthermore, *the major changes occurred among young people who had identified themselves as radical or liberal prior to joining.* Although 23 persons had retrospectively characterized themselves as radicals and 19 as liberals before joining, only 3 said they were radicals (and one said liberal) after joining. These young people who collectively were not particularly politically-oriented (in terms of activity) before joining, became even less so after joining. Most had not been very involved in politics in their society, or in vigorous attempts to challenge or change the system before joining, and they became even more politically uninvolved after joining. After joining, the perspective of members was overwhelmingly "people changing." Eighty-six percent were totally unconcerned with politics, only 15 indicated any political identification, and 11 of these identified as either moderate or conservative. None were then active in any political organizations or activities.

One reason for this strong deemphasis of things political is that the source of and solution for the problems of the individual and the society were viewed in religious terms, as described in our earlier discussion of CCO ideology. Most respondents saw the main problem in the world today as sin (35%) or nonacceptance of the Lord (47%). Only 6 persons felt that the main problem was of a more political or social nature (i.e., war, crime, racism, or poverty). Their solution to the problems facing the world was "to bring more people to the Lord." With such a nonsecular perspective as this, it is not surprising to find that persons were not involved in direct confrontations with the world. As Stark (1965) and Gary Marx (1967) would suggest, we should expect persons with an other-worldly orientation to be generally uninvolved in this world. Religious utopias imply no social overhaul. They customarily sanction, at least implicitly, the prevailing institutions and are implicitly committed to the status quo. Withdrawal from the world physically or in terms of non-participation is more likely than confrontation with the world.

Given these views of the world, it may appear initially contradictory that members felt it was possible to change this world, and that such should be attempted. However, both the problems and their solutions are defined in religious terms, and even that was a "special interpretation" (see the Introduction's discussion of the growth and spread of a generalized belief for more on this notion). The major problems of sin and nonacceptance of the Lord can be solved through the acceptance of Jesus by more people. Seventy-two (82%) of those interviewed indicated that the acceptance of Jesus and God would provide the solution for the major world problems. Apparently, attempts to change or replace the societal institutions are seen as meaningless and in contradiction to the Lord's command of conformity to them. According to CCO members interviewed, any change in society must come, not from institutional change, but from a change "in man's heart." If members felt they could not change the society in which they lived, how did they feel about man's ability to change his own life? Over half (57%) said that man could change his life while 35 (39%) said he could not. Twenty-five (72%) of those persons who said man could not change his life felt that only God can change man. Furthermore, of those who felt man could change his life, a few explained that man has free will, but 70% indicated that man could change himself only through coming to the Lord, and the rest indicated that man needed God's help to change himself.

CONCLUSIONS

The Jesus movement emerged during a period of violent ruptures within American society. It shared with other social movements an awareness of the difficulties of war, racism, drug addiction, violence, and other social problems. But its message was generally one of disengagement rather than confrontation. The solutions were not to be found through changes in the society, a suggestion which may have made a certain amount of sense to some of these young people who had been part of the more bloody confrontations, or who were so acutely aware of the meaning of the killings at Kent State and Jackson State. The solution was to come through individual change (see the Introduction). The only way to change society was to change men's hearts. Wicked and sinful people, non-Christians, would by necessity create and maintain a world of sin. Major social problems, drug addiction, war, and the like could be solved only if people took Jesus into their hearts, not by marching, protesting, petitioning, or burning draft cards. The temporal conjunction of the Jesus movement with other social movements and its emergence during a particular historical period had led some authors to view the Jesus movement as drawing its members primarily from the ranks of the disenchanted radicals and politically involved young people. The assumption seems to have been that persons who were actively engaged in attempts to change society recognized the futility of their efforts and through disappointment, or a sudden insight into the "real" situation, recognized that individual change was the only possibility. Such authors as Pederson (1971), Plowman (1971), and Blessit (1971), for example, report that the Jesus movement gained large numbers of recruits from political activists. Some authors, including Streiker (1971, p. 10) view the Jesus movement as the last alternative for its members—"having tried everything—drugs, sex, politics, materialism, Krishna consciousness, transcendental meditation, surfing, racing, and hippie communes—and found nothing, they have turned to Jesus" (an idea with some promise—see chapter 9). Journalistic reports and other media coverage stress prior political involvement of the Jesus people. Jesus movement publications and books stressed the movement's success in recruiting political radicals and transforming them into peaceful, law-abiding, loving Christians. It might also occur to readers that perhaps state and federal agencies had incorporated this view—hence their direct and indirect support of the movement, as evidenced by the tax-free status of CCO (and other such organizations), its establishmeni as an alternative service organization, its status as a labor camp, and the like.

Other more theoretical work on the relationship between politics and religion would not support the popular position that politically involved persons are particularly amenable to membership in a religious group. Eric Hoffer's "true believer" philosophy and those who share his perspective aside, most studies have indicated an *inverse relationship* between political involvement and religious involvement. Gary Marx (1967) found a lack of political involvement among active churchgoers and Glock and Stark (1965) assert that persons who look forward to an afterlife are not likely to become deeply involved in the social and political activities of this one.

These more scholarly treatments are helpful in understanding why most commentators were plainly wrong in their assessments of the movement as being made up of converted political activists (if our data are at all generalizable). However, the "afterlife" idea as an explanatory device lacks precision and seems too seductive. Peter Berger, in his insightful writings about alienation, has, we think, contributed greatly to an understanding of *why* the "afterlife" notion is related to political inactivity. His work seemed directly applicable to this segment of the Jesus movement, and thus we were led to try out on a limited scale some of his ideas, and potentially even to extend and specify them a bit.

It seems to us that the admittedly rather rough-hewn measurements and indicators of alienation employed in our research support, in general, the relationship between alienation and religion which Berger posits (his "de-alienation" qualification notwithstanding). The religious perspective apparently held by many CCO members prior to joining would be indicative of alienation in Berger's terms, and this perspective becomes pervasive after affiliation. We anticipated that there might be a relationship between the type of religious socialization and alienation, although Berger does not explicitly state that, within the context of the United States, conservative religions would alienate more than liberal or moderate ones. We thought, however, that his analysis of religion could support a view that conservative religions might alienate to a greater degree than moderate or liberal ones. We found, however, very little association between religious affiliation and responses to the questions on alienation. Persons with conservative affiliations before joining were slightly more likely to see this country as guided by God in the area of world politics than were others. Prior religious affiliation had no effect on responses to the other questions used in our brief "alienation scale." It may well be that the Judeo-Christian religions incorporate alienating factors to the extent that denominational differences are of little or lessening significance, as the work of Herberg (1955) and Lee (1960) implies. It may also be that the CCO philosophy and rhetoric were incorporated quickly and thoroughly by all members upon affiliation or shortly thereafter, thus blurring any distinctions based on prior religious affiliation.

No association between length of membership and alienation was found. We had hypothesized that alienation would be high among group members, but that it would increase as length of time in the group increased. Failure to find such an association has several possible explanations. The instrument designed to measure alienation was unsophisticated and preliminary, perhaps not capable of discerning any fine differences. Alienation, however, may not increase over time among members of the group. A third alternative is that alienation may be very high at the point of entrance into the group, so that any increases over time would be minor by comparison. We have presented evidence for the description of respondents as alienated. Since there is little change over time, we suggest that their alienation was high before joining the group and was probably related to prior religious socialization, or alternatively, that within the first few months, weeks, or even days of membership, members incorporated an alienated philosophy and/or rhetoric to such an extent that little increase over time was possible or measurable.

All of the foregoing material indicates that members of this group were alienated. We found some support for Berger's theoretical analysis. The group philosophy of nonparticipation in the world and acceptance of that world, coupled with doctrinal support for nonquestioning and acceptance of society's structures, seems to have been readily incorporated by these young people. These are generally peaceful, benign, accepting, unquestioning people—and they are alienated, as Berger uses the term. They seem far different from the "de-alienated" youth who marched in the streets demanding an end to racism, paternalism, and war. For some, this conclusion will offer solace; for others, sadness.

NOTES

1. Berger points out (1967, p. 197) that he takes issue with Marx's "pseudo-theological notion that alienation is the result of certain historical 'sins' of the social order or in his utopian hopes for the abolition of alienation ... through the socialist revolution." Berger adds that, "we cannot go along

Alienation and Political Orientation

with Marx's notion (further vulgarized later on by Engels) that alienation *historically succeeds* a state of non-alienated being." Berger also considers that his own treatment of religion and alienation (to be discussed herein) is much more "balanced" than that of Marx, who, Berger says (1967, p. 96), refused to accept the fact that religion can and does sometimes contribute to *de-alienation* (see Scharf, 1970, pp. 84-87) for a somewhat different view of Marx's appreciation for the "de-alienating" propensity of religion).

2. See Musgrove (1975) for a thorough and more balanced, albeit still somewhat biased, study of a similar population of study as that used by Rigby.

3. Rigby does admit that some vulgarizations of Marx must also be categorized as "alienated utopians," what with their emphasis (1974, p. 56) on "the working class as the embodiment of some historical necessity," a clarification that makes even more narrow the "gates of heaven."

4. Berger is not without his critics, it should be noted, and we do not totally support all his ideas and presuppositions. However, especially since his ideas have been so little tested, it seems that this is a valuable exercise. See Scharf (1970), Harvey (1973), Cairns (1974), Gill (1974), Light (1969), Hammond (1969), and Clanton (1974) among others who have critiqued Berger's work.

5. Berger himself seems to have "recanted" a bit, with his *Rumor of Angels* (1969), and especially by his signing the now famous (or infamous) "Hartford Theses." See Clanton (1974) and Harvey (1973) for relatively thorough interpretations of the evolution of Berger's thought up until the last two or three years.

6. After this somewhat hastily devised but moderately successful attempt at measuring some of Berger's notions, we are planning a more systematic and thorough approach to scale building in this area.

7. This response could, of course, indicate a general revulsion against killing that derives from sources more general than the specific group ideology. Such an interpretation does not detract from the fact that this question involving killing produced the strongest negating data in terms of our ideas derived from Berger. Apparently (and some will say hopefully) there is a "limit" to the alienating propensities of this type of religion. However, we would caution against too much rejoicing, given the fact that most of the young men involved would probably have served if drafted (we failed to ask that specific question), and given the findings of Milgram (1974) concerning obedience to authority, not to mention our own findings concerning personality assessment of CCO members (see chapter 7). It is intriguing to consider that such a "pressing to the limit" by those in "questionably sacred" positions (for example, military leaders), might well be something of a "trigger" that encourages or allows the profound and even awe-inspiring process of *de-alienation* to begin. This idea was not pursued in this study, however.

PART D

CONVERSION AND AFFILIATION

Part C has presented much information on the backgrounds and personalities of CCO members. Implied in that discussion and in the other parts of the book (including the Introduction) has been some theorizing about why such individuals would join a group such as CCO. In Part D, which is chapter 9, we will present our ideas concerning the conversion process that operated in this movement. As a part of this effort, we present and critique two conversion models of some import in the literature—those of Lofland and Stark (1965), and Gerlach and Hine (1970). Then we amplify this earlier work by suggesting some ideas that seem especially useful in explaining why people convert to groups such as CCO and other contemporary movements. A more general model of conversion is suggested, and then some elements of the general model are applied to the members of CCO in an effort to yield better understanding of the conversion process. A summary of part of this chapter appeared earlier (Richardson & Stewart, 1977).

9

Conversion Models: A Critique, Extension, and Partial Test

Some have characterized these times as an age of "true believers," or so it seems from reading and viewing popular media treatments of the Jesus movement and some related phenomena. All kinds of esoteric groups have gained a foothold in modern Western society, and in some instances, that "beachhead" has been developed into a virtual "conquering" of certain social groups, ready to try something (anything?) new (or even old) in their quest for security and meaning in life. Here we will not try to chronicle all the various groups that have developed and gained followings in recent times. In fact, we will not even fully delineate the development of the Jesus movement and the commune movement (see the Introduction). What we will do here is to focus on the *process whereby new members are absorbed into such movements*. This process is not *movement specific*, as very similar things are found anytime people are persuaded to affiliate with a new movement, whatever the movement. The vehicle for our investigation of this phenomenon will be, of course, the religious and communal organization which is the subject of this book—Christ Communal Organization (CCO)—and some data relevant to the idea of conversion [1] will be presented from our study. However, we think our work has broader application, and the general model suggested can be used to study recruitment of new members by many different types of social groups.

In discussing conversion,[2] many areas of scholarly work are germane, including sociology of religion, of course, but also the broad areas of social movements and collective behavior, socialization (and resocialization), deviancy, attitude change (broadly defined to include such phenomena as "thought reform," and belief and value change), and some other areas of social psychology. Psychologists have also been involved directly in conversion studies, and through related work in such areas as personality change. We cannot begin to incorporate material directly from all these areas, but will rely on them implicitly, while focusing directly on a defineable literature of conversion that is generally social psychological in nature, but which typically uses conversion to overtly "religious" groups as a medium of study. Specifically, the literature on which our discussion will draw directly includes the work of Lofland and Stark (1965), Gerlach and Hine (1970), Gordon (1974), Glock (1969) Travisano (1970), and Parrucci (1968), with some attention being paid to other related works.

The literature just cited can generally be grouped into one of two categories. One category, including the work of Lofland and Stark and of Gerlach and Hine has focused on the *process of conversion,* or the reasons why conversion occurs. The other literature—work by Parrucci, by Travisano, by Gordon (and, less directly, by Glock) has given major attention to *types of converts and conversion.* Our present attempt has as its major thrust a focus on the first of these two traditions, but some attention will also be paid to the "typologists." The "process theorists" have generally focused on just one or two groups or movements, and this has led to the development of somewhat limited models of the conversion process. On the other hand, the "typologists" have made some attempts to integrate process with types, being forced, by recognition of the presence of qualitatively different types of converts in nearly all movements, to explain where they came from. Notable (and supportive of our point about the split between the two traditions) is the fact that there is virtually no cross-referencing between works of the two traditions—the only exception to this being a minor reference in Parrucci's paper to the work of Lofland.[3]

Before proceeding with a detailed critique and integration of available conversion models, some of the more important and/or most cited work to which we have just referred will be presented briefly. We will compare and critique Lofland and Stark (1965), and Gerlach and Hine (1970), since they are the most ostensibly inclusive conversion process models in the literature.

THE PROCESS OF CONVERSION

Lofland and Stark's Model

Lofland and Stark (1965) after extensive study of an eclectic religious cult called the "Divine Precepts," outlined seven factors, the *accumulation of which* is both a necessary and a sufficient cause for conversion. They conceive of conversion as a *funneling* and *sifting process* in which the number of persons who may become converts is increasingly diminished by the effects of the elements of their model. The factors which Lofland presents are *not* ordered in terms of temporal occurrence; rather the ordering principle is one of "activation," an approach similar to Smelser's (1963) "value-added" method.

The following factors are seen as necessary background or *pre-disposing characteristics:*

1. Perception of considerable long-term tension, strain, deprivation, or frustration (felt needs).
2. Possession of a "religious" rhetoric and problem-solving perspective (constrasted to "political" or "psychiatric" perspectives, which are "secular definitions").
3. Self-definition as "religious seeker" (involves rejection of traditional religion and more "secular" definitions as solutions to felt problems).

The *situational factors* which arise from interaction between potential converts and cult members were seen by Lofland and Stark to be essential factors in the conversion process:

4. "Turning point" reached (old lines of action no longer operable, and contact with a cult member begins).
5. Development (or pre-existence) of affective bonds between "preconvert" and cult members (beginning of serious consideration of cult ideology).
6. Relatively weak or neutralized extra-cult affective ties (or existent ties were with other "seekers" who encourage continued contact)—culminates in "verbal conversion."
7. Intensive (usually communal) interaction with cult members culminates in "total conversion," and person becomes "deployable agent."

Gerlach and Hine's Model

Gerlach and Hine (1970), in a model that is more overtly "chronological" than that of Lofland and Stark, identify seven major steps in what they refer to as a "commitment process." Their model is derived from a lengthy study of the neo-Pentecostal and "Black Power" movements. The model explicitly disallows predisposing characteristics (although they incorporate such considerations in an unsystematic and implicit way), and begins with "initial contact."

1. Initial contact with a participant (regardless of predispositions of potential convert).
2. Focus of needs through demonstration (redefining the potential convert's needs, desires, or discontents in terms of specific ideology of the group).
3. Re-education through intense group interaction. (Recruited into specific "cell," not the movement as a whole).

    a. Provides basis for cognitive reorientation.
    b. Facilitates development of in-group ties.
    c. Encourages formulation of normative expectations.

4. Decision and surrender of old identity (can be gradual or sudden; if sudden, steps 1-4 occur together and much support needed immediately).
5. The commitment event (an overt act that sets the individual apart and "burns bridges" with the past), accompanied by an "identity-altering" experience.
6. Testifying to the experience (objectifies a subjective experience and "fixes" it as a reality—both to convert and group).
7. Group support for changed cognitive and behavioral patterns (must develop and continue, as commitment process is open-ended).

Comparison and Contrast of the Models

Much more detail could be given about the models, and we recommend that readers refer to primary sources for additional information (see Lofland, 1966, 1977; Hine, 1969, as well). However, this brief presentation of the basic elements of both models does allow some comparisons to be made. An important point of contrast with substantive implications is that the two models were developed from studies of considerably different populations of study—Lofland and Stark studied the "Divine Precepts," which was the beginning of Reverend Moon's Unification Church in America, while Gerlach and Hine researched the Black Power and contemporary Pentecostal groups.[4] Another obvious thing about the two models is that they "begin" and "end" at different "places" in the overall conversion process. This comment is something of a criticism of the two models, as both were attempts to be inclusive of all important elements in the process.[5] Nonetheless, it must be stated that the models overlap each other, with the Lofland and Stark model "starting sooner," as a result of their explicit consideration of predisposing characteristics, and the Gerlach and Hine model "ending later," as a result of their apparent greater appreciation for the open-ended and continuousness of the process (see their step 7). We will discuss the lack of overlap at the beginning of the process in more detail in a following critique of how Lofland and Stark handle predisposing characteristics. However for now, suffice it to say that this situation of areas of nonoverlap suggests that the two models might be integrated into a more inclusive model. Both models are also apparently developed post hoc and thus have not been adequately tested and "proved," although most references to either imply that they have. (The only claims of which we are aware for explicit tests of either is by Austin (1977) and Seggar and Kunz (1972), both of whose applications of the Lofland-Stark model is itself open to serious questions.)

Another distinction between the models is that Lofland and Stark's is, interestingly enough, somewhat more individualistic or even psychological in orientation, with its focus on predisposing characteristics and on individual mental states. (Their very small population of study may have contributed to this orientation.) Lofland and Stark do incorporate a strong social psychological emphasis with their situational factors, but Gerlach and Hine, although anthropologists, are the more generally social psychological, with their assumption that interaction is the key variable. This thrust is evidenced in nearly all their "steps," especially the "initial contact" stage and the last stage involving continuing group support.[6]

Both models, as do others in the "process"tradition, use a relatively undifferentiated concept of conversion (or commitment), and thus do not adequately distinguish *types of converts,* a problem deriving at least in part from their respective data bases. Particularly in the case of Lofland and Stark, the homogeneity of the population of study apparently influenced them to draw some conclusions of limited application to members of other social categories. Gerlach and Hine also use a rather simplistic concept, as has been noted by Harrison (1975, p. 404). Even though they obviously had greatly differing types of people involved in their study (i.e., old-line Pentecostals and neo-Pentecostals), they allowed the apparent similarity of the glossolalic experience to override such considerations in parts of their study. This oversight is a major detraction from their valuable study. Their decision to overlook predisposing factors was made mostly on the basis of some psychological-type considerations, and it apparently also led them to disallow, at least in part, some important social background considerations as well.[7] Lofland and Stark make a distinction between "verbal" and "total" converts, and Gerlach and Hine distinguish only between two types of converts on the basis of the effects of conversion on interpersonal relationships.

The "focus of needs through demonstration" (step 2) and "re-education" (step 3) which Gerlach and Hine propose are related to Lofland and Stark's ideas of "religious perspective" and the "self-definition" as a "religious seeker," although the timing of the factors differs somewhat in the two models. Both models, however, take rather passive views of the potential convert, which do not treat the potential convert as an active agent deliberately seeking new affiliations. Lofland has since adopted a more humanistic view (Lofland, 1977), and others have emphasized the more positive view of seekership as well (see Balch & Taylor, 1977; Taylor, 1976; Strauss, 1976).

Both models emphasize the formation of affective bonds with group adherents—Gerlach and Hine see this personal contact as an initial factor, whereas Lofland stresses the importance of it later in the process of commitment. Both also place importance on the decrease of extra-cult ties; Gerlach and Hine incorporate this into their "bridge-burning" concept. Intensive interaction with cult adherents is seen by both as crucial. Gerlach and Hine describe in more detail the significance of these intergroup supportive ties in terms of support, fellowship, and explanation or interpretation of events and experiences. However, both stress the importance of interaction to the study of conversion or commitment, a view shared by White (1968) and by Austin (1977).

The Gerlach and Hine model does not follow the major emphasis of most conversion literature in that it does not stress emotional, physical, or psychological needs of potential converts which would predispose them to commitment.[8] However, their introduction of the term "bridge-burning" and their coupling of it with an identity-altering experience as the two components of commitment seems an important contribution in terms of detail in the interactional approach to conversion. Nevertheless, it must be said that they do not draw the full implications of the bridge-burning act, for they seem unaware of the implications of this act in terms of dissonance theory and the possible impact of action on belief. Both the models being discussed seem to accept the common view that people act *from* or *as a result of* their beliefs, attitudes, and values, rather than the perspective that accepts beliefs, values, and attitudes as *deriving from actions,* as individuals try to rationalize their actions (or, in the language of dissonance theorists, to reduce dissonance resulting from an incongruity between actions and cognitive (or previous behavioral) elements. (See Kiesler, 1971, for a good presentation of such a perspective.)

Admittedly Gerlach and Hine seem more intuitively cognizant of this view than Lofland and Stark, whose focus on predispositions (a focus probably deriving from their population of study) "traps" them into focusing on the past, rather than on the contemporary experience of converts. Although this concentration on predispositions has much to recommend it (and we fault Gerlach and Hine for their explicit disregard of such considerations), there are problems with the approach offered by Lofland and Stark, in terms of applying their model to some contemporary movements. We want to examine this part of their work in some detail, as a preliminary to developing some of our own ideas.

Critique and Extension of Conceptualization of "Predispositions"

Although Lofland and Stark explicitly and insightfully focus on predispositions, they (and certainly not Gerlach and Hine) do not take full advantage of the basic insight that people view things from different perspectives. They also do not indicate a full appreciation of the complexity of the "basic perspective" concept. This problem is directly related to the just-discussed use of a little-differentiated concept of conversion, but it involves other considerations as well, especially the homogeneity of their population of study. Another possible reason for this lack of full development is that Lofland and Stark wanted to develop the situational factors more fully, instead of attending only to what they called factors "pushing" people into deviant groups. Their attention to the "pulls" of situational factors is admirable, but we think their basic and important work on predispositions should also be developed. Specifically, we think that (1) Lofland and Stark delineated too few basic perspectives, (2) the concept of a basic perspective was not elaborated as fruitfully as it might have been, (3) the perspectives used were viewed as relatively static instead of continually evolving and potentially rapidly changeable, and (4) the implications for and complexity of the "religious" perspective in terms of its contribution to the "felt tensions" was not made explicit.

At least one major "new" perspective needs to be added to Lofland and Stark's three, and another, briefly discussed but not delineated in their work, needs to be more carefully explicated if the model is to be generalized. These "new" perspectives are in addition to (but at the same level of abstraction as) their three—the *psychiatric,* the *political,* and the *religious*—only one of which, the religious, was used in a major explanatory way in their research. For purposes of clarity and contrast, the brief definitions given these three perspectives will be quoted (1965, p. 867). "In the first, the origin of problems is typically traced to the psyche, and manipulation of the self is advocated as a solution. Political solutions, mainly radical, locate the sources of problems in the social structure and advocate reorganization of the system as a solution. The religious perspective tends to see both sources and solutions as emanating from an unseen and, in principle, unseeable realm."

A major addition to the three perspectives suggested by our research is what we refer to as a *physiological perspective,* which we define as including particularly the use of elements or activities to effect the body and mind in a way that furnishes some "meaning" for the person. One might be tempted to refer to this perspective as hedonistic or "withdrawal," but to do so would belie the serious and active approach to life taken by many devotees of this orientation. Also, such terms as "withdrawal" have a generally negative connotation, and we prefer a neutral stance on such issues. While the physiological perspective may include as important elements sex and drugs, there are other activities that also can and should be classified as a part of this view of life. For instance, the use of alcohol and such things as health food "trips," dieting, vitamins, exercise, yoga, and other "body therapies" should be included. The overriding tie between such activities is the doing of things that somehow include and affect the body in an attempt to achieve meaning, whether that meaning is derived from orgasms, jogging, natural foods, or some innovative combination of such activities.

Another perspective that should be more carefully delineated *and* appreciated is what might be termed the "muddle through" perspective, although dubbing it *conventional* might be better. Lofland and Stark (1965, p. 867) say: "Because people have a number of conventional and readily available definitions for, and means of coping with their problems, there were, in the end, very few converts to D.P." Later they mention some "normal" things that potential converts can do to alleviate their situations short of conversion. They can, they say (1965, p. 868), "persist in stressful situations with little or no relief," or "take specifically problem-directed action to change troublesome portions of their lives, without adopting a different world view to interpret them" or such person can take advantage of "a number of maneuvers to 'put the problem out of mind.' " This latter situation they describe as "compensations for or distractions from problems of living" and specifically mention such things as mass media addiction, child rearing, immersion in work, and, more spectacularly, alcoholism, suicide, and promiscuity. We would only add a few more examples of the use of such a perspective to solve problems—such things as getting a divorce, getting married, moving, changing jobs, taking a holiday, dropping out of school, and affiliating with a conventional religious (or other type of) group (or changing such affiliation). The basic thrust of this idea is that there are more or less acceptable ways that most people deal with their problems, and that sometimes these quite "normal" activities are deliberate or even unconscious attempts to solve felt problems. We would even suggest tenative hypotheses that most people will try to "muddle through" before dealing with their problem in more dramatic ways, and that "muddling through" is actually something of a quiescent state to which people regularly return when more dramatic solutions do not resolve problematic situations.

Thus we suggest five major perspectives for interpreting and dealing with felt problems—*psychiatric, political, religious, physiological,* and *conventional*—all conceptualized at the same level of abstraction. However, it seems plain that there are various ways of viewing these several perspectives, fitting them into what, for want of a better term, we will designate *general orientations.* Lofland and Stark talk about their three perspectives in such a manner, referring to the political and psychiatric as both being "secular," but this seems of little value. We want to develop other more general ways of grouping the perspectives that will be of help in discussing the various types of conversions.

One seemingly fruitful way to view the several perspectives is to focus on the most basic unit used in defining problems and solutions to problems. This leads us to the use of the admittedly simplistic but still valuable dichotomy of *individualism-collectivism.* Much has been written about this dichotomy, and great import is given the distinction by some,[9] especially in discussions of Western and American history, views that support our decision to employ the distinction in an analysis of contemporary conversion phenomena (also see the Introduction). Using this dichotomy, it seems that all but one of the five perspectives would be usually classified as an *individual level* approach to defining and solving felt problems. To use a term with some contemporary credence in the literature, the individuals possess or develop *individualistic world views.* Only the political perspective, particularly as defined by Lofland and Stark to mean more radical political views, seems potentially classifiable as a *collectivistic world view.*[10]

We do not deny that there are some problems in applying the individualism-collectivism dichotomy, and that in one sense, it is a "false dichotomy." For instance, plainly some more or less conventional religious groups take different positions on a continuum that has individualism and collectivism as polar types at either end, although most should probably be classified as closer to the individualistic end of the continua.[11] And it is just as plain that one would be foolish to classify all politically-oriented solutions as collectivistic, for many (if not most) such solutions in our society involve a large dose of so-called American individualism. In order to resolve such difficulties with our scheme, one is forced to treat each case individually and to qualify some categorizations.

By adopting the position that nearly all "religious" views are individualistic, we might engender wrath from more conservative apocalyptic religious groups (such as CCO), who talk in somewhat structural terms when they describe the results of the "second coming." We have some reservations about disregarding this claim, for we do think that the claims of people about what they are doing should be taken seriously. In the immediately following paragraphs, in fact, we try to use such a phenomenological perspective to aid in understanding. However, for purposes of our discussion of whether or not religious solutions are collectivistic, we must, while admitting that Western history has a few such examples (in theocratic situations), state that we do not accept such claims made by most contemporary millennial groups. What such groups say and the claims they make are, we think, best viewed in the light of Glock's statement (1969, p. 29) that *religious* solutions to felt problems "are more likely to occur where the nature of the deprivation is inaccurately perceived or where those experiencing the deprivation are not in a position to work directly at eliminating its causes." Insight into such claims can also be gained from considering them as indicative of a state of false consciousness à la Lukacs (1971). And as discussed in an earlier chapter, such views seem to illustrate well what Berger (1967) means when he talks about the "alienating propensity of religion."

But that issue aside for the moment, we are still left with the difficulty of political events possibly being classifiable as either individualistic or collectivistic. To resolve this obstacle, we think it advisable to assume a more phenomenological perspective and ask what the general interpretation given by groups and individuals to their activities and beliefs is in terms of *support for* the social system. Do they view what they are doing as generally supportive to the social system of which they are a part, *or* do they consider that their beliefs and actions are opposed to that system?

Such an approach to the problem does not solve all the inherent difficulties, for there will be obvious disagreements between so-called "objective observers" and members of certain groups about the meaning of what the groups are doing and what they believe. Such difficulties will again require that some qualifications be made regarding certain groups, for there are different ways to view the same thing.

What some groups might claim is extremely radical behavior, an observer may categorize as completely system-supportive, at least in terms of its *latent* consequences. This fundamental-level argument cannot be addressed here. We find both perspectives contain some value, and we will at this juncture employ the former in attempting to come to a better understanding of conversion.

With this caveat in mind, the following typology is presented. It contains, for illustrative purposes, the classification of several groups, movements, and types of individual action *according to our judgment* about the general type of world view, and using *our assessment of the typical view of group members and leaders* about the way their group or movement relates to the greater social system. We have chosen to list specific groups because the five perspectives cannot be so easily classified into the fourfold table relating type of ideology and relationship with American society.

One possible limitation to the scheme is the apparent need for a "neutral" category between "opposed" and "supportive." For example, most "group sex" groups apparently make no explicit claims concerning the variable of relationship to society. However, we have refrained from including such a category because it seems to us that, unless explicit claims are made concerning opposition to the greater society, at least tacit support is being given. Indeed, with regard to the objective-subjective argument just alluded to, even some groups that make explicit claims of opposition to the society are sometimes only engaging in rhetorical self-justification.[12] Another possible limitation involves the fact that groups can possibly shift rapidly from the opposed to the supportive category, and vice-versa. A hypothetical example of such a shift would be the possible movement of most right-wing political groups to the opposed category (and some left-wing groups to the supportive) if McGovern had won the presidential election in 1972. Some such groups did shift closer to the opposed category even when Ford was president! Such shifts do not vitiate our argument.

Thus we are enabled, through this scheme, to talk on a more general level about the content of belief systems and ideologies, while at the same time tapping the basic emotive element illustrated by the overt and latent animosity that some members of American society, including many Jesus movement adherents, have had toward the greater society. Some implications of our scheme for conversion are probably obvious, but perhaps we should point out a few possible implications of applying our fourfold typology. First it is obvious that, if there is any import to the distinctions made, movements of people and groups among and between the various cells of the table (conver-

TABLE 9.1

Relationship of Groups to American Society and the General Type of Ideology Espoused by the Groups

Type of Ideology	Relationship to American society*	
	Opposed	Supportive
Individualistic	Jesus movement Drug subculture Most Eastern religious groups Some fundamentalist groups A few "conventional solutions" of more disaffected people	"Popular" or "lay psychology" movement groups Most ecology groups Most right-oriented political groups Neo-Pentecostal movement Anti-ERA groups Most conventional groups
Collectivistic	Most left-oriented radical political groups Some more radical "women's lib" groups	Some of the more radical ecology groups Some more radical right-wing groups

*based on implicit or explicit claims of groups listed.

sions) are *qualitatively different*. Although important qualifications must be made in terms of specific content of certain beliefs, generally we will be suggesting that movement within a category is "easier" to accomplish than movement across one of the two important more general "boundaries" that we have set up with our use of the two dichotomous variables. Whether or not the "opposed-supportive" boundary is more inviolate than the "individualistic-collectivistic" is an empirical question as yet unanswered. However, at this point, we will state that we think movement *within* categories is more likely to occur (when not strictly prohibited by specific strongly accepted belief content elements) than is movement *across* either the "individualistic-collectivistic" or the "opposed-supportive" boundaries. Movement across the individualistic-collectivistic boundary seems directly related to the *intensity* of the support or opposition dimension, as well as to some other elements such as affective ties. If the emotive or affective element vis-á-vis the greater society was quite intense, then one might expect the supportive-opposed "boundary" to be the most inviolate of all, resulting in comparatively "easier" movement across the other major boundary and within cells. However, the affective element vis-á-vis group members and nonmembers might operate quite differently. We will develop this discussion of "conversions" from one group and/or one cell to another more when discussing the dynamic nature of basic perspectives (also see Richardson, 1977, for a fuller discussion). But first, one more important problem in using our fourfold scheme requires comment.

This problem is what might be termed *multiple commitments*. Our age has been characterized as that of the uncommitted (Keniston, 1965), and this type of consideration has been echoed in the sociology of religion literature by the growing attention being paid to the concept of the cult, since one of the basic defining characteristics of a cult is its lack of definite behavioral and belief boundaries.[13] The reason for this theoretical interest in the cult is the simple realization that many (perhaps even most) groups in contemporary society do *not* require total allegiance of participants, as is thought to be the case in traditional sects. Another term which allows for "part-time" *partial* or *temporary* commitment is needed, and "cult" is such a concept. In terms of our fourfold scheme, this multiple or partial commitment means that specific persons (and possibly even some groups) can simultaneously occupy different cells in the table. In our sense, this was not a tremendous problem for our research, as CCO rapidly became sect-like in its approach to commitment (it is "all or nothing"). However, since we are explicitly trying to develop a model of conversion that is more general, the problem of multiple commitments must be acknowledged.

There is also an overriding substantive reason for addressing the problem. Many, if not most, members of the more prominent Jesus movement groups derived from a population that had multiple commitments. To overlook this fact might lead us to miss something of real theoretical value in terms of understanding conversion (and the movement as well). Many individuals were at one and the same time involved in varying degrees in the drug subculture and to some degree in left-oriented political groups and activities (or at least they were sympathetic). This situation is, we would suggest, one of inherent tension and "dissonance arousal," and attempts to resolve the difficulties may have been very important in explaining origins of the Jesus movement and the conversion of many individuals to this belief and behavior system that obliterates such tensions. Gordon's (1974) insightful work speaks to this question with particular reference to the Jesus movement, and we will return to his paper later. We think there are basic phychological drives or needs that eventually cause many (but significantly not all) people to make a commitment to a group that occupies only one cell of our table. Groups with a firmly stated position would seem to have a great deal of appeal to individuals who have been jumping back and forth to groups within a category, or who have tried to simultaneously occupy places in two (or more) cells of Table 9.1. This leads us directly into a discussion of such switches of perspective and orientation, and to this we now turn our attention.

Lofland and Stark seem rather static in their approach to perspectives (and general orientations), a situation probably deriving from the type of people on which they were doing their study—people with a deeply inculcated "religious" world view who were affiliating with a somewhat deviant religious group. The only shift involved is *within* a perspective that we would categorize as "individualistic-opposed" (fully realizing that some, perhaps even Lofland and Stark, would disagree with this assessment). What seems to us to be of great import, given the "tenor of the times," is to develop a model that can adequately incorporate the shifts *across* our two major boundaries of Table 9.1, and *within* all the cells as well.

The only shifts Lofland and Stark discuss, aside from the shifts within the individualistic-opposed category, are some "movements" that are more "conventional," be they opposed to society (suicide is an extreme example of such an "opposed-conventional" move), or basically supportive (changing jobs, etc.). They recognize that they are not talking about any other types of shifts, for they say (1965, p. 826) "we think the model suggests some rudiments of a general account of conversion to deviant perspectives. But the degree to which this scheme applies to shifts between widely held perspectives must, for now, remain problematic." Also, the lack of basic shifting across general orientation boundaries is demonstrated in their comments about the social origins of most converts and the type of perspective held by the converts they studied. Most converts were (1965, p. 863) "primarily white, Protestant, and young (typically below 35); some had college training, and most were Americans of lower middle-class and small-town origins." Lofland and Stark claimed that there are few, if any, specific elements of belief that tie the new beliefs of the converts to old thought systems. They state (1965, p. 869) that the "concrete pre-convert beliefs varied a good deal," a point we would caution readers against overinterpreting, as most if not all "pre-converts" shared a perspective that is of an individualistic orientation. Pre-converts, they claim, shared two "postulates about the nature of ultimate reality. . . . First, they believed that spirits of some variety come from an active supernatural realm to intervene in the 'material world.' . . . Second, their conception of the universe was teleological . . . each person must have been 'put on earth' for some reason. . . ."

Thus, Lofland and Stark insightfully note a correspondence between the basic perspective of their preconverts and that which the converts came to accept. They were *not* saying that there had been a major shift in orientation that would, in our terms, lead to a crossing of the boundary between the individualistic and collectivistic categories in Table 9.1. A case might well be made for their at least implying a recent shift across the "opposed-supportive" boundary. but even that seems problematic from reading some of their "case histories," which indicate an "opposed" mentality not of recent origin. We think that any general model of conversion must not only recognize that different types of "conversion" occur, but that such shifts of perspective and orientation occur more than once in the life of a person. "Once saved always saved" or "eternal security" may be an important theological tenet of some groups and a basic desire of many more groups of all kinds, but it simply cannot be accepted as a full explanation of contemporary conversion phenomena.

A full explanation of conversion must be cognizant of the impossible multiple-conversion history of many contemporary individuals (see Richardson, 1977). To take this great amount of *ideological mobility* that is typical of some groups and individuals in contemporary society into account, we suggest a concept of *serial alternatives*.[14] This concept (which has some similarities to the notion of serial monogamy as a way of characterizing modern marriage) seems valuable for incorporating the dynamic element in modern-day conversion phenomena. The serial alternative approach will, we think incorporate shifts within the basic four categories we have outlined, as well as the more dramative shifts across some of the more general boundaries such as the two we have delineated. The literature on brainwashing (Lifton, 1963; Schien, 1957), and resocialization (i.e., McHugh, 1970; Dornbusch, 1955) demonstrates that such major shifts can occur. The extreme fragmentation and pluralism of modern American society (especially in the 1960s) leading to the increased availability of potentially acceptable "general orientations" and "perspectives," suggests that such dramatic cognitive shifts might occur with rapidity and *more than once,* as various sets of beliefs are tried and rejected as inadequate (or even dangerous). We live in a time-space social environment that is a virtual supermarket of ideas which might be discussed in terms of a large and differentiated *opportunity structure* of possible ways to interpret and resolve felt problems. (See Parrucci, 1968, p. 150, for a similar, but not adequately developed idea.) And the social situation of the 1960s virtually guaranteed that many new solutions would be defined into existence, and that, paradoxically, few of them would be worthwhile and lasting solutions for members of certain social groupings. As might be guessed from our fourfold classification scheme of Table 9.1, the few solutions that were deemed useful and acceptable (and not so personally dangerous) can be characterized as being in about any cell *except* the "collectivistic-opposed" category. This, of course, means that the specific group we studied was (and still is) classifiable in one of the more "acceptable" cells of Table 9.1. Efforts—usually not direct—are being made by some CCO members and by certain segments of the greater society to get them to move into an even more acceptable cell—"individualistic-supportive"—a move that maybe under way even now.

Given the common social origins and personal experiences of most participants in the Jesus movement and in CCO, it seems possible to construct typical *conversion careers* or *trajectories* for most participants. Plainly, one would expect some common or typical conversion career patterns in terms of tried and rejected series alternatives, as individuals sifted through the opportunity structures of potential allegiances available to and acceptable by them. Adams and Fox (1972), in a research report that briefly addresses this question, found such patterns, although they do not give enough detail to allow a thorough test of our idea. They were surprised with their findings, as the following quote illustrates: "Before beginning this study, the writers had theorized that Jesus people who are ex-dopers had participated in a succession of social movements: they began in the peace movement, had dropped out into the drug scene and finally joined the religious revival. The data, however, refute this assumption about the sequence of membership in the various movements, for the use of drugs almost always had preceded participation in the peace movement."

Thus, a typical conversion career for a majority of their respondents was discernible, even though the pattern of memberships was apparently unexpected. They also found yet other patterns in other classes of respondents. Gordon (1974) also found discernible typical conversion careers in his study of a small Chicago Jesus movement group. Conversion patterns are *not* random for CCO converts, and probably the same can be said for converts to other groups or movements as well. We think it possible to develop a rather sophisticated, even somewhat "mathematical-model" approach to this problem of conversion—an approach that could perhaps associate probabilities with certain conversion careers or trajectories and with certain types of switches *within* a pattern, since many patterns would probably involve several "conversions" (see a somewhat similar attempt to establish general probabilities by Parucci, 1968).

The basic elements of such a model would fall into three broad categories: (1) prior socialization, (2) contemporaneous experiences and circumstances, and (3) the opportunity structure available for problem definition and resolution. Prior socialization is related to what we have referred to as predispositions, in that all individuals are "given" a basic perspective which they apply in their life but may sometimes modify. A change or disavowal of such a perspective results usually from a negative interpretation being given to contemporaneous experiences and circumstances, and the change must follow certain lines of opportunity. It seems a truism to say that people cannot convert to a different perspective unless they are aware of it, but nonetheless this should be stated (the potentially important but empirically rare case of the charismatic leader with an individual "religion-starting" mystical experience notwithstanding).

All of these elements working together represent, we think, a more sophisticated view of what is usually meant by the use of the concept "predispositions." Some may claim that including the notion of opportunity structure in predispositions is incorrect, and that it (and even "circumstances") should more rightfully be considered part of "situational factors." We disagree, and would further suggest that the dichotomous treatment of predispositions and situational factors by Lofland and Stark is possibly misleading. Plainly, they mean it only as an analytical device, for it seems unsound to assume that prior socialization does not affect one's view of "circumstances" or one's view of available "opportunities." It seems obvious that certain kinds of socialization preclude the interpretation of some circumstances as being frustrating, while other circumstances are felt to be intolerable *because of* the prior socialization (more on this later). And certain "opportunities" are precluded by some world views, while yet others are seemingly *obvious solutions* to certain problems. Types of early socialization obviously differ, not only in terms of content, but perhaps as importantly, in terms of *methods used* in inculcating the content, and that these differences have important implications for what we have been saying. An interaction between types of early socialization and the experiences of life should not be unexpected. Only if this is well-understood can more precise modeling of conversion experiences be accomplished.

An example of what we mean in this regard would be the case where a person was involved with strong religious socialization in his or her childhood. Such a situation could result, in certain circumstances, with a not surprising rejection of the perspective or even orientation, and the adoption of a new and radically different one, at least for a time. Yet at the same time, socialization theory (and findings such as those of Gordon, 1974) would suggest that strong training stands a good chance, again given certain circumstances, to prevail eventually with the person "returning home" (thus adding meaning to the use of the "trajectory" analogy). In short, such strong early training may indeed be able to override most situational contingencies more than less rigorous socialization. Situational contingencies (which, as stated, achieve "reality" only through the basic orientation) may determine the route taken to "go home," but they do not usually become a permanent "home" themselves. Our saying this means, of course, that we basically agree with the thrust of the "socialization hypothesis," although we are not doctrinaire socializationists. We think that, "if you raise a child in the way that he or she should go, then he or she *usually* will not depart from it, *unless* circumstances develop which produce a more attractive and viable alternative way."

The ideas just developed have, we think, special application to our study and to that of Lofland and Stark, and leads us to our next point. This fourth criticism of Lofland and Stark's work is admittedly more speculative and is not adequately tested in our research. Nonetheless, we think it important within the context of our research.

The "way" of import to our study and that of Lofland and Stark is that of fundamentalist Christianity. It seems apparent that many if not most of Lofland and Stark's fifteen subjects had such a religious background. Their small-town, lower middle-class, Protestant origins seem congruent with such a notion, as does the characterization of their basic perspective, which we have already discussed. An added point of support from their beliefs is that they believed in Satan as an active spirit (1965, p. 869). Another reason to attend to fundamentalist Christianity is that most descriptions of the Jesus movement have so characterized the movement (see Enroth, Ericson, & Peters, 1972; Gordon, 1974, for a few examples). Such descriptions raise, particularly for the sociologist, an interesting question. Could it be that, contrary to some popular discussions of the movement, most of the members are "just" "returning fundamentalists?"

Our research and that of Gordon (1974) suggest that such is quite possible, and this idea, coupled with knowledge that most of Lofland and Starks' converts were probably also originally fundamentalists, suggests yet another line of inquiry. Is it possible that such a background makes people more predisposed toward deviant affiliations? Does such a perspective usually result in more personal problems in such an age as this, where a fundamentalist world view is certainly in the minority? [15] And even more fundamentally, does the fundamentalist world view contain elements that made such a world view especially subject to refutation during the turmoil of the 1960s in America? If the answer to the last question is "yes," then we are faced with the paradoxical situation of being led to suggest that fundamentalism—that "rock from whence most of us were hewn"—may actually have *contributed* to the severe problems which developed in the 1960s in America (and it also seems to be contributing to the "solution" of the severe problems, which adds to the paradox). Needless to say, this view of the meaning of religious background for the conversion process differs from the emphasis in Lofland and Stark that such experiences contribute "only" a religious perspective. Such a difference of meaning needs to be examined in more detail, and this we will attempt, using the work of Peter Berger (1967), some of whose work has already been presented in chapter 8.

Berger suggests, as has been stated, that religious socialization inculcates people with the view that their world is sacred and therefore relatively immutable. Implicit in his statement is the notion that certain variations of religious socialization would be "worse" than others in this regard. That is, we might expect that fundamentalist or conservative religious groups would be the "worst offenders," especially given the coming together of certain conservative religious groups with far right political views (see Jorstad, ·1970) that has occurred in the past few decades.

This "alienated perspective" of those that have undergone conservative religious socialization would, if Berger is correct, leave them with the deeply-held belief that institutions were sacred and unchangeable (or irrelevant and therefore not worthy of attention).[16] If they perceived problems within these institutions, then dealing with the problems would be more difficult for the individuals involved. They would be quite prone, particularly if attempts at dealing with problems with which they were involved were unsuccessful, to withdraw from grappling with the "sacred institutions." Their withdrawal would predictably be to something that did not challange the institutions, and to something with which they were fairly familiar in terms of life styles, beliefs, jargon, and so on. The Jesus movement generally fits this description, even though some participants try to present a case for it as a religious "revolution," a claim that we think helps rationalize joining the movement for a great number of people who perceive problems with many institutions, including institutionalized religion. Most Jesus movement groups do dress differently than their counterparts in organized fundamentalist religion, and their life-styles may differ since the movement tends to be communal, but the basic belief system is similar and leads, we suggest, to similar results—an ascetic life style that is latently supportive of the status quo. (See Richardson, 1979b for more on similarities between the movement and the dominant culture.)

To summarize this point, we think that being raised as a fundamentalist possibly makes people more prone to encounter frustration in their lives. This idea also receives support from the work of Fromm (1950), in which he makes his classic distinction between authoritarian and humanitarian religions. Fromm, whose definition of authoritarian religion seems to fit fundamentalism, offers an element, Marxian in derivation, of "self-alienation" to our study. He says (1950, p. 53), "The real fall of man is his alienation from himself, his submission to power, his turning against himself even though under the guise of worship of God." His description is of a person deabilitated by a set of beliefs that degrade man and lead to dependency. Such a person would be prone to encounter problems living in a world such as ours, caught up in such rapid change and disorder. The excellent literature review and presentation of data by Pattison (1970) is also supportive of this view of fundamentalism.[17]

The ties between such theorizing and the material in chapter 7 depicting a "dependency-prone" personality type seem clear. Such persons would have great difficulty functioning in a society where the authority structures had invalidated themselves through ill-considered "actions" (i.e., the Vietnam war) and "inactions" (i.e., persistent and unresolved racism). Individuals of this "problem-prone" background would, we think, experience a high and persistent level of tension and frustration in the face of the catastrophic middle and late 1960s in America. The several accumulated catastrophes resulted in a situation that, following Berger (1967), can be thought of as a "generational unit" (Mannheim's term, used by Balswick, 1974, with reference to the Jesus movement) experiencing a total failure of a well-inculcated theodicy. The tumultous 1960s overwhelmed the personal theodicies of many youth, and thereby demonstrated on a personal level insufficiencies in fundamentalist theodicy.

Such a view receives some indirect support from Lofland and Stark's claim (1965, p. 867) that, although felt problems did not appear objectively to be overly severe, "pre-converts felt their problems were quite acute, and they experienced high levels of tension concerning them over long periods." The authors never made the connection, developed herein, between prior religious socialization and the present tension-filled state of their converts. Instead, they simply asserted (1965, p. 867), "Most people probably have some type of frustrated aspiration, but the pre-converts *experienced* (emphasis theirs) the tension rather more acutely and over longer periods than most people do."

Perhaps fundamentalism represents an important case of what Toch (1965, p. 128-29) refers to as "oversocialization." He notes that all converts are previously disillusioned people, and defines a disillusioning experience as "the perception of discrepancy between conventional beliefs and psychological and physical realities." His description of the types of beliefs and situations resulting in disillusionment for certain types of people seems apropos of fundamentalism. He summarizes his discussion of the types of beliefs, situations, and people by saying: "A person will tend to become disillusioned if he becomes actively involved in life situations for which he has been ill-prepared by socialization" (Toch, 1965, p. 128). He then closes his provocative discussion of "oversocialization" with a paragraph that seems to have been written with fundamentalism and the Jesus movement in mind:

> Although there are many deficits in the socialization process, its most general defect is overambitiousness. Persons who have been oversocialized, in the sense that too many absolutes have been inculcated in them, are most likely to experience subsequent clashes with reality. The extreme instance of this rule is the true believer, for whom life becomes a constant struggle to impose shaky dogmas on slippery facts. In general, a person who de-

mands that conventional society conform to his mold soon finds that he must either revise his expectations or transform the social order. He may try both (Toch, 1965, pp. 128-29).

Fundamentalist religious socialization, as has been said, emphasizes deep personal commitment, and such socialization often is rigorous, if not "oversocialization." By way of summary, it would seem that many persons with this background who are (1) dissatisfied with a lack of emotion and the sterility of their world, (2) searching for meaning and fellowship, (3) suffering from depression or isolation, (4) unable to find other viable alternatives, and (5) unable to relate to or accept existing institutions, would find communal fundamentalist religious sects appealing.

Situational Factors in Conversion

We have focused mainly on the Lofland and Stark model of conversion in the discussion of predisposing characteristics. We will now examine briefly one area of *situational factors* in conversion, an analytical area that includes the latter several elements of the Lofland and Stark (1965) model and virtually all of the model developed by Gerlach and Hine (1970). One especially important concept from the analytical area of situational factors is that of *affective ties*. This variable has been deemed of great import by most writers in the conversion process literature, but its operation has not been adequately specified for contemporary conversion phenomena.

Gerlach and Hine note that conversion usually occurs to specific "cells" of movement, not to movements as a whole, and Lofland and Stark's study illustrates this key point, as does our own work. Affective ties must usually be developed between a potential convert and members of a specific group to which that potential convert may be predisposed. While we are hesitant to say that such ties to group members preclude affective ties between potential converts and people outside the group, it seems obvious that a situation of weak ties with nongroup members such as those with whom one would usually be expected to have positive affective ties (family members, spouses, classmates, etc.) would contribute to the propensity of a person to convert, as is assumed by Lofland and Stark, among others. The typically expected relationship of the variable of affective ties with group members and the variable of affective ties with nongroup significant others can be demonstrated by using a trichotimization of both variables as in Table 9.2. Work such as that of Lofland and Stark and of

Gerlach and Hine suggests that those individuals in cells 2 and 3 would be most prone to convert, whereas those in cells 7 and 8 would seem least likely to undergo conversion. The "conversion potential" of the other cells in the table is not clear without more information, as little research has addressed such questions.

An interesting possible interaction of the variable "affective ties with group members" with the variable "affective ties with nongroup significant others" would occur when a nongroup member with whom the potential convert had positive affective ties was either positive (or at least neutral) toward the group which the potential convert was considering joining. In such an instance, a positive affective tie with someone *outside* the group might actually *contribute to* conversion. A similar effect *might* be found if a *negative* affect with significant nongroup others was associated with a *negative* evaluation of the group by the nongroup others. This line of thought, which seems to specify considerably the operation of the variable of affective ties with nongroup members, can be presented somewhat simplistically in tabular form, as in Table 9.3.

We would expect conversions to occur (other things being equal) more frequently with individuals classifiable in cell 1, with perhaps those from cells 1 and 4 being next in expected frequency of conversion. However, as indicated, those in cell 9 might also especially be prone to convert. Those in cells 3 and 7 would probably be less prone to undergo conversion. Cell 5 seems a moot or inconsequential type.[18]

Table 9.4 attempts to present in summary form some possible relationships of predisposing elements with this crucial element, affective ties. Admittedly, the variables in the tables are simplified abstractions, but nonetheless, we hope the tabular scheme conveys the importance of both predisposing and situational variables, along with a demonstration that conversion can occur in several qualitatively different situations vis-á-vis the two variables. Note that while "congruence" is used mainly as a cognitive kind of variable, we would suggest that the term would also include behavioral elements as well. Also note that Table 9.4 does not attempt to integrate the important point made in Table 9.3.

Plainly, individuals (or groups) finding themselves classifiable in cell 1 of the table would be most prone to convert, while those in cell 9 would be less prone to convert. The ranking of the rest of the cells on a continuum of "proness to convert" is more problematic, however. Lofland and Stark's work, with its heavy emphasis on predisposing factors, seems to imply that those in cell 1 might be relatively prone to convert, whereas Gerlach and Hine's work seems to suggest that those

TABLE 9.2
Relationship of Affective Ties with Nongroup Significant Others and Affective Ties with Group Members

Affective ties with group members	Affective ties with non-group significant others		
	Positive	Neutral	Negative
Positive	1	2	3
Neutral	4	5	6
Negative	7	8	9

TABLE 9.3
Relationship of Affective Ties with Nongroup Members and Evaluation of the Group with Significant Nongroup Others

Evaluation of group by the significant nongroup other(s)	Affective ties with significant nongroup other(s)		
	Positive	Neutral	Negative
Positive	1	2	3
Neutral	4	5	6
Negative	7	8	9

in cells 1, 4, and 7 would be about equally prone to convert, although it should be said that Gerlach and Hine do not explicitly take a variable such as "congruence" into account in their scheme, which seems to imply that "initial contact" and "refocusing of needs" operate the same on just about anyone. Both models (and the work of White, 1968) suggest that those falling in cells 3, 6, and 9 will not convert.

TABLE 9.4

Relationship of Affective Ties with Group Members and Congruence of Group with Predispositions of Potential Converts

Congruence of Group with Predispositions of Potential Convert	Affective Ties with Members of Group to which Conversion is Contemplated		
	Positive	Neutral	Negative
High	1	2	3
Medium	4	5	6
Low	7	8	9

What is not clear is their respective positions on those included in the other cells (except cell 1, on which they agree).

In terms of general *types* of conversions and converts, we might suggest that those converts falling in row 1 of the table could be classified as cognitive converts, while those falling in column 1 might be classified as affective converts. This would suggest that converts in cell 1 would be "double" converts, both cognitive and affective, a situation dramatically different from that with other conversion (for instance, in propensity for converts to "stay converted").

Two significant comments should be made about the operation of the two major variables in Table 9.4. First, individuals (and groups) may move over time to different cells in the table. People may change their affective ties with group members (indeed, we would usually expect movement in a "positive" direction on the affective ties variable if affiliation occurs), and the degree of congruence may change as well, as new group members come to understand and accept a given group's ideology. Thus, if affiliation does occur (for reason of extreme felt needs or lack of alternatives that have yet to be disproved as viable alternatives), then we would expect a gradual (or perhaps even quite abrupt) "drift" toward cell 1 of the table for most individuals. Any movement counterdirectional to this tendency would be reason to expect eventual disaffiliation or "deconversion" (a worthy subject for investigation itself—see note 1).

A second comment is related to the first. The two major variables in the table are *not* independent of one another. Extant or developing affective ties may lead to more congruence, just as initial congruence may contribute to the development of affective ties with group members. Which variable usually has the strongest effect—and thus explains more conversion—is subject to some debate, as we have noted. Much more research needs to be done on this point, but we would suggest that one may have a stronger effect under certain circumstances, whereas the other will show more influence in yet other circumstances. For instance, relative social isolates desiring affective ties may not attend to congruence factors as much as individuals with a strong (well-inculcated) commitment to certain orientations and perspectives. It is at least theoretically possible that individuals in the latter category could seek out and convert to a group with which they had no positive affective ties initially. It is also theoretically possible, even predicted according to the Gerlach and Hine model, that individuals with high needs for affective ties (and possible other basic needs such as food and shelter) would convert to a group with which they had no basic cognitive or behavioral congruence. We think there are examples of both these extreme possibilities to be found in the history of CCO, along with many other examples that fall somewhere between the extremes.

A GENERAL MODEL OF THE CONVERSION PROCESSES

Now we will summarize our efforts at developing a model of the conversion process especially applicable to CCO and the Jesus movement, as well as other contemporary movements. We will use particularly the insights furnished by our examination of the work of Gerlach and Hine (1970) and Lofland and Stark (1965), along with input from other approaches. The model presented will not necessarily be chronological, but will instead adopt the Lofland and Stark principle of "activation" or the Smelser (1963) "value-added" perspective. This means that while the model may appear to be a temporal sequence, such is not necessarily the case. Some parts of the model may occur before others, some may occur simultaneously, and some elements may be of greater importance in explaining a given type of conversion. All the elements of the model must be taken together to explain most instances of conversion (including "group conversion"), and we think that just about any given instance of conversion occurring in contemporary society can be explained by the confluence of the factors contained in the model. Note that the separate elements are analytical parts of the conversion phenomenon, and thus are not totally independent of each other.

Major Elements in General Conversion Model

Prior Socialization

Any model of conversion should attend to the importance of prior socialization, Gerlach and Hine (1970) and Hierich (1978) notwithstanding. We do not intend that this variable be treated in a simplistic and/or deterministic fashion, but instead would suggest that the operation of this important predisposing variable would be quite movement specific and temporally specific. Prior socialization furnishes what Lofland and Stark (1965) refer to as *perspectives* for defining problems and solutions to problems, and as has been discussed, prior socialization also contributes a basic general orientation to people.

In this chapter, we have developed general orientations using two cross-classified dimensions—*individualistic-collectivistic* and *supportive-opposed*—and we have suggested two additional "perspectives"—*physiological* and *conventional*—to complement the three presented by Lofland and Stark (religious, political, and psychiatric). Generally, we would expect that conversion processes would involve individuals moving *within* general orientations and perspectives, unless a traumatic experience disallowed further consideration of that orientation or perspective, or there were no available alternatives within a problemation general orientation or perspective. We also noted that certain general orientations and attendent perspectives can be direct *causes of* perceived difficulties at times when a basic orientation and perspectives associated with it in a given culture do not "work" any longer (i.e., do not allow an individual to function effectively).[19] General orientations and perspectives can also make individuals and groups more susceptible to appeals from certain kinds of groups and movements, and conversely, less susceptible to other groups and movements.

Prior socialization cannot be considered a simple concept. We must know the kinds of content to which a person has been socialized, the amount, timing, and "intensity" of exposure to that content, the level of personal commitment developed toward the specific content area, any previous shifts from one general perspective to another, and any previous "multiple" and simultaneous commitments to different general orientations and/or perspectives (see Richardson, 1977, for more discussion of these points). Although difficult to state unequivocally, we would generally expect that early, more lengthy, and intense socialization experiences that had developed strong personal commitments toward certain general orientations and perspectives would have the most lasting effects, effects that would generally be expected to manifest themselves in later conversion experiences.

Perceived Personal Difficulties

A second major element concerns perceived personal difficulties or problems. As indicated, such may be the result of the direct interaction of certain prior socialization experiences with temporal conditions. The perceived difficulties can be quite specific, or they may be of a more general or amorphous nature or, in a situation suggestive of a maximum propensity toward conversion, a person (or group) may feel *both* general and specific tensions. Glock's (1969) work on types of deprivation furnishes some insight into types of tensions or frustrations that might result in the perception of a personal difficulty, as does Parrucci's (1968) work dealing with the relationship of societal integration and societal regulation vis-à-vis conversion. The psychological and religious concept of guilt may also be employed in explicating perceived difficulties, as demonstrated by Gordon (1974) and Richardson, Simmonds, and Harder (1972). Note that particularly in modern society, there may well be a *continual* perception of personal difficulties and problems for many people. This aspect of modern society may aid in an understanding of why there seems to be such a plethora of new movements developing constantly. There seems to be a kind of *continual conversion* process from one group to another operating for many individuals as they seek a resolution to perceived general problems, problems which may not be soluble in the classic sense. Thus, this time in American society might well be characterized as an "age of conversion."

Resolving Perceived Difficulties

A third element involves the perception that a certain movement and/or movement organization may furnish a way to resolve perceived difficulties. This element incorporates the notions of defining oneself as a certain type of "seeker" and of reaching a "turning point" from Lofland and Stark, with the ideas of "initial contact" with a movement participant and "focusing of needs" from Gerlach and Hine. Obviously, there is a relationship between elements one and two of the general model being here presented and this element. Prior socialization can help make one aware of certain problem-solving orientations and perspectives alternatives, while precluding other perspectives and orientations. There is a predisposition toward some movements and movement groups because of prior socialization. However, particularly in situations where the "felt needs" are more amorphous and little understood, simple *contact* with certain groups may define a problem and a solution to the problem. (Gerlach and Hine seem to adopt such a view.) The relationship between elements one and three of our model has been alluded to in the discussion of element one. Assuming the operation of element two as something of a "trigger," we would expect most individuals to seek solutions to perceived problems within the same perspective and orientation before going to other perspectives and/or another general orientation,[20] unless such alternatives had already been tried and disproven, and unless such perspectives and orientations were consciously defined as "part of the problem."

Some other important aspects of this element of our general model need to be further delineated. Some individuals in contemporary society seem prone to move from one "solution" to another in a serial-like fashion—serial alternatives is the term used earlier in the chapter. This movement, which illustrates the immense *ideological mobility* of modern life, seems to result directly from the relatively large number of alternatives available in modern pluralistic society (the existence of a large opportunity structure) and the inability of any one "way" to definitively assert itself as *The Way* to resolve personal difficulties. This serial alternative approach dictates that instead of just focusing on one movement and/or group and its converts, and on one "conversion event," we must examine the *conversion careers* or *trajectories* of participants as they move from one group to another if we are to fully understand conversion phenomena and what is happening in our society.[21] *Conversion to any given contemporary movement and/or group should be thought of as one in a series of steps, not as an ultimate goal.* This means that the defining of a particular movement and/or group as a way to solve perceived difficulties may be a temporary occurrence, and that such probably transitory events should not be reified by social scientists studying them. Such a tendency to freeze movements in and out of groups does little justice to the dynamism of contemporary society.

Loss of Meaningful Ties with Society

A fourth analytically important element of our general model concerns the lack or loss of meaningful positive ties with society. Obviously this element does not operate chronologically (occurring only after the first three elements have become operational), but instead is related to all the first three elements. Prior socialization can contribute to a person's feeling isolated from the greater society, and this isolation can be made manifest in terms of general or specific tensions felt by individuals. Further, encountering a given group that is developing in contrast to the greater society or some of its specific institutional structures can help convince a person of their isolation. These concerns for the interrelationship of this element with the first three (and the next one) notwithstanding, we still think it valuable enough to attend to separately, a view shared by some theorists in this area.

We do not want to be accused of disallowing cognitive elements in the conversion process and have in fact emphasized them in the first three elements of this general model, all of which deal with the operation of *predispositions,* some of which are certainly cognitive, in the conversion process. The fourth and fifth elements are much more *situational,* to use Lofland and Stark's term, and also incorporate activity or *behaviors.* Given that individuals and groups are predisposed toward certain movements and/or groups as ways to solve perceived difficulties, the operation of the variable *affective ties* will help explain why and how conversion occurs. And first, we will briefly look at how affective ties work with reference to the greater society.

This element has been discussed somewhat in our comments about the operation of affective ties, which will be the focus of our fifth and final general analytical element. It was noted that, generally, converts have weak ties with nongroup members, which implies few ties with the greater society of which the person is a part. Lofland and Stark's work emphasizes this view, with the explicit inclusion in their conversion model of the notion of weak affective ties with "noncult members." Gerlach and Hine suggest something similar with their emphasis on the commitment event, which seems to imply the relatively small importance of outgroup social, economic, kinship, and friendship ties. White's (1968) works suggests that interaction with non-group members must lessen for conversion to occur. Thibaut and Kelley's (1959) work suggests that the "comparison level of alternatives" must be high in order for a change of group allegiance to occur, a position that also seems indicative of relatively weak or weakening nongroup ties.

The only exception that we have noted to the usual operation of this variable is in the interesting case of a potential convert having a positive affective tie with someone outside a given group who holds a positive view of the group. This situation might well furnish some encouragement for a person to join who has some strong ties with nongroup members. With this one exception, we generally expect that converts will have weak ties to nongroup members, or that ties extant at the time of contact will lessen in importance.[22]

"Pulling" Effect

The fifth element of the general model concerns the "pulling" effect of the operation of developing affective ties between potential converts and group members, an effect contrasted to the "pushing" effect of the typical operation of affective ties with nongroup members. The literature of conversion abounds with references to this variable. Both Lofland and Stark and Gerlach and Hine emphasize the importance of developing positive affective ties with group members, as do others such as White (1968) and those in the "brainwashing" tradition.

Our discussion of the fourth general element contains several points germane to the operation of this variable, but we also want to move beyond that treatment and focus on the way in which ingroup affective ties are developed. Lofland and Stark stress as their last factor "intensive interaction" and say that such usually occurs in communal situations where the potential convert (or "verbal convert") moves into a living situation with some group members. Gerlach and Hine include "re-education through intense group interaction" and note that the individual is recruited into a given small cell, not into a movement as a whole. The entire brainwashing tradition appears to agree about the necessity of severely limiting interaction with anyone except those chosen to be a part of a group. The "revolutionary colleges" developed in China shortly after the takeover of the communists amply demonstrates their appreciation of the importance of intense interaction to "conversion" (see Lifton, 1963). And White's (1968) paper focuses on the interaction model of religious influence, implying that this is the process whereby affective ties are developed between potential converts and group members. All this literature thus leads us to emphasize the importance of *intense interaction between potential converts and group members* on initial conversion, and the possibly even greater importance of interaction on maintaining a new member in a group and making that person into what Lofland and Stark refer to as a "deployable agent."

We would point out that this interaction variable, which can be operationalized in many different ways, functions with the fourth element of our general model as well. If interaction is minimal (for whatever reason) between potential converts and nongroup members, this will usually mean that affective ties with nongroup members will weaken. There is, of course, no rule of human behavior that says affective ties are directly related to amount or intensity of interaction.

However, especially in cases where some volitional element enters the picture, it seems that one might usually expect a positive relationship between affective ties and amount of intensity of interaction. The volitional element is important, in part, because of the implications for volition in the dissonance literature. Once a decision has been made by an individual to allow contact with a group, then there may well be tendencies to encourage interaction and the development of ingroup affective ties, at least partially to justify (or perhaps to "test") the initial decision to allow the contact.

RESULTS OF PARTIAL TEST OF MODEL

The general model developed by combining parts of the Lofland and Stark and the Gerlach and Hine models and extending them is difficult to test fully. This difficulty arises because of the type of information that must be obtained and because of methodological difficulties associated with field research on a phenomenon such as the Jesus movement (see Appendix A). An attempt was made, however, to apply parts of the model to CCO members in an effort to explain why members joined. Each of the five elements of our general model will be discussed in turn, not as specific hypotheses, but more as expectations.

First Expectation

The data, some presented in chapter 6, indicate that members to a large extent had experienced considerable *religious socialization.* As indicated, the majority of CCO members did attend church in their early years, and they generally attended frequently, even if the majority (60%) were not from strictly fundamentalist backgrounds. Data on length of time involved in this early religious socialization is not available, although other data cited (such as type of church to which they belonged and frequency of attendance) substantiate our idea that religious socialization would be important to most members. Thus, many apparently could be thought to possess an individualistically-oriented religious perspective.

The fact that religious socialization is important in the background of most participants seems indisputable. However, the meaning of this involvement is subject to great debate. We know of no research other than our own that has attempted to address the specific theory of Berger's that such socialization leads to alienation, and the notion that the degree of alienation varies by type of religious socialization. We were able to gather some suggestive data from our population of study, but this data can certainly not be treated as a conclusive test of the Berger (1967) theory, even though in general it supports the theorizing. Our tentative data, presented in chapter 8, support the view that most members thought of the institutional structure as sacred, implying that they were alienated, as Berger uses the term. Another type of evidence for the notion of the possible deabilitating effects of conservative religion such as that of CCO was gathered by using Gough's Adjective Check List, some of the results of which are presented in chapter 7.

Although such results are certainly subject to differing interpretations, some would say that these results are in accord with Fromm's (1950) theories about the deabilitating effects of authoritarian religion. They also mesh with the Berger theorizing, as they give the impression of people not very adept or interested in effecting change in the institutional structure of society.

One explanation for the somewhat unexpected finding of more persons with religious socialization in "moderate" groups, as was reported in chapter 6, is related to socioeconomic class. Most members were from middle class or upper-middle class families using the criteria of parents' average annual income, and father's occupation and years of education. According to Stark (1964), Demerath (1965), and others, conservative denominations are largely composed of persons in the lower and working class. Thus our finding of only 40 percent conservative (including Catholics) should not have been so surprising, given the class-of-origin makeup of CCO.

Second Expectation

Our second expectation is that young persons who convert to CCO will report experiencing some form of *major difficulty or dissatisfaction in their lives prior to joining*. In addition, there may be other specific indicators of situational disruption such as divorce of parents, bad drug experience, or high mobility.

Several questions were asked for the purpose of indirectly assessing disruptions in the lives of the respondents. Such events and circumstances as parental deaths, divorces, high mobility, poor relationships with parents or siblings, and bad drug experiences, especially those occurring shortly before their contact with the group, were seen as possible indicators of stress which could be resolved through affiliation with a warm, supportive group.

At the risk of appearing to oversimplify, the data (presented in chapter 6) indicate some general state of frustration or tension for most members, a situation probably not dissimilar to that of many American youth in the 1960s. However, the data do indicate considerable disquiet by the majority of members in the six-month period just prior to joining CCO. Bad drug experience was the most prevalent such problem.

Immediately before joining (the last few days before), 19 (22%) reported highly disruptive situations such as use of alcohol or drugs, or being frightened or upset; 28 (32%) reported moderately disrupted lives, such as traveling, being on the streets, or hitchhiking; and 22 (35%) reported no disruption, such as staying with family or friends, working, or going to school.

Thus, although members did not report excessively tension-filled or disruptive relationships with parents and siblings, many reported that during the period immediately prior to contact with the group, they were depressed or upset by specific circumstances. This information provides limited support for the contention that preconverts perceived disruption or crisis in their lives prior to joining. Gordon's (1974) study also revealed a pattern of some major personal loss preceding affiliation, but Hierich (1978) opposes such a view.

Third Expectation

Our third expectation was that these young people would perceive a *fundamentalist-oriented religious group (such as CCO) as offering a possible solution to their felt problems.* This expectation may seem a bit nonsensical, since our data represent a post hoc test which reveals that 100% have adopted a *religious perspective* in defining and solving personal difficulties. However, we want to move beyond such a simple concern and examine the conversion histories of some CCO members, along with presenting data on how they may have sifted through certain other possible ways of defining and solving felt difficulties.

In the terms of the latter concern, recall the several possible perspectives presented by Lofland and Stark, and our own formulation of two other perspectives. These perspectives, we suggested, could fruitfully be characterized in terms of either individualistic or collectivistic general orientations. Our data indicate that many members of CCO had sifted through several alternatives "on their way" to CCO. All of the several perspectives discussed seem to have been tried by some members of CCO at some time in their quest for meaning.

Lofland and Stark's *psychiatric perspective,* which is of course individualistic in orientation, was tried by some. Forty-one (47%) of the respondents had at some time in their life been to a psychiatrist or psychologist, although only 8 had been in the year prior to the interview. Only 6 respondents felt, in retrospect, that the experience had been beneficial, while 32 of the 41 (78%) said it did not help them. Respondents reported that the main reason the counseling was not beneficial was that the psychiatrist was incompetent or lacking in ability. Twenty of the 32 (62%) gave this response. Four felt that the experience had caused them even more problems. Those who had attempted to deal with their problems in this manner were not pleased with the results. We can suggest then that most respondents did not have a psychiatric perspective before joining (contrast this to Anthony et al., 1977, who discuss the confluence of interest in psychiatry and interest in Eastern-oriented religious groups). Quite a few had "tried it," but for most the alternative was not viable. At the time of interview, only 10 (11%) of the respondents felt that psychological counseling would be of benefit for a person who was deeply troubled. Fifty-nine (67%) of the members felt that such a person should "seek Christ or "ask the Lord for help."

The *political perspective,* which can be either individualistic or collectivistic in orientation, was tried by some, although fewer claimed to have been involved in this alternative than was the case with the psychiatric perspective. Only 28% claimed to have been involved in any political activities before conversion, as was reported in chapter 8. Very few of those who were involved were "very active." As a group, CCO members became even less political when they joined, with 71 of those interviewed saying they were totally uninterested in politics (see Table 8.3), and 67 saying that nothing can be accomplished by being politically active. Thus we see a pattern of some trying this alternative and giving it up shortly, but with the majority simply not defining political definitions and solutions to problems as being possible. Note that this, the one alternative perspective with a *possible* collectivistic general orientation, attracted less than half the members who had tried the individualistic-oriented psychiatric perspective. Gordon (1974) found *no* Jesus movement members with a radical politics background in his small population study. Such information seems to support our idea that crossing the major boundary between collectivistic and individualistic orientations is more difficult and therefore less frequent than "movement" within a general perspective. And, as stated earlier, these data do *not* lend much support to the contention of some commentators that Jesus movement groups converted many young people from a life of political activism.

The newly delineated *physiological perspective,* an obviously individualistic general orientation, was tried by many CCO members prior to joining. We have already presented data on drug usage in chapter 6, data that indicate about 90% of CCO members interviewed had used drugs prior to joining. Recall that this drug usage was in most cases taken quite seriously and involved, in many cases, long-term use of relatively hard drugs. Apparently, this is a familiar pattern in the movement, since Adams and Fox (1972) also noted this kind of finding among these subjects, as have other researchers. Although our data are not as systematic as we would like concerning some other possible activities contained within the scope of the physiological perspective, we have, through our long-term contact with group members, learned that many had considerable sex experience before joining CCO, and several were also into other individualistically-oriented activities such as health foods and "nature trips." Thus this perspective was tried by most (if not all) but was given up in favor of the latent religious perspective.

An important point has been suggested in the writings of W. H. Clark (1969), who thinks that the use of drugs has evoked a religious type of experience for many young people, who in our culture have been taught not to have such experiences. He sees some contemporary religious groups among the young as being the product of a natural evolution from unfeeling, irreligious young people to religious-feeling people through drugs. As evidence, he says that many people in new religious movements decided to stop using drugs before getting involved in a religious group. They simply became more interest in their religious experiences than in drugs that induced the experience. Our data lend some support to this analysis, as does the study of Adams and Fox (1972), and also Austin (1977). This approach furnishes a theoretical prediction about the type of conversion trajectory followed by many participants, a prediction borne out by Adams and Fox's data on the history of participants' movements from drugs to the Jesus movement.

Our data concerning the exact pattern of movement through the several perspectives (including the *conventional perspective,* which we have not discussed in this section) are less thorough than we need to establish the proportions of members who followed certain specific *conversion trajectories.* However, we can make some speculative comments. Plainly, many members went from an individualistic general orientation with a religious perspective to other individualistically-oriented perspectives such as the physiological one, and then "returned home" to a religious perspective similar to that of their rearing. A few took a "detour" into the collectivistic-oriented political arena but returned to more familiar turf. A considerable number included a sojourn with the psychiatric perspective in their movement through a conversion career, and we suspect that all used a conventional "muddle through" perspective at some time during their movement from one orientation to another or from one perspective within an orientation to another. Table 9.1 offers many suggestions about possible conversion trajectories, and the listings in the cells of that table are by no means complete. Further research along these lines of thought needs to be done before we can be firm in our position, but it is safe to say that our ideas about serial alternatives, conversion careers and trajectories, and conversion opportunity structures offer some promise.

Fourth Expectation

Our fourth expectation was that persons who become converts would have *tenuous ties with society which would be further loosened or broken in order for them to become members.* Some data relevant to this expectation have already been presented in chapter 6 and in the discussion of the second expectation. However, we want to give more detailed information on this important analytical element of our general model.

Seventy (79%) persons reported that they had friends to whom they felt very close before coming to CCO. Twenty-six (37%) of these said they had many close friends and 28 (40%) said they had at least one or two. Fifty-two (74%) of these persons said they could go to their friends and talk about deep personal problems, 9 said they sometimes could and 12 said they could not. In all, 61 (69%) of the respondents felt as though they had at least one close dependable friend, so it cannot be concluded that they were isolates, as Lofland and Stark found in their study. It is possible that although the respondents were not friendless, they and their friends were mutually isolated from rewarding interactive ties. Thus the member and his or her friends may both have been members of an "isolate class." Direct information concerning this question was not gathered.

Over half participated in activities at school, primarily sports or music and drama. Seventy-five (85%) of the respondents dated or went out before they joined, 36 (48%) of these very often (at least every week-end), and 11 (15%) at least twice a month. Fifty-six (64%) of the respondents reported that they had serious romantic involvements before joining the group. It should be noted, of course, that these self-descriptions were for a period often not immediately prior to joining the group. Recall the data about personal disruptions just prior to affiliating.

Despite some indications that the converts were not total social isolates, their ties with others did not appear to be excessively rewarding. Forty-seven (53%) of the respondents characterized their lives before joining as unhappy or very unhappy. Of course, this evaluation was retrospective and may have been influenced by the situation at the time of interview: eighty-two (91%) of the respondents characterized their present lives as happy or very happy. One further indication that social ties on the outside may have been lacking in warmth or strength is the indication by 31 (35%) of the respondents that the warmth, closeness, and love were the factors which first attracted them to the group. Thirty-eight (43%) gave religious reasons such as "the Lord's will" or "people doing the Lord's work." Such reasons might be viewed as rationalizations by some.

We also investigated the question of whether outgroup ties were broken. There are several indications that ties were loosened or broken with non-members. Fifty-five (64%) of the members said that they felt more distant from friends than they did before joining. Length of membership had little effect on whether respondents saw friends as often as they used to, with almost 100% in each membership category seeing friends from outside CCO less often. Feelings of distance or closeness to friends did not appear to change over time. Respondents in all categories felt more distant from friends. Eighty-six (98%) said they no longer saw their friends as often as they used to, which was, of course, at least partially attributable to spatial separation.

Although respondents indicated more distance from friends, their relationships with parents were described as *closer* than before joining for 54 (61%) of the members, a significant finding, especially when coupled with the finding that 51 reported that their parents approved more of the lives their children were now leading than they did of the lives they had led prior to affiliation. Twenty-two (25%) said that they felt more distant from their parents. There was no difference between males and females. Feelings of distance from or closeness to friends did not appear to change significantly with time in the group, with respondents in all categories feeling more distant from friends. Those who had been members from six months to one year, however, felt slightly closer to their friends outside the group than persons who had been members for more or less time, an intriguing finding.

Most respondents felt that people in general either disapproved of the group and groups like it or were ambivalent in their feelings. Only 13 (15%) said that they thought most people had positive feelings toward such groups, which may indicate a break with or lack of ties to the greater society. Fifty-seven (65%) of the respondents indicated that they felt weaker ties with American society than they did before joining. Only 12 (14%) persons felt stronger ties with American society. Length of membership did not appear to influence the respondents' reports of the ties they felt to American society.

A change in significant others from outside the group to within the group indicated the breaking of ties with the old. Forty-one (47%) persons said that before joining there was an individual who had a great influence on them. For 27 (66%) of these, the influential person had been a friend. Only 5 (12%) of the original 41 persons said that that individual still had a strong influence on them.

Thus our data indicate that sect members were not isolated from their society to the extent that Lofland and Stark found in their study. However, many members did not have especially rewarding ties, and most such ties were generally weakened or broken at least for a time after a person became a member of the group.

These data are not surprising given the physical isolation of the group, the relatively authoritarian structure, and their world view, all of which encouraged the weakening of outgroup ties. The group encouraged its members to "find fellowship among fellow Christians," to "shun things of this world," and the philosophy of the group was otherworldly in orientation, calling members to spend their energies getting "closer to the Lord" so that they may "live forever with Christ." Members not surprisingly reflect a disinterest in politics, social problems, and other worldly occurrences. The growth of interest in nongroup family members that seems to occur with some members after they have affiliated does not vitiate this general conclusion, since the phenomenon may be explicable in other terms (see note 2). Also, the fact that the organization is undergoing some changes in terms of ties with society does not affect an explanation of why members joined during the earlier years. A theory to explain current conversions might differ somewhat, especially concerning the operation of affective ties with significant others (see Table 9.3).

Fifth Expectation

Our fifth expectation was that *maintenance of membership depends on the development of rewarding ingroup ties.* The development of affective ties with group members is important in explaining who converts to and remains in the group. It was expected that the group must become the member's reference group if he or she was to remain a member. Strong positive interactional ties between sect members which are more rewarding than outgroup ties provide the basis for maintenance of faith.

In the group, kinship terms were used consistently and a familistic atmosphere was deliberately fostered. Members were addressed as brother or sister, an indication, we think, of closeness. Members overwhelmingly reported that they were happy and satisfied with their lives as members, although most persons were materially better off before they joined the sect. Only one person said that he was not happy.

Members did not report that they joined the sect in order to enter a fellowship of warmth, security, and acceptance. Sixty-four (72%) of the members said that they joined to be close to the Lord or because it was the "Lord's will." Only 4 (6%) said they joined to be with the people or because of the fellowship. However, other data suggest that these reports may have been rationalizations. As reported already, 31 of the members (35%) were first attracted by the fellowship and warmth. Thirty-six (41%) were attracted by "the people doing the Lord's work" or by the "presence of the Lord." In addition, 74 (84%) persons said that if they had to leave the group, they would miss most the fellowship and the brothers and sisters.

An indication of close interactional ties within the group was the statement by 76 (86%) of the respondents that most of the persons to whom they felt closest were also members of the group. Of these, 35 (40%) said that *all* of the persons to whom they felt close were fellow members. All members felt close to some other members of the group. More new members said that most persons to whom they felt close were not group members than did older members, although most persons said all or most of the persons to whom they felt close were group members.

A further indication of close ingroup ties was gained from a question related to whom persons felt like talking to when they were depressed or unhappy. Of the 37 persons who said they felt like talking to someone when they were depressed or unhappy, 34 (92%) said that person was a member of the group.

Members appeared to have developed strong in-group ties, which is not surprising, given the communal life style of The Farm. For most, the persons to whom they felt closest were other CCO members; the fellowship and brothers and sisters would be most missed if they had to leave; and they described their lives as very happy. These data lend support to the importance of the development of strong ingroup ties for commitment to occur. We plan to continue our research in an effort to test ideas about the importance of such ties to maintaining long-term commitment, a point stressed by Gerlach and Hine (1970).

CONCLUSIONS

By no means are we suggesting that these data allow a full test of all aspects of the model of conversion or commitment that we have developed, based particularly on the work of Lofland and Stark (1965) and Gerlach and Hine (1970). We are missing data that would allow full confidence in our theorizing, although the available data suggest that our approach is sound. One major problem is that of a possible "ecological fallacy" (Robinson, 1950), since what we have done is present group percentage data which, of course, can be misleading. We do hope and plan to do such a "cohort analysis" in the future. For instance we might take just the group of individuals who did not fit our initial expectations and see if they "fit" the model in other ways. Recall our notion of serial alternatives. We have tentatively developed a "crash pad hypothesis" involving such people. Simply stated, we would expect that persons, even if they had no background of religious socialization, would, if they "crashed" with the group (which always welcomes visitors) at a time when alternatives to problematic situations seemed unavailable, be prone to affiliate. Only further analysis of our data and more research can speak to this idea.

In spite of the disclaimers that have just been issued about our study, it is apparent that there is some support contained in the data for most of our ideas about conversion which, admittedly, are not all that new, but which have been newly organized with reference to CCO and some other contemporary groups.

NOTES

1. It is obvious that "conversion" typically involves withdrawing from some other group, however amorphous, and that from a theoretical point of view the process of "deconversion" is just as interesting and potentially fruitful as that of conversion. We will follow the usual practice of focusing on conversion *to* a group. At a later time, the deconversion implications will be more fully developed in a separate paper. For specific attempts to deal with the deconversion phenomenon, see especially Weiss (1963), White (1968), Mauss (1969), and Toch (1965). The latter classic work includes an entire chapter entitled "The Dynamics of Disaffection."
2. The term conversion, as we use it here, has something of a technical meaning involving rapid and dramatic change of identity and allegiance. The meaning of this term is not unanimously accepted even in the schol-

arly literature, and quite often the term conversion is used to refer to any type of change, however inconsequential and gradual. In such instances, terms such as affiliation or recruitment are sometimes used as synonyms. The brief and simple definition of conversion given has been accepted for use in this study because rapid and dramatic changes have been common in CCO. The fact that such changes have been widespread in our society in recent times, as people have "flipped" from one group affiliation to another, is the major reason that we think our work has broader implications and is not group or movement specific.

3. It is sad to also have to admit that there is also little cross-referencing *within* the two traditions of study. For instance, Weiss's (1963) provocative work has been totally ignored by others in the "process tradition," as has the important work of Parrucci, which is not cited at all by either Gordon or Travisano. We should add that we did not deliberately select an unrelated set of articles and books to make this point. We have selected, on qualitative grounds, from a rather large literature on the subject, omitting a number of works that seemed to add little substance.

4. The groups studied have been examined by others as well, with the immense literature on civil rights type groups being directly related to the "Black Power" aspect of Gerlach and Hine's study, and the studies of the neo-Pentecostal movement (see Kildahl, 1972; McGuire, 1974; Harrison, 1975; and Fichter, 1975 for good examples of such work). The "Divine Precepts," which, as stated, is a pseudonym for the now worldwide and notorious Unification Church initiated by the Korean Sun-myung Moon, has been researched more recently by Cozin (1973); Beckford (1976); and Robbins, Anthony, Doucas, and Curtis (1976); a brief discussion of them is included in Ellwood (1973).

5. Both the models being discussed were developed post hoc, and as a result they "fit" the data of their respective studies well. Neither of the teams of researchers being discussed made explicit claims that their models would be all-inclusive of other related phenomena (quite to the contrary, in fact, with Lofland and Stark, 1965, p. 862, a point overlooked by Austin, 1977). However, the literature on conversion has, when citing either, tended to treat them as more general models. Also, the use of the term "commitment" by Gerlach and Hine explains their "longer" process, since the term usually has a slightly different connotation than does conversion, which is usually thought of as a more abrupt and temporally limited event with a recognizable duration. Our own preference is to encompass the dramatic conversion event, but to also take into account that the event is part of a much larger and continuing process. We are interested in how and why people convert *and* in how and why they "stay converted."

6. It is possible to categorize some of the references cited in terms of major focus—psychological or social psychological—but this seems of little value, as most of the works have a strong social-psychological emphasis. Careful reading of such works, however, does suggest implicit underlying psychological assumptions, and we recommend such an exercise.

7. This is evident in the book by Gerlach and Hine and especially in the article authored by Hine (1969). See Richardson (1973) for a critique of the psychologically-based aspects of their work and for an examination of

literature on psychological correlates of religious behavior, especially glossolalia.

8. Gerlach and Hine's deemphasis of predisposing factors has gained implicit support in the interim since their work by the well-done statistical study of conversion by Hierich (1978) who, using a control group design, could find little to distinguish converts to charismatic renewal groups from matched nonconverts.

9. See especially the insightful discussion of individualism in Martin (1965), and also the work by Miller (1967). It should be stated that after the development of this basic approach to conversion, we found the Parrucci (1968) paper, which also makes use of the distinction, but in a way at odds with our application. His use is, we think, actually misleading, and is a problem in his otherwise valuable but usually overlooked paper.

10. "World view" is, of course, made most popular through the work of Peter Berger and Thomas Luckmann (1966). Trying to integrate their conceptual scheme with the one being presently employed is challenging, but also intriguing. For instance, it is conceivable that they would claim we have misapplied their notion of world view, and that it should be used with the specific perspectives. In that case, their notion of "plausability structure" would probably have the most correspondence with our own term "general orientation."

11. Our saying this may upset some more liberal religionists who claim to be involved in structural change, but their view of what they are doing does not necessarily coincide with our own conclusions about the meaning of their activities.

12. Some would make the claim that any group working within a society is supportive of that society, even if they are building bombs for use in terrorist activities. There may be some logic to this view, but we still think it of value to accept, at least momentarily, the claims that people make for themselves and their actions.

13. See Nelson (1969), Jackson and Jobling (1970), Campbell (1972, 1977), Wallis (1974, 1975), Eister (1972), and Richardson (1979a, 1979b) for recent theorizing on the cult concept.

14. We have in several places deliberately used the phrase "groups and individuals" when talking about conversion. We do this because, in an attempt to develop a truly general model of conversion, it is apparent that "group conversions" must be considered. There are some interesting, even classic, instances of groups converting in mass to new beliefs as a result of circumstances affecting the entire group. Such instances, illustrated by the adoption of Christianity by entire tribes, families, or villages in India and Africa, should not be dismissed as shallow and meaningless for the individuals involved. Indeed some of these "rice Christians" have been so sincere that their beliefs have been maintained through many generations in India (see the work of Sharma, 1968, in this regard). The circumstances surrounding the mass conversion usually involve severe deprivation of various kinds (see Glock, 1969, for the best discussion of kinds of deprivation), coupled with a strong legitimate authority structure. Given the tremendously rapid conversion (or "reconversion") to Christianity of so many former drug devotees at the beginning of the Jesus movement, it is

possible (and potentially theoretically fruitful) to build a case for there being something quite akin to group conversion in recent American history. Since there was no apparent legitimate authority structure present, we might conjecture that the "felt deprivations" of the social category affected must have been great indeed.

15. The concept of "cognitive minority" is apropos here. Perhaps the best discussion of it in terms of germaneness to this study is that of Meredith McGuire (1974), who develops the concept in her analysis of the Catholic neo-Pentecostal movement.

16. This latter parenthetical idea, which has potentially important theoretical implications not systematically developed herein, was suggested to us by Ralph Grippin.

17. For more discussion of fundamentalism, see also our earlier treatment (Richardson, Simmonds, & Harder, 1972), in which we discuss fundamentalism as a form of what Lifton (1963) calls "religious totalism."

18. Plainly, Tables 9.2 and 9.3 have implications for any theory of "deconversion" or disaffection. However, such implications will be delayed for now but will be developed in a later separate paper.

19. This notion, as well as the companion idea to be discussed in element 2 of "tension," seems indicative of what Smelser's (1963) concept of "structural strain." Thus we see some direct confluence of conversion models with his general model of collective behavior and social movement development.

20. Such easy solutions as those involving movement within a given perspective, or even within one general orientation, should perhaps not be called conversion, according to some such as Travisano (1970) and Gordon (1974) who would reserve the term for more dramatic changes of identity. See Richardson (1977) for a fuller discussion of this distinction.

21. The concept of cult as presented, especially as discussed by Eister (1972), seems to mesh nicely with this notion of "continual conversion" that seems to characterize our age. Also see Strauss's (1976) discussion of the seeker and Campbell's (1972) treatment of the "cultic milieu."

22. This exception is noteworthy, especially with regard to some contemporary groups which encourage members to reestablish ties with relatives who are nongroup members, partially in an effort to convert them, but also in an attempt to secure support of various types from these nongroup members. Such encouragement would not be given unless the groups thought they had a good chance of controlling and even using the reestablished ties for the good of the group.

PART E

FUTURE OF THE ORGANIZATION

We have examined in considerable detail several aspects of Christ Communal Organization. Part A focused on an organizational-level analysis, while Part B gave attention to what life in CCO has been like, with special attention given to the "marriage and family" cultural configuration. In Part C, we presented detailed information on the individual members, their backgrounds, beliefs, and attitudes. Also in that part, we presented information about personality assessment of members, along with a special examination of the political orientation of members discussed in terms of the concept alienation. Part D contained a more social psychological emphasis, as we examined the conversion experience of individual members and developed a critique and extension of the "conversion literature" in the process. In this closing section, we want to return to something of an organizational level of analysis for the specific purpose of predicting whether or not we think CCO will continue to exist as an organization for the foreseeable future. We will make use of Kanter's (1972) thoughtful work on what factors contribute to the "success" of communes in this effort, which seems a fitting way to bring this report of our research on CCO to a close.

277

10

An Application
of Kanter's Model to CCO

We would be remiss not to refer to Kanter's work (1972) on communal commitment mechanisms more systematically in this study, and we choose to close our book with an application of her insightful theorizing, which will be used as a basis for predicting the "success" or continuation of CCO. Her model is especially apropos, since it was developed out of her study of nineteenth-century utopian communes, a general type similar in many respects to CCO. In one sense, her work does not "fit," in that her definition of a successful commune was one lasting thirty-three years or more. However, we will be applying her findings in an attempt to *predict* whether or not CCO will last that long or longer, and will thus be *applying* her model, not really testing it. With this in mind, we should also note that this cannot be a thorough examination of her model, since our data are too limited to constitute a real test of her theorizing.[1]

Kanter's model makes some useful distinctions concerning the way in which a communal group can implement three analytically separate types of commitment—*instrumental, affective,* and *moral* (1972, p. 69)—which are to foster, respectively, the solution of three potentially independent problems facing any commune—*continuance, cohesion,* and *control* (p. 66). These three types of commitment operate in an additive fashion. She says, "Groups with all three kinds of commitment, that is, with total commitment, should be more successful in their maintenance than those without it" (p. 69). Each of the types of commitment makes use, Kanter says, of two analytically separate mechanisms—one to "attach" the person to the group, and the other to "detach" the person from other commitments. These mechanisms are listed in Table 10.1, which is a summary of the theoretical model developed by Kanter. Each of the six mechanisms was operationalized in various ways for application in Kanter's specific comparison of "successful" and "unsuccessful" communes, and we will use as many of the same indicators as possible in our study. However, in this brief treatment, we will group her indicators somewhat, as discussing in detail the entire list of over one hundred indicators she used seems unnecessary.

SACRIFICE

The act of sacrifice, among other things, severs ties with that which is sacrificed and thus "detaches" the person. Kanter treats sacrifice in a rather straightforward "cognitive consistency" manner, claiming (1972, p. 76), "the more it 'costs' a person to do something, the more 'valuable' he will consider it, in order to justify the psychic 'expense' and remain internally consistent." The specific categories and measures used by Kanter to indicate sacrifice were (1) *abstinence*—oral abstinence, celibacy, and "other" abstinence; and (2) *austerity*—building

TABLE 10.1

Basic Elements of Kanter's (1972) Model of Commitment: Types, Mechanisms, and Effects

TYPES	MECHANISMS	EFFECT OF MECHANISM
Instrumental Commitment	Sacrifice	Detaching
	Investment	Attaching
Affective Commitment	Renunciation	Detaching
	Communion	Attaching
Moral Commitment	Mortification	Detaching
	Transcendence	Attaching

own communal buildings. CCO would be classified as requiring oral abstinence (no alcohol, tobacco, and drugs), although members do take meat and have few aversions to "rich foods" (now that they can afford them), coffee, and tea. Because of the "subjective weight" of the rules about alcohol, drugs, and the austere existence vis-à-vis food which lasted for several years, we think that CCO should be considered "abstinent" on this indicator. Sexual abstinence is practiced to a degree in CCO since no premarital sex is allowed, and sex is permitted only within the monogamous marriage. However, Kanter makes much of the fact that celibacy should be required for a group to be placed in the celibate category. Since such was the case for the large majority of members for the first few years of the organization's history (since most were unmarried), we consider the group to meet a minimal standard on this indicator, and we classify them as celibate. We would suggest that rigorous sexual regulation might be a more generally applicable variable in commune studies instead of absolute celibacy, for however short a period of time. "Other" abstinence is also practiced in CCO, with there being a general feeling of subjugation of the individual to group needs and group ideology. Admittedly this aspect has been changing, and the growing materialism of the group, coupled with the increasing de facto private ownership of material goods, causes us to think CCO has evolved so much in the past few years on this indicator as to be considered "mixed" on the "other abstinence" indicator. But certainly in the early history of the group, "other" forms of abstinence were practiced. The data we have presented on personality assessment of members seem germane here as well.

We consider CCO "austere" in that members have built many of the buildings, and the presence of the CCO construction crews indicates that this will probably continue in at least a limited way. CCO members are also generally frugal in their life-style and do not engage much in "conspicuous consumption" (unless lower-middle class living standards are so considered). There are counterindications, however, as we have already noted the growing materialism of some group members, especially married couples. Also, the group is now buying or renting many of their properties. However, using Kanter's indicator, CCO is classified as "austere."

INVESTMENT

Kanter says (1972, p. 80), "The process of investment provides the individual with a stake in the fate of the group community. He commits his 'profit' to the group, so that leaving it would be costly." She developed nine separate indicators of investment, in three major categories—(1) *physical participation,* (2) *financial investment,* and (3) *irreversibility of investment.* The only indicator of the first was the prohibition of nonresident members, which is the general rule in CCO communes. Seldom are nonmembers welcomed for any length of time, although special categories of people are allowed to visit for short periods (parents of members, and ourselves, for instance). CCO also compares well on the second major category, as personal possessions must be turned over to the group at the time of joining. There is, as has been stated, a growing tendency toward de facto ownership, even though the organization maintains legal ownership of most things. The meaning of the de facto ownership is not clear to us at present, but its possible importance might suggest another needed modification in Kanter's scheme, a modification related to degree of group affluence.

We have some difficulty in assessing the indicators of irreversibility of investment, since our access to CCO's financial records has been limited. However, our best information (and guesswork) is that (1) records of contributions are kept (CCO leaders have a penchant for keeping financial records, partially caused by their status as a tax-exempt organization); (2) defectors are not usually reimbursed for property given to the group or for labor furnished the group, although reimbursement is allowed (and is considered an act of charity). Again some qualification is needed, as the new policy of paying some male members a salary from CCO coffers could be easily interpreted as a *quid pro quo* for "services rendered." But in the main, CCO requires a relatively large personal investment of its members and works to keep nonmembers out, unless they accept the group tenets and join, giving up their possessions (and future labor) as they do so.

RENUNCIATION

Renunciation involves the relinquishing of relationships that are potentially disruptive to group cohesion, thereby heightening the relationship of individual to group (1972, p. 82). Kanter adds, in her discussion of "insulating mechanisms," that most successful communities overtly sought specific renunciations of potential members. Our data indicate that CCO does encourage renunciation through its teachings about the evil nature of the world and the sinfulness of all individuals, especially nonbelievers, and through the requirement of confession and repentance of those who join. There are also clear-cut behavioral and belief boundaries between "the world" and the group, and much is made of these differences. Geographic or "ecological isolation" is a part of CCO life and culture, particularly during the first months of a new member's life in the group. Close monitoring of contacts with the outside world and the pattern of trying to maintain work teams made up only of members illustrate this emphasis.

The latter illustration also seems to demonstrate what Kanter calls "institutional completeness" (a term from Stinchcomb, 1965), although she used only group-provided medical services as the major indicator. CCO meets this criteria as well, as the group now has their own doctor and nurse staff, and have allocated resources to equip a medical office for use by group members in the home area. Other communes around the country use nonmember medical personnel, although the thrust is definitely in the direction of providing for health care within the group whenever feasible. This emphasis and things as the developing fellowship halls, work teams, and such demonstrate an attempt to be relatively "institutionally complete" and thus take care of most needs of group members.

Other indicators of renunciation used by Kanter also generally predict "success." No uniform is worn by members, although they do share a casual or "hippie-like" mode of dress. A special jargon has been developed within the group, and the use of outside publications (such as newspapers) is discouraged, especially among newer members. American holidays are not completely ignored (especially Christmas), but there is a rather casual treatment of Sunday as a sacred day.

The second major category—*cross-boundary control*—is also evidenced with CCO. The average member seldom leaves the group, except "on assignment," although this can and does sometimes mean working outside the community at "secular" jobs. The work-team and small-service business approach helps mute the possible negative effect of this contact, however. There are also rather strict rules for interacting with visitors and nonmembers, although such rules seem to be changing in the direction of greater tolerance of others. The move toward single-family dwellings also indicates a weakening of boundaries, but the rapidly developing fellowship hall approach mitigates this tendency to some extent. At least CCO leaders seem aware of problems in this area, and they are taking steps to counteract such trends.

We have already talked at length about the third and fourth major categories under renunciation, those being *renunciation of the couple and of the family* (see chapter 5). The allowance of "dyadic intimacy" with the encouragement of affective ties and sexual relationships between "marrieds" seems counter to communal interests. However, as Kanter notes, successful communities in the past have allowed such ties, although the tendency is to regulate them rather strictly and to subjugate such interests to the group through ideological teachings. In CCO and some other Jesus movement groups (such as the Children of God), there is a tight control on married couples and a strong emphasis that marriages and families are subject to a higher authority—that being talked about in terms of the loyalty to Christ, to God, and to CCO itself (and, in the case of the Children of God, to Moses Berg or "Mo"). The ready availability of close affective ties with other commune and organization members, coupled with other mechanisms to maintain loyalty to the collectivity, seem so far to counteract the potential for disruption caused by developing familism. However in sum, we must say that the picture regarding these two categories of renunciation is decidedly mixed, and only time will tell which way CCO will develop vis-à-vis such concerns.

COMMUNION

This specific "attaching" mechanism illustrates the analytical nature of Kanter's scheme, as some of her indicators of communion are also incorporated into other of the six mechanisms. By communion, Kanter seems to mean the degree to which communities share and work toward a "we-feeling." She says (1972, p. 93), "the emphasis of communion mechanisms is on group participation, with members treated as homogeneous, equal parts of a whole rather than as differentiated individuals." Her first major category of specific mechanisms—*homogeneity of membership*—seems to lack some conceptual clarity but does seem applicable to CCO. Specifically mentioned are similarity of religious background, economic and educational status, and ethnic background, along with the prior acquaintance of members. As indicated, members are from a relatively homogeneous social grouping. However, as has been noted, there is a growing tendency toward the development of some potentially important internal differentiation in terms of marital status. This tendency may be vitiated by the fact that, apparently, most members actually aspire to the status of being married and assume that they will marry someday. This use of the marriage as a "reference status" seems of crucial importance, as the long-term presence of a large group of people who did not or could not marry would be potentially divisive.

The second major category—*communal sharing*—is implemented quite well within CCO in that most possessions are owned by the group and used by members according to their needs. This is particularly the case with single members. Only personal effects are officially designated as owned by the individual, although we have already noted the problem of de facto ownership and its possible meaning. The third category—*communal labor*—also suggests the continued success of this group. The new salary motif may indicate important changes, just as do the allowance for developing expertise at specific tasks brought about by the lack of a systematic plan of job rotation, and the few males who have taken "secular" employment. Nevertheless, we think the overall tendency has been, and still is, toward communal labor, as illustrated by the large communal work efforts such as apple picking, tree planting, "house raisings," janitorial-service businesses, and the team approach to evangelism.

The fourth category of communion mechanisms—*regularized group contact*—is closely related to the notion of familism previously discussed. Most members do live communally for part or most of their experience in CCO, but many also live separately and have considerable privacy. Regular group meetings (such as Bible studies) and other shared activities, and an emphasis on intragroup communication help counter this anticollectivist tendency. But as stated, it remains to be seen whether or not the planned regularized group contact among marrieds through fellowship halls will be sufficient to encourage continuation of the group over the long term. We would classify CCO, however, as having considerable regularized group contact even now, and such was even more the situation in earlier years.

The fourth communion mechanism—*shared rituals*—raises some problems, as the culture of the group does not as yet contain a great number of rituals of celebration. Perhaps these will develop, but possibly the very nature of the "hang-loose" group culture will mitigate against the development of many obvious rituals. There are a number of less obvious rituals engaged in by the group, however. Perhaps the most important are the regular Bible studies and prayer times. Also, each class of graduates from the schools described in chapter 2 has special activities associated with the change of status brought about by the completion of the required studies. Marriage is also treated as an important ritual to be shared by the group, and perhaps it illustrates a tendency to simply reapply "normal" rituals within the group context. Also, several hundred CCO members meet yearly (in August) for a regular celebration that combines elements of a large family reunion, a "religious Woodstock," and a Fourth of July picnic. A state park is reserved, and several hundred members come great distances for this much-anticipated event.

Some difficulties are also encountered in applying Kanter's ideas on the fifth communion mechanism—*persecution experience*. Or perhaps it is better to say that CCO does not meet rigorous criteria on this indicator. Although members as separate individuals apparently perceived themselves as something of a persecuted class *before* joining the group, the response of the greater society toward CCO and other organizations like it has been decidedly positive (a major exception is the generally negative response toward the Children of God). There is some question of balance required in terms of persecution and positive treatment, however. As indicated in the introduction, the positive response of the greater society has been crucial to the group's continuation and growth. However, Kanter's point, which is similar to some ideas from the MO literature (see chapter 3), is that too much positive treatment can seduce an organization into giving up its distinctive character and becoming instead just a somewhat different part of the greater society's institutional structure. Only a strong emphasis on ideological differences can maintain a "cognitive minority" status in the face of such a welcome by the greater society as has greeted most of the Jesus movement.

MORTIFICATION

Mortification could well be thought of as a process whereby the old self is destroyed. Kanter makes it sound like a rather simple process, but in reality, this may be sometimes a nasty and distasteful process (depending on your point of view), with similarities to brainwashing techniques described so well by Lifton (1963) and applied to the Jesus movement in general in our earlier paper (Richardson, Simmonds, & Harder, 1972). Such techniques have been in the news now as a result of the Hearst trial and the current debate about "deprogramming" (see Shupe, Spielman, & Stigall, 1977, for a discussion of the anticult or deprogramming movement). Kanter develops twenty specific indicators of mortification arranged in four major categories—*confession and mutual criticism, sanctions, spiritual differentiation,* and *deindividuation.*

Vis-à-vis confession and mutual criticism, we think CCO adequately implements what Kanter intends by mortification. Members are expected to confess upon conversion, which often coincides roughly to the time of joining. The confession would be made to the group members involved in the conversion, and group leaders would regularly be informed about the new member—including his or her confession. Also, there is a certain expected regularity to confession thereafter, with members required to confess "trials" and difficulties to house or fellowship pastors as they arise. We have been informed that group confession is also practiced, especially among newer members, and we are convinced that Kanter's term "mutual surveillance" is also practiced. Members are inculcated with group beliefs that they are responsible for each other and that this includes reporting (for the person's own good, of course) any "trials" that the person undergoes but fails to report. We have seen this system function, as a few persons thinking about leaving the group and returning home were "reported" by fellow group members. And there is certainly surveillance by group leaders, who are much more involved in the lives of members than, for example, a typical pastor of a suburban church. The only possible disclaimer to this pattern is the new situation of married couples living apart from the group. As has been stated, this new living situation carries with it not only a loss of direct surveillance, but the possibility (probability?) of developing affective ties between family members that could counter the pervasive claims of the organization. On the whole, however, we think CCO certainly should be considered as practicing confession and mutual criticism.

Sanctions are also practiced when members are "deviant." We are not aware of such drastic actions as having people shave their heads (as sometimes is done in Synanon), but there is a rigorous adherence to the rules of the group. Violators are expected to confess, and this confession becomes public knowledge and serves as an example for others. We have also been told that persons have been asked to leave the group on rare occasions, but like many other such groups in past history, there are relatively few cases of deviance. Once the person has agreed to join and is accepted, there is an expectation that he or she will adhere to group norms. This expectation is usually met.

Spiritual differentiation, another mortification mechanism, is also an integral part of CCO life. Older members are considered to be "older in the Lord," which means that they are "closer to the Lord" and thus occupy a relatively elite status within the group. Members come to think of their leaders as being truly guided by God in decisions and actions, and there is little questioning of authority. When someone fails to fulfill an assigned task, he or she is thought to be spiritually weaker than the others and is "mortified" at being so designated. The CCO leadership structure is actually defined within the organization in something of an inverted fashion, with leaders being described as the "servants of all," chosen by God to serve the group. To be a servant (leader) is to be closer to God, and to be an "ordinary member" is to be constantly striving for the elite status of servant. We are not aware of such overt indicators of spiritual differentiation as the use of special seating arrangements at communal meetings, a technique used in some communal organizations described by Kanter, but even in this relatively "hang-loose" group there is still much differentiation along "spiritual" lines.

Some of the other indicators Kanter uses for spiritual differentiation also are found in CCO. There is a serious attempt made to teach the rules and doctrines to new members, and members are expected to learn the doctrines. Also, new members are segregated for a lengthy time as they proceed through the schooling designed to resocialize them, and they are put through something of a probationary period even before the schooling starts. Because of the relatively unskilled nature of much of the work done by members during CCO's first few years, there were few status distinctions on the basis of skill or intelligence. However, we have observed some status distinctions developing in recent years as certain people gain skills and are placed in supervisory positions over other less-experienced members. This, however, is the only counterindication of the notion of spiritual differentiation as the concept is delineated by Kanter.

Deindividuation mechanisms seem to be in a state of flux in CCO, although the emphasis is still more "deindividuating" than not. While there is no uniform *required,* all members are expected to dress rather informally, and we have seen no one formally dressed. We have already related the rather rigorous requirements concerning dress for females, and even though there has been some relaxation, it still seems to us that there are some strict norms of female dress, at least. It has also been the practice that all CCO members live communally, share communal dining facilities, and eat the same meals. However, this is changing some, as we have discussed, and thus deindividuation mechanisms seem to be loosing some influence. The personality data indicating "dependency-proneness" of member self-characterizations (chapter 7) suggest that the deindividuation techniques are functioning to either produce such persons, or to maintain them, as such, if they are already "deindividuated" when they join.

TRANSCENDENCE

Mechanisms for transcendence (a term with apropos religious connotations) are supposed to accomplish the opposite of mortification mechanisms. They are designed to develop a feeling of being a part of the organization. In short, the person is given a new identity—an identity welded to the group definitions of reality. Transcendence, Kanter says (1972, p. 113), ". . . requires, first, the experience of great power and meaning residing in the community." She uses the term "institutional awe" further in her discussion to explain what is meant by this key term transcendence. She then divides transcendence into five major categories—*institutional awe through ideology, institutional awe through power and leadership, guidance, ideological conversion,* and *tradition*—some of which have as many as eight specific indicators.

Institutional awe through ideology is certainly demonstrated by CCO. They adopted, with some modifications, a well-developed ideology which is a modified form of fundamentalism (described in chapter 1) containing all the major elements considered essential by Kanter. There is a definition of humanity as sinful before God and as needing redemption through individual salvation. The thought system is complete and well-articulated, in that all possible things encountered by group members can be "explained" by this system. It is "totalistic," as demonstrated in our earlier paper dealing with thought reform (Richardson, Simmonds & Harder, 1972). All things are "locatable" in the thought system, even if their "place" seems rather simplistic to outside observers. CCO leaders are vested, through the ideology, with special powers of communication with God and are thought to have magical (spiritual) powers as a result (the power to sometimes "work miracles"). The history of CCO contains several single instances of visionary experiences which guided the group, through its leaders, to its present position of relative power and success. Demands on members are sanctioned through the use of the ideology, and we have heard many of them explain that they were doing some arduous task because it was their calling, given to them by God (usually through the leadership). Members, through the notion of "priesthood of believers," are also defined as potentially possessing all the magical powers of leaders. If and when they can demonstrate these powers, they are much more prone to become upwardly mobile in CCO through the process of being selected by the leadership for greater responsibility. Also, there is the feeling that God will demonstrate satisfaction with members by allowing his power to "flow through" them as the members accomplish various tasks given them to do. And all decisions are explained and justified in terms of the pervading beliefs. This is most evident in everyday conversation with members, but also the several pages of Scriptural justification that preface the financial plans and regulations for CCO demonstrate this approach. In fact, we have yet to see any kind of group policy document that is not justified through the use of Scripture. Printed material describing the experimental "in-house" bank, with no interest charged or paid, contained more Scripture references than anything else.

Perhaps the most important indicator of institutional awe through ideology, at least from the point of view of CCO, is the idea that the organization has direct ties with important historical figures and happenings. The person of Jesus Christ is pushed to the forefront of most discussions, and CCO members and leaders truly believe that CCO (and perhaps it alone) is living the true Christian life. References are made to the Book of Acts with its descriptions of early Christian communal living to explain why the group lives as it does. Even the recent change with reference to married couples was justified using ideological considerations (the male as head of his household)! Thus CCO seems to meet all the requirements posited by Kanter, and with "room to spare."

Institutionalized awe through power and authority is also to be found in CCO. The group has a definite authority hierarchy, which has been described. CCO is so new that it has not changed leadership at the very top, but it seems plain that several leaders are defined as possessing special powers and thereby having the ability to enter into top-level policy decisions. There are also special leadership prerogatives in terms of life-style and other privileges. Such leaders are considered stronger and "closer to the Lord," thus helping make them immune from usual problems and temptations. The leaders also usually live separately, as demonstrated by the commodious quarters at The Land for some leaders. There are few special forms of address for leaders, however, as we have only heard them referred to by their first names (the usual treatment of all members). Decisions made by leaders often have a quality of mystery and magic about them. However, the continued success of the organization validates the decisions and apparently serves as further proof to members that CCO is indeed guided by God. We are completely unaware of any sort of impeachment provisions for upper-level leaders, although some lower-level leadership have been demoted, at the direction of top leaders, for poor performance of assigned tasks. We would add one other point that Kanter does not discuss. Because CCO has continued to expand and change through most of its history, there has always been the possibility of upward mobility through the sacred hierarchy of the organization. We think this possibility is important to CCO, in that it seduces otherwise more independent members to stay within the organization (and thus helps validate the structure) instead of engaging in schismatic activities that would perhaps destroy the structure. A structure that keeps most of its members and allows them to think that they too might someday occupy the upper levels of leadership seems to be more permanent than one in which leadership positions are filled and there is no possibility of upward mobility.

The indicators for "guidance" are not met with as much rigor, but we think that the "spirit" of the idea is maintained within CCO. There is certainly a fixed daily routine of activities for most members (although a few "troubleshooters" have unroutinized lives). We have described typical daily routines in chapter 4. There have also been (and still are) strict personal conduct rules, as have been demonstrated in several sections of this book. The only indicator not fully supported concerns detailed specification of the daily routine. There seems quite a bit of flexibility in terms of doing an accepted task, and there is no strict set of rules for each job. We would, in fact, question the efficacy of this indicator, as it seems somewhat dysfunctional in a large organization to try to specify all possible behaviors, and it goes against the spirit of getting members personally involved in organizational life in a meaningful way.

Ideological conversion is also required by CCO, as the group is a part of the revivalistic tradition in America. This tradition focuses on individual conversion, and all CCO members are expected to have undergone a thorough conversion experience. We have heard nearly countless tales of the dramatic conversion experienced by members and the immediate effects of the experience. New members are expected to make vows of allegiance to the person of Jesus, and this is in fact also a vow to the organization, which represents, according to group beliefs, "His presence on earth." There is a procedure for choosing new members, with fairly specific criteria (total commitment to God and Christ, allegiance to his chosen instrument, CCO, and adherence to group norms and beliefs). Potential members who cannot or will not meet the criteria are not allowed to join. We do not know, of course, what will be required of the children of members in order for them to become full members, but indications are that a conversion experience of some type will be expected.

In terms of tradition, this group has the "ultimate." It considers itself heir to the 2,000 year-old history of Christianity and regularly hearkens back to scriptural references in its governance. Much is made of the fact that CCO has found again "the true way," and that the group is helping "prepare the way" for the second coming of Christ. This view is, according to our data, pervasive of all group members, who believe that the "second coming" is near, and that they have a special mission to perform prior to that time.

CONCLUSIONS

Our examination of the Kanter commitment mechanisms leads us to the conclusion that Christ Communal Organization will last for the foreseeable furture. This conclusion is not meant to suggest that the organization will not have its difficult moments, for we think it will have some problems. we are particularly interested in observing how they handle the growing familism emphasis and affluence But we must admit that, based on several years of fairly close obseryation of CCO, we think they will overcome these difficulties and continue to exist as an organization. We base our conclusion not on the number of specific indicators of "success" found (a large majority were found, but a few were not), but on the idea that CCO has put together what seems a coherent group of commitment mechanisms. Kanter herself says (1973, pp. 136-37):

> Successful nineteenth-century groups used most but not all of the commitment mechanisms outlined. Each group made its own selection, and put together a "commitment package" out of all the possible ways to build commitment. There were always commitment mechanisms that certain groups did not utilize.
>
> Moreover, most of the successful nineteenth-century groups retained some private space. . . . In fact, it was the unsuccessful rather than the successful groups that more frequently developed communal households in which all members lived together in one space, this being the only instance in which a higher proportion of unsuccessful group utilized a commitment mechanism.

This insightful quotation suggests that if a communal group used all possible commitment mechanisms, such would be dysfunctional, as members would perhaps be driven away from, instead of attracted to life in such a group. Few communal experiments of any success were "total institutions." They were voluntary organizations trying to attract and maintain members by striking a balance between costs and rewards. The latter quoted paragraph indicates that the growing familistic tendencies in CCO may not be as great a potential hazard to continued existence as might first be thought. Perhaps CCO can actually turn the desire for more familistic concerns to its ultimate benefit (as the Mormons appear to have done). The high degree of member satisfaction we have found during recent visits would so indicate.

CCO seems to have found a successful commitment formula and struck a reasonable enough balance to continue to grow. The presence of this "balanced situation," coupled with Kanter's observation (1972, p. 136) that all the successful communal groups she studied had a religious basis, leads us to predict that CCO will be around for some time to come. We hope that we will be allowed to observe them in their future growth and change.

NOTES

1. There are some possible ways to critique Kanter's work, although it obviously has much merit. One could critique her definition of success, which is based only on length of existence of a communal group. There are other criteria of success, and indices of success that contained some other considerations could be built. Her typological scheme could also be critiqued on the basis of its relatively static nature, among other things. The analytical distinctions between the separate mechanism used in Kanter's model are also sometimes quite blurred, as is illustrated by the occasional use of the same specific indicator for different mechanisms. Some will also not like the way in which qualitative and quantitative distinctions are intertwined. We are not told, for example, why certain indicators and groups of indicators were selected, and there is no explanation for the fact that some mechanisms have more indicators than others. But these comments notwithstanding, Kanter's work is a major contribution to this field of study. Our appliction of the Kanter model does contain some suggestions about possible improvements, but such ideas are incidental to our major purpose, that being a make a prediction about the continued existence of CCO.

APPENDIX A

The Research Project:
Methods, History, and Special Features

Our study has yielded a great amount of data, unique both in terms of type and amount gathered. These unusual features of our research, coupled with its length, made us think that recounting a chronology of the research experience would be of interest to readers. However, as we began writing the history of research, it became obvious to us that we had over the years of the research faced some of the classic problems forever being discussed in method courses and books, and further, that sometimes, our solutions to these problems might be considered innovative. It seemed to us that a discussion of the unique features of our research and how we dealt with them (and they with us) could be useful to future studies of similar types of phenomena. Therefore, rather than presenting just a simple chronological history of the research project, we also address some substantive issues raised by research of this nature, and also include a frank discussion of why we have been able to continue our research on such a group as CCO for so long.

Classic problems addressed herein include ethics in research—phrased in terms of deception versus honesty—and subjectivity versus objectivity. Also, we address claims of various kinds of methodology used in our research and are especially attentive to the issues (including ethics) surrounding the use of "qualitative methodology." (See Filstead, 1970 p. 7 for a definition, and the entire book for some provocative discussions of issues raised by this approach.)

Our experience justifies as well some comment on Bellah's (1970a, 1970b, 1974) defense of "symbolic realism" as the best, possibly even only, way to approach the study of religious phenomena. Several commentators have taken issue with Bellah, including Burtchaell (1970), Klausner (1970), and Nelson (1970). We, however, will be most concerned with the report of Robbins, Anthony, and Curtis (1973) who discuss the concept in relation to their research on a "deviant" group with many similarities to that which we have been studying, and which also originated in the Jesus movement. Hopefully, our treatment will serve both as a balance for the report of Robbins, Anthony, and Curtis, and as a link between discussions of symbolic realism and some traditional concerns (especially ethics) in the area of methodology.

Closely related to our discussion of symbolic realism is a possibly unique contribution to the methodology literature—our examination of the importance of beliefs and behaviors of a subject or a group of study in contributing to the success of a research project. It is now plain to us that our initial decision to study an evangelical sect made research *easier* (or at least possible) because of (not *in spite of*, as Robbins, Anthony, & Curtis, 1973, suggest) some of their beliefs and practices. We would guess that other researchers have had similar experiences, but we are unaware of any systematic discussions of this in the literature on methodology. We will also discuss some of the special problems *caused by* beliefs and practices of the type of group we have been studying.

Before presenting our "research history," we will first briefly reiterate the different methodological approaches used in our research.

SPECIFIC METHODS USED

Something of an eclectic approach was used in our research in an effort to test some hypotheses developed prior to the research, and to gather as much information as possible about group members and the CCO organization itself. Thus while a part of the project was quite structured along the lines of survey research and personality assessment, a complementary part that can best be described as nondeceptive participant observation was also employed. This latter approach allowed us to develop new hypotheses in the field and check them out quickly. It also gave us ideas for later, more structured approaches for gathering information about the group. Our participant observation has been very successful, in that the group had allowed us to participate in nearly every group activity, including Bible studies, evangelism classes, orientation sessions of new members, drama rehearsals, meals, recreation times, visits in group leaders' homes, and working the fields. And of course, we have lived with the group during all our visits, sleeping in their dormitories, communes, and houses, eating with them, and generally being relatively accepted by the group leaders and members, most of whom have been very open with us.

Also used in the study were intensive, lengthy, and recurring interviews with certain leaders of the group. These interviews have been continuing over the years with some leaders. They have taken many forms, including taped sessions where a preestablished series of questions were asked; informal visits in their homes, places of work, and airport waiting rooms; and even a continuing correspondence in which questions were posed in letters. The contact with the leaders has been essential in terms of maintaining rapport so that the research might continue. The focus of these interviews has been a study of group origins and evolution, group structure and organization, group decision making, group beliefs, group plans, and other such general information, as well as gathering data on the individual group leaders.

Other methods used include some content analysis of group printed matter (including especially their bimonthly journal) and taped "educational" materials. (They have an extensive tape ministry which produces multiple copies of dozens of selected talks, sermons, and Bible studies for distribution across the country to branches of the organization). Personality assessment has also been incorporated and has resulted in what we think is the only such data gathered on members of a Jesus movement group. The specific inventories used include the Marlowe Crowne social desirability scale (Crowne & Marlowe, 1960), Spielberger's (1968) State Trait Anxiety Index (STAI), and Gough's (1952) Adjective Check List (ACL). These inventories have all been administered at least twice, with the ACL being used during three different research trips.

The structured interviews administered to group members included questionnaires designed to test some preestablished hypotheses, to do some "exploratory work" in some other areas of theoretical interest, and to gather as much background information as possible about group members, along with information about present beliefs and lifestyle so that changes could be assessed. The first research visit, which took place in the summer of 1971, included the use of a 265-item questionnaire which had as one major purpose the testing of a model of conversion synthesized from some of the major writings in this area. It took *at minimum* 45 minutes to administer, and most interviews took longer (some took hours). Eighty-eight people were interviewed with this instrument, over 90% of those present at The Farm, a major branch of the group. The next summer, in a June visit to The Farm, a 115-item questionnaire was administered to 96 members, virtually 100% of those present at The Farm. A 46-item follow-up questionnaire was used during the second visit to The Farm in August of 1972, and this was given to 53 members who had previously taken the June questionnaire. (Since the harvest season was ending, many of those assessed in the June visit had moved out of the area to other branches and could not be located due to constraints of time and finances.) Also during this visit, a 90-item "supplementary questionnaire" was administered to a few members who had been interviewed during the 1971 visit. Copies of all these instruments are available from the authors upon request by researchers.

The personality inventories were included in the research as follows: the first visit to The Farm (summer 1971) included administration of the ACL to 83 members one evening prior to a group Bible study. This is virtually a "population study" of those at The Farm at that time, as only those involved in chores the evening chosen for the administration of the inventory were not included. The second major visit (June 1972) included the use of the ACL, the STAI, and the Marlowe-Crowne scale, all of which were administered to ninety-six members at The Farm (again a population study). These same three inventories were administered in August of that summer of some fifty-three members who had previously been administered the instruments in June.

Comment on Interpretation of Retrospective Data

Before closing this specification of methods, one point should be made. We are aware of the fact that some of our data are largely retrospective in nature, and that, from the perspective of some, these data are not worthy of being used to test hypotheses. The questionnaires used included many questions that required the respondent to rely on memory (and simultaneously required that we rely on the honesty of the respondent). The greatest problem we faced in this troublesome area of retrospective data was not simply faulty memory, however. Berger (1963) and Goffman (1961) have both written perceptively about the conscious and unconscious "reconstruction or construction of biography." Goffman's work focuses on the interpretation of behaviors of a person *by others*. He discusses the relatively common occurrence of interpreting behaviors in a way that is consistent with past classifications of mental patients. For example, if a person in classified as paranoid, behaviors which "demonstrate" unreasonable fear or anxiety and unfounded accusations might be noted, while behaviors inconsistent with this classification might be ignored, or perhaps even go *unperceived*. This type of "construction" of biography seemed less a problem with our type of data, although we were conscious of such tendencies as we sought to interpret our data.

We felt that our major difficulty would be in the possible reconstruction of biography that persons being interviewed would do *for themselves*, and that the group leaders and members might also "reconstruct" the group's history as well. There has been some discussion in the literature of deliberate attempts to give wrong data, but we felt we were up against a more subtle phenomenon. We anticipated that individuals would, without malice or attempting to mislead, reinterpret their past history in a way that would cast them in a favorable light. Research on response bias has demonstrated that respondents may try to describe themselves in such a favorably disposed way, and/or they may try to answer as they think the interviewer desires. We saw no reason why we would be exempt from such unmalicious and undeliberate attempts to describe past histories, although we have since come to believe that the group culture, which fostered honesty, openness, and acceptance (even of researchers!) may have *helped* us gather more valid information than would have been possible in a research situation where such "Christian virtues" were not a part of the group culture. (More on this and related issues later.)

However, there may have been a hidden cost of the positive effects of the group culture. Our gathering valid information on group history and on individual histories had to take into account the important specific beliefs in a fundamentalist religious group about individual sinfulness and the great change that is claimed to occur with conversion from the prior sinful state. One member of the research team (Richardson) with previous personal experience in fundamentalist culture was particularly aware of the fact that, for some individuals in such a culture, there seemed to be an implicit high association between the degree of sinfulness (or the amount of past sin of "degeneration") and the "strength" of the conversion experience and subsequent evaluation as a Christian. More than once, he had observed in fundamentalist churches and revivals what might be termed "negative bragging sessions," as various members staged an implicit "contest" to see who could describe themselves as being the most sinful before their conversion (an analogy to a lying contest would not be out of order here). Some seemed very "proud" of their past sinfulness, and much ado was made about it. There seemed to be an unstated view among some that the worse one's past, the better one's present as a Christian. Since one had paid such a "high price" to "wash away all those sins," it seemed reasonable (to some) that one was potentially worth more as a Christian and was even a better Christian for having experienced all those sins, but having then found the strength to give them up. The degree of past sinfulness was thus sometimes used as a way of establishing a status hierarchy within some fundamentalist circles, as one could easily tell by listening to introductions given some revival speakers. Also, people of such vast "worldly" experience are sometimes especially sought after and defined as counselors for personal difficulties in their "areas of expertise." Thus, a rehabilitated alcoholic might be found in charge of a rescue mission for alcoholics. Simply put, in some circles the past life is important in establishing the credentials for activities in the present religious situation.

In our research, we had to contend with this phenomenon and realize that some respondents might, in attempts to have us evaluate them as "good Christians," use subtle (or even deliberate) attempts to make their pasts appear worse than they actually were. This type of effect of group ideology on the reconstruction of biography seems to compound the difficulty described by Berger (1963) and may be a special and extreme case of this phenomena. Thus the effect of reinterpreting one's history (or the history of the group) may be more of a problem when group beliefs such as those we have outlined combine with a general desire to be viewed in a good light by others. This tendency may have been countered somewhat by group norms *against* extensive talk about one's past. Group leaders stated that members, especially new converts ("lambs"), might "compete" in terms of their past wicked lives. Such open recognition of their type of problem only increased our original caution not to take everything said about the past at face value and to attempt cross-validation of such information.

Our questionnaire construction, interviewing, and analysis of data have all been done with such special problems in mind. Where possible, we have gathered corroborating evidence on individual histories and on the history of the group. Skillful interviewing, which included pressing a bit on points of information that seemed dubious, was our major method of handling these problems. Most importantly, care has been taken in the analysis of data to take into consideration difficulties such as those described, including Goffman's (1961) idea of the interpretation of personal histories by others in a way that "fits" previous ideas.

HISTORY OF THE RESEARCH PROJECT

This section presents a brief history of our research on "Christ Communal Organization." This presentation attempts to describe the research process as it has actually been conducted. Usually, there are considerable discrepancies between the actual research process and the report of the research, a difference illustrative of Kaplan's (1964) distinction between "logic-in-use" and "reconstructed logic." An attempt to describe a specific research history with all its pitfalls and surprises will hopefully remove the usual veil of secrecy from the research process.

Initial Entrée

At the time of our first contact with CCO in 1970, it consisted of over forty communal houses located throughout the United States and claimed a "full-time" membership in excess of five hundred, although at the time we were completely unaware of the extensiveness of the group. The organization had been in existence for over two years, having been founded in southern California in the late 1960s. After organizing and operating several houses in southern California, the leadership felt "led" to another Western state where they reestablisehd their headquarters and started establishing houses in other areas (see chapter 1 for more details on early history).

One of the authors (Stewart, whose last name at that time was Harder), intrigued by the media's attention to the Jesus movement and also interested in the area of deviance, considered in late 1970 the possibility of researching the Jesus movement from a sociological perspective for a dessertation. As with many research endeavors, chance circumstances played a role. One member of a local Chistian house associated with the group contacted her about the possibility of doing lawn work at her place of residence (most male members—"brothers"— of the house worked at odd jobs such as raking leaves, washing cars, washing dishes, and the like). Stewart was able to get acquainted with the brother and had several long informal talks with him. Consistent with the group's modus operandi, he attempted to convert the author, and she expressed interest in knowing more about the group. Following an invitation to visit the local commune, Stewart spent several afternoons and evenings at the house becoming acquainted with other members, the operations and structure of the organization, the language and group's views about their purpose, and other matters.

Stewart initially did not fully explain her interest in the group as a research topic, but it soon became apparent that one could not remain in contact with the commune for any period of time without expressing a growing commitment "to the Lord" through withdrawal from the world, verbal expressions of commitment, a change in language style and demeanor, and the like. She questioned the advisability of this approach both on practical and ethical levels. The necessary indications of commitment seemed unfeasible for various reasons. As a Ph.D. candidate attempting to study the group sociologically, she felt it would be impossible to meet the demands of overt commitment, especially withdrawal from the world. Family and school responsibilities seemed to preclude such involvement, even if beliefs had allowed it. The interest of the research focused initially upon the structure of the group, but also upon the religious, political, and experiential backgrounds of the members. Continual questioning of members about such things as their drug use, social activities, relationships with parents, and the like was likely to create suspicion about the motives of the author. In addition, as was already discussed, group norms discouraged members discussing their past lives in any detail with each other. The researcher also recognized the emotional and ethical difficulties of maintaining a deception for an extended period of time, especially when those being deceived seemed honest, open, and trusting.

After about three weeks of contact with the group and some discussions with her advisor (Richardson), it was decided to approach the local group leader or "pastor" and attempt to gain his permission to study the group. Had his response been negative, the study would probably have ended at that point. However, participation in the group had provided the researcher with knowledge of the group's desire not to gain any sensational publicity, their language style, their sensitivity to being termed "freaks," and the problems they faced in gaining acceptance within the community. Stewart approached the house pastor with a proposal to study the group in depth in order to present a more comprehensive and detailed picture of these young people who had chosen to join. The pastor agreed to the study and requested the brothers and sisters in the house to cooperate fully with the research.

A Move, A Change in Plans, Regaining Entrée

Stewart planned initially to gather in-depth information on each of the approximately twenty members of this local Christian house. Initial interviews focused on the members' backgrounds and previous life-styles, but they were loosely structured. Responses to these interviews were taped and provided general descriptive information on members and the organization, which when coupled with more theoretical support, provided the foundations for a more formal interview schedule.

Although Stewart maintained almost daily contact with members of the local commune, after a week-long absence during the summer, she returned to find the house deserted and no trace of the members. Some members later told us that their move was a response to the Lord's call to them to engage in more promising work elsewhere. Other observers place more significance on local police harassment of the members, lack of community cooperation, and the complaints of the neighbors. Some of the group members had been arrested for loitering while distributing tracts and witnessing to tourists who were visiting the area.[1]

We were surprised to find that the group had disappeared even though they (sensitive to the harassment and lack of acceptance) had mentioned the possibility of "the Lord calling them" to return to the organization's headquarters. The disappearance of the group caused concern, since by now Stewart had made a decision to use the group for her dissertation research. After much searching, one of their old buses, painted brightly with Scriptures and symbols, was found in a vacant lot. A nearby resident said that she had allowed the young Christians to put their vehicle there because she admired their efforts. She revealed their forwarding address and telephone number after assurance that the author knew and liked the young people of the group.

By contacting the group headquarters through several phone calls, we were made aware that members of the house were scattered to many different organizational communes and that some were at a farm (The Farm, described in chapter 1) leased by the organization. A decision was made to proceed with the research, a prospectus was written and approved, and a small travel grant was secured from the university social psychology doctoral program. Lengthy interview schedules (265 items) were carefully prepared based on the earlier interviews with a few members of the local house.[2] Soon thereafter, the researcher left on the research trip, accompanied by another doctoral student (Simmonds), and a friend to help with interviewing.

Initial plans called for interviewing as many group members as possible wherever they could be found. The first stop, arranged by phone, was at an organization house in a medium-sized town where each member of the research team went through an interview in order to help familiarize themselves with the schedule and with the interview setting. After spending the night at this house, the team went on to a larger city where contact was established with CCO headquarters, which at that time was in a downtown office building. The afternoon that day was spent at a local CCO commune, and later in the day, the team journeyed to The Farm, which was two or three hours drive away, located outside a small town. The decision to proceed to The Farm was prompted by information that this was the place of largest concentration of members at this time. Thus the research team decided to alter the research design to include intensive interviewing of persons at The Farm. In order to do this, it was necessary to gain the cooperation of the "Pastors' Council," which directed the many separate operations of the organization. Prior contact with the local house had given considerable insight into the special concerns and sensitivities of the organization, as well as a knowledge of the structure of the organization, and this information proved very valuable. Thus the research team, headed by Stewart, was able to gain the cooperation of the leaders using an approach similar to the one used earlier. Group leaders insisted that anonymity be maintained in all publications about the group, but they promised continued cooperation with the research.

Interviewers arrived at The Farm late one evening just as a prayer meeting was ending and introduced themselves to leaders and several curious members. Leaders at The Farm were very reluctant to allow interviewers to talk to members, however, since they had not been informed of the arrival and research plans by the Pastors' Council, with whom discussions had been held by the research team only earlier that day. They cordially provided them with sleeping space and indicated that they would contact headquarters to seek clearance for the research. As the team members were shown to their separate sleeping areas, it became clear that they had left one world and entered another. They were met with greetings of "praise the Lord," and "Jesus loves you." It was apparent that the role of researcher, although important to the researchers, was of little significance to members, who were more concerned with evangelizing than with their interview schedules or dissertations.

Data Gathering on the First Major Visit

Once permission for the research was received from headquarters, The Farm pastor called all the brothers and sisters in the group together, introduced the researchers, and instructed members to cooperate with them in every way. He told the members to drop whatever work they were doing when an interview was requested and to freely give all the information asked. The expectation that members comply without question to directions from leaders (more on this later) resulted in excellent cooperation. The group's cultural beliefs, as we have said, included an emphasis on honesty, a consideration which we think generally increased the validity of responses. In addition, the members' perception of self as "no longer of the world" and as "saved," also seemed to minimize reluctance to discuss sensitive areas about their pasts, including even premarital sexual experiences, homosexual experiences, use of drugs, arrest records, and the like.

The interview team was successful in getting interviews and some personality assessment data with over ninety percent of the residents at The Farm that first visit. The omissions were mostly random, although the one black member present at The Farm refused to be interviewed. This first visit lasted about one week and was considered successful, in that rapport was maintained and a high response rate was obtained. In addition to the important qualitative information obtained, the questionnaire produced a great deal of data. This information has been used directly in one dissertation (Harder, 1973), in several papers and publications, and serves as the major bulk of data on individual members presented herein. One of the first public presentations of systematic data on the Jesus movement resulted from this first visit. A descriptive paper containing highlights of the data was presented in October 1971 at the Society for the Scientific Study of Religion annual meetings at Chicago.

Continuation of the Research

It became obvious to all concerned that this organization deserved more attention. The advisor and committee chairman of Stewart's dissertation (Richardson), a faculty member at the University of Nevada, Reno, made a visit to The Farm during the 1971-72 academic year. This was his first visit to the area, but he was welcomed by the group and was shown around The Farm by group leaders during a short stay there. Simmonds, who had served as an interviewer during the first trip, also made another visit to The Farm during that academic year. He found the group to be still very open and cooperative and made a decision to pursue a dissertation topic through more study of the group, also working with Richardson as advisor and committee chairman. Simmonds had been involved in questionnaire construction and the interviewing of the first phase of the project (the 1971 summer visit), and he also had asked to include a personality assessment instrument (ACL) in the 1971 research. His continuing interest in the area of personality assessment and change (among others) has been of great value to the overall project.

During the spring of 1972, Simmonds prepared a prospectus which focused on personality change in the group, and his dissertation research began. It included a new questionnaire of some 115 items and a "supplementary questionnaire" (46 items) for those interviewed the previous year, in an effort to follow up on the earlier work as well. The plan was to interview members and administer personality inventories at The Farm in late spring and early summer, just after most had arrived (only a few stayed there all winter, the rest being sent there during growing season), and then return toward the end of the summer and readminister the instruments in order to assess personality and other changes.[3] The several personality instruments which have been described were the primary instruments, although the interview schedules also provided valuable information. Special attention was to be paid as well to gathering information about CCO group structure and functioning, and plans were made to visit other segments of the organization, to observe them, and to have interviews and discussions with leaders to gather this additional information of interest.

The first data-gathering trip of 1972 was taken in early June. It and the second trip in August 1972 were supported by the Research Advisory Board at the University of Nevada, Reno, whose support was nearly essential. They gave some $2,300, which included small stipends for Richardson and Simmonds, plus travel expenses for them and an interview team of five college students recruited and trained by these two authors.

Data Gathering on Second Major Visit

Although there had been some forewarning to Farm leaders who had granted permission to come, Richardson and Simmonds were doubtful about rapport continuing when they arrived with seven people in two vehicles, one of which was a large pickup camper. The first summer's research team had consisted of only three people in one vehicle, and we feared the group would view the new situation as an unwanted invasion.

Since earlier commitments to allow the research had been made, however, the team was allowed to begin interviewing, and this was begun on the day of arrival. Some Farm leaders seemed dubious about the project, and this was expressed by comments concerning our disrupting the life and work of The Farm too much. Some of this concern was a result of our having sought and received permission for the research from group leaders other than the pastor of The Farm. Although he never complained directly, we became convinced that he was somewhat upset at having us appear without first discussing the matter with him. (The reason for this apparent oversight was a lack, at that time, of full understanding of the authority relations among "house pastors"—such as the pastor of The Farm—and other leaders.)

Because of these problems of rapport, several tactical decisions were made. One was to do the interviewing as quickly as possible with no unnecessary delays. Another was to volunteer to help with the work on The Farm whenever we could in an effort to be as help and non-disruptive as possible. (See Blum, 1970, for a discussion of some of the benefits of this approach.) This led to an informal division of labor among the research team, with a few people helping more than others with the work of The Farm. Others on the team focused on interviewing. A third decision resulted in yet another division of function on the research team. Richardson did most of the interviewing of leaders in an effort to gain maximum information and also to try to allay their concerns about the research. Some of these interviews were trying affairs, as a few leaders seemed to view our visit with suspicion or were concerned about our interfering with the operation at The Farm. However, we managed to maintain rapport and convince the leaders that we meant no harm, and that we would attempt not to disrupt farm operations. Simmonds served as head of the interviewing team and worked out of the camper. He, along with doing some interviewing, supervised the interview team, assigned people to interview, and double-checked every questionnaire and set of personality inventories immediately after it was done. If there was missing or incomprehensive information given, the interviewer was sent *immediately* to complete the interview. This approach, which we strongly recommend for use in any interview research, was a result of problems of missing data done by the one inexperienced interviewer used in the summer 1971 visit. It worked very well and there were very few problems of missing data.

The "division of labor" approach worked amazingly well, and complete information was gained on all 96 members present at The Farm during the visit. Several interviews and discussions with leaders were taped for later transcription, and much information was gained by the interviewers working with the group at its daily tasks. All interviewers were also instructed to keep their eyes open, and when some information that seemed of value was obtained, this was reported to Simmonds or Richardson and was taped as field notes.

Upon leaving The Farm in June 1972, Richardson and two interviewers visited another major segment of the group that was rapidly becoming a major center of group activities. This segment, known within the group as "The Land," was about two and one-half hours drive from The Farm. It is a ninety-acre parcel of land on which the organization has built a number of buildings. It is home for several major group activities, including some other agricultural operations and some group educational activities. Life at The Land is described in more detail in other parts of this book, but suffice it to say that the trip there was quite informative and also helped strengthen and maintain rapport. After this stopover, we continued homeward, glad to be going home, but deeply impressed by what we had learned during our visit.

The Next Major Visit

Another major visit to the group took place in late summer of 1972, when follow-up data was obtained on over half of the persons interviewed in June. Simmonds and two interviewers returned for a few days, only to find that many members had been transferred to other parts of the organization because work at The Farm was lessening due to crops having been harvested. He had to trace down some people at other organization communes and operations, but he also found a number still at The Farm. About fifty-three usable interviews and sets of personality inventories were obtained after a great deal of effort, and these data served as the basis of Simmonds's dissertation, which was completed in 1977.

Unexpected Visit and Other Contacts

During the early spring of 1973, Richardson had an interesting contact with the group that bears mention, if only because it indicates continuing rapport with the group. After the 1972 summer visits, a few letters had been exchanged with some group leaders. Even so, it was a bit surprising one day to receive a call from the Reno airport from a group leader whom we had known for the entire life on the study. This leader said he was stopping by on his way home and invited Richardson to come to the airport for a short visit. This Richardson hastened to do for several reasons, one of which was the publication a few months prior of our first paper on the research. (This will be discussed further.) Upon arrival at the airport, he was surprised to find four young men, all of whom were flying in a newly acquired airplane owned by the CCO. They had been touring the region, visiting some CCO communes, and were on their way home. An amiable chat was held lasting over an hour. Then the four flew homeward leaving Richardson pleased and marveling at the experience.

Later in the summer of 1973, Richardson, Simmonds, and another graduate student who was new to the project visited the area again in order to study changes within the organization. We had concern that organization leaders might be upset with us because, in the interim since our last research visit, the aforementioned paper, a lengthy feature article in the December 1972, issue of *Psychology Today* (Harder, Richardson, & Simmonds, 1972) had appeared. The decision to publish this article was one made only after much discussion, and the decision was the cause of much concern among us and others who knew of our study. We will discuss this paper further herein, but suffice it is to say that we were quite concerned about the effects of publication on our rapport with the group. As it turned out, we were better treated than ever during that summer 1973 visit. We did not go to The Farm again but instead focused on seeing segments of the organization that we knew less about. We stayed at The Land, studied its many facets, and took guided trips to other units, most of which were located within fifteen or twenty miles of The Land. This trip was the first in which we were allowed any access to financial records (and even this was limited). We also visited a goat dairy farm owned for several years by the group, saw the group's complicated financial accounting system, toured their new cannery (which canned 170 *tons* of fruits and vegetables produced by them that year), examined a new preschool for group members' children, and learned much more about all the other agricultural enterprises of the group. We left astonished at their growth and evolution, and extremely pleased that we were still being treated as friends. We also subscribed to a new journal which was then being published by CCO and which allowed us to gain much more information about the group. (See chapter 2 for more on the journal and other operations of CCO.)

Stewart and Richardson visited the organization's center again in the summer of 1974. They were treated as special guests, sharing food and lodging with some of the leaders, who continue to be quite open to us and our research. During the visit, we were shown The Land, a newly leased "Financial Center," a newly leased vacant church used for married couples' activities—"Fellowship Hall"—and other facets of the organization. We were taken to a rehearsal of an astonishingly good drama production being readied for local television and live performance (their second such production). Also, we were allowed to sit in on the last session of a "teams school" and the orientation of a new class for "lambs school" (See chapter 2 for more detail on the schools.) All in all, it was a very fruitful visit.

Since that time, Richardson has made two othe visits to CCO operations. In the summer of 1976, such a visit was undertaken, as well as in the fall of 1977. These periodic research trips, plus contact via CCO publications and personal letters, has allowed relatively close scrutiny of organizational evolution, as reported particularly in chapter 2. We plan for there to be even more contact in the future, as follow-up research is done on members interviewed earlier.

Problems (and "Blessings") of Publication of Findings

As stated, the first decision to publish some results of the research was one of great concern. Although we had openly said to group leaders that publications might result from the study, we were fearful of what effect the first article might have, especially since it appeared in a more popular magazine with a large circulation (Harder, Richardson, & Simmonds, 1972). The group leaders had insisted on anonymity in any publication. They felt that receiving publicity would have a deleterious effect on them and that seeking of such publicity was unscriptural and un-Christian. We had agreed to this stipulation and had honored our agreement in the first article (and in subsequent publications).

The article in *Psychology Today* attracted much attention, with stories based on it appearing in many major newspapers around the country. Also, some radio and television networks and national newsmagazines contacted us in an attempt to find out about the group so they could do a program or story on them. We refused to divulge their whereabouts and were successful in protecting the group, although we had some surprising happenings. Once, Richardson was surprised to hear himself on a national radio news program. A phone call interview held that very morning with a reporter who wanted to know more about the group had been taped without the knowledge or permission of Richardson, and parts of it were being played back on the newscast. Nothing had been said that jeopardized the anonymity agreement, but nevertheless, the experience was disconcerting.

Thus, we were successful in guarding the group's identity and location, except for one breach by *Christianity Today*, which received a letter of rebuke from us taking issue with their casual use of what they knew to be privileged information. The response of *Christianity Today* was somewhat bemusing. The letter writer said (*Christianity Today*, 1973), "I am ... sorry if (the review) has caused the ——— people any disturbance. My guess is that it has not. The TV people don't read us, and besides, we didn't pinpoint any of (their) locations." The letter went on to protest that the group was already relatively well-known, and besides, "While your written report involved scholarly research, ours involved *news.*" Apparently defining something as "news" destroys any responsibilities that one might have toward those being written about. The letter closed with a very questionable statement. "I recognized your subject as ——— when I read the report, and no one told me I should keep it a bit secret." What had actually happened is that the person writing for *Christianity Today* had made an educated guess, based on his own research, as to the identity of the group. Then he called the first author of the *Psychology Today* article (Stewart) to confirm his guess. The first author had indicated that he was correct, but had asked him *not* to reveal this in print. This request was ignored, for whatever reasons.

It turned out that group leaders had read the *Christianity Today* review and were upset at it (although not at our article itself). We gave them a copy of our letter to the magazine and also a copy of the response, which some group leaders read very carefully. This seemed to satisfy them that we had kept our word as best we could.

The group's response to the *Psychology Today* article itself was interesting. We had notified them that it was out but later found out that they had seen the article several days before our letter. We deliberately waited to tell them about the forthcoming paper because we felt strongly that no censorship of our writing was acceptable, a position at odds with that of Barnes (1970), who calls for clearing manuscripts with those most directly involved. In some situations, such controls might be called for but not, we thought, in this one, as we could foresee no harm coming from our research reports and we had not been asked for censorship rights.

The article instantly made the group one of the best known (even though anonymously) groups in the entire Jesus movement. (*Psychology Today* published, we understand, about 450,000 copies of that issue.) CCO leaders realized this and seemed not to mind as long as they were not bothered. Also, they seemed to delight in reading our analysis of them. Some things in the paper they thought strange, inconsequential, or even funny, but others they took much more seriously. For instance, they were apparently impressed that we had, over the two years of study at that point, noticed changes in the sex-role relationships within the group. They told us that after our first visit (but not because of it), they had had an important meeting of pastors and other leaders that led to an "upgrading" of females in relation to males. We had noticed changes in this area and chronicled them, and they seemed pleased.

Group leaders were also obviously pleased that people were joining the group *because of* the article. This fact initially astonished us, but after thinking about it, we decided that the very large readership of *Psychology Today* would include some people interested in just the type of life-style described as objectively as possible in the article. These people wrote to us (or to *Psychology Today*, which forwarded such letters to us), and after much discussion about what to do with these letters, we sent them to the group, since we were bound not to reveal the name or location of the group. Our decision to send such letters on to CCO is, of course, questionable on purely methodological grounds, but we felt compelled to make a more "human" decision and not just destroy the letters. When we arrived in the summer of 1973, there were a few new members there who joined after first hearing of CCO through publication of the article, a fact somewhat disconcerting to us because we were determined to effect the group as little as possible. We still get an occasional letter from someone who just read the piece, and we still forward such mail to the group. These letters (over fifty at last estimate), although totally unplanned for and even unwelcome, have probably been of some import in maintaining rapport with the group. From the group's point of view, they demonstrate that we and our work are being "used of God." This notion will be examined in depth in the following section, which addresses a little-discussed but important consideration in research of this nature.

IMPORTANCE OF GROUP PRACTICES
AND IDEOLOGY TO OUR RESEARCH

A sometimes unnoticed, or at least usually uncredited, item of importance to a research project involves the openness of the "culture" of a group (or the personality of a specific subject) to the research and the researcher. In the section on the history of the research project, we mentioned some of the ways in which the group beliefs and behaviors helped us, and here we desire to pull these together into a more cogent discussion of this important issue.

It is obvious that normal rules of courtesy aid any researcher who asks permission to interview a potential subject. Chances are usually quite good that the potential subject will treat the researcher with courtesy, and this plainly gives an initial advantage to any researcher willing to intrude into another's life. Further Milgram's research on obedience (1974) has demonstrated that many (most?) people will obey requests that go far beyond the realm of normal courtesy, an occurrence that aids potential researchers who cloak themselves in the robes of scientism. Also, it is just as obvious that, sometimes, research is allowed because it can possibly be used to good advantage by the one (or the group) being researched. The tradition of research on such captive populations as the armed services fits this latter category, but also much research in industry (the Hawthorne studies) and in sociology of religion (or "religious sociology") could be so described. Also, we are all aware of the problems brought about by the desire of some to be studied with the resulting tendency to volunteer for studies (Rosenthal & Rosnow, 1975), or the so-called "Hawthorne effect" illustrated by workers continuing to put together complex devices in near darkness. However, when we talk in this instance of the value of group culture to research, we mean something more overt (but in some ways more subtle) than the kinds of things just mentioned.

Of great import in this research has been the authoritarian structure of CCO, a style of organization that may be based partially on necessity, but which is certainly justified by reference to beliefs through the medium of quoting certain Scriptural verses that support such a prescription for group life. Because of this definite authority structure, we were not faced with having to justify our existence to every individual subject in an effort to convince him or her to grant an interview. Instead, we had only to persuade certain group leaders that our project should be allowed. When they decided that it was acceptable, they then instructed the members to allow us to interview them. We had very high response rates (approaching 100%), and it is worth admitting that the response rate would probably have been virtually zero if we had not used the tactic of getting permission from leaders. This is plainly a place where some knowledge of the group ideology helped a great deal. If we had not known or found out that the group was authoritarian in nature, we might have begun attempting interviews with selected subjects, a tactic that would have virtually guaranteed the failure of the project. So in a sense, CCO was easier to study than a group in which each individual could make up his or her own mind about whether or not to be interviewed. This latter situation is, of course, analogous to just about any survey research where interviewers go from house to house trying to interview as many members of a sample as possible. The low response rates of some such studies exemplifies our point.

The actual interview situation and the situations of the administration of personality assessment instruments was eased considerably because of group beliefs and practices. Because the subjects really believed that their past life had been "washed clean" by virtue of their "conversion to Christ," they were very willing to talk about it. It seemed as if this past life could no longer harm them in any way, and they could treat it in a very objective fashion (the problem of sometimes making it sound worse than it actually was notwithstanding). Also, their new beliefs contained a strong emphasis on honesty in personal relations, and especially since we were "approved" by the leaders of the group, the respondents were extremely open to us, a fact that we have had to take into account in comparing some of the results of personality inventories with "normal" populations, which we assumed might not to be so honest.[4]

All this being the case, it is even more interesting to "go behind" the decision that we were to be welcomed by the group and see how the decision to be open to us was made. We, of course, do not have secret tape recordings of deliberations of the group leaders as they were trying to decide what to do with us. However, we do have enough knowledge of how the group functions and of its belief system to, we think, fairly well construct key elements of the probable scenario.

The Jesus movement groups generally adopt the traditional dualism of fundamentalist Christianity. (See Robbins, Anthony, & Curtis 1975 for a good discussion of this perspective and a contrast to eastern "monism") This system of thought is one of few categories and may be described as simplistic in nature. Things are good or bad, black or white, the "work of the devil" or the "work of the Lord." This lack of differentiation served us very well, especially when taken *in conjunction with* some other important group beliefs and practices. The group is very evangelical and defines as a (possibly *the*) major goal the conversion of "sinners" (which, simply defined, means those who do not believe as the group does). Also, the ideology of the group is very "God-centered" and historical in that they believe that God is in control of everything and that God takes an active role in the affairs of the world (including their personal and group life), and *at least* "permits" all that happens. This even includes their interpretation of every contact with a nonbeliever (including us) as being an opportunity, even responsibility, sent by God so that the nonbeliever might be witnessed to by them.[5]

The dualism of fundamentalist Christianity does extend, of course, to include the concept of an "anti-God" who can also move in human history, but we were fortunate enough not to be categorized as being a part of this evil contingent. Instead, partially because of our openness and our real interest in what was taking place in the group, and because the group members were honestly concerned about us, we were classified in just about the only other possible category in this simplistic system of thought with its inherent lack of differentiation (and hence of other categories). We were classified generally as potential converts—converts who obviously were to be "won to Christ" by members of this group, a situation similar in some ways, but also significantly different, to that of the researcher described in Robbins, Anthony, and Curtis (1973). Thus members and leaders of CCO were led partially by their own beliefs to assume that God had sent or directed us (even against our own wills and without our knowledge) to them. The least they thought was that God had permitted us to come there and had thereby given us over to this group as a part of their Christian responsibility.

It is possible, of course, that we could have been considered a "test" sent from God in a manner akin to the boils visited upon Job, but if some had this thought we were unaware of it. And even if some had this thought, *it would still have most likely resulted in our being able to stay with the group,* simply because we desired to do this and intended to stay until asked to leave. In short, group beliefs rendered them somewhat *passive* in the face of a concerted effort to study them. We, the active agents in all this, were apparently assumed to be tied somehow up with "the will of God," and which group member or leader was going to try to thwart that? In addition to this kind of consideration, it must be stated that personal ties between ourselves and some members and leaders have developed, interjecting an element of basic trust into our relations with the group.

Because of such ideological circumlocutions and developing personal ties, we were welcomed with sincere concern and even feted (to the extent that group resources allowed). Their usual practices of making potential converts welcome (at least for a time) seemed sometimes to be carried to the extreme. This may have been facilitated because of our relatively high status positions "in the world," because most of these were "young Christians" used to doing a lot of "witnessing," or simply because they trusted us and cared for us (more on this latter point later)

It seemed that there was an implicit contest going on to see who could convert one of us first. Nearly every interview was a contest of wills (and patience—on both sides), and we regularly heard our names mentioned in prayers in their public gatherings during our first few visits. The importance of this issue to the group was graphically illustrated when rumors of the impending conversion of a member of one of the June 1972 interview teams swept The Farm. There was much premature rejoicing among group members, who plainly assumed that the real purpose of our being there was to "get converted." We should add that this incident led to much discussion among the interview team members so that none of us would do anything to encourage such interpretations of our activities. Apparently, what had happened was that an interviewer member had expressed an interest in finding out more about the group ideas, and he had started to read the Bible during his spare time. Just the sight of him reading the Bible seemed enough to set the rumor mill in motion. In some of our later visits, people have still asked about this interviewer, desiring to know if he finally decided to convert. The tenacity of such ideas demonstrates their importance to the group (just as the continuing interest of that interviewer in the group evidences the effect the research experience had on him).

Comment on "Loving Subjects"

The personalistic episode just described is indicative of yet another unique feature of this project, one that should be addressed openly in a discussion such as this. We have earlier mentioned the great concern shown by group members for us. They truly wanted us to share their way of life and they made this abundantly clear in their interactions with us. A more human and honest way to describe this situation would be to say that apparently some of them quickly came to care for us as close friends. Their beliefs led them to place us in a category of people who were to be openly loved, and this many of them did with no apparent hesitation. Seldom in research do researchers find themselves in such a position. In some ways, our enviable situation was also our greatest predicament. We were overjoyed at being so well-treated, since we are only human and nearly all humans enjoy being loved, *and* since this contributed so plainly to our expressed goal of doing research on the group. On the other hand, we were also human enough to feel guilt about taking such advantage of the group as to accept their love and concern. Never in the experience of any of us had the subject-object dichotomy so often used in research been so strained. We went with the purpose of studying the group and its members as objects of social scientific interest. We placed them under the microscopes of our instruments and inventories and watched them continually. They, in return, sometimes treated us somewhat as objects to be converted, but they did it in such a skillful and sincere manner that many of those of both persuasions got caught up in a subject-subject type of relationship that might well be referred to in terms of Martin Buber's "I-thou" relationship. As the case of the one interviewer who became openly interested in their beliefs illustrates, some of those on the research team were considerably affected by their experience, and all of us were forced to consider the value of what we were doing, especially from the point of view of the ethics of research.

Once safely ensconced back in our offices studying results of the research, and away from the loving atmosphere of the group, it is much easier to deal with the influences some of us felt at the time. It is even possible to write reports of the research experince in which we suggest that the problem of "loving subjects" is one that must be dealt with in future research of this nature. (See Lofland, 1977, for a discussion of one new religious group—the Unification Church—using "loving" [or affective ties] as a deliberate recruitment tactic.)

INTERPRETATION OF OUR RESEARCH EXPERIENCE

A few more comments are in order about our research, lest the reader be misled about the problems associated with such research. We are convinced that research on evangelical religious groups may be among the most difficult of all possible research because it deals with an area of great personal importance to many—religion—and this is compounded by the beliefs and behaviors of the evangelical group. In some ways, our experience was not unlike that of Robbins, Anthony, and Curtis (1973), although their experience appears generally more "dramatic" than our own (more on this later).

Much pressure to convert, both overt and covert, was brought to bear on us throughout our stay. In many ways, the overt pressure was easiest to handle. Nearly every interview involved attempts to convert the interviewer. We had warned the interviewers about this, but even so, some were rather unprepared for the intensity of some attempts. All of us were asked repeatedly what we believed and why we didn't "believe in Christ." Open disdain was shown by a few CCO members for the value of what we were doing. They simply defined our presence there as being sent to them by God for conversion. The "subject" often totally reversed the usual respondent/interviewer relationship, making the interviewer become the "subject" of an intense witnessing and conversion attempt. Most interviewers were successful in handling such attempts, but problems arose as a result of this overt pressure. Some interviewers were caught up in the situation and wanted to argue with some particularly forceful group members. We continually counseled against *argument per se,* but it was a problem, particularly for some of the more politically conscious and articulate of the interviewers, some of whom had very strong negative feelings about the "dropout" type of existence being lived by members of the Jesus movement group. (The June 1972 visit was during the time of the hard fought California primary, and we were all conscious of this important political battle. Members of the group, however, were oblivious to this contest, an upsetting fact for some of us.)

Some few others of the interview team had a different type of problem. As has been said, one person in particular was influenced by the situation to the point of considering converting and staying in the group, and was somewhat hard-pressed when it came time to decide whether or not to return home after the interviews were completed. (Interestingly, this person was one who did a great deal of work with group members during our stay. He enjoyed physical labor and also liked talking with group members, so we allowed him to be one of the "workers.")

The last statement illustrates the other more subtle pressure. We did not take groups of weak, incompetent people on research trips to be used as interviewers. Instead, being somewhat aware of the possible problems of this type of research we had chosen carefully among selected mature undergraduates for our interview team (especially the larger one in June 1972). We talked with them about what to expect and tried to prepare them for the interviewing. The fact that one considered staying and that a few others found themselves responding so strongly only illustrates the problems caused by dropping people literally into a "new and different world."

This new world was one where life outside of The Farm was viewed as worthless. The fundamentalist-oriented world view had everything defined and ordered in a way considerably different from what the interviewers were used to. The most compelling aspect of this new world was its total permeation with peace and love. It was obvious to all of us that the people enjoyed being there, and that they loved one another dearly. *And*, as we have said, they "loved" us as well and treated us as "prodigal sons and daughters." They welcomed us with open arms (notwithstanding concern by the few group leaders discussed), fed us, worked with us, furnished us a place to sleep, and constantly expressed great concern that we should come to share their "peace that passeth understanding." One has to be hardhearted indeed not to be moved when his or her name is mentioned in earnest prayer before meals and during Bible studies. This loving and caring atmosphere was hard to ignore and different people responded differently to it.

As a group, we made serious and systematic attempts to maintain the "thin thread of conversation" (Berger, 1967), so that our view of reality would be reinforced. In the June 1972 visit, researchers met every evening and during breaks during the day in the camper, which was generally "off limits" to group members (except by special invitation), and talked about the experiences of the day. (We also drank a little wine and told a few jokes just for good measure). These meetings in the camper were *essential*. If we had not had the camper along, we would have been forced to seek refuge by withdrawing from The Farm and going to a nearby town, as the researchers of summer 1971 had done. As it was, we had a "retreat" on The Farm which allowed us to withdraw quickly if desired, but at the same time, we were continually around to observe group activities and participate in informal conversations with members and leaders.

One final comment on this subject. More than one member of the 1972 research team left the group with very mixed feelings, which included for some a large measure of sadness. The total openness of most group members and their obvious concern for us had contributed to the development of affective ties between some members of the research team and some group members, even though we were only there for a few days. Also, for some of us who had temporarily left the university "rat race," life at The Farm had a certain idyllic appeal. The maintenance of a subject-object relationship between interviewer and interviewee, and between research team and the group of study, was no longer possible even if it had been desirable We had, for a brief time span, entered their life and they had entered ours. The mutual intrusions gave some in both camps pause for thought.

WHY HAVE WE BEEN ALLOWED
TO CONTINUE THE RESEARCH?

Many readers may be justifiably interested in how we have managed to continue our research for these several years without practicing overt deception or without converting to the beliefs and practices of the group being studied. This is a reasonable question, because we have reported in our earlier publications the rather terse and final way that potential Jesus movement converts who refused rapidly to convert were dealt with (see Richardson, Simmonds, & Harder, 1972; and Harder, Richardson, & Simmonds, 1972 for examples). Also, the only report in the literature specifically about such research (Robbins, Anthony, & Curtis, 1973) graphically points out possible problems or research on such evangelical and exclusive sects, leaving the impression that to continue for any length of time would be nearly impossible without conversion. We will further in this paper critique the Robbins et al. report, but it would be unfair for now to simply leave the impression that somehow we were better researchers than they, and that this is the only anwer to this apparent difference between their team of researchers and ours.

One reason that we have been able to continue our research is that we have worked very hard to maintain rapport, spending a great deal of time and energy maintaining good contact with the group, and especially with selected leaders. We, all of whom are trained researchers, have visited them, written letters, shared our own lives to a considerable extent with them, and just generally expressed a continual interest in finding out about the organization and its members. This effort has borne much fruit in terms of the continuation of our study. The effort has, of course, been facilitated by geographic proximity, since the group has its headquarters only a few hundred miles from the university where one author has a position and the other two did doctoral work, and luck has also been important.[6]

We would also suggest that the continuance of the project is one of the fruits of the honesty with which we have dealt with the group. As Blum (1970, p. 84) has noted, "if [the researcher] has given evidence that he [can be] trusted as a human being he can get more information than an insider." We have treated them as we agreed and have, as we described, even defended their interests with others. Also, the way we have so far reported our results in publications has been viewed somewhat positively by the group (although this was not our aim). Again, we see the effect of their beliefs because, particularly when some members were obtained through our publications, they apparently decided we were being "used of God," and that we should not be stopped in our research (although some continue to raise questions about specific aims of the research). We even suspect that some group members like the anonymous fame they have achieved through our publication of some results, and they desire to see this fame grow. Or, more benignly, we think that some group leaders (with whom we have had periodic discussions about the anonymity requirement, at least as far as seeking permission to use the real name of the group) are beginning to think of us as possibly being "sent" to chronicle the history of the group, again illustrating the positive effects on us of their ideology that includes a God active in human history. Some have indicated to us that they realize that someone will eventually "tell their story," but so far they have maintained the position that this will be done by a group member.

Also, it is plain that certain group members have continued to be personally concerned about us, and their desire to see us become Christians of their particular variety has aided us in our research. This concern for us has interacted with some other considerations (such as those just mentioned) to allow the waiving of some usual practices applied when dealing with recalcitrant potential converts. Thus in the minds of some group members, we still seem to be potential converts who are to be shown God's love through their actions towards us.

We have also been aided in the continuance of the project by the effects of the mere passage of time. Now when we visit the group, we immediately begin talking with some of the leaders of the group that we have known for some time and some new leaders who were ordinary members when the project started. New members who do not know us see us being warmly greeted and well treated by these group leaders. The new members, even though often the most evangelical, assume that we have some special status, and they too treat us with some deference. It would only be fair to say that it is common for such new members to assume, in fact, that we are members of the group from afar or at least "friendly" professing Christians. Some of our later visits have had their embarrassing and trying moment when something was said to dispel this opinion. This occasional "mistaken identity" has caused some problems for us, for it has led to a tendency to only interact with those who have stopped trying to convert us. Because of this, we have had to be careful not to shelter ourselves too much from the "rank and file," and not to seek only information given by leaders we know, who perhaps have a vested interest in maintaining a certain view of the group in their minds and in ours. This tendency of some new members to view us as group members has also perpetuated the never-ending problem of being ethical and not taking advantage of the naiveté of the new members. All in all, however, it is plain that the passage of time, coupled with past good rapport with some group leaders, has worked to our advantage in dealing with the group.

We would be greatly remiss not to mention one other way that the passage of time has aided our continued contact with the group. It is obvious that the group has changed a great deal since we first had contact with them. Many of these changes have already been chronicled in this book so details will not be reiterated. Suffice it to say, however, that the group has become quite strong in terms of capital assets and membership, and they are understandably more self-assured in their dealings with outsiders. They are not so fearful of scrutiny any more and have become more open to worldly contacts of many kinds. For instance, they encourage visits from interested people, including parents of members, and they are reaching out to the greater society as a group more, allowing members to have more contact with the outside world (evidence their drama troupe and their many commercial ties with the greater society). They are generally more tolerant of nearly all outsiders (see Martin, 1965, for a discussion of the meaning of tolerance in religious groups), and this, of course, includes us. This evolution of the group, which some would describe in theoretical terms as indicating change toward becoming more like a denomination than a sect, has been fascinating to watch, and has also been very useful to us in terms of the continuance of the research project.

COMMENT ON "SYMBOLIC REALISM" DEBATE

Robert Bellah (1970), in a very provocative article, claimed that "religion is a reality *sui generis*. To put it bluntly, religion is true" (p. 93). Bellah thus made a plea for treating religious phenomena as real when doing research on them, stating that, "symbolic realism is the only adequate basis for the social scientific study of religion," a position that is disagreeable to some who think that taking this position is not essential to doing good work on phenomena of research interest (see especially Klausner, 1970). It is apparent that this argument over the so-called "symbolic realism" that Bellah calls for is but another chapter in the continuing "insider-outsider" debate (see Merton, 1972), and that it has obvious limitations, especially since Bellah does not clearly point out how such research would be accomplished and apparently does not appreciate inherent problems with the approach.

Some of the limitations of Bellah's position have been addressed by Robbins, Anthony, and Crutis (1973), who studied a Jesus movement group—the Christian World Liberation Front (CWLF) in Berkeley. The researchers try to draw out the methodological implications of symbolic realism and illustrate the inherent problems of the position for research on certain types of religious groups, such as evangelical

Jesus movement groups.[7] They note that Bellah is apparently supportive of an emphatic or phenomenologically based methodology (p. 260), but point out that such an approach has inherent limits in that there are problems in understanding highly emotional or "mystical" experiences like conversion, "without oneself having had a similar experience. Moreover, a defining criterion of such experiences is that they *compel* belief" (p. 261). Robbins et al. continue by suggesting that such experiences on the part of a researcher would make the researcher sympathetic to such perspectives. This they do not view as necessarily bad, but they go on to note: "in highly sectarian settings the *degree* of sympathy of identification with the religious meanings of subjects can have a crucial effect upon the course of participant observation research. In such settings, symbolic realism and a empathic field methodology may not be conducive to harmonious conditions, empathic symbolic realism can threaten or traumatize subjects as seriously as the most cynical, reductionistic approach" (p. 262).

Then Robbins et al. present the experience which one of them had while studying and interviewing members of the CWLF, a traumatic experience both for the subjects and the researchers. Subjects lost their tempers at the researcher because of frustration caused by his apparent authentic acceptance of their reality as valid, but his simultaneous refusal to accept the beliefs personally. The research situation began amicably enough, with subjects actually asking to be interviewed. However, it deteriorated into shouting matches on occasion, after it became obvious that the researcher not only would not convert, but even refused to discuss his personal religious views with the subjects. The researcher, after undergoing increased pressures accompanied by guilt feelings, finally returned in kind, getting angry with subjects and taking an obviously (and admitted) negative view of the group and its members. Robbins et al. indicate that they think such research is some kind of "limiting case" in terms of the use of symbolic realism. They imply that the stronger a set of beliefs are held by group members, the greater the difficulty in taking such an approach. In other words, the more well-defined the group ideological boundaries, the worse the problems of using a symbolic realist approach, a summarization that may be an extension and generalization of their view. They seem to imply that the intensity with which the beliefs that define the group boundaries are held obliterates the distinction claimed by them and other social scientists between empathy and sympathy.

Robbins, Anthony, and Curtis (1973 p. 269) claim that the refusal of the researcher to become a believer, "imperiled their sectarian ideology and threatened the subjects' total belief structure," causing "cognitive dissonance," claims that seem unsubstantiated. We would suggest, alternatively, that while it is possible some subjects felt threatened by the presence of the researcher, probably what was happening is that the people were more upset at the *refusal of the researcher to deal with them in what they defined as a fair manner,* reciprocating the treatment that they were giving the researcher. Our assessment is based in part on the discussion of Robbins, Anthony, and Curtis (p. 269) of the options they saw for the researcher when difficulties arose.

> At this point the researcher had three options, all of which have obvious drawbacks: (1) He could have lied to the subjects and conducted "disguised observation" by feigning conversion, a strategy which he viewed as unethical; (2) He could have openly asserted his adherence to his own conflicting beliefs, which would have antagonized subjects and probably have terminated the study; (3) He could, as he did, refuse to discuss his own beliefs, which seemed contrary to the spirit of his empathic stance, and moreover simply led to increased tension between him and the subjects.

We would suggest that there are other options than those listed, and further, that options one and three are not as far apart as Robbins et al. seem to think. It also seems plain that by choosing option three, *the researcher may not have been practicing Bellah's idea of symbolic realism* at all. Another option (especially after our own research experience) would be for the interviewer to be allowed, in certain situations, to openly discuss his beliefs, and even enter into serious conversation about his or her beliefs in special circumstances.

This approach appears more humane, more ethical, and is a demonstration that the researcher probably *takes the beliefs of the other seriously*, which is part of what Bellah seems to mean by his idea. From a practical point of view, such an approach is one of honesty and will usually bear the fruits of honesty in human interaction. Also, much information may be directly gained in such discussions. In our own research, we discouraged interviewers from engaging in serious discussion (because we feared what Robbins, Anthony, and Curtis feared—that such might terminate the research project), but we did not totally rule them out. Some interviewers and all three of the authors took part in such exchanges on occasion, especially with some group leaders who were especially curious about what we were doing. It was obvious that we did not fear being questioned, and this openness was appreciated by those on whom we were doing research. Thus, instead of being seriously hindered by group beliefs and practices (as Robbins et al. thought they were), we actually gained from them, as has been already discussed.

It is also possible to fault the Robbins et al. paper as being derived from a narrow data base, since the data of their paper are based on only a single "case study" lasting two years. The person involved obviously had some idiosyncratic features that might have been expected to cause problems in this type of research—the fact that he was a devotee of Meher Baba (1973, p. 263) for instance. We will not press this point, however, since it is obvious that the experience of the researcher is important and worthy of attention, and may have even been more "intense" than our own, especially since he apparently had no fellow researchers to furnish personal support. Nevertheless, we would point out to the reader that our own discussion of methodological problems associated with research on such groups is based on about seven years of contact with CCO and on the experiences of about a dozen different people, three of whom (the authors) have seen considerable intense contact with many different group members. It is worth noting (as Robbins & Anthony have pointed out to us) that none of the investigators or interviewers had strong commitments to any given set of religious beliefs. Thus perhaps such research may have been easier for us than for Anthony.

Ethics and Symbolic Realism

It would be unfair to all concerned to close this section without a more explicit discussion of the ethical problems of symbolic realism, and of the approach that we took to our research. Neither Bellah nor Robbins, Anthony, and Curtis systematically address the issue. We think that our research experience may have been closer than that of the Robbins-Anthony team to what Bellah claims to mean by symbolic realism, and we assert that it certainly solved some of the practical difficulties with which the researcher of the Robbins team found himself faced. However, to claim that our approach was completely ethical, *and* to put forward such claims for symbolic realism in general, seems to us to be a serious mistake.

We would suggest that Bellah's approach is open to charges that it can be *simply another technique whereby "nonbelieving" researchers can gain access to groups and subjects on whom information is desired.* Symbolic realism may just be a more refined version of the "outsiders' role" (Trice, 1970). Anyone with average interaction skills can, through the use of a technique that expressly appreciates the views of others, manage to maintain interaction (and thus gain information) with just about anyone or any group. But by respecting (or appearing to respect) the subjects' views in such circumstances, do we ultimately reject his or her "humanness?" Far from solving the ethical difficulties of research with his approach, Bellah's approach has only demonstrated how profound such ethical problems really are.

We have no solution to offer for this problem, but we do agree that we and other researchers adopting such techniques should not fool ourselves and make grandiose claims for being more ethical than those who would use more deceptive methods. About the only thing that can be said about the appraoch used by us is that it *is* more open and *apparently* more honest than much research. It is not necessarily to be thought of as more ethical, however. That is an ultimate question for which we have no answer.

NOTES

1. The harassment by the police has occurred with other parts of the Jesus movement. In this instance, the "final local chapter" of this group's history was written when an article appeared in a local paper quoting some law enforcement officers who were lamenting the demise of the group, since it had been, they said, the only place available to send transient young women and be assured that they would be safe.
2. Special thanks is given to Doris Ginsburg for help in constructing the questionnaire.
3. We are well aware that this time span of two-and-one-half months may seem to some to be an insufficient time for there to be meaningful changes, but would counter by pointing out that groups such as this one claim that changes of great import occur almost immediately upon conversion. Also, our work had to be completed within certain time constraints involving location of subjects and doing the research during a summer when interviewers were available for such work. The value of such short-time studies of personality change has been amply demonstrated by the work of Lovekin and Malony (1974), who studied personality changes in a somewhat similar type of religious group (neo-Pentecostal Catholics) over a three-month period. See Simmonds (1977) for some assessment of changes (or lack of same) over time.
4. We also had take into account another problem presented by group beliefs. In responding to some of the personality inventories, many respondents would ask if we wanted them to respond as they were prior to their conversion, or after. Because of our intent, we always said "now" in response to such questions, but hindsight has made us realize that we might well have gathered some more valuable information if we had instead said "both" and gotten them to go through the inventories (such as the ACL) once for before conversion and once for after.
5. The definition of researchers as potential converts on whom great attention is lavished seems the ultimate example of the benefits of the "out-

sider" role discussed by Trice (1970). The problem, of course, is in maintaining this privileged status for a long enough time to do the research (and in resolving the ethical problems inherent in this position).

6. We have mentioned that luck played a part in our research, although we would certainly question anyone who drew the conclusion that this was the major factor in explaining our research project. The fact that we chose to study a group of this type was "lucky" (because they have been relatively "easy" to study), but the choice was deliberate. Based on our knowledge of the culture of the group and our own training, we felt that the research could be done. In the course of the research, a number of specific events happened that allowed us to continue or facilitated the work in some way. However, we encouraged many of these to occur through the application of interaction skills, or simply through perseverance. Also one virtue of our eclectic approach is that it builds maximum flexibility into the research and allows the resercher to take maximum advantage of serendipitous happenings. We were not "locked in" in terms of methods, or even of questions we wanted to research. These facets of openness and flexibility has resulted in some of our most interesting findings.

7. Bellah (1974) and Anthony, Robbins, and Curtis (1974) continued the debate over this issue in papers that appeared after the first draft of the preceding comments were written The debate has been carried into a more substantive as opposed to practical arena, especially by the solid Anthony, Robbins, and Curtis paper, which claims that Bellah's position is basically untenable. We will not go into detail about their discussion here, but would say that we tend to agree with the substantive critique of Anthony et al. while still generally maintaining our own critique of the earlier work of Robbins et al. (1973). For more discussion of this issue, see our paper presented at the 1975 American Sociological Association meetings under the title "The *Lack* of Limits of 'Symbolic Realism': More Evidence from the Jesus Movement" (Richardson, Harder, & Simmonds, 1975).

APPENDIX B

Testing Specific
"Movement Organization" Hypotheses

This appendix is presented for those readers interested in a more detailed approach to the "movement organization" literature. In an effort to further contribute to this area of study, we will now address some specific hypotheses developed by Zald and Ash (1966), and some offered since by Zurcher and Curtis (1973) and Curtis and Zurcher (1974), using CCO and the larger Jesus movement as a vehicle. Note that *the testing will be done using our own conceptualizations of certain variables as delineated in chapter 3,* a fact that may mean we will not do justice to some of the earlier work of Zald and Ash and Zurcher and Curtis. Care will be taken to note important differences between our own and earlier interpretations of variables when such differences seem germane to the particular test being made. This examination of relevant hypotheses will follow the general format of the Zald-Ash paper, since this is the base on which the subsequent work discussed has been built. The numbers attached to the basic hypotheses derive from Zald and Ash and are retained to allow easier integration with this earlier literature, although we will substitute our own preferred terms where applicable.

THE ZALD-ASH PROPOSITIONS

The first proposition from Zald and Ash is very general and nearly a truism. It says:

> Proposition 1: The size of the organizational potential support base, the amount of societal interest in the social movement and its MO's, and the direction of that interest (favorable, neutral, or hostile) directly affect the ability of the organization to survive and/or grow.

Plainly, all the variables mentioned in the proposition were important to the Jesus movement and to CCO. Details will not be offered here, but we would point out the great value of considering the demographic variable of potential size of target population and the general positiveness with which the greater society has greeted the movement and most of its MO's (movement organizations). We would add, however, that there are other crucial reasons for MO survival and success, as well as those mentioned (see the Introduction and Richardson, 1974, for more on these points).

Proposition 2 has already been discussed briefly (see note 5 of chapter 3).

> Proposition 2: The more insulated an organization is by rigorous membership requirements and goals aimed at changing individuals, the less susceptible it is to pressure for organizational maintenance or general goal transformation.

With CCO, the part of the proposition dealing with "pressures for organizational maintenance" simply does not hold, just as it did not in the Zurcher and Curtis test. We see no logical reason why or evidence for the idea that organizations with rigorous membership requirements and people-changing goals should be less susceptible to such pressures for organizational maintenance. We also do not understand why there would be less goal transformation, if one allows a definition of transformation that includes differentiation of goals, especially when some of the newer goals are plainly directed at external target groups (using an "individualistic mode" of attempting to change society).

The third proposition does gain support from CCO.

> Proposition 3: Goal and tactic transformation of a MO is directly tied to the ebb and flow of sentiments within a social movement.

The inter-organizational competition for support leads to a transformation of goals and tactics.

We have noted that the interests of CCO married couples, for instance, have resulted in the reallocation of certain group resources. Note, however, that most of the first married couples involved males in leadership positions, demonstrating again the importance of leadership in such amorphous MO's.

We also believe the fourth proposition to be supportable but would admit to having somewhat limited data.

Proposition 4: MO's created by other organizations are more likely to go out of existence following success than MO's with their own linkages to individual supporters.

It is our impression that a number of groups related to the Jesus movement were organized by churches during the past few years (both here and abroad) in a "mimic response" to the movement's "success." And it is also our impression that many if not most of these groups have failed to survive (which *may* indicate "failure"). Groups such as CCO (and the Children of God), which early severed ties with the institutional church structure have lasted longer and appear to be gaining strength. Whether or not they will continue to survive stressing such independence probably depends on many factors, both external and internal to the groups. We would hasten to add one point to this discussion, however. It seems to us that some ties with the external society are required (nearly by definition), and that such ties can be of great importance to MO groups. We need to think of "degrees of relationship" with other groups, instead of just the simple dichotomous "created by not created by" variable. But as far as this hypotheses goes, our data support it.

Proposition 5 suffers from the problem of distinguishing between specific and diffuse goals, a point over which we labored long in chapter 3.

Proposition 5: MO's with relatively specific goals are more likely to vanish following success than organizations with broad general goals.

Nonetheless, the notion finds some support in our work, if only because the group has developed more than one specific goal (or has at least differentiated its most important goal of evangelism) and it has lasted. The broadness and generalness of the goals are open to some interpretation, however, as we have stated. Most commentators might assume that evangelism is a broad and unspecific goal, and if this is accepted, then CCO certainly supports the proposition. It must be noted, however, that some Jesus movement MO's with this broad goal have *not* lasted, indicating again the importance of other variables in such considerations.

> Proposition 6: MO's which aim to change individuals and em-. ploy solidary incentives are less likely to vanish than are MO's with goals aimed at changing society and employing mainly purposive incentives.

We think proposition 6 is untestable, given our definition of the terms and recognition that MO's like the one we studied have both major goals and employ *both* types of incentives (and material ones as well). It makes little sense, as we have said in chapter 3, to assume that purposive incentives serve only groups with a more "structural" orientation toward social change. Such a position possibly reveals some bias in the literature vis-à-vis "religious" MO's.

> Proposition 7: Organizations with easy conditions of membership are likely to fade away faster than ones with rigorous conditions; the latter are more likely to take on new goals.

Proposition 7 gains support from our study and from the Jesus movement literature, given the substitution of our own concepts for "exclusive" and "inclusive." It does appear that groups which early developed rigorous resocialization procedures have shown more survival ability.

> Proposition 8: A becalmed movement is most likely to follow the Weber-Michels model because its dependence on and control of material incentives allows oligarchization and conservatism to take place.

The "becalmed movement" hypothesis finds some support from our data and from other movement groups of which we are aware. However, it would be misleading to think of the movement as totally "becalmed" and to consider CCO as "becalmed." It and some other groups are still quite vigorous in their "reaching outward," and we have no direct evidence that growth in numbers of converts is slowing down (although the "type of convert" is undergoing some change). Its chances of "success" have not become any more "dim" than they always were, as Zald and Ash (1966, p. 333) state in defining a becalmed MO. *But* if one thinks of "becalming" as a *process,* then there are tendencies for such to occur in most movement groups we know about. Interestingly enough, in more authoritarian groups, this tendency can be dramatically checked, at least temporarily, by the implementation of decisions handed down by an "absolute" leader or cadre of leaders. Such happened in the COG in 1974-75, with some very large colonies being broken up into small groups, many of which were ordered to move to other locations (see Davis & Richardson, 1976).

> Proposition 9: MO's with easy conditions of membership are more likely than those with rigorous ones to participate in coalitions and mergers.

The ninth proposition is supported by the fact that this "rigorous" organization has avoided forming mergers or coalitions with other groups (although it does have some other groups with which it occasionally interacts in a minor way on an organizational level). However, some other less rigorous MO groups in the movement have merged, as will be discussed in the next paragraph on the related proposition 10.

> Proposition 10: Coalitions are most likely to occur if the coalition is more likely to achieve goals or lead to a larger resource base—when success is close or when one indivisible goal or position is at stake.

The related proposition 10 seems somewhat inapplicable to CCO, but we have some supportive data on the rest of the movement in this regard. The proposition does raise an interesting question concerning the meaning of coalition. Does such a union require formalization or can (should) informal ties be treated as a coalition? Most groups have shown an interest in developing certain kinds of ties when it suited their purposes, but we are unaware of any instances of formal ties developing between CCO and other such groups. Some merging has taken place within the movement: a large Seattle group and an Atlanta group merged with the COG, mergers provoked by the relative attractiveness of the COG in terms of the accomplishment of certain goals. This example may indicate a possible specification of propositions 9 and 10. In the instance cited, more "easy" groups merged and surrendered identity to a larger much more "rigorous" group, the COG. Thus, perhaps we could suggest that "easy" groups are more prone to form mergers—especially with more "rigorous" groups—and that more "rigorous" groups might be more prone to form coalitions (and retain individual group identity) in certain circumstances such as mentioned in the proposition.

> Proposition 11: The less the short-run chances of attaining goals, the more solidary incentives act to separate the organization into homogeneous subgroups—ethnic, class, and generational. As a corollary, to the extent that a becalmed or failing MO is hetero- geneous and must rely heavily on solidary incentives, the more likely it is to be beset by factionalism.

Our data lend some support to proposition 11, given that converting everyone is a goal with little chance of early total accomplishment, although it must be noted that such groups can certainly possess a subjective feeling of *relative* success when important progress—that is, increased numerical and financial strength—has been made, as is the case with CCO. There is also the aforementioned problem (see chapter 3) in treating only solidary incentives in this context. The corollary is not testable yet, except to the extent that having a single and a mar- ried group within the organization constitutes heterogeneity (which is not what Zald & Ash appear to mean, 1966, p. 337). As stated, we do not consider CCO to be yet becalmed, and it certainly is not "failing," which in a sense makes the corollary inapplicable. However, the *lack* of factionalism in the "unbecalmed" group does lend some weak indi- rect support to the corollary.

> Proposition 12: The more the ideology of the MO leads to a questioning of the bases of authority the greater the likelihood of factions and splitting.

Proposition 12 seems supportable, if only because CCO has had very few schisms since its very early history when the original leader was trying to establish his authority, as described in Chapter 1. Once he was "enthroned," few tried to unseat him. Group ideology defines him (and other leaders) as "chosen by God," a common pattern in the Jesus and related movements.

> Proposition 13: MO's with rigorous conditions of membership are more likely than those with easy ones to be beset by schisms.

We have no evidence to suggest that schisms have occurred since the early history of CCO, even though the group is rigorous in its

membership requirements. Thus, this proposition is *not* supportable
with our data. We would go further and suggest that if one of the
requirements of membership is the acceptance of authority, then members who enter a "rigorous" group are probably *less* oriented toward
radical restructuring of the group. Nonetheless, proposition 13 from
Zald and Ash may well be true (and even a truism) *if* the "easy"
groups have little over which the members are concerned and over
which they might potentially split the group. But such groups also
might have attracted a heterogeneous membership, which could lead to
factionalism. In short, the hypothesis seems to require much qualification.[1]

> Proposition 14: Routinization of charisma is likely to conservatize
> the dominant core of the movement organization while simulta-
> neously producing increasingly radical splinter groups.

Proposition 14 gains no support from our study, although the test
may be a bit early in terms of the relatively short history of CCO,
especially since the original leader (or cadre of leaders) has not been
replaced. This fact means that, technically, proposition 14 is not testable using this group (or most others in the movement). However, since
Zurcher and Curtis included this test in their paper—even though neither group leader died and/or was replaced—we felt we should also.

> Proposition 15: If a leadership cadre are committed to radical
> goals to a greater extent than the membership-at-large, member
> apathy and oligarchical tendencies lead to greater rather than
> less radicalism.

Proposition 15 seems possible but very unlikely, unless the group
members in certain kinds of organizations were so apathetic as to
actually not constitute an organization anymore. This would, in a
sense, free the leaders of the defunct organization to do as they
pleased, and they might choose a radical path of action (see Shibutani,
1966, for a discussion of this situation). Such has not occurred in
CCO. The recent decision of COG leadership to scatter members from
larger colonies may illustrate the possibility of the proposition being
valid under certain conditions, such as a strong, legitimate leadership
with much authority. Note that the major example used by Zald and
Ash regarding this proposition (labor unions) involves a situation with
some basic democratic character. Probably their proposition will hold
in such groups, but its applicability to nondemocratic groups (such as
CCO and most other major Jesus movement groups) seems question-

able since such groups are, by definition, relatively oligarchical from their inception, and the members occupy a state of relatively "forced apathy." [2]

> Proposition 16: An MO with rigorous conditions of membership is almost certain to have a leadership which focuses on mobilizing membership for tasks, while one with easy conditions is readier to accept an articulating leadership style.

We do not think proposition 16 is sound. We see no reason why outwardly focused, vigorous, and "rigorous" organizations such as the one we have studied cannot be thought to possess a combination of leadership styles, since such a group must "mobilize" its members and relate to the greater society toward which it directs much energy.

> Proposition 17: The MO oriented to individual change is likely to have a leadership focused on mobilizing sentiments, not articulating with the larger society. Organizations oriented to changing the larger society are more likely to require both styles of leadership, depending on the stage of their struggle.

Proposition 16 is similar to proposition 17 in that it also seems untestable given our understanding of major terms. We think CCO illustrates the last sentence of the proposition—*if* there is an appreciation of the oft-repeated notion that this group is trying in its own way, however unsuccessfully, to change the greater society. Its "mode" of attempting change differs from that apparently preferred by the Zald-Ash scheme, but it is still an attempt to change society.

Now that we have examined the seventeen propositions of Zald and Ash, a summary of our results seems useful. Such a summary is presented in Table B.1, along with the findings of the Zurcher-Curtis test as well. We will be examining the Zurcher and Curtis paper in more detail, but since it is the only other systematic attempt to test the Zald-Ash scheme of which we are aware, it seems valuable to include it here. We, as did Zurcher and Curtis, admit that the Zald-Ash scheme was developed to apply to relatively large and stable MO's. Although the group we studied is "national," it is still young and relatively small. Also note that *in our test some of the major terms have been redefined somewhat* (see discussion in chapter 3), which means the two tests are not always similar in interpretation. In contrast, Zurcher and Curtis generally *accepted* the conceptualizations of major variables proposed by Zald and Ash. Another difference between our test and

TABLE B.1
Results of a Test of the Zald and Ash (1966) Propositions Concerning Social Movement Organizations, with Zurcher and Curtis (1973) Results Included

Proposition Number	Our Test	Zurcher & Curtis Test
1	Yes	-[4]
2	No	Y & N[5]
3	Yes	-
4	Yes	Yes
5	QY[1]	Yes
6	NT[2]	Yes
7	Yes	No
8	QY	-
9	Yes	Yes
10	QY	-
11	QY	-
12	Yes	-
13	No	Yes
14	QN[3]	Yes
15	NT	-
16	NT	Yes
17	NT	-

[1] A "QY" means yes with qualifications—see specific discussion of such propositions.

[2] A "NT" means that for reasons presente in the specific discussion the proposition was not deemed sound and/or not logical and was, therefore, not testable in our applications.

[3] A "QN" means no with qualifications—see specific discussion of the proposition

[4] Not examined at all in the paper (see Zurcher and Curtis, 1973:176).

[5] This proposition was divided into subhypotheses, resulting in support for a part and no support for a part. Technically the proposition, as stated in Zald and Ash, was not testable by Zurcher and Curtis, neither of whose groups of study met the basic criteria of groups for which the hypothesis dealt ("exclusive" and "people-changing"). Their test found support for the relationship hypothesized for one of the two criteria variables ("exclusiveness"), but not for the other. Our own test, which was done with a group meeting both criteria, resulted in a negative finding.

that of Zurcher and Curtis is that their test was more of a comparison of two specific organizations, whereas our own test used mainly data gathered on one group, CCO, with supplementary but sometimes not strictly comparable information on other Jesus movement groups. One last important caveat is that some of the Zald-Ash propositions are really several hypotheses in one, and that sometimes not all parts were involved in the test, or certain elements and interpretations of variables predominated in the specific test.

What should be said about this test of the Zald-Ash propositions and the comparison of our test with that of Zurcher and Curtis? First, it is obvious that the Zald-Ash propositions have *some* basic validity, as is evidenced by the number of "yes's" and "qualified yes's" listed in the table. Particularly, this is evident in the Zurcher-Curtis test, in which the Zald-Ash basic conceptualizations were used, and only one and "one-half" of the tested propositions were found not to be supported. In our test, six "yes's" and five "qualified yes's" resulted, in comparison with only two "no's" and one "qualified no." This generally positive view of the Zald-Ash scheme should not, however, conceal that we believe there are some basic problems with their conceptualization of some variables and with the development of those variables in subsequent work by the Curtis-Zurcher team. The six "qualified" results of our testing, coupled with the fact that we found four of the propositions not sound and/or not logical and therefore not testable (not to mention the two "no's") indicates that, although Zald and Ash have done a great service to the field with their attempt at structuring such knowledge, much work remains to be done. They recognized this in their original paper in their call for "a systematic testing of the propositions, using large numbers of historical and contemporary case studies" (1966, p. 341). We hope our meager effort has contributed to more understanding of this important area of scholarship.

In terms of specific criticisms of the general scheme offered by Zald and Ash, it seems to us, as it did to the Curtis-Zurcher team, that the variables involved must be ranked in some fashion. All the possible independent variables used in the propositions are not of equal weight, a fact plainly appreciated by Zald and Ash and certainly by the Zurcher-Curtis team. Some variables are much more crucial than others. Zurcher and Curtis suggested (1973, p. 186) that the three variables of greatest importance in relatively small and unstable MO groups were leadership orientation, goal specificity, and incentive structure. We too think those variables are important, but would point out that *they are all relatively "internal" variables, and therefore seem to assume external constancy.* The same comment can be made about the scheme they present later in the Curtis and Zurcher paper, which we have already critiqued, even though the authors do make an explicit claim to the contrary (1974, p. 359). They do discuss effects of "hostile" and "reinforcing" environments on certain "congruent" types of MO's (1974, pp. 364-65), but the focus of their paper seems to be on internal mechanisms. We would also incorporate a strong element of *quality of leadership* here, for a small and unstable MO will survive only if the leadership can maneuver the group through the various internal and external pressures that it must face. Such a situation seems typical with most MO's. MO leaders evaluate situations and plan accordingly. If they have planned well, *and/or* have "luck" on their side, the MO will probably maintain itself and even grow. We mention "luck" in all seriousness, for we think that sometimes (possibly often) a strictly rational (and possibly psychologized) model of social movements and MO's makes no sense. Conditions and forces over which MO members and leaders have no control (or even, sometimes, no knowledge of) effect what happens to MO's. The "accidental" discovery of the "successful" but only later well-justified tactic of nonviolence by the civil rights movement, discussed in Washington (1964), is but one example of this kind of "luck." In the instance of CCO, it seems very important that they moved into an area with a prosperous economy with many kinds of available work of the nonskilled type (agriculturally-related, generally). And their obtaining of their first real property (see chapter 1) was a real "stroke of luck." [3] They were also "lucky" in that societal conditions (including postwar birth rates) had furnished them with a large constituency of disenchanted youth of a certain type from which to recruit, and that "society" generally responded so favorably that they could prosper.[4] These illustrations highlight a major conclusion. *External conditions are crucial, and how leadership responds to such conditions seems of special importance, especially at the inception of a group,* a position supported by the first Zurcher-Curtis paper (Zurcher & Curtis, 1973, p. 183). After achieving some stability, internal factors such as membership makeup, desires, and needs will play an increasingly important role and must also be handled effectively by leadership.

We would also reiterate that religious groups need to be treated more seriously and realistically in analyses such as that of Zald and Ash. The implicit assumption that most religious groups are small, weak, and nearly inconsequential misleads. Also, the assumption that such groups are "inward" focused and "expressive" (as opposed to instrumental) with diffuse goals simply does not hold up when examined in the light of our data. (See chapter 3 for more on these points).

ZURCHER-CURTIS HYPOTHESES

It is perhaps unfair to treat the Zurcher and Curtis set of hypotheses separately (1973, pp. 186-87) given their later theoretical paper (Curtis & Zurcher, 1974). However, since the later paper did not explicitly refute the hypotheses or suggest systematic modifications, we think they should be examined, for completeness' sake if no other. We will quote the two sets directly:

> The small or emergent social movement organization, when the leadership is oriented toward goal specificity and purposive incentives, will manifest the following characteristics: task orientation; bureaucharisma; conservativeness in strategies and tactics; exclusiveness in membership recruitment; homogeneity of membership characteristics; no mergers or coalitions with other social movement organizations; schisms; a short duration, or a duration terminated upon goal attainment; resistance to pressures for organizational maintenance; no goal transformation; society-or community-changing goals; existence of a parent organization.
>
> The small or emergent social movement organization, when the leadership is oriented toward goal diffuseness and solidary incentives, will manifest the following characteristics; expressive orientation; charisma; radicalism in strategies and tactics; inclusiveness in membership recruitment; heterogeneity of membership characteristics; mergers or coalitions with other social movement organizations; long duration; susceptibility to pressures for organizational maintenance; goal transformation; person-changing goals; no parent organization.

Before doing any specific "testing," a general comment should be made. These sets of hypotheses suffer from the same problems of conceptualization that we have criticized vis-à-vis the Zald-Ash propositions and the Curtis and Zurcher scheme. The Zurcher-Curtis conceptualization was not, of course, informed by our understanding of the goals of MO organizations, and it suffers from the problem of trying to dichotomize the "purposive-solidary" incentive conceptualization of Clark and Wilson (1961). Those comments notwithstanding, it still seems to us that one set of the hypotheses is testable using our data. This is the first set developed specifically for MO's whose leadership is oriented toward goal specificity and purposive incentives. To us these criteria simply mean, in terms of CCO, that this group has specific goals (note the plural) and tries to implement its values, both inside and outside the group. With this understanding, we will proceed with our test of the apropos set of hypotheses. Since the results of this test are in many ways predictable given our just-completed test of the Zald-Ash scheme, we will treat our examination of the set in a more discursive fashion, in order to conserve space and avoid unneeded repetition.

CCO definitely (1) has a strong task orientation, (2) does exhibit "bureaucharisma," [5] (3) is "exclusive" (now has rigorous membership conditions), (4) has a very homogeneous membership in terms of class, race, and prior experiences (although as stated, it is "dividing" into a married and single group), (5) has not participated in any mergers or coalitions with similar MO's, (6) does have and tries to implement society or community-changing goals (though in the "individualistic" mode), and (7) had for a short time connections with what might be termed a parent organization (see chapter 1).

However, some important parts of the supposedly coherent scheme offered by Zurcher and Curtis are called into question by data on CCO. First, CCO has experienced no schisms in the past several years, and the earlier rare ones were really more a part of a "boundary definition" process. Second, CCO still exhibits a general orientation that cannot be categorized as especially conservative in strategy and tactics. The group is economically strong and "takes chances" in attempts to implement its goals. Third, it certainly *cannot* be thought of as a short-term organization, even though it has been relatively (and certainly subjectively), successful.[6] Fourth, much of their energy has gone into maintaining the organization. Fifth, there has been some goal transformation (or at least goal differentiation and/or elaboration).

It must be admitted that Zurcher and Curtis would probably not allow our classification of this group as having specific goals, and they might also take issue with the idea that it is mainly "purposive." Technically, if one or the other of such comments were held to be valid, then the set of hypotheses could not be said to be strictly testable using our data. However, it should be noted that *if the group is classified as having diffuse goals and stressing solidary incentives, the relevant (second) set of hypotheses does just as poorly in a test,* if not more so. Thus, we are left with the conclusion that the Zurcher and Curtis scheme has serious problems, making it (or parts of it) inapplicable to such groups as CCO. This means to us, of course, that the scheme is not general enough and needs a thorough-going revision to be made general enough to incorporate both this test and the one done on the antipornography organizations examined by Zurcher and Curtis. Such a revision will not be attempted here, but we would suggest that comments made apropos the Zald-Ash scheme would seem to hold here also.

CURTIS-ZURCHER HYPOTHESES

We have already commented at length in chapter 3 on the Curtis-Zurcher typological scheme and its underlying theoretical conceptualizations. In this section, we will carry the discussion a bit further by examining some specific hypotheses that seem relevant to CCO and to the movement of which it is a part. We will also offer comments about why some ostensibly applicable hypotheses from Curtis and Zurcher do not "fit" in this instance.

That last point seems a good place to start, as it is germane to any specific testing that we will do. Recall that Curtis and Zurcher developed nine types of MO's and then further divided the nine into two categories—congruent and incongruent—on the basis of their admittedly arbitrary designation of certain types as being "congruent" (1974, p. 367). Then they discussed the various types in terms of their dichotomous classification of congruency. We have critiqued this classification as not being particularly logical and especially fitting for organizations such as the one described herein. Our criticism implied that much of the Curtis-Zurcher scheme might be inapplicable for our purposes, even though their general scheme (with our conceptual modifications) was useful to us. The specific problem is that Curtis and Zurcher spend much of their effort talking about their congruent types, which they say are "exclusive-expressive" and "inclusive-instrumental." We are unwilling to classify CCO as either of these now (although, as stated, it was "easy" and "instrumental" for a short time), as we have already indicated indirectly. We think there is some support for our position within the Curtis-Zurcher paper itself, for they indicate (1974, p. 364) some problem in treating the Jehovah's Witnesses as "exclusive-expressive" (or they at least imply that they do not readily "fit" their conceptualization).[7] This example of a poor fit also implies that including such organizations as CCO in their scheme is somewhat problematic, since the group has managed to maintain itself, and it is quite "outgoing" and "vigorous." We think such organizations should be classifiable as "rigorous-outward" and "instrumental" (using our terms and conceptualizations), and that such organizations should be treated as "congruent" and "natural," instead of being "awkward fits" or "incongruent types." With that qualification, we will now move to an examination of Curtis and Zurcher's general type of "exclusive-instrumental," which seems most applicable to our purposes (even though we do take issue with its being considered an incongruent type).

In their own paragraph about exclusive-instrumental types (rigorous-outward in our terms), Curtis and Zurcher (1974, p. 356) use the example of "several civil rights organizations" of the 1950s and 1960s. They suggest that such groups "must maintain a relatively extensive set of prescriptions for member participatory behavior." We agree, as our data strongly support such a notion. They add: "The combination of instrumental goal orientation with a highly disciplined membership tends to emerge in situations where goal achievements demand a highly structured interaction with the environment. The stresses upon the members, however, are severe . . . [T]he personal demands must be equated with the movement purposes in order to justify or explain the stresses." (1974, p. 356).

We agree with most of this. The focus on evangelism has led to the development of a highly disciplined membership in CCO. Members are rigorously inculcated with group ideology in an attempt to ready them for their expected and deliberate encounters with the external environment. The great costs to the organization of resocialization are justified on the grounds that evangelical activity is "required" of a Christian. The only part of the quote we think requires some qualification concerns the stress on members. Evangelistic activity seems inherently stressful on face value, but care must be taken in carrying such an assumption too far. If the activity is carried out in an environment that is positive toward it, then it may not be so stressful and may even be rewarding. Also, if evangelizers are thoroughly trained and inculcated with the organization's ideology, and if the organization has been "successful" in such efforts (and other ways), then it seems that evangelizing might also not be so stressful. Our own experience in being rigorously evangelized by respondents (see Appendix A), the enthusiasm shown by members at news that a witnessing "trip to town" was planned, and the continual CCO efforts to "convert everyone in sight" cause us to think that this group, at least, has made evangelism into a positive thing. Stress occurs if evangelism activities are limited! [8]

In their discussion of noncongruent types with "mixed components" (types 2, 4, 5, 6, and 8 in Table 3.1) Curtis and Zurcher suggest that such combinations raise the possibility of schisms (1974, p. 366). Although CCO has been and presently is "mixed," we can only repeat that schisms have not occurred in the recent history. Some relatively minor schisms did occur early in the organization's "prehistory" when it was more amorphous, and this fact may lend some credence to the idea of Curtis and Zurcher, especially since what few schisms did occur took place when the organization was moving into a more "rigorous" position, as the organization was moving through cells 5 and/or 6 of Table 3.1 or Table 3.4.

Also in their discussion of "mixed" types, Curtis and Zurcher discuss the great complexity of some organizations having mixed components, and they cite the intriguing example of the Sierra Club as an organization that combines instrumental and expressive orientations. They note that the different local chapters of this national organization emphasize different orientations, an observation that seems also apropos to CCO. As indicated in chapter 2 (and in other portions of the book), various subsets of the CCO's members do evidence different orientations. Some subsets (such as married couples or certain communes) might well be more "inward" and/or expressive, while others might be less so.

In the conclusions of their paper, Curtis and Zurcher (1974, p. 368), after suggesting that, "the congruent types are more likely to operate 'within the system' and to become institutionalized in some fashion . . . ," add that "the noncongruent types (especially the exclusive-instrumental), on the other hand, may be at the cutting edge of social innovation." We do not want to appear biased about the group we have studied, but it does seem to us that Curtis and Zurcher are correct vis-à-vis CCO (which is best characterized in their terms, we think, as exclusive-instrumental), although in ways that they might now "allow" in terms of their perspective. CCO has demonstrated the efficacy of living communally and of developing, mainly on their own, a complex organization staffed nearly entirely by youth. From the point of view of the group, they have demonstrated that their beliefs have credence and relevance for this age. We would say, somewhat less dramatically, that they have indeed demonstrated that such a life-style and ideology can be maintained in this age, at least for the relatively short run.

One last point from the Curtis-Zurcher work. In their discussion of congruent types, they comment briefly but insightfully on the effects of "reactions of the community of concern." Even though we, as stated, do not agree that CCO is one of their congruent types, it does seem to us that their comments have relevance to all types of groups, with some qualifications. They state that a "hostile environment" will increase insulation, making groups more exclusive and expressive in orientation. Alternatively, a "reinforcing environment" will encourage more instrumental orientations and weaken insulating mechanisms. We think these two generalizations have basic validity, and even think that latter one to be a partial explanation of the continual "instrumentalness" of CCO,as well as its lessening concern for maintaining isolation from external society. However, we think that the first generalization about hostile environments needs some qualification. In the instance of CCO, even though there was a rapid, even if muted, appreciation for the positiveness with which the greater society responded to such groups, there was still a rather deliberate move to isolate itself from "external influences." This decision was made by the leadership and again illustrates our point that the key variable with relatively small and new MO's is leadership style and "quality." Whether or not the experience of CCO is generalizable at all remains to be seen, however.

NOTES

1. Although it does not appear directly in any of the Zald-Ash propositions, some comment seems in order concerning their idea that concern for doctrinal purity is one of two basic reasons that splits and schisms occur (heterogeneity of "social support base" being the other). It seems to us that concern for doctrinal purity may be and often is more of a justification or rationalization for changes than a basic independent cause of such changes. Washington's (1964) fine book on black religion demonstrates that schisms often occur as a result of people trying to exert themselves in order to gain authority, and that such people may well use ideological justifications of such power-gaining attempts. CCO has been beset by few if any schisms in the past several years, mainly because there has been little desire on the part of members to challenge the leaders, who are themselves dedicated to maintaining "purity." There has been plenty of "authority" to go around, as the organization is growing and thus opening up new leadership positions regularly. There has also been a growing affluence which is shared, to varying degrees, by all members. This growing affluence and increase in numbers have demonstrated to members the validity of the organization and has thereby muted disputes that might have arisen and been couched in terms of doctrinal purity. If CCO ceases to grow, or if resources get so scarce that serious battles develop over their distribution, then schisms might well be expected—and such schisms would probably be rationalized in doctrinal terms. Note, however, that both the mentioned possible causes of such schismogenesis have their origins in considerations more external than internal to the organization.

2. The theorizing concerning apathy raises an interesting question about the meaning of the term. Apathy can be "forced," as when members are not allowed to take part in group leadership. But this notion involves an element of "access to power" in defining apathy. We would suggest that apathy needs to be carefully defined before being used in the context of religious groups (or most others). Does this term just mean "inactive" or

does it mean "not allowed to be involved in decision making?" Certainly, CCO illustrates that members who have little access to power can be very active in other ways. Are they to be considered apathetic because they have accepted the authority structure of the organization, or at least do not choose to challenge that structure even if they are still quite "active"? We think not, although this assessment should not be interpreted as an endorsement of the group's ideology and authority relationships. See Etzioni (1965) for more discussion of the crucial variable of power in organizations.

3. As stated earlier, CCO leaders claim to have always been guided by God in decisions, a claim that does not, we think, disallow our analysis.

4. We are not here trying to delineate all the "causes" of the Jesus movement; instead we are only trying to illustrate our general point that external factors are of crucial importance, especially at the inception of a movement and its MO's. Such causal analysis is possible if done within certain limits (see Richardson, 1974; Balswick, 1974; and the Introduction), but we do not want to get trapped into seeming to say something as nonsensical as "the Jesus movement was caused by World War II (because of the postwar baby boom)."

5. Bureaucharisma is defined by Zurcher and Curtis (1973, p. 183) as "an admixture of enthusiastic and contagious commitment and a knowledge of, experience with, and practical ability in the use of organizing and organizational techniques." See Zurcher (1967, p. 416) for more details.

6. Zurcher and Curtis (and Zald and Ash, 1966, before them) seem unaware of the implications for their scheme of the possibility that one of the primary specific goals of an MO might be the continuance of the organization. This is the case in CCO, and the specific goal is enthusiastically implemented by the leadership through many different tactics.

7. We have earlier mentioned that there is the possibility of bias when discussing religious groups (see note 4 in chapter 3). The Curtis and Zurcher (1974) paper may illustrate such tendencies, as indicated by their categorization of the Witnesses as an exclusive-expressive group, when they seem so "outward" and instrumental in their orientation.

8. We have already stated that, particularly for certain subgroups within CCO, there seems to be less emphasis on evangelism. But the comments still hold for the organization as a whole and certainly for certain subgroups within CCO.

About the Authors

James T. Richardson is professor of sociology at the University of Nevada, Reno, having been there since 1968, when he received his Ph.D. from Washington State University. He received both his B.A. and M.A. from Texas Tech University, where he taught a year after receiving the M.A. in 1965. His major present research interests include the sociology of religion, sociology of knowledge, social movements, conversion processes, and alternative life-styles. He has studied new religious groups for several years in America and overseas, focusing on the so-called Jesus movement and the neo-Pentecostal movement. Earlier publications include articles authored or coauthored in the *American Journal of Sociology, Sociometry, Human Relations,* the *Journal for the Scientific Study of Religion, Sociological Analysis,* the *Review of Religious Research, Social Compass,* and *Psychology Today,* among others, along with one coauthored textbook in the area of computing. He recently edited a special issue of *American Behavioral Scientist* on "Conversion and Commitment in Contemporary Religion."

Mary W. Stewart is assistant professor of sociology at the University of Missouri, Kansas City, having taught previously at Kearny State College in Nebraska and Colorado State University at Fort Collins. She earned her B.A. from the University of Nevada, Reno, her M.A. from Temple University (1968), and her Ph.D. in social psychology from the University of Nevada, Reno (1972). Her current research interests include sociology of women, the Jesus movement groups, deviance, and family violence. She has authored and coauthored work in several journals, including the *Journal for the Scientific Study of Religion, Psychology Today, International Review of Modern Sociology,* and *Social Compass.*

Robert B. Simmonds, an assistant professor of sociology at the State University of New York, Cortland, specializes in deviant behavior, personality assessment, methodology, interpersonal processes, and small group analysis. A native of San Bernardino, California, he received his B.A. in psychology from the University of California, Riverside, and his Ph.D. in social psychology from the University of Nevada, Reno, in 1977. Currently residing in Ithaca, New York, he plans to continue his research with contemporary religious movements and in personality and social structure. He has authored or coauthored papers in *Social Compass, Journal for the Scientific Study of Religion, Youth and Society, Psychology Today, American Behavioral Scientist,* and the *International Review of Modern Sociology.*

Bibliography

Adams, Robert Lynn, and Fox, Robert John. "Mainlining Jesus: The New Trip." *Society* 9 (February 1972): 50-56.

Anthony, Dick; Robbins, Thomas; and Curtis, T. E. "Reply to Bellah." *Journal for the Scientific Study of Religion* 13 (1974): 491-95.

Austin, Roy L. "Empirical Adequacy of Lofland's Conversion Model." *Review of Religious Research* 18 (1977): 282-87.

Balch, Robert W., and Taylor, David. "Seekers and Saucers: The Role of the Cultic Milieu in Joining a UFO Cult." *American Behavioral Scientist* 20 (1977): 839-60.

Balswick, Jack. "The Jesus People Movement: A Generational Interpretation." *Journal of Social Issues* 30 (1974): 23-42.

Barker, Eileen. "Inside the Unification Church: Followers of the Reverend Sun Moon in Britain." Paper read at the Fourteenth International Conference for the Sociology of Religion, August 1977, Strasbourg, France. Mimeographed.

Barnes, J. A. "Some Ethical Problems in Modern Fieldwork." In *Qualitative Methodology,* edited by W. J. Filstead, pp. 235-51. Chicago: Markham, 1970.

Beckford, James A. *The Trumpet of Prophecy: A Sociological Study of Jehovah's Witnesses.* New York: Wiley, 1975.

―――. "British Moonies on the Wane." *Psychology Today,* British Edition (August 1976): 22-23.

―――. "Through the Looking-glass and Out the Other Side: Withdrawal from Rev. Moon's Unification Church." Paper read at the Fourteenth International Conference for the Sociology of Religion, August 1977, Strasbourg, France. Mimeographed.

Bell, Robert. *Marriage and Family Interaction.* Homewood, Ill.: Dorsey Press, 1971a.

―――. *Social Deviance.* Homewood, Ill.: Dorsey Press, 1971b.

Bellah, Robert N. "Christianity and Symbolic Realism." *Journal for the Scientific Study of Religion* 9 (1970a): 89-96.

―――. "Response to Comments on 'Christianity and Symbolic Realism.'" *Journal for the Scientific Study of Religion* 9 (1970b):112-15.

―――. "Comment on 'The Limits of Symbolic Realism.'" *Journal for the Scientific Study of Religion* 13 (1974): 487-89.

Berger, Bennett M., and Hackett, Bruce M. "On the Decline of Age Grading in Rural Hippie Communes." *Journal of Social Issues* 30 (1974): 163-83.

Berger, Peter. *Invitation to Sociology.* New York: Doubleday, 1963.

―――. *The Sacred Canopy.* New York: Doubleday, 1967.

―――. *Rumor of Angels.* New York: Irvington, 1969.

―――. "Some Second Thoughts on Substantive versus Functional Definitions of Religion." *Journal for the Scientific Study of Religion* 13 (1974): 125-33.

Berger, Peter, and Luckman, Thomas. *The Social Construction of Reality.* New York: Doubleday, 1966.

Blau, Peter. *Exchange and Power in Social Life.* New York: Wiley, 1964.

Blessit, Arthur. *Turned-on to Jesus.* New York: Hawthorne, 1971.

Blum, Fred H. "Getting Individuals to Give Information to the Outsider." In *Qualitative Methodology,* edited by W. J. Filstead, pp. 83-90. Chicago: Markham, 1970.

Broom, Leonard, and Selznick, Philip. *Principles of Sociology.* New York: Harper & Row, 1968.

Brown, D. G., and Lowe, W. L. "Religious and Personality Characteristics of College Students." *Journal of Social Psychology* 33 (1951): 103-29.

Brown, James C. "An Experiment in Role-Taking." *American Sociological Review* 17 (1952): 587-97.

Burtchaell, James T. "A Response to 'Christianity and Symbolic Realism.'" *Journal for the Scientific Study of Religion* 9 (1970): 97-99.

Cahill, Tim. "True Believers and the Guises of the Weasel." *Rolling Stone,* no. 136, 7 June 1973a, pp. 1, 42-50.

———. "Infiltrating the Jesus Army." *Rolling Stone,* no. 137, 21 June 1973b, pp. 50-60.

California Legislature Senate Select Committee on Youth and Children, Mervyn M. Dymally, Chairman. Hearing at California State College at Northridge, August 24, 1974.

Campbell, Colin. "The Cult, the Cultic Milieu, and Secularization." In *A Sociological Yearbook of Religion in Britain,* edited by Michael Hill, pp. 119-36. London: SCM Press, 1972.

———. "Clarifying the Cult." *British Journal of Sociology* 28 (1977): 375-88.

Christianity Today. Personal Letter, 1973.

Clanton, Gordon. "Peter L. Berger and the Reconstruction of the Sociology of Religion." Unpublished paper, 1974.

Clark, P. B., and Wilson, J. W. "Incentive System: A Theory of Organization." *Administrative Science Quarterly* 6 (1961): 129-66.

Clark, W. H. *Chemical Ecstasy: Psychedelic Drugs and Religion.* New York: Sheed & Ward, 1969.

Corry, Geoffrey. *Jesus Bubble or Jesus Revolution: The Growth of Jesus Communes in Britain and Ireland.* London: British Council of Churches Youth Department, 1973.

Cottrell, Leonard S., Jr. "Individual Adjustment to Age and Sex Roles." *American Sociological Review* 7 (1942): 618-19.

Cowen, E. L. "The Negative Concept as a Personality Measure." *Journal of Consulting Psychology* 18 (1954): 138-42.

Crowne, D. P., and Marlow, D. "A New Scale of Social Desirability Independent of Psychopathology." *Journal of Consulting Psychology* 24 (1960): 349-54.

Curl, Roger. "Change and Adaptation in a Jesus Movement Group: The London Jesus People. Unpublished paper, 1975.

Curtis, Russell, L., Jr., and Zurcher, Louis A. "Social Movements: An Analytical Exploration of Organizational Forms." *Social Problems* 21 (1974): 356-70.

Davis, Rex, and Richardson, James T. "The Organization and Functioning of the Children of God." *Sociological Analysis* 37 (1976): 321-39.

Demerath, Nicholas J. *Social Class in American Protestantism.* Chicago: Rand McNally, 1965.

Dittes, J. E. "Psychology of Religion." In *Handbook of Social Psychology,* edited by G. Lindsey and E. Aronson, pp. 602-59. Reading, Mass.: Addison-Wesley, 1969.

Dornbusch, Sanford M. "The Military Academy as an Assimilatory Institution." *Social Forces* 33 (1955): 316-21.

Douglas, Jack. *Research on Deviance.* New York: Random House, 1972.

Drakeford, J. W. *Children of Doom.* Nashville, Tenn.: Broadman Press, 1972.

Eister, Alan W. "An Outline of a Structural Theory of Cults." *Journal for the Scientific Study of Religion* 11 (1972): 319-33.

Ellwood, Robert S. *One Way: The Jesus Movement and Its Meaning.* Englewood Cliffs, N.J.: Prentice-Hall, 1973.

Enroth, Ronald; Ericson, Edward E.; and Peters, C. Breckenridge. *The Jesus People: Old Time Religion in the Age of Aquarius.* Grand Rapids, Mich.: Eardmans, 1972.

Etzioni, Amatai. "Organizational Control Structure." In *Handbook of Organizations,* edited by J. G. March, pp. 650-77. Chicago: Rand McNally, 1965.

Fairfield, Richard. *Communes U.S.A.* Baltimore: Penguin, 1972.

Farber, Bernard. *Family Organization Interaction.* San Francisco: Chandler, 1964.

Fichter, Joseph. *The Catholic Cult of the Paraclete.* New York: Sheed & Ward, 1975.

Filstead, William J., ed. *Qualitative Methodology: First Hand Involvement with the Social World.* Chicago: Markham, 1970.

Flacks, Richard. "The Liberated Generation: An Exploration of the Roots of Student Protest." *Journal of Social Issues* 23 (1967): 52-74.

Fromm, Erich. *Escape from Freedom.* New York: Avon, 1941.

———. *Psychoanalysis and Religion.* New Haven, Conn.: Yale University Press, 1950.

Gans, Herbert J. *The Urban Villagers.* New York: Free Press, 1962.

Garrett, William R. "Troublesome Transcendence: The Supernatural in the Scientific Study of Religion." *Sociological Analysis* 35 (1974): 167-80.

Gerlach, Luther, and Hine, Virginia. *People, Power and Change: Movements of Social Transformation.* Indianapolis, Ind.: Bobbs-Merrill, 1970.

Gill, Robin. *The Social Context of Theology.* London: Mowbrays, 1974.

Glock, Charles Y. "The Role of Deprivation in the Origin and Evolution of Religious Groups." In *Religion and Social Conflict,* edited by Robert A. Lee and Martin Marty. New York: Oxford University Press, 1969.

Glock, Charles Y., and Bellah, Robert. *The New Religious Conscious-ness.* Berkeley: University of California Press, 1976.

———. *Patterns of Religious Commitment.* Berkeley: University of California Press, 1968.

Glock, Charles Y., and Stark, Rodney. *Religion and Society in Tension.* Chicago: Rand McNally, 1965.

Goffman, Erving. *Asylums.* Garden City, N.Y.: Doubleday, 1961.

Goldenberg, Sheldon, and Wekerle, Gerda R. "From Utopia to Total Institution in a Single Generation: The Kibbutz and the Bru-derhof." *International Review of Modern Sociology* 2 (1972): 224-32.

Gordon, David F. "The Jesus People: An Identity Synthesis." *Urban Life and Culture* 3 (1974): 159-79.

Gordon, Wayne C., and Babchuk, Nicholas. "A Typology of Volun-tary Organization." *American Sociological Review* 24 (1959): 22-29.

Gough, H. A., and Heilbrun, A. B. *The Adjective Check List Manual.* Palo Alto, Calif.: Consulting Psychologists Press, 1965.

Gouldner, Alvin. *The Coming Crisis in Western Sociology.* New York: Basic Books, 1970.

Greil, Arthur L. "Previous Dispositions and Conversion to Perspectives of Social and Religious Movements." *Sociological Analysis* 38 (1977): 115-25.

Gusfield, Joseph. *Symbolic Crusade.* Urbana: University of Illinois Press, 1963.

Hammond, Phillip. "Peter Berger's Sociology of Religion." *Soundings* 52 (1969): 415-24.

Harder, Mary White. "The Children of Christ Commune: A Study of Fundamentalist Communal Sect." Ph.D. dissertation, University of Nevada, Reno, 1973.

Harder, M.W., Richardson, J. T., and Simmonds, R. B. "Jesus Peo-ple." *Psychology Today* 6 (December 1972): 44ff.

———. "Life Style: Sex Roles, Courtship, Marriage and Family in a Changing Jesus Movement Organization." *International Review of Modern Sociology* 6 (1976): 155-72.

Harrison, Michael. "Sources of Recruitment to Catholic Neo-Pente-costalism." *Journal for the Scientific Study of Religion* 13 (1975): 49-64.

Harvey, Van A. "Some Problematic Aspects of Peter Berger's Theory of Religion." *Journal of the American Academy of Religion* 41 (1973): 75-93.

Heilbrun, A. B., Jr., and Sullivan, D. J. "The Prediction of Counseling

Readiness." *Personnel and Guidance Journal* 41 (1962): 112-17.

Herberg, Will. *Protestant, Catholic and Jew.* New York: Doubleday, 1955.

Hierich, Max. "Change of Heart: A Test of Some Widely Held Theories About Religious Conversion." *American Journal of Sociology* (forthcoming 1978).

Hill, Michael. *A Sociology of Religion.* New York: Basic Books, 1973.

Hine, Virginia. "Pentecostal Glossolalia: Toward a Functional Interpretation." *Journal for the Scientific Study of Religion* 8 (1969): 221-26.

Hollenwegen, Walter. *The Wisdom of the Children: The Jesus People, Pentecost Between Black and White.* Belfast, Northern Ireland: Christian Journals, 1974.

Horowitz, Irving Louis. "Science, Sin, and Sponsorship." *Atlantic* 239 (March 1977): 98-102.

Jackson, John, and Jobling, Ray. "Toward an Analysis of Contemporary Cults." In *A Sociological Yearbook of Religion in Britain,* edited by David Martin, pp. 94-105. London: SCM Press, 1970.

Jacob, Michael. *Pop Goes Jesus: An Investigation of Pop Religion in Britain and America.* London: Mowbrays, 1972.

Jacobsen, Cardel, and Pilarzyk, Thomas. "Croissance, Developpement et fin d'une Sect Conversioniste." *Social Compass* 21 (1974): 255-68.

Jacobson, R. K., and Pilarzyk, T. J. "Faith, Freaks, and Fanaticism: Notes on the Growth and Development of the Milwaukee Jesus People." Paper presented at the annual meeting of the Society for the Scientific Study of Religion, 1972, Boston.

Johnson, Benton. "Do Holiness Sects Socialize in Dominant Values?" *Social Forces* 39 (1961): 309-16.

———. "Ascetic Protestantism and Political Preference." *Public Opinion Quarterly* 26 (1962): 38-44.

Jorstad, Erling. *The Politics of Doomsday: Fundamentalists of the Far Right.* Nashville, Tenn.: Abingdon Press, 1970.

Judah, Stillson. "Attitudinal Changes Among Members of the Unification Church." Paper presented at the annual meeting of the American Association for the Advancement of Science, February 1977, Denver, Colorado. Dittoed.

Kanter, Rosebeth Moss. *Commitment and Community: Communes and Utopias in Sociological Perspective.* Cambridge, Mass: Harvard University Press, 1972a.

———, ed. *Communes: Creating and Managing the Collective Life.* New York: Harper & Row, 1972b.

Kelley, Dean. *Why Conservative Churches Are Growing.* New York: Harper & Row, 1972.

Keniston, Kenneth. "Social Change and Youth in America." *Daedalus* (Winter 1962): 145-71.

———. *The Uncommitted: Alienated Youth in American Society.* New York: Harcourt, Brace & World, 1965.

Kiesler, Charles A. *The Psychology of Commitment: Experiments Linking Behavior and Belief.* New York: Academic Press, 1971.

Kildahl, John P. *The Psychology of Speaking in Tongues.* New York: Harper & Row, 1972.

Klausner, Samuel Z. "Scientific and Humanistic Study of Religion." *Journal for the Scientific Study of Religion.* 9 (1970): 100-5.

Kohn, Melvin L. "Social Class and Parental Values." In *The Family: Its Structures and Function,* edited by Rose L. Coser, pp. 472-94. New York: St. Martin Press, 1964.

Lee, Robert. *The Social Sources of Church Unity.* Nashville, Tenn.: Abingdon Press, 1960.

Lifton, Robert J. *Thought Reform and the Psychology of Totalism.* New York: Norton Press, 1963.

Light, Ivan. "The Social Construction of Uncertainty." *Berkeley Journal of Sociology* 14 (1969): 189-99.

Lofland, John. " 'Becoming a World Saver' Revisited." *American Behavioral Scientist* 20 (1977a): 805-18.

———. "The Boom and Bust of a Millenarian Movement: Doomsday Cult Revisited." In *Doomsday Cult,* enlarged edition edited by John Lofland, pp. 279-352. New York: Irvington, 1977b.

Lofland, John, and Lofland, Lynn. *Deviance and Identity.* Englewood Cliffs, N.J.: Prentice-Hall, 1969.

Lofland, John, and Stark, Rodney. "Becoming a World-Saver: A Theory of Conversion to a Deviant Perspective." *American Sociological Review* 30 (1965): 862-75.

Lovekin, Adams, and Malony, H. Newton. "Religious Glossolalia: A Longitudinal Study of Personality Changes." *Journal for the Scientific Study of Religion* 16 (1977): 383-930.

Lukács, Georges. *History and Class Consciousness.* Transcribed by Rodney Livingstone. Cambridge, Mass.: MIT Press, 1971.

March, James G., and Simon, Herbert. "The Theory of Organizational Equilibrium." In *A Sociology of Complex Organizations,* edited by Amatai Etzioni, pp. 77-86. New York: Holt, Rinehart & Winston, 1969.

Martin, David. *Pacifism: An Historical and Sociological Study.* London: Routledge & Kegan Paul, 1965.

Marx, Gary. "Religion: Opiate or Inspiration of Civil Rights Militancy Among Negroes." *American Sociological Review* 32 (1967): 64-72.

Maslow, Abraham. *Toward a Psychology of Being.* Princeton, N.J.: Van Nostrand, 1962.

Mauss, Armand. "Dimensions of Religious Defection." *Review of Religious Research* 10 (1969): 128-35.

Mauss, A. and Petersen, D. "Les Jesus Freaks et Le Retour a la Respectabilitie, ou la Predication des fils Prodigues." *Social Compass* 21 (1974): 283-301.

McGuire, Meredith. "An Interpretive Comparison of Elements of the Pentecostal and Underground Church Movements in American Catholicism." *Sociological Analysis* 35 (1974): 47-65.

——— "Toward a Sociological Intepretation of the Catholic Pentecostal Movement." *Review of Religious Research* 17 (1975): 94-104.

McHugh, Peter. "Social Disintegration As a Requisite of Resocialization." In Social Psychology Through Symbolic Interaction, edited by G. Stone and M. Farberman, pp. 699-708. New York: Wiley, 1970.

McPherson, William. *Ideology and Change: Radicalism and Fundamentalism in America.* Palo Alto, Calif.: National Press Books, 1973.

Merton, Robert. "Insiders and Outsiders: A Chapter in the Sociology of Knowledge." *American Journal of Sociology* 78 (July 1972): 9-47.

Messinger, Sheldon L. "Organizational Transformation: A Case Study of a Declining Social Movement." *American Sociological Review* 20 (1955): 3-10.

Milgram, Stanley. *Obedience to Authority.* New York: Harper & Row, 1974.

Miller, David L. *Individualism: Personal Achievement and the Open Society.* Austin: University of Texas Press, 1967.

Murray, H. A. *Explorations in Personality.* New York: Oxford University Press, 1938.

Musgrove, Frank. *Ecstacy and Holiness: Counter Culture and the Open Society.* Bloomington: Indiana University Press, 1975.

Nash, Dennison, and Berger, Bennett. "The Child, the Family and the Religious Revival in Suburbia." *Journal for the Scientific Study of Religion* 2 (1962): 85 ff.

Needleman, Jacob. *The New Religions.* Garden City, N.Y.: Doubleday, 1970.

Nelson, Benjamin. "Is the Sociology of Religion Possible?" *Journal for the Scientific Study of Religion* 9 (1970): 100-6.

Nelson, Geoffrey K. "The Spiritualist Movement and the Need for a Redefinition of Cult." *Journal for the Scientific Study of Religion* 8 (1969): 152-60.

Nettler, Gwynn. "A Measure of Alienation." *American Sociological Review* 22 (1957): 670-77.

Nisbet, Robert. *Community and Power.* New York: Oxford University Press, 1962.

Nolan, James. "Jesus Now: Holy Water and Hogwash." *Ramparts,* August 1971, pp. 24-26.

Nordhoff, Charles. *The Communistic Societies of the United States.* New York: Dover, 1966.

Parrucci, D. J. "Religious Conversions: A Theory of Deviant Behavior." *Sociological Analysis* 29 (1968): 144-54.

Parsons, Talcott, and Bales, Robert. *Family Socialization and Interaction Process.* Riverside, N.J.: Glencoe Free Press, 1955.

Pattison, E. M. "Ideological Support for the Marginal Middle Class: Faith Healing and Glossolalia." In *Religious Movements in Contemporary America,* edited by I. Zaretsky and M. Leone, pp. 418-55. Princeton, N.J.: Princeton University Press, 1970.

Pederson, Duane. *Jesus People.* Glendale, Calif.: Royal Books, 1971.

Peterson, D. W., and Mauss, Armand. "The Cross and the Commune: An Interpretation of the Jesus People." In *Religion in Sociological Perspective,* edited by Charles Glock, pp. 261-79. Belmont, Calif.: Wadsworth, 1973.

Plowman, Edward A. *The Jesus Movement.* New York: Pyramid, 1971.

Prothro, E. T., and Jensen, J. A. "Inter-relations of Religious and Ethnic Attitudes in Selected Southern Populations." *Journal of Social Psychology* 32 (1950): 45-49.

Rabkin, Leslie, and Rabkin, Karen. "Children of the Kibbutz." *Psychology Today* 3 (September 1969): 40-46.

Reidy, M. T. V., and Richardson, James T. "Comparative Studies of Neo-Pentecostalism." Paper read at biannual meeting of the International Conference for the Sociology of Religion, 1975, Spain.

———. "Neo-Pentecostalism in New Zealand." *Australian and New Zealand Journal of Sociology* (forthcoming 1978).

Reiss, Ira. *Family System in America.* New York: Holt, Rinehart & Winston, 1971.

Richardson, James T. "Deprivation, Alienation, and Contemporary Glossolalia Movements." Paper read at annual meeting of the Society for the Scientific Study of Religion, 1971, Chicago. Dittoed.

———. "Psychological Interpretaiton of Glossolalia: A Re-examination of Research." *Journal for the Scientific Study of Religion* 12 (1973): 199-207.

———. "The Jesus Movement: An Assessment." *Listening: Journal of Religion and Culture* 9 (1974): 20-42.

———. "The Jesus Movement Outside America." Paper read at annual meeting of the Association for the Sociology of Religion, August 1975, San Francisco. Dittoed.

———. "From Cult to Sect: A Theory of Qualitative Change in Social Groups." *Pacific Sociological Review* (1979a).

———. "The Cultic Origins of the Jesus Movement." *Annual Review of Social Sciences of Religion* vol. 2. The Hague: Nouton, 1979b.

———. "Types of Conversion and 'Conversion Careers' in New Religious Movement." Paper read at annual meeting of the American Association for the Advancement of Science, 1977, Denver.

———. "Comment on Empirical Adequacy of Lofland's Conversion Model." *Review of Religious Research* (forthcoming 1978).

Richardson, James T.; Harder, Mary W.; and Simmonds, R. B. "The Lack of Limits of 'Symbolic Realism': More Evidence from the Jesus Movement." Paper read at annual meeting of the American Sociological Association, 1975, San Francisco.

Richardson, James T., and Reidy, M. T. V. "Comparison and Contrast of Two Glossolalic Movements." Paper read at annual meeting of the Society for the Scientific Study of Religion, October 1976, Philadelphia.

———. "Neo-Pentecostalism in Ireland." *Social Studies: The Irish Journal of Sociology* 5 (1977): 243-61.

Richardson, James T., and Simmonds, Robert B. "Personality Assessment in New Religious Groups: Problems of Interpretation." Paper presented at the meeting of International Association for the Psychology of Religion, August 1977, Uppsala, Sweden.

Richardson, James T.; Simmonds, Robert B.; and Harder, Mary White. "Thought Reform and the Jesus Movement." *Youth and Society* 4 (1972): 184-202.

Richardson, James T., and Stewart, Mary W. "Conversion Process Models and the Jesus Movement." *American Behavioral Scientist* 20 (1977): 819-38.

Rigby, Andrew. *Alternative Realities: A Study of Communes and Their Members.* London: Routledge & Kegan Paul, 1974.

Robbins, Thomas; Anthony, Dick; and Curtis, Richard. "The Limits of Symbolic Realism: Problems of Empathic Field Observation in a Sectarian Context." *Journal for the Scientific Study of Religion* 12 (1973): 259-72.

―――. "Youth Culture Religious Movements: Evaluating the Integrative Hypothesis." *Sociological Quarterly* 16 (Winter 1975): 48-64.

―――. "The Last Civil Religion: Reverend Moon and the Unification Church." *Sociological Analysis* 37 (1976): 111-25.

Roberts, Ron. *The New Communes: Coming Together in America.* Englewood Cliffs, N.J.: Prentice-Hall, 1971.

Robinson, W. S. "Ecological Correlations and the Behavior of Individuals." *American Sociological Review* 15 (1950): 351-57.

Rosenthal, Robert, and Rosnow, R.L. *The Volunteer Subject.* New York: Wiley, 1975.

Scharf, Betty R. *The Sociological Study of Religion.* London: Hutchinson, 1970.

Schien, E. H. "The Chinese Indoctrination Program for Prisoners of War." *Psychiatry* 12 (1957): 149-72.

Seeman, Melvin. "On the Meaning of Alienation." *American Sociological Review* 24 (1959): 783-91.

Sharma, S. L. "Comparative Styles of Conversion in Major Religions in India." *Journal of Social Research* 13 (1968): 178-84.

Shibutani, Tamotsu. *Improvised News: A Sociological Study of Rumor.* Indianapolis, Ind.: Bobbs-Merrill, 1966.

Shupe, Anson, Jr.; Spielmann, Roger; and Stigall, Sam. "Deprogramming: The New Exorcism." *American Behavioral Scientist* 20 (1977): 941-56.

Simmonds, Robert B. "Conversion or Addiction: Consequences of Joining a Jesus Movement Group." *American Behavioral Scientist* 20 (1977a): 909-24.

―――. "Maladaptive Implications of Affiliation with a Jesus Movement Group." Paper read at annual meeting of the American Psychological Association, 1977b, San Francisco. Mimeographed.

―――. "The People of the Jesus Movement: A Personality Assessment of Members of a Fundamentalist Religious Community." Ph.D. dissertation, University of Nevada, Reno, 1977c.

Simmonds, Robert B.; Richardson, James T.; and Harder, Mary W. "A Jesus Movement Group: An Adjective Check List Assessment. *Journal for the Scientific Study of Religion* 15 (1976): 323-37.

Skolnick, Arlene. *The Intimate Environment: Exploring Marriage and the Family.* Boston: Little, Brown, 1973.

Smelser, Neil. *Theory of Collective Behavior.* New York: Free Press, 1963.

Smith, Chuck, with Steven, Hugh. *The Reproducers: New Life for Thousands.* Glendale, Calif.: Regal, 1972.

Spielberger, C. D. *The State-Trait Anxiety Inventory.* Palo Alto, Calif.: Consulting Psychologists Press, 1968.

Spiro, Melford E. *Children of the Kibbutz.* Cambridge, Mass.: Harvard University Press, 1958.

Stark Rodney. "On the Compatibility of Religion and Science: A Survey of American Graduate Students." *Journal for the Scientific Study of Religion* 3 (1963): 3-20.

———. "Class Radicalism and Religious Involvement in Great Britain." *American Sociological Review* 29 (1964): 698-706.

———. "Psychopathology and Religious Commitment." *Review of Religious Research* 12 (1971): 165-76.

Stein, Barry S. "The Internal Economics of Communes." In *Communes: Creating and Managing the Collective Life,* edited by R. M. Kanter, pp. 264-76. New York: Harper & Row, 1973.

Stinchcombe, Arthur. "Social Structure and Organization." In *Handbook of Organizations,* edited by James G. March, pp. 142-93. Chicago: Rand McNally, 1965.

"Street Christians: Jesus as the Ultimate Trip." *Time,* 3 August 1970, pp. 31-32.

Strauss, R. "Changing Oneself: Seekers and the Creative Transformation of Life Experience." In *Doing Social Life,* edited by J. Lofland, pp. 252-72. New York: Wiley, 1976.

Streiker, Lowell D. *The Jesus Trip: Advent of the Jesus Freak.* Nashville, Tenn.: Abingdon Press, 1971.

Talmon, Yonina. "Family Life in the Kibbutz: From Revolutionary Days to Stabilization." In *Communes: Creating and Managing the Collective Life,* edited by Rosabeth Moss Kanter, pp. 318-33. New York: Harper & Row, 1973.

Taylor, Brian. "Conversion and Cognition: An Area for Empirical Study in the Microsociology of ʼReligious Knowledge." *Social Compass* 23 (No. 4 1976): 5-22.

Thibaut, J. W., and Kelley, H. H. *The Social Psychology of Groups.* New York: Wiley, 1959.

Toch, Hans. *The Social Psychology of Social Movements.* Indianapolis, Ind.: Bobbs-Merrill, 1965.

Travisano, R. "Alternation and Conversion as Qualitatively Different Transformations." In *Social Psychology Through Symbolic Interaction,* edited by G. P. Stone and M. H. Farberman, pp. 594-606. New York: Wiley, 1970.

Trice, H. M. "The Outsiders' Role in Field Study." In *Qualitative*

Methodology, edited by W. J. Filstead, pp. 77-82. Chicago: Markham, 1970.

Vachon, Brian. *A Time to be Born.* Englewood Cliffs, N.J.: Prentice-Hall, 1972.

Wallis, Roy. "Ideology, Authority, and the Development of Cultic Movements." *Social Research* 41 (1974): 299-327.

———. "Scientology: Therapeutic Cult to Religion Sect." *Sociology* 9 (1975): 89-99.

Ward, Hiley. *The Far-Out Saints of the Jesus Communes.* New York: Association Press, 1972.

Washington, Joseph. *Black Religion.* Boston: Beacon Press, 1964.

Weber, Max. *The Protestant Ethic and the Spirit of Capitalism.* New York: Scribner's, 1958.

Weiss, Robert. "Defection from Social Movements and Subsequent Recruitment to New Movements." *Sociometry* 26 (1963): 1-20.

Wilkerson, David. *The Cross and the Switchblade.* New York: Pyramid, 1968.

Wilson, Bryan. "A Typology of Sects." In *Sociology of Religion,* edited by Roland Robertson, pp. 361-83. Baltimore: Penguin, 1969a.

———. *Religion in Secular Society: A Sociological Comment.* Baltimore: Penguin, 1969b.

Winch, Robert T. *The Modern Family.* New York: Holt, Rinehart & Winston, 1971.

Wood, W. W. *Culture and Personality Aspects of the Pentecostal Holiness Religion.* The Hague: Mouton, 1965.

Yankelovich, Daniel. *The New Morality: A Profile of American Youth in the 70's.* New York: McGraw-Hill, 1974.

Yinger, Milton. *The Scientific Study of Religion.* New York: McGraw-Hill, 1974.

Zablocki, Benjamin. *The Joyful Community.* Baltimore: Penguin, 1971.

———. "Some Models of Commune Integration and Disintegration." Paper read at annual meeting of the American Sociological Association, August 1972, New Orleans.

Zald, M. N., and Ash, Roberta. "Social Movement Organization: Growth, Decay and Change." *Social Forces* 44 (1966): 327-41.

Zald, M. N., and Denton, P. "From Evangelism to General Service: On the Transformation of the Y.M.C.A." *Administrative Science Quarterly* 8 (1963): 214-34.

Zurcher, Louis A., Jr., and Curtis, Russell L. "A Comparative Analysis of Propositions Describing Social Movement Organizations." *Sociological Quarterly* 14 (1973): 175-88.

Index

Activism, 102-103
Addictive personality, 198
Adjective Check List: use and results, 188-199, 297-298
Affective ties, 82, 233, 236, 252-256, 260, 268-271, 319
Afterlife: belief in, 223
Age characteristics, 172-173
Agriculture experience, 9, 12, 24, 27-28, 31-35, 58, 101
Airplanes, 36, 100, 309
Alamo's Christian Foundation, 5, 37, 76, 172
Alcohol use, 9, 147, 238, 264, 281
Alienating propensity of religion, 205-207, 240, 249-250
Alienation, 201-225, 262-263
Alienation Scale, 213-225
Allotment System, 60
Anonymity, 12, 37-38, 304, 310-311
Antinomian heresy, 19
Anti-intellectualism, 20, 81
Anomy(ie), 202-203
Apocalyptic beliefs, 44
Apotheosis process, 54

Associate communes, 87
Authoritarianism, 55, 313
Authoritarian religion, 196, 250, 263
Authority Structure, 46-49, 139
Aviation Ministry, 36

Becalmed movement, 332-333
Beliefs and Ideology, 17-21, 42, 54, 66, 82, 88, 138-146
Bias against religious groups, 95, 114, 115, 122, 205, 339, 346
Bible, 17-18, 54
Bible studies, 8, 69-71, 73-74, 87, 130-131
Birth control, 157
Black Power, 234, 272
Boot camp, 33
Bridge burning, 234-236
Bruderhof, 68, 80, 139, 171, 174
Bureaucharisma, 341-346

Calling, 49-50
Calvary Chapel Church, 6, 37-38, 183
Calvinism, 19

Campus Ministry, 26, 86-87, 90
Cannery, 27-28
Career plans, 174
"Catch as catch can" evangelism, 82-83
Catholic Church, 166, 181-183
Celibacy, 148, 280-281
Charisma: routinization of, 335
Charismatic Renewal, 198-272
Chicken-picking, 101-102
Child care, 22, 27, 29, 78-81
Child evangelism, 76, 78-81, 85-86
Children, 156-158
Children of God, xxvii, 5, 6, 21, 37, 76, 90, 100, 118, 160, 163, 173, 179, 210, 284, 286, 331, 333, 335
Children's Schools, 27, 78-81, 158
Christ Communal Organization (CCO): Beliefs and ideology, 17-21, 42, 54, 66, 82, 88, 138, 146, 312-316; Courtship and Marriage, 145-158; Conversion to, 251-274; Characterized using MO concepts, 116-120; Daily life, 127-135; Early history, 5-16; Evangelisim methods, 82-89, 343; Future of, 279-293; Goals, 42-46, 108-122, 339; Leadership structure, 46-56, 139; Living arrangements, 64-68; Membership characteristics, 171-225; Organizational differentiation, 21-37; Orientation, 158-165; Personality assessment, 185-199; Political orientation, 201-225; Sex roles, 137-146; Support method, 56-64; Training and resocialization, 68-81
Christian World Liberation Front, 172, 322
Christianity Today, 311
Church-Sect theory, 91-94
Civil Rights, xx
Class origins of members, 174-175
Coalitions, 333-334
Coast Guard Academy, 132
Cognitive minority, 274-286
Collective reintegration, 98
Collectivism, 159-165
Collectivistic world view, 115, 239, 265-267
Commitment package, 292

Commitment process, 233-236, 279-293
Commitment, types of, 279-293
Communal lifestyle, xxv, 65-68, 133-134, 159-165
Commune Federations, 94
Commune Movement, xv, 203-204
Commune Theory, 91, 94, 279-293
Commune Typologies, 94-97, 203-204
Communes, 35, 42, 87
Communications ministry, 29, 70-71
Communion, 284-285
Comparison level of alternatives, 260
Computer, 25
Conditions of membership, 108-110, 117, 330, 332-336
Congruency, 108, 117-118, 121-122, 342
Construction company, 58
Contact with environment, 108, 119-120
Contemporaneous experiences, 247
Content analysis, 297
Contract labor, 35, 59
Conventional perspective, 238, 266
Conversion, 251-274; Careers, 246, 259; Continual, 258; Converts and conversion types, 232, 235, 255; General model, 256-271; Process, 232, 235; Trajectories, 246, 259, 266-267
Counseling Readiness, 193-195
County farm, 26-28, 79
Courtship, 137, 147-152
Crash-pad hypothesis, 271
Cult, 92, 273-274
"Cultic milieu," 43
"Culture class," 73

Daily life in CCO, 127-135
Dating, 147
Deacon, 47
Deaconess, 47
De-alienation, 212-213, 223-225
Deconversion, 255, 271, 274
De-individuation, 288
Demographic concerns, 102, 172-175
Denomination tendencies, 92, 322
Dependency proneness, 250
Deprogramming, xvi, 286

Deviance, 287
Division of labor: among communes, 50, 84, 138; within communes, 48-49
Divorce, 156, 166
Donations, 56
Draft: military, 216-217
Drama troupe, 30, 45, 87
Dress codes, 142
Drug experiences, xxi, xxii, 179-180, 264-266
Dualism, 314-315
Dysfunctionality, 198

Economic support, 56-64
Educational background, 174
Ethics in research, 295, 302, 312, 325
Evangelism, 29, 43, 82-89, 331-332, 343; Indirect, 88; Teams, 71-78, 83
Expressive goals, 111-121, 339, 342
External conditions, 339

Falling from grace, 19
Familism-collectivism, 67, 117, 145, 155-156, 159-292
Family: as independent variable, 165
Family life, 154-156
Fellowship Hall, 29-31, 35, 68, 79, 90
Finances, 15-16, 56
Financial center, 26
Fishing industry, 36
Forestry ministry, 51-52
Freedom of choice, 80
Fundamentalism, xxiii, 17, 38-39, 42-43, 138, 248-252, 264, 289, 299-300, 314, 318, 374

Gathering (outreach) houses, 35-36, 75
General orientations, 239
Glossolalia, 7, 186, 198, 212
Goals, 42-46, 108-122, 330, 336
Goat dairy, 31-32
God's will, 18-19, 55, 312, 315
Goodwill, 56
Governmental support, 56
Group conversion, 273-274
Group survival and maintenance, 43-44

Hawthorne effect, 313
Helps' ministry, 74-75, 78, 132
Heterogeneity of membership, 110, 118-120, 334
Holy Spirit, 18
Homogeneity of membership, 118-120, 137, 173, 284
House of Acts, 7
House of Miracles, 7
Humanistic religion, 196
Hutterites, 139

Ideal descriptions, 193
Ideological mobility, 245, 259
Ideology of Jesus Movement, 20, 54
Incentives for membership, 108, 119-121, 332-334
Individualism-collectivism, 239, 265-267
Individualistic world view, xxiii, 19, 115, 239, 265-267, 330
Individual support, 60-64
Institutional awe, 288-290
Institutional church ties, xxvi, 10, 38, 331
Instrumental goals, 108-121, 339, 342
Integrative hypothesis, 97-99
Interaction, 261-262, 269-271
International efforts, 90
Investment, 281-282
Irreversibility of investment, 282
IRS, 90-91

Jehovah's Witnesses, 115, 346
Jesus-centered, 17-18
Jesus Movement, xv, xix, 113; Causes, xix-xxvii, 346; Characteristics, 171-175; Effects, 97-99; Glossolalia, 186; Goals, 113; Ideology, 38, 172, 222, 312-316; Outside America, xxvii; Size, xxvii
Jobs: furnishing, 62
Job's ministry, 75
Journal, ii, 29-30, 39, 84, 87, 99

Kent State, vi, xx, xxii, xxiv
Kibbutz, 80, 160, 163-164
Killing: revulsion against, 225
Kiononia Bank, 61-62
Kitchen operation, 99-100

Lamb's school, 72-75, 131
Leadership: Charismatic, xxv; Disputes, 10; Structure, 46-56; Style, 108, 118-120, 336
Levels of Education, 76
Living arrangements, 64-68
"Loving subjects," 316-317
Luck: role in research, 327

Magical tendencies, 92
Maladaptive personality, 196-197
Maladaptivity, 196-198
Male superiority and dominance, 48, 139-146, 153-154
Manipulationist response, 92
Marlowe Crowne Social Desirability Scale, 297
Marriage, 134, 152-154
Marxian perspective, 202-205, 224-225, 250
Mauss and Petersen's work, 97-98
Media, xxvi
Medical care, 23
Meher Baba, 97
Member characterisitcs, 171-225, 233
Membership incentives, 108, 119-121, 332-334
Membership requirements, 67, 118-120
Minorities, 173, 305
Mobility, 52, 54-56, 60, 62-64; Horizontal, 55; Vertical, 55
Model personality, 194-195
Montessori, 210-211
Moody films, 102
Mormons, 115, 166
Mortification, 286-288
Movement organizations, 106-122, 329-346
Multiple commitments, 243
Murray's need-press system, 188, 191-193, 195
Mystical religion, 212

Naturalistic explanations, 38
Need-press system, 188, 191-193, 195
Neo-Pentecostal movement, 272
Net worth, 45
Night School, 78
Nineteenth-century communes, 279

Nonprofit status, 14-15, 48
Nuclear family, 155-165

Oligarchical tendencies, 335
Oneida, 161
Opportunity structure, 246-247
Outreach houses, 35
"Outsiders' role," 325-327
Oversocialization, 251-252

Parents: ties with, 175-179; marital relationship, 177
Participant observation, 297
Pastors' Council, 15, 47, 52, 54, 74, 84, 90, 144, 304
Patroness, 48
Peach orchard, 31
Pentacostal groups, 234
Personality: assessment of members, 185-199, 297-298, 306
Physiological perspective, 238, 257, 266
Political affiliation, 181
Political orientation and involvement, 102, 180-181, 201-225, 265
Political perspective, 237-265
Political self-characterizations, 218-222
Pragmatic approach, 42
Predisposing characteristics, 233
Predispositions: critique and extension, 237-252
"Priesthood of believers," 55
Prior socialization, 247, 257-258
Property ownership, 161-162
Protestant backgrounds of members, 181-183
Protestant ethic, 49-50
Psychiatric perspective, 237, 264-265
Psychology Today, 309-312
Psychopathology, 186-187
Pulling effect, 261-262

Quaker, 210

Racial intermarriage, 173
Racism, xxi
Reconstruction of biography, 298-299
Recycling leaders, 71

Reintegrative hypothesis, 91, 97-99, 103
Religiosity and personality, 185-187
Religious affiliation, 181-182
Religious alienation: propensity of, 205-207
Religious perspective, 236
Religious seeker, 236
Religious socialization, xxi, 181-183, 249, 262-263
Renunciation, 282-284
Research methods and history, 295-327
Resocialization, 36, 68-81, 147
Response bias, 299
Retrospective data problems, 298-301
Revolution by tradition, 54
Rituals, 285
Role expectation, 137-146, 153; For brothers, 144-146, 165; For sisters, 139-144, 151-152

Sabbath, 99, 130
Sacrifice, 280-281
Salary plans, 61-62
Salvation Army, 12, 56
Satanic forces, 18
Schisms, 8-10, 55, 67, 82, 334-335, 341, 343-345
Schools, 23-24, 36, 71-81
SDS, 181
Sects: Types of, 92; Characteristics of, 102
Secular education, 32, 79, 81
Self-actualization, 95, 197-198
Self-descriptions, 188-199
Serial alternatives, 245
Service business, 59
Sex differences, 188
Sex ratio, 149
Sex roles, 48, 134, 137-146, 159-160, 165
Sexism, 48, 66, 79, 138-144, 153-154, 174
Sexual intercourse, 147, 177
Shakers, 161
Sheep farm, 32-33
Shepherding houses, 35-36
Situational factors, 233-237, 252-256

Smelser's model of collective behavior, xix-xxvii, 233, 256, 274
Smith, Chuck, 6, 10-11
Smoking, 147
Social control, xxvi
Social movement organizations, 106-122, 329-346
Socialization hypothesis, 210, 248
Society for the Scientific Study of Religion, 305
Sociology, 38
Sociodrama, 76
State Trait Anxiety Index, 297
Steward structure, 48-53, 139
Stratification by marital status, 133, 159
Street witnessing, 7
Student protest movement, xxii
Support methods, 56-64
Symbolic Realism, 296, 322-327

Tape's ministry, 23, 29, 71, 87
Tax exempt status, 15, 57, 90-91, 100
Team's (Sheep) School, 71-78, 83-84, 132
Teen Challenge, 6, 37
The Farm, 33-35, 39, 50-51, 56-59, 65-66, 78, 101, 128-131, 134-135, 298, 303-307, 318
The Land, 15-16, 21-25, 50-51, 58, 68, 72-80, 83, 99, 131-133, 308
Thought reform, 70
Tolerance, 92, 322
Total institution, 80
Training, 68-81
Transcendence, 288-291
Transportation facilities, 36-37
Types of authority, 54

Unification Church, 90, 234, 272
University house, 25-26
Utopia, 44

Vice-president of Financial Affairs, 15, 81, 90
Vietnam War, xxii, 215, 217
Visions, 13, 14
Visitors' rules, 134-135
Vocational counseling, 74

Weathermen, 181
Weber/Michels model, 107, 332
Widows' houses, 27, 65
Wilson's work, 92-94
Witnessing, 130; By example, 45, 88
Women's place, 48

Work emphasis and philosophy, 7, 57-58, 100-101, 129, 134

Yankelovich survey, 175, 217-219

Zablocki's theoretical types, 96

DATE DUE

MR 16'81			
	Withdrawn From		
	Ohio Northern		
	University Library		
GAYLORD			PRINTED IN U.S.A.

HETERICK MEMORIAL LIBRARY
306.6 R523o   onuu
Richardson, James T/Organized miracles :

3 5111 00078 4326